THE CONVOLUTIONS
OF HISTORICAL POLITICS

THE CONVOLUTIONS OF HISTORICAL POLITICS

Edited by
Alexei Miller and Maria Lipman

Central European University Press
Budapest–New York

© 2012 by Alexei Miller and Maria Lipman

Published in 2012 by

Central European University Press

An imprint of the
Central European University Limited Liability Company
Nádor utca 11, H-1051 Budapest, Hungary
Tel: +36-1-327-3138 or 327-3000
Fax: +36-1-327-3183
E-mail: ceupress@ceu.hu
Website: www.ceupress.com

400 West 59th Street, New York NY 10019, USA
Tel: +1-212-547-6932
Fax: +1-646-557-2416
E-mail: mgreenwald@sorosny.org

All rights reserved. No part of this publication may be reproduced,
stored in a retrieval system, or transmitted,
in any form or by any means, without the permission
of the Publisher.

ISBN 978-615-5225-15-4 cloth

LIBRARY OF CONGRESS CATALOGING-IN-PUBLICATION DATA

The convolutions of historical politics/edited by Alexei Miller and Maria Lipman.
   p. cm.
  Includes bibliographical references and index.
  ISBN 978-6155225154 (hardbound)
  1. Historiography—Political aspects—Europe—Case studies. I. Miller, A. I. (Aleksei I.) II. Lipman, Maria.

D13.2.C66 2012
907.2094--dc23

2012024339

Printed in Hungary by
Prime Rate Kft., Budapest

Table of Contents

Introduction. Historical Politics: Eastern European Convolutions in the 21st Century
Alexei Miller 1

German History Politics and the National Socialist Past
Stefan Berger 21

Poland's Institute of National Remembrance: A Ministry of Memory?
Dariusz Stola 45

Jedwabne, July 10, 1941: Debating the History of a Single Day
Maciej Janowski 59

The Memory of Trianon as a Political Instrument in Hungary Today
Gábor Gyáni 91

The "Politics of History" as a Case of Foreign-Policy Making
Alexander Astrov 117

The "Nationalization" of History in Ukraine
Georgiy Kasianov 141

The "Politics of Memory" and "Historical Policy" in Post-Soviet Moldova
Andrei Cusco 175

Interventions: Challenging the Myths of Twentieth-Century Ukrainian History
John-Paul Himka 211

Caught Between History and Politics: The Experience of
a Moldovan Historian Studying the Holocaust
Diana Dumitru 239

The Turns of Russian Historical Politics, from Perestroika to 2011
Alexei Miller 253

Politics of History in Turkey: Revisionist Historiography's
Challenge to the Official Version of the Turkish War of
Liberation (1919–1922)
Şener Aktürk 279

The Politics of History in Contemporary Japan
Jeff Kingston 309

List of Contributors 347

Index 349

INTRODUCTION

Historical Politics: Eastern European Convolutions in the 21st Century

ALEXEI MILLER

In the early 1980s, the new West German Chancellor Helmut Kohl, who had a doctorate degree in history, made the revisiting of some key interpretations of the recent past a crucial element of his "moral and political pivot" policy. This policy line, effectuated under the motto of consolidating German patriotism, was aimed at fortifying his victory over the Social Democrats in official historical discourse. As the polemics stepped up, which grew into the famous *Historikerstreit*, or the "battle of historians," shortly after that, opponents labeled the policy as *Geschichtspolitik*. (See Berger's article in this volume.)

In 2004, a group of Polish historians politically close to the Kaczyński brothers' Prawo i Sprawiedliwość (Law and Justice) party proclaimed that *polityka historyczna* (historical policy) was important for Poland. They made a conscientious choice as they translated the notion of *Geschichtspolitik* literally, although it had a derogatory label in Germany, while Kohl's supporters never used it for self-identification. It was then that the broad use of history for political purposes, so typical of Eastern European countries in the early 2000s, got its name.[1] Soon afterwards, the notion of historical policy spread across Polish borders to neighboring countries.

---

[1] The term "Eastern Europe" is used here just to refer briefly to all post-Communist countries, except the former Yugoslavia, where political use and abuse of history has important specificity, linked to the dissolution of Yugoslavia and the subsequent wars in the region. We do not engage here with protracted discussion about the terms "Eastern Europe," "Central Europe," "East-Central Europe."

The phenomenon we are dealing with is an individual case of the *politicization of history* that has transformed into a global tendency.[2] Each individual element of the political interpretation of history in Eastern Europe over the past decade most likely has parallels in other parts of the globe as well. (Articles on Germany, Turkey and Japan in this volume provide plenty of such analogies.) Moreover, each Eastern European nation has its own specificity in this sense. At the same time, intertwining all the elements of politicizing history in a single region is quite unique. The intensity with which neighboring countries have borrowed the techniques and forms of this policy from one another over the past decade has not been matched; neither has the establishment of a mechanism to escalate the politicization of history in interstate relations or inside each particular country. Thus, why do we not manipulate the notion of *historical politics* yet again and use it as an analytical term in our research to denote the regional specificity of politicizing history in Eastern Europe at the beginning of the 21st century?[3]

After Communism, After the Empire.
Post hoc ergo propter hoc?

First, it would make sense to note some specific features the region inherited from the decades of Communist domination. The description of recent history, above all the period between the two World Wars and during World War II, was subjected to harsh censorship in all Communist countries. That was the result of a struggle with the enemies of the regime and, partly, of a desire to refine the history of the Communist movement. Although the Communists as such were not involved in the Holocaust, they would typically not talk about the extermination of the Jews—mostly for ideological "anti-Zionist"

---

[2] Studies of "politics of memory," "historical politics," "wars about history," etc., became a separate institutionalized field. There are journals, devoted exclusively to this topic (*History and Memory*). Recently we have even got predictions (obviously wrong) of the coming out of fashion and collapse of the "industry of memory studies." See Rosenfeld, "A Looming Crash or a Soft Landing?" 122–158.

[3] The first attempt to use the term *Geschichtspolitik* as an analytical tool dates back to 1999. See Wolfrum, *Geschichtspolitik in der Bundesrepublik Deutschland*.

reasons—and often avoided the touchy aspects of participation by the local population in these crimes. Taboos were also imposed on prewar and wartime ethnic conflicts, as these issues were deemed out-of-place in the "fraternity of peoples of the Socialism camp."

Still, the existence of large blank spots, which should rather be referred to as the "minefields" of collective memory in many cases, a surge in nationalistic emotions during the disintegration of the Warsaw Pact, and subsequently the Soviet Union, cannot explain the sharp intensification in historical policy in the 2000s. By the beginning of the 21st century, most of the previously taboo topics became subject of many scholarly publications and were broadly presented in mass media. New national narratives were embedded in official discourse and school textbooks. Old monuments had mostly been pulled down, to be replaced by new ones reflecting national pride, or at least as far as their authors could understand the notion.

Among the changes that occurred after the collapse of Communism, the new status of history and historians in society stands out. Strictly speaking, the notion of historical *politics* as such is worth applying only to societies that are democratic, or at least pluralistic, since the latter demonstrate some degree of commitment to democratic values, including freedom of speech. It is precisely these conditions that give rise to politics as a competition among different actors, parties and viewpoints. In Soviet-style authoritarian societies, the authorities meddled with the study of history and memory policies, proceeding from the official presumption of ideological monopoly, the mechanisms of omnipresent censorship, and administrative control over professional historiography. Dissenting historians were subjected to harsh reprimands at party meetings, and persistent dissidents were fired from their jobs.

All these mechanisms undergo transformation in a society that claims to be democratic. Unlike the former Communist party-state system, a group or a party holding power at a given moment is no longer synonymous with the state. The public sphere becomes pluralistic and the government can no longer aspire to have full control, even more so repressive control. A new set of norms is endorsed at the official level. School education becomes pluralistic, since history teachers are free to choose textbooks and interpret historical events and processes on the basis of official educational standards. As a rule, legislation protects schools from the influence of political parties. Historians are entitled to independence and intellectual freedom. State funds allocated for historical research are distributed based on expert decisions made by the community of professional historians. State financing of education and research does not presuppose the right of the group or party in power at a given moment to dictate the content of education or research programs. That funding does not come from party funds, but is provided by the state budget, that is through public taxes. The political force holding power cannot lay claims to an ideological monopoly. Access to the archives is supposed to be universal and regulated by laws, not by administrative decisions.

The former system of strict party control over the historical science, historical publications, and history as a school subject was demolished right after the collapse of the Communist regimes. One might say that the 1990s became a kind of transitional period in many Eastern European countries when historians were left free, also free to earn what and how they could, however meager. Politicians did not have the time or the opportunity to interfere. Moreover, they still had to master all the diversity of methods of historical policy.

Naturally, not all post-Communist societies managed to transform themselves into genuine democracies. More-or-less steady democratic systems took shape only in countries that were quick candidates for NATO and EU membership, and which were later admitted to those organizations. Other post-Communist countries, which remained on the sidelines of EU expansion, demonstrated various forms of political plurality and soft authoritarianism that largely relied on a social contract with the population, rather than on repression. The facade democracy practiced by the elites of those countries for domestic and international legitimization raised the costs of repressive policies. Even in the most authoritarian countries of the region, the current situation is marked by a greater degree of freedom than during Communist rule.

Eastern European countries are no longer subject to official censorship; nor is there state control over publishing houses, or a single, ideological power monopoly. The government does not steer the activity of professional historians and research institutions, and it does not have monopoly over the channels of financing. It is also important that the state does not risk making open claims about the restoration of a system regulating scientific research, even if it wants to do so. (The legacy of the previous regime that manifests itself in intellectual habits and reflexes is found in all Eastern European countries). The Internet is something the government cannot control and it has acquired new significance everywhere. In other words, even though historical policy in Eastern Europe is rooted in many ways in the legacy of the old Communist period, it represents a new set of practices concerning the political utilization of history typical only of pluralistic non-Communist societies. It is quite another thing that the makeup of political regimes and civic society there stands in marked contrast to old democracies in the West.

This is exactly what deserves detailed discussion. Interpretations of the very nature of the phenomenon we call "historical policy" usually put all the emphasis on the Communist legacy. In other words, current political manipulations of history are interpreted as the legacy of past abuses, as a consequence of lingering habits formed previously, or as a natural evolution of the countries that have freed themselves from Moscow's imperial domination. The latter ostensibly presupposes focusing efforts on the consolidation of ethnic self-identity. However, such interpretations diminish the novelty of the phenomenon.

Furthermore, it is exactly the *political* nature of historical policy as a phenomenon that makes researchers pay more attention to the actors, institutions and methods of this policy, rather than diverse interpretations of the *past* in its format. These issues have usually escaped the attention of scholars so far. Of course, it would be unfair to claim that our approach is totally new. Although the majority of publications on collective memory or memory politics still concentrates on narratives and narrative strategies,[4] recently several important projects have addressed politics of history and/or politics of memory exactly as a political phenomenon.[5] However, most of this research rather looks at how collective memories influence political attitudes and strategies, and pays less attention to how historical narratives and collective memories have been manipulated by various political actors

---

[4] See Parker, et al, *A European Memory,* for one of the most recent example of narrative-concentrated approach.

[5] See Müller (ed.) *Memory and Power in Post-War Europe*; Kratochwil, "History, Action and Identity;" Lebow et al., *The Politics of Memory in Postwar Europe*; Art, *The Politics of the Nazi Past in Germany and Austria,* The Annals of the American Academy of Political and Social Science. Philadelphia, 2008, vol. 617, no. 1.

to pursue their goals in domestic and international politics. Nobody has yet addressed systematically these issues based on material provided by the post-Communist countries of Central and Eastern Europe during the recent decade. We consider the present volume to be a contribution to this research perspective, as we focus on actors, institutions and political strategies involved in political use/abuse of historical issues and collective memory.

Multiform Post-Communism

The post-Communist and/or imperial legacies have been viewed as a universal rationale for the forms that the politicization of history acquired in Eastern Europe at the beginning of the 21st century. However, this leaves out a crucial circumstance—the marked diversity of the nature of political plurality across Eastern European countries.

First, some Eastern European countries are seeing a split along cultural and/or ethnic lines. Importantly, in some countries (such as Ukraine) this split is the center of political life, while in others it has been driven to the political periphery (in Estonia and Latvia, where a considerable number of ethnic Russians are still banished from official politics). Moldova combines the two options: the split between "Romanianists" and "Moldovanists" has penetrated the very core of the political sector, while the Transnistria region stands apart from it. In other words, the overall "post-imperial" or "post-colonial" situation should not overshadow the considerable differences in the character of challenges that Eastern European countries run into as they seek to build their collective identities.

Second, Poland, Hungary (to mention the countries analyzed in this volume), as well as other post-Communist nations that are members of the EU are relatively stable democracies, although they sometimes face serious challenges to democratic order. This democratic stability is bolstered, among other things, by a powerful external factor in the form of influences wielded by EU institutions. Ukraine and Moldova have pluralistic systems, where the outcome of elections is not always predetermined by the people holding the reins of power when the votes are counted. Still, democratic institutions are underdeveloped and highly unstable in this region. Russia has an authoritarian regime, in which political struggle is neither explicit nor conventional, and is replaced by what can be called "the struggle between the Kremlin's towers." Nonetheless, Russians enjoy considerable freedom of speech. Belarus has demonstrated a considerable similarity with tough authoritarian regimes in Central Asia. All these differences naturally leave imprints on the historical policy in different countries.

Diversity of Actors

The field is crowded with all kinds of players: political leaders, political parties, new specialized institutions (such as the Institutes of National Remembrance, and a number of museums established under the patronage of particular parties over the past twenty years), traditional research organizations like the Academy of Sciences, various non-governmental organizations (from the Memorial Human Rights Center to Aleksandr Dyukov's Historical Memory Foundation), associations (including associations bringing together the victims of repressions and their descendants), the mass media (especially those that view historical problems as indispensible highlights), and politically active ethnic communities. The champions of historical policy from the milieu of professional historians deserve a special remark. There is a wide variety of people among their ranks, ranging from profoundly committed enthusiasts to career professionals, who will service any political client in exchange for positions and remunerations. It would be interesting to trace the role of the generational factor in this. Especially amazing is the new type of young people who bear a strong resemblance to Soviet-era Young Communist League functionaries. These personalities are strikingly similar in different nations (Piotr Gontarczyk, Sławomir Cenckiewicz and Paweł Zyzak in Poland; Volodymyr Vyatrovych and Ruslan Zabily in Ukraine; Aleksandr Dyukov and Pavel Danilin in Russia; and the list continues).

The issue of who the active operators and/or actors are is crucial for analyzing historical policy, but too often remains marginal in the works devoted to the problem known as the "politics of history," the "politics of memory," or "political wars around history." For our book the question about actors is central: some articles focus on individual political leaders (see Kasianov on Yushchenko and Cusco on Ghipmu) or political parties (see Berger and Gyáni). Other articles pay special attention to new specialized institutions and traditional structures, like Academies of Science (see Stola on Polish Institute of National Remembrance, Gyáni on museums, Miller on the institutional dimension of Russian historical politics), media (see Janowski on Polish debates about Jedwabne) and politically mobilized diasporas (see Himka and Kasianov). Individual activists of historical politics also deserve special study, but this topic gets only fragmentary treatment in our volume.[6]

As the editor of this volume, I particularly value the articles by John-Paul Himka and Diana Dumitru, who, based on their own experience, describe possible individual strategies to resist historical politics and describe the price one should be ready to pay for doing that. Resistance to historical politics deserves a detailed study. We can see perfectly well that professional historians in some countries—for instance, in Poland—put up organized counteraction, sometimes through the mass media. On some occasions historical policy bumps into covert sabotage from traditional scientific organizations, especially the Academies of Sciences. One should stress the crucial role public opinion—and especially some Internet publications—plays in opposing historical politics. Of course, the Internet is also gradually turning into an arena and instrument to spread historical politics. This calls for in-depth consideration, since the ways this medium functions and the styles of statements made on the Internet have a specificity of their own.

Generally speaking, in Eastern Europe attempts by politicians to interfere in education and the public functioning of history have not met with strong resistance from society. This becomes especially clear if one compares the situation with that in Britain, where active debates on how to teach history at schools have been going on for more than twenty years.[7] Moreover, the problems of national identity and state interests occupy an important place in those debates.

Active participation by politicians in these debates is seen in the criticism of school history curricula, which emphasize the history of

---

[6] Georgiy Kasianov provides a perfect analysis of activities and motivation of historian Stanislav Kul'chitskii in his recent *Danse Macabre*, 162–188.

[7] See Phillips, *History Teaching, Nationhood and the State*; Andrews and Mycock, "Dilemmas of Devolution"; and Waldman, "The Politics of History Teaching in England and France during the 1980s."

everyday life rather than the "glorious victories" of the British Army and Navy. One can regularly hear concerns over the failure of history lessons to play a large enough role in the patriotic upbringing of youth and the shaping of national identity. However, the most powerful participants in these debates are organizations like the National Council for School Curriculum and Assessment and the National Association of Head Teachers, which are prepared to resolutely defend their interests. As a consequence, politicians are unable to impose an agenda of their own, to say nothing of dictating certain decisions. They are compelled instead to take part in professional debates and to abide by their rules if politicians want to win voters over to their side. In other words, politicians have to discuss the tricky and ambivalent issues of teaching history as *res publica* (an asset of public good), without primitive political slogans or persecution of those who think differently.[8]

Borrowings

Diverse political conditions in Eastern European countries raise an important question: What mutations do the institutions and methods of historical politics undergo when spreading across borders? The instances of mutation are myriad. The Institute of National Remembrance, set up by Poland relying on the experience of Joachim Gauck's commission in Germany, has seen changes in its legal status in the context of inter-party political struggle. (See Stola's article.) However, once it was transferred to Ukraine the Institute turned into a self-mockery: instead of steering the study of the Communist Security Services' archives, it was transformed into a subdivision of Ukraine's Security Service. I show in my article on Russia how the idea of creating such an institute in Russia fueled very different institutional arrangements, with

---

[8] Politics by definition are not dialogue, but war, competition, negotiation and deals. In other words historical politics inevitably undermine understanding of history and past as *res publica* and subject to dialogue, that is interaction in which the sides express themselves, or *give* themselves to the partners in dialogue, in words. The key issue here is whether social actors are strong enough to prevent politicians from imposing the rules of politics on dealing with history and past, and able to save the space of dialogue.

the infamous Presidential Commission for "Fighting against Falsifications of History" as the center of the complex network.

Another institutional idea consistently borrowed from country to country was the formation of commissions to investigate the crimes of totalitarian regimes, which mostly engaged in compiling lists of Soviet crimes. The scale of the crimes was often assessed in dozens of billions of U.S. dollars, which the commissions proposed getting in compensation. These commissions functioned for many years in Estonia, Latvia and Lithuania. Moldova's acting president Mihai Ghimpu formed the body in 2010. It was given the unambiguous task of producing the report in six months' time, on the eve of the parliament elections. The political pragmatism of this initiative was never concealed.

One more example of the institutional dimension of historical policy and intensive cross-border borrowings is the creation of museums under the patronage of certain political forces. (See Gyáni's article.) Any alternative positions on what such museums would display are ignored outright. Take for instance the Warsaw Uprising Museum, founded by the Kaczyński brothers; the House of Terror in Budapest, set up by Hungarian right-wing groups; or the Museum of Soviet Occupation in Ukraine (including the standard design exhibition of the Holodomor, the man-made famine in the Ukraine in the 1932–1933), established under the patronage of former president Victor Yushchenko. Historical narrative in general and museum exhibitions in particular often focus on martyrology, or the image of an enemy, which most typically is tailored on an association with contemporary political forces inside and outside the country. Quite often these are museums of invasion and/or genocide.

Almost all post-Communist countries except Russia see a political task for themselves in showing off titular nations as victims of 20th century genocide. When the epidemic of manipulating the notion of genocide reached Russia during the August 2008 war in Georgia, it produced a brief, but very intensive, splash, which was manifested in attempts to describe the Georgian Army's attack on South Ossetia in terms of genocide. It is noteworthy that Warsaw's municipal authorities have recently rejected the Museum of Communism project endorsed by the Kaczyńskis' Law and Justice party. The municipality is controlled by the Platforma Obywatelska (Civic Platform) party that has assimilated a moderate line towards historical policy recently.

Historical policy manifests itself at the legislative level, too, when national parliaments pass laws establishing an interpretation of events as the only correct one. Sometimes these bills—and even the laws after endorsement—stipulate criminal punishments for those who call these interpretations into question. This practice is not only typical of Eastern Europe. Legislative acts that regulate historical interpretations exist in some countries of western Europe (France is the most telling example). Similar laws exist in Turkey. (See Aktürk's article.) Their authors will typically refer to Holocaust denial laws adopted in some Western countries. Such references are conscientiously plotted manipulations, since Holocaust denial laws prosecute the refutation of the very fact, rather than attempting to make interpretations.

Methods

The methods of historical policy are in many ways clear from what we said earlier. One can divide them into five groups. Obviously, the classification proposed below is rather conventional, since all the methods listed are closely intertwined.

First, the setting up of specialized institutes which are used to impose certain interpretations of past events beneficial for a political force. The problem of financing presents a special interest in this sense. If a party has its own financial resources which it allocates for research it finds necessary or deems correct in historical orientation, it has the right to do so, just like any other sponsor would. This sponsorship must be transparent and subject to common regulations. However, the principles of transparency are frequently disregarded and—most importantly—Eastern European countries often use money from federal budgets controlled by political forces holding the levers of power. A dubious, and often illegal, use of finances—and especially budget money—is a characteristic feature of historical policy.

Second, there is political interference in the mass media. This is by no means a specific feature of Eastern Europe, since such practices take place in countries like France, Japan and Turkey. (See Kingston's and Aktürk's articles for examples.) In some cases such interference is fraught with serious trouble for politicians, while in Eastern Europe it rather constitutes an undeclared norm. Although instances of outright censorship in the form of deleting sections from books and movies are rare, widely used methods include marginalizing opponents, and blocking access to television and the most widely read papers.

Third, archives are manipulated, partially by labeling many state archival materials as classified documents, although the law states that researches should have access to them. Priority, or sometimes exclusive, access to archival documents is given only to historians who lean towards one or another political force. Materials are retailored for publication and experts do not have an opportunity to verify them.

Fourth, new measures are devised and used to control the work of historians. In addition to moral pressures on opponents, an entire system emerges of official and non-official bonuses for historians close to certain political parties. In some cases, this presupposes privileged salaries and status; for instance, for the staff members of Institutes of National Remembrance. While on the government payroll, researchers at these institutes enjoy much larger salaries than their counterparts at regular research institutes or universities. Part of this special status is a much higher level of "discipline" and risk of losing one's privileges. In other cases, people with a merit record in terms of historical policy can expect to receive support in getting key posts at academic institutions. The reader will find telling examples in almost all the articles in this volume.

Fifth, there are instances of political interference in the content of textbooks and curricula, up to overt encroachments on the law. This was exactly the case with a chapter on "sovereign democracy" in the Danilov/Filippov textbook in Russia that portrayed an element of the ruling party's ideology as an objective and even scientifically grounded concept. (See Miller's article.)

The aspect all these methods have in common is the use of state administrative and financial resources in the field of history and historical policy to serve the interests of the ruling party.

Ideological Grounding

Political manipulations with history in the new conditions demand a new ideological grounding. The ideological foundations of historical politics reveal stark similarities in all Eastern European countries and are based on four principal postulations.

First, history and memory (remembrance) are regarded primarily as an arena of political fighting with enemies, both domestic and external. This leads to the conclusion that "history is too important to be left to the care of historians."[9] This in turn means that historians need to be placed under the control of people more sophisticated in political issues. Historians as such do not have the right to refer to the principles of professional ethics in order to claim independence from politics.

Second, there is an assertion that "everyone is doing it." Thus an attempt is made to justify in the public eye an obvious infringement on the principles accepted in democratic societies of how social science functions. The true and imaginary instances of manipulations in the sphere of historical consciousness and collective memory in other countries are invariably cited to substantiate the thesis that the politicization of history is an "unavoidable evil," not as something of which the nation should be apprehensive.

Third, there is a belief that historians have a duty to put up "solidarity resistance" to interpretations of history that are detrimental to the homeland and are used by external enemies. It is only natural that polemics with opponents at home gives way to personal assaults, accusations of complicity with the enemy, or attempts to pass the opponent off as an alien. (See Miller's, Janowski's and Himka's articles.) As a consequence, any room for dialogue about the problems of history inside the country is destroyed and—let us reiterate—the productive instruments of public discussion of the past as an asset of common heritage are broken, too.

The mechanism for destroying the space for dialogue is applied to relations with the outside world, as well. The adepts of historical politics on both sides of the border initiate a heated war of words with each other. They sometimes conduct this war under the motto of a "dialogue of national historiographies." A standoff like this usually boils down to defending mutually exclusive arguments. Since neither side wants to convince or understand the other, these discussions only aggravate the conflict and eventually serve as a means of legitimizing the adepts of historical policy inside each country. This, in

---

[9] See elaborations on this issue by Marek Cichocki, an ideologist of historical politics and adviser to late President Lech Kaczyński in Stobiecki, "Historians Facing Politics of History. The Case of Poland,"182.

essence, replicates a characteristic feature of Soviet propaganda, where increased brainwashing inside the country became the main technique of responding to the "malicious ideological designs of the enemy." In the past no one in the West except for postgraduate students with bizarre tastes would read Soviet critiques of "bourgeois historiography." Nor does anyone today in the Baltic States read the rancorous tirades of Russian champions of historical politics, which they spearhead at coeval Baltic fighters with Soviet totalitarianism.

The aftermath of this approach is highly destructive both for professional historians and for public morals. It breeds a conviction in society that a craving for objectivity in historical research and assessments is little more than a facet of naivety, or a hypocritical camouflage for ethnic or political partiality. Those who allegedly conduct discussion in the format of historical politics are, in fact, engaged in imitating it, as they address their own target audiences instead of addressing opponents in reality.

Ukrainian historian Georgiy Kasyanov, who conducted a brilliant survey of the Holodomor as a specific form of cultural reality, listed the following generic features of the discourse: ethnic exclusiveness; confrontational orientation; elements of xenophobia; preponderance of ideological forms over scientific ones; accentuating the martyr's mission of the own nation; imparting a sacred nature to ethnic torments; equating the nation to a human body; the domination of moralistic rhetoric; and a justificatory pathos that relegates the main responsibility for the harm sustained to external factors, primarily to Russian Communism.[10] All the nine signs of the syndrome inevitably show up in discourses molded in the format of historical politics in all Eastern European countries.

Fourth, the justification of historical politics is made under the pretext of an allegedly pitiful state of patriotism and the inconsistent teaching of history at schools. The same cunning explanations stand behind proposals to jettison (provisionally) the plurality of views from textbooks and concepts, so that "our children could at least learn the basics." Regarding "the basics," priority is given to fostering patriotism, not the critical civic stance. Naturally, patriotism is to be fostered

---

[10] Kasianov, *Danse macabre*, 209–212.

with the aid of the historical narrative that highlights the moments of a nation's glory and sufferings, and carefully erases the guilt of some of its members. Many articles in this volume, particularly those by Himka, Dumitru and Janowski, analyze these discursive strategies.

Internal Political Objectives

In reality, however, concern for public interests will typically disguise the sheer party-oriented goals of historical politics. The "truly patriotic" version of history is unfailingly lucrative for a definite political force. Take Poland, for example, where the supporters of historical politics used it as an instrument in fighting with contenders over the Kaczyński brothers' right to be considered the sole genuine successors to the Solidarity movement. In Ukraine, the interpretations of the history of the Ukrainian Insurgent Army (UPA) and the famine of 1932–1933 voiced by Victor Yushchenko provided support for him in the struggle with the opposition and helped (in the opinion of the authors of this policy) to install a concept of the Ukrainian nation that matched the ideas espoused by the former president and his political associates. As for Russia, the historical policy conducted from 2007–2009 overtly served the objectives of "sovereign democracy" that was (or maybe still is) an element of the United Russia party's political program.

Historical policy is instrumental in struggling for votes and eliminating competitors on the basis of lustration laws or in the absence of such laws. This partly results from the sterilizing of meaningful agendas, in which case the desire for votes appeals to interpreting the past, rather than resolving the acute problems of contemporary development. This also works the other way, when the real life situation throws in a convenient theme for a campaign from a different sector. In this case, historical policy is shelved immediately, such as what happened in Poland after Lech Kaczyński's death in a plane crash near Smolensk. Later, when the idea of a Putin-Tusk plot to assassinate the Polish president was to some extent floated, the issue of allegedly genocidal character of the Katyń massacre of Polish officers in 1940 was exploited again.

It is a persistent fact that the intensification of historical politics in the early 21st century is mostly linked to the activities of right-wing parties. Right-wingers are active players in the field of nationalism and patriotism, where they take on the role of "defenders of the homeland." They often invoke alarmist motives of a threat to national sovereignty, dignity, and traditional national values. The subjects of "historical injustice" and "genocide" are devised in such a way that the role of victim is assigned exclusively to their own ethnic group or nationality, while demands for repentance are regulated to external forces. Today's liberals are more inclined to raise the problem of historical responsibility of their own group, and it is much more fruitful for fostering public morality and for relations with neighboring countries. This does not mean that liberals or left-wingers want to refrain from implementing some methods of historical policy, especially in modeling the public discourse about the past. However, on the whole, the set of means is much closer to those used by right-wing rather than left-wing forces.

Foreign Policy Objectives

As a rule, historical policy plays a less important role in foreign relations, although its supporters will usually claim the opposite. If deep splits emerge along political, cultural, or linguistic lines due to discord within a certain polity, then internal political tasks almost certainly become historical policy priorities, even in cases where the debates and manipulations formally focus on relations with the outside world. (See cases of Moldova, the Ukraine, Turkey, Hungary, Poland, addressed in this volume.) However, as Alexander Astrov has shown in his article on Estonia, in some cases IR priorities become highly important. Usually, the main target of historical claims is not the main target of the political message, which is addressed instead to public opinion in the leading western countries in order to prevent them from "forgetting" or trading the interests of the "small and weak."

At the same time one should not underestimate or—and this happens quite often—oversimplify the role the international factor plays in Eastern Europe. The foreign policy factor has never exerted an influence in one dimension only. Highlighted is usually the post-imperial dimension of the situation, i.e. the tensions between Russia, on the one hand, and the former Soviet republics or Warsaw Pact countries, on the other. Although this aspect is self-evident, it will hardly help understand the dynamics of current developments, as it does not explain in any way the sharp increase in historical policy in 2003–2004, and its noticeable decline in 2009 and 2010.

Eastern European countries found themselves in a previously unknown situation in 2003 and 2004, when the war in Iraq jolted the unity of the West and the rest of the world, prodded on by Donald Rumsfeld who started speaking about Old and New Europe. (See Astrov's article for discussion of this situation.) The "smaller" Baltic States—Estonia, Latvia and Lithuania—were always concerned by what they believed to be insufficient guarantees of security they had received from the West, while joining NATO and the EU. These apprehensions intensified after the NATO and U.S.-led invasion of Iraq had exposed deep divisions between Washington and its leading European allies. In these conditions, actively exploiting the theme of victims of Soviet totalitarianism and of betrayal on the part of the liberal West on the eve of World War II, or immediately after it, was addressed precisely to Western public opinion, since it mirrored the willingness of "smaller" countries to ensure security guarantees from leading Western powers. (See Astrov's article.)

Georgia's Rose Revolution in 2003 and the Orange Revolution in Ukraine in 2004 also raised the stakes in Eastern Europe. This was the time when historical policy sharply intensified and received its name.

There is hardly any doubt that the new U.S. administration in 2009, and the ensuing changes in the course and rhetoric in U.S.-Russian relations, strongly influenced the situation. The Obama administration made it absolutely clear to the New Europe that it had no interest in a further growth in tensions in those countries' relations with Moscow. The change facilitated steps towards a "détente" in some cases, and this applies to efforts undertaken by Moscow and the Polish government led by Donald Tusk since 2008. This in turn prompted the Russian authorities to make serious adjustments in their own approach to historical issues. (See more in Miller's article.)

At the same time, warmer relations between Moscow and the major European powers, which have been interpreted as a return to *Realpolitik,* are yet another reason for using historical policy as far as the Baltic states are concerned. It is worth noting that, contrary to Poland where certain political forces proved ready to supplement the "resetting" of relations between Washington and Moscow with a "détente" between Warsaw and Moscow, the leaders of the Baltic States have kept up the previous line—in spite of U.S. recommendations to lower passions. A fear that their interests may turn into a subject for bargaining compels smaller Eastern European countries to continue employing historical policy as an instrument of influencing public opinion in the West.

One can presume that the 2012 presidential elections in the U.S. will become a landmark for historical policy in Eastern Europe regardless of who wins the White House. The Obama administration's policy will either be reaffirmed and détente—including in the field of historical policy—will continue, or we will see a new surge of this policy. In any case, the annals of historical policy are far from exhausted.

It is difficult to predict the future of historical policy today. The intensity of "historical wars in Europe" has decreased since 2009, but the process could still be reversed. First of all, it is not at all clear how long the resetting of relations between Moscow and Washington will last. Second, it is becoming increasingly obvious that there is a crisis in European integration. This has already ignited a growth in nationalistic economic sentiment all across Europe. In time, this may call into question achievements made in historical reconciliation and the surmounting of past divisions, which underlies the European Union. It is still very likely that history will be used as a tool for political disputes among EU member-states and in conflicts with immigrant communities inside European countries. Eastern Europe beyond the EU continues to be quite unstable—politically, economically, and even with respect to borders and the countries per se. Given this situation, reverting to extremely aggressive, conflict-prone and destructive methods of historical policy is still a realistic threat.

In conclusion, a few words about the structure of this book. It includes articles about Germany, Japan and Turkey, which address in long chronological perspective the experience of politicization of history in these countries. Each of this cases resonates in various ways with experience of Eastern Europe. Discussions of historical politics in Eastern Europe often refer to German experience, usually to its idealized and imagined version. Japan is also often mentioned in these discussions in opposition to Germany as a country which consistently rejects the *Aufarbeitung der Vergangenheit*. The Turkish case is also very instructive in the context of problems of Eastern Europe, particularly in the part which deals with the cult of Kemal Atatürk as the paternal figure, founder of the nation. Many countries in Eastern Europe, most obviously Russia, are struggling with similar problems.

The major part of this volume is devoted to Eastern Europe. Two articles deal with Poland, whose experience with historical politics often served as a reference point both for the adepts and opponents of historical politics in neighboring countries. Another case of EU-member country where historical politics are actively employed both in international and domestic arena is Hungary. Estonia is among those three former Soviet republics, who became the members of EU. The book also analyses the cases of Russia, Ukraine and Moldova—three post-Soviet republics, which remain outside EU. We have also included into this volume the article of John-Paul Himka, which describes the experience of a historian, who lives in Canada, but focuses on Ukrainian history in his research and is closely linked to Ukraine and to Ukrainian diaspora in Canada. We didn't try to cover all the Eastern European countries, because attempts to give a comprehensive overview of the whole region usually suffer from unequal quality of the articles. Our task was to use case studies to study the phenomenon, which got the name of "historical politics."

The editors acknowledge with gratitude the financial support of the Open Society Institute and organizational assistance of Carnegie Endowment for Peace (Moscow). We personally thank Tatiana Barabanova for her organizational assistance.

BIBLIOGRAPHY

Andrews, R. and A. Mycock. "Dilemmas of Devolution: The 'Politics of Britishness' and Citizenship Education." *British Politics* no. 3 (2008): 139–155

Art, D. *The Politics of the Nazi Past in Germany and Austria.* Cambridge: Cambridge University Press, 2006.

Kasianov, G. *Danse Macabre. Golod 1932–1933 rokiv u polityci, masovoi svidomosti ta istoriografii (1980-ti–pochatok 2000-h).* Kyiv: Nash Cash Publishers, 2010.

Kratochwil, F. "History, Action and Identity: Revisiting the 'Second' Great Debate and Assessing Its Importance for Social Theory." *European Journal of International Relations* vol. 1, no. 12 (2006): 5–29.

Lebow, R.N., W. Kansteiner, and C. Fogu, eds. *The Politics of Memory in Postwar Europe.* Durham, NC: Duke University Press, 2006.

Pakier, M. and B. Stråth. *A European Memory. Contested Histories and Politics of Remembrance*. New York, Oxford: Berghahn Books, 2010.

Müller, J.W., ed. *Memory and Power in Post-War Europe. Studies in the Presence of the Past.* Cambridge: Cambridge University Press, 2004.

Phillips, R. *History Teaching, Nationhood and the State. A Study in Educational Politics*. London: Cassell, 1998.

Rosenfeld G. D. "A Looming Crash or a Soft Landing? Forecasting the Future of the Memory 'Industry'" *The Journal of Modern History* vol. 81, no 1. (March 2009): 122–158.

Stobiecki R. "Historians Facing Politics of History. The Case of Poland" in *Past in the Making: Historical Revisionism in Central Europe After 1989*. Edited by M. Kopecek. Budapest–New York: Central European University Press, 2007, 182.

Waldman A. "The Politics of History Teaching in England and France during the 1980s." *History Workshop Journal* vol. 68, no. 1 (Autumn 2009): 199–221.

Wolfrum, E. *Geschichtspolitik in der Bundesrepublik Deutschland. Der Weg zur bundesrepublikanischen Erinnerung 1948–1990*. Darmstadt: DarmstadtVerlag, 1999.

German History Politics and the National Socialist Past

STEFAN BERGER

Introduction

On November 10, 1988 the president of the West German Bundestag, Philipp Jenninger, gave a speech in the parliament to commemorate the 50th anniversary of the Night of Broken Glass (Reichskristallnacht). During the speech, several members of parliament from the opposition—but also from the ruling coalition—left in protest. All parliamentary parties met on the following day to discuss the "scandal." Jenninger ultimately resigned his post stating that he did not want to damage his office and that many had not understood his speech in the way that it was meant. What was he accused of? The criticism focused on his use of language: by taking over National Socialist terminology and adopting the perspective of the perpetrators without adequately distancing himself from this perspective and contextualising it, he had given the impression as though he was giving a speech entirely inappropriate for the occasion. Seen with hindsight and without the hype attached to the event immediately afterwards, any observer reading the speech now could be excused for wondering what all the fuss was about. After all, Jenninger did not condone the pogroms, and he was not apologetic about the National Socialist past of Germany.[1]

What the alleged scandal surrounding the Jenninger speech underlined was the degree to which talking about the National Socialist past had become a political and moral minefield in Germany after 1945. The speech came on the tail-end of one of the biggest public

---

[1] Siever, *Kommunikation und Verstehen*.

history debates to rock German society in the post-Second World War period—the so-called Historians' Controversy (Historikerstreit), which raged in the German media for almost two years between 1986 and 1987.[2] This essay will review the controversy as part and parcel of German history politics,[3] but it also seeks to contextualise it in a longer durée perspective on German discussions about the National Socialist past from the foundations of the two Germanies to the present day.

What is noticeable about all of the public history debates reviewed below, is that they are never purely scholarly ones. They have a political agenda and they get their lifeblood from their associations with particular causes which affect wider groups than merely historians. They are frequently driven by party-political agendas which seek to functionalize history for their own purposes. Quite often they are related to setting up or breaking down alleged taboos in society and they frequently deal with traumatic events in the past. They are about extending or limiting what can be said publicly about the past. This does not mean that debates on history politics cannot have scholarly consequences. Arguably, the Historians' Controversy led to a new focus in scholarly research on the perpetrators, especially on the Wehrmacht,[4] and also on comparative genocide research.[5] In this sense it would be facile to dismiss history politics as irrelevant for scholarly history. But history

---

[2] It has been very widely dealt with in several books and articles. See, for example, the collection of original newspaper articles entitled *Forever in the Shadow of Hitler? Original Documents of the Historikerstreit, the Controversy Concerning the Singularity of the Holocaust*; Baldwin, *Hitler, the Holocaust and the Historians' Dispute*; Eley, "Nazism, Politics and the Image of the Past"; Evans, *In Hitler's Shadow*; Maier, *The Unmasterable Past*.

[3] I use the term "history politics" in analogy to the German term "Geschichtspolitik," and would like to express the proximity of a particular historical perspective to political agendas. They do not have to be, but often are closely aligned to party political agendas and amount to the functionalisation of history by politics.

[4] The roots of the famous Wehrmacht exhibition can be traced back to the Historians' Controversy and publications still portraying the German army as a professional and honorable institution. On the Wehrmacht exhibition and its impact on changing perceptions of the Wehrmacht in Germany, see Heer and Naumann, *Vernichtungskrieg: die Verbrechen der Wehrmacht, 1941–1944*.

[5] Bergen, "Controversies about the Holocaust," 141–174.

politics debate are not essentially about scholarliness; they use scholarliness to legitimate and delegitimate particular political positions which are being debated because of their wider relevance to society.

History Politics and the National Socialist Past in Germany, 1949–1982

The foundation of two Germanies in 1949 meant that both states had to position themselves against the National Socialist period. They did so very differently. The Federal Republic of Germany (FRG) consciously portrayed itself as the successor state of the German Reich which had ceased to exist in 1945. It took over its obligations, and, under considerable pressure from the Western allies, it agreed to pay reparations to the Jewish World Claims Conference and the state of Israel—a measure which was unpopular with the vast majority of West Germans. Of the three main post-war political parties in West Germany, the ruling Christian Democrats (CDU) under Konrad Adenauer consciously distanced their Christian worldview from that of National Socialism, but they also insisted that the vast majority of Germans had no guilt in the National Socialist atrocities and their lenient policies ensured the relatively smooth integration of many former Nazis into the Federal Republic.[6] The sometime coalition partner of the CDU, the Free Democrats (FDP), was a party in which many former middle-ranking Nazis were active in the post-war period, and they had no interest in lingering on the past too much. The opposition Social Democrats (SPD) emphasized their anti-Fascist credentials, portraying themselves as morally justified to speak on behalf of the new democratic Germany, but their post-war attempts to represent German interests vis-à-vis the victorious Allies also were not conducive to a prolonged engagement with the complicity of large sections of the German population with National Socialism. Hence, in the absence of party political pressure to engage the German population more directly and more self-critically with the National Socialist past, many West Germans, well into the 1950s, remained privately convinced

---

[6] Frei, *Vergangenheitspolitik*.

that Hitler was the greatest German statesmen ever, and that he was merely ill-advised by his surrounding lieutenants. Memories of the 1930s were overwhelmingly positive, and the National Socialist ideology of Volksgemeinschaft continued to influence German perceptions of "self" and "other." The Holocaust and German atrocities committed in the Second World War were not part of the collective memory of the nation. Instead Germans commemorated their own victims of the Second World War—those who had endured the bombing war against German cities, those who had been ethnically cleansed from East Central and Eastern Europe, and, above all, the prisoners of war still languishing in Soviet POW camps. Popular novels, such as Heinz G. Konsalik's *The Doctor of Stalingrad* confirmed the public image of the honest and suffering German soldier and the Asiatic, barbarous Russians that had been part and parcel of National Socialist propaganda. The image of the man with the shaven head behind barbed wire, which every school child today would immediately associate with the Holocaust, was instead widely associated with German prisoners of war in 1950s West Germany.[7]

Historians in the West made the National Socialist period an important part of their work almost immediately after the Second World War. One of the most respected doyens of German historiography, the octogenarian Friedrich Meinecke, published a little booklet in 1946 entitled *The German Catastrophe* that amounted to a critique of German traditions that allegedly led to the succes of National Socialism, especially German militarism and the famous *Untertanengeist* of the Germans, i.e. their subservience to authority.[8] Meinecke talked about the need to maintain a staunch anti-Communism, but he also talked about the necessity of Germany to turn "west" and adopt a more western political culture, whilst at the same time retaining the allegiance to what was best in German culture (hence his concrete suggestion at the end of the book to set up Goethe societies as a means of moral renewal). The book still contained some remarkably insensitive comments on German Jews, and it portrayed the Second World War

---

[7] Moeller, "War Stories."
[8] Meinecke, *The German Catastrophe*; on Meinecke see also Ritter, *German Refugee Historians and Friedrich Meinecke*; and Frey and Jordan, "Inside-Out."

in terms of a natural desaster, thereby avoiding questions of agency and responsibility. It was clearly written out of patriotic concern, but nevertheless, the reaction to his book by some of his fellow historians showed that even mild self-criticism was not on the agenda. Meinecke was accused of fouling his own nest and other doyens of German historiography, such as Gerhard Ritter and Hans Rothfels rallied to the defence of the German nation. They argued that the success of National Socialism in Germany was rooted in European modernity, in the theories of the French Revolution, in Italian Fascism and in an overharsh Versailles Peace Treaty; in other words: there was nothing wrong with peculiarly German traditions. The defence of Ritter and Rothfels was so effective, because, unlike most of their colleagues in West German history departments, they had not lent their pens in support of the National Socialist regime. Ritter was involved in the coup of July 1944 seeking to topple Hitler and would have been minister of culture in a post-National Socialist government, had the coup been successful. Rothfels had to flee National Socialist Germany in 1938, because of his Jewish origins, and continued a very succesful career at the University of Chicago. Both were German nationalists, keen to defend the traditions of the German nation against claims that National Socialism represented those traditions. Hence they focused in their own work on the national-conservative opposition to Hitler which, to them, represented the good Germany against the bad (and un-German) National Socialists.[9]

With support of the Bavarian Land and the Federal governments of West Germany, the Institute of Contemporary History was founded in Munich in 1947 with the explicit aim of investigating the National Socialist period.[10] In fact, it spent much of its early history in producing expert reports for legal proceedings to do with the aftermath of the Third Reich. It did become an early center for research on National Socialism, but it very much focussed on the Nazis' political system and on totalitarian rule. The holocaust was not a focus of its work until much later, and indeed, it has been shown that the German directors

---

[9] Ritter, "The German Opposition to Hitler"; Rothfels, *The German Opposition to Hitler*; on Ritter see Cornelissen, *Gerhard Ritter*; on Rothfels, see Eckel, *Hans Rothfels*.

[10] Möller and Wengst, *50 Jahre Institut für Zeitgeschichte*.

of the Institute marginalized Jewish historians because they were convinced that Jewish colleagues would not be "objective" enough to do research on the National Socialist period.[11] But even Germans found it difficult to get published in the Institute's book series, if their books were too critical of German traditions. So, for example, Kurt Sontheimer's by now classic volume on anti-democratic thought in the Weimar Republic,[12] was rejected by the book series of the Institute.

In the Communist German Democratic Republic (GDR), historians, tightly controlled by the regime, busied themselves with demonstrating the entanglements of West German historians with National Socialism—sometimes being rather inventive with the sources, but at other times also problematizing pasts that colleagues in the West had been burying after 1945.[13] Tainting West Germany with the brush of Fascism was part and parcel of the GDR's strategy to undermine the legitimacy of West Germany and present itself as the "better Germany." The East German government had adopted anti-Fascism as one of the key official ideologies of the state and promoted it whenever possible. The Communist Party was portrayed as a stalwart of anti-Fascism in the 1930s and 1940s. Its leader, Ernst Thälmann, had been incarcerated and murdered in a National Socialist concentration camp, Buchenwald.[14] If, in official discourse, the Communist Party represented all that was good in German national history, then all the negative aspects were attributed to political forces still active in the capitalist West.[15]

---

[11] Berg, *Der Holocaust und die Westdeutschen Historiker*.
[12] Sontheimer, *Antidemokratisches Denken in der Weimarer Republik*.
[13] Nationalrat der Nationalen Front des Demokratischen Deutschland. Dokumentationszentrum der Staatlichen Archivverwaltung der DDR (ed.), Braunbuch: Kriegs- und Naziverbrecher in der Bundesrepublik und West-Berlin, Berlin (Ost), 1965.
[14] There has been considerable debate surrounding Thälmann's death in Buchenwalt. For a long time, West German historians in particular argued that he was killed by an allied bombing raid. However, the latest research on Thälmann argues convincingly that he was killed by his National Socialist torturers. See Norman LaPorte's forthcoming biography of Thälmann. I am grateful to Dr. LaPorte for sharing this information with me.
[15] On the manichaen nature of the GDR's history politics see the contributions in Sabrow, *Erinnerungsorte der DDR*.

This was entirely in line with the official history politics espoused by Communist East Germany. Its government saw the GDR as a new German state which had nothing to do with the German Reich. Hence it denied all responsibility for the actions of the old Reich government. It adhered to a view of history according to which you could divide German history neatly into two traditions: one positive and one negative.[16] The positive one incorporated the Peasant's War, opposition to absolutism and feudalism, the democratic revolutionary tradition, the early labor movement, the revolutionary wing of the Social Democratic Party in Imperial Germany, the Communist Party in the Weimar Republic and its anti-Fascism which ultimately culminated in the foundation of the GDR. The negative one stretched from feudalism, absolutism, militarism, the Prussia of Frederick the Great to Bismarck, Hindenburg and Hitler and this tradition, GDR history ideologues argued, was still alive in the FRG. The consequences of such a history politics for East German citizens were considerable: they could feel safe in the knowledge that they and their state stood in the anti-Fascist tradition and were not tainted by association with National Socialism.[17] As in the West, positive national traditions (albeit different ones) were emphasized leading to the marginalization of some of the most problematic legacies of National Socialism. The Holocaust did not become a prominent topic among GDR historians and in wider historical consciousness of East Germany until the 1980s.[18]

We can conclude then that from very different ideological positions, both German states sanitized the National Socialist past during the long 1950s. Whilst this continued in the GDR, the 1960s and 1970s brought a decisive break with this history politics in the West. The Auschwitz and Eichmann trials in Frankfurt (1963–1965) and Jerusalem (1961) respectively, literary events, such as the publication

---

[16] On this particular division of history into two juxtaposed traditions, see Dorpalen, *German History in Marxist Perspective*.

[17] On anti-Fascism and its role in GDR discourse on historiography and historical consciousness, see Berthold, *Marxistisches Geschichtsbild*, which allows revealing insights into the official self-understanding of the GDR.

[18] On the marginalisation of the holocaust in the GDR and its discovery as a topic during the 1980s, see Groehler, "Der Holocaust in der Geschichtsschreibung der DDR"; also more generally *Timm, Hammer, Zirkel, Davidstern*.

of Günter Grass's *The Tin Drum* (Die Blechtrommel, 1959) and Rolf Hochhuth's *The Deputy* (Der Stellvertreter, 1963) and the historical controversy surrounding Fritz Fischer's book (*Griff nach der Weltmacht*, 1961) on Germany's attempts to achieve world hegemony through world war in 1914 heightened public awareness of problematic continuities in German history and of the involvement of ordinary Germans in the regime's crimes. If historical consciousness was already changing during the early 1960s, history politics was transformed through the student protest movement of the late 1960s. The students accused their parents' generation of complicity in National Socialist crimes and of sweeping this complicity under the carpet in a post-war West Germany obsessed with the economic miracle and all its facets of crass materialism. They accused the political establishment of restaurationist tendencies after 1945 and perceived a very real threat of the capitalist Federal Republic returning to authoritarian and perhaps even Fascist policies in the context of debates on the Emergency Laws.[19]

While this belated anti-Fascism of the West German students' movement had many of its own problems, it helped to shift the ground of the official discourse on the National Socialist past. This discourse had always been more contested and less prescribed than the GDR's discourse on the Third Reich, but the official West Germany now began to commemorate the more problematic aspects of the National Socialist past, to teach it in schools and to develop a national consciousness of contrition, which differed sharply from the forgetfulness of the 1950s. "Coming to terms with the past" (Vergangenheitsbewältigung) became a project into which considerable resources and energies were invested. The advent of the Social Democrat-led government of chancellor Willy Brandt was marked by three courageous new beginnings: in foreign policy it marked the breakthrough of Neue Ostpolitik; in domestic politics it was about laying the groundwork for a more democratic society; and in its history politics, it was about making the contrition about German crimes under National Socialism a much more important element of German historical consciousness. Willy Brandt's famous act of contrition in Warsaw, when he fell to his

---

[19] On 1968 and reinterpreting the history politics of the National Socialist past, see Lüdtke, "Coming to Terms with the Past"; see also Herf, *Divided Memory*, 334.

knees in front of the Memorial to the Warsaw Ghetto Uprising, was the most significant symbolical act marking this change in the official history politics of the FRG.[20]

Of course, Brandt's gesture was extremely controversial in Germany. The center-right newspaper *Die Welt*, for example, interpreted this act of humility and penance as "capitulation and subjugation." A survey of the weekly *Der Spiegel* showed that the majority of Germans thought that Brandt's gesture was unnecessary and overdoing it.[21] During the 1969 election campaign the Christian Democrats sought to gain political capital from attacking Brandt for changing his name from Frahm to Brandt in the Second World War and returning to Germany in the uniform of a Norwegian military officer. The allegation that Brandt had somehow betrayed his fatherland in the Second World War stuck with those national-conservative circles who also vigorously opposed any acts of contrition in relation to Germany's responsibility for the atrocities of the Second World War, including the Holocaust. In the late 1960s and early 1970s Germany was still a heavily divided nation when it came to conceptions of memory politics surrounding the Second World War. It was, however, an important signal from the head of government that a younger generation of Germans, to whom Brandt appealed and who included his strongest supporters, wished to move to a more self-critical understanding of Germany's responsibility for war and genocide. It undoubtedly helped that sections of the German media moved towards a more critical attitude towards history politics in the course of the 1960s. Thus, liberal flagship weeklies, such as *Der Spiegel* and *Die Zeit* were amongst those journals which vigorously supported a more self-critical history politics vis-à-vis the National Socialist past. Whereas the German Social Democrats were influential in bringing about this shift in West-German history politics, the Austrian Social Democrats under Bruno Kreisky helped to maintain the silence of Austrian complicity in National Socialism, as they needed political allies many of whom were directly implicated in National Socialism.[22]

---

[20] On Brandt's history politics, see Merseburger, *Willy Brandt*.
[21] Kruse, *Der Kniefall von 1970*.
[22] Art, *The Politics of the Nazi Past*.

The *Historikerstreit* in the Context of Attempts to Renationalize German Historical Consciousness in the 1980s

It was against this change in the official history politics of the FRG during the 1960s and 1970s that we have to contextualize the attempts of the newly elected Christian-Democrat-led government of Helmut Kohl, coming into office in 1982, to revise the history politics associated with 1968. In his first programmatic speech as chancellor, Kohl announced plans for a "spiritual-moral renewal" of Germany. It was to end what he perceived as the dominant libertarianism and antinationalism of the 1970s and mark a return to more traditional values of church, family and nation.

The promotion of a new patriotism in Germany necessitated the relativization of the National Socialist past from its pivotal anchor point from which to interpret the whole of German history. This was the aim of one of the closest advisors of Kohl in all history politics affairs, the Erlangen-based professor of modern history, Michael Stürmer. Stürmer was no apologist of National Socialism. He was not against making the National Socialist past an important element of German historical consciousness. But he was adamant that it should not be the only element and even that it should not be allowed to dominate German historical consciousness. As he repeatedly argued in a series of influential articles in the *Frankfurter Allgemeine Zeitung* and elsewhere, Germans had a lot to be proud of, and events, movements and cultural icons, such as the Reformation, the Prussian reform movement and Immanuel Kant should not be forgotten in a historical consciousness, which, according to Stürmer, increasingly narrowed to the twelve darkest years of German history.[23]

This kind of reasoning found expression in a history politics that promoted the establishment of two new history museums in the FRG: a general German history museum in West Berlin and a history museum depicting the history of West Germany in Bonn. Whilst the former was to present a longue-durée view of German history that was to overcome the alleged fixation of German historical consciousness

---

[23] Stürmer, "Geschichte in geschichtslosem Land."

with the National Socialist past, the latter was to celebrate the achievements of the Federal Republic, from economic recovery to the establishment of a thriving liberal democracy. To the critics of the project, of whom there were many, the identitarian aspects of both museums were deeply problematical. In particular those left-liberal historians, who were often closely associated with Social Democracy and the turn of history politics in the 1960s and 1970s, wrote about the dangers of renationalizing German historical consciousness.[24]

Had the history museums already stirred left-liberal sentiments, the joint visit of Kohl and the American President Ronald Reagan to a German soldiers' cemetery near the town of Bitburg fanned the flames. The cemetery included graves of members of the Waffen-SS, and in his determination to push ahead with the visit, Kohl and his advisors made a series of public statements which indicated that they saw German soldiers, including members of the Waffen SS, as victims of Hitler and the Second World War. To those who had promoted the new history politics of the 1970s, this must have sounded like yet another attempt to sanitize the National Socialist past. In line with many international protestors and spokespersons for Holocaust survivor groups, they raised their voices in protest. The Bitburg visit damaged Kohl's reputation internationally and confirmed suspicions regarding his history politics leading to an apologia for National Socialist crimes.[25]

It was in the midst of all this that the historian Ernst Nolte published an article in the *Frankfurter Allgemeine Zeitung*, in which he argued that the Holocaust should be seen as rooted in anti-Bolshevism and the justified fears of the middle classes of the class war that a victory of Communism would unleash upon Germany. The class war of the Bolsheviks in the Soviet Union, Nolte maintained, preceded the race war of the National Socialists. The prominence of Jews among the Bolsheviks meant that the Nazis combined anti-Semitism and anti-Bolshevism. And Nolte left no doubt that the National Socialists' anti-Bolshevism was a legitimate response to a totalitarian threat. Critics of Nolte were quick to point out that such an argument might easily be

---

[24] The debate surrounding the Berlin museum is carefully documented in Stölzl, *Deutsches Historisches Museum Berlin*.
[25] On Bitburg, see Hartmann, *Bitburg in Moral and Political Perspective*.

misconstrued as justification of the Holocaust, and was, at any rate, a serious attempt to relativize the uniqueness of the criminal energies unleashed by the Nazis on Europe's Jewish population.[26]

It was an article in *Die Zeit* by the prominent philosopher and public intellectual, Jürgen Habermas, which started the Historians' Controversy. Habermas was close to the Social Democratic Party (SPD), and his intervention was rooted in history politics rather than the desire for scholarly controversy. He wanted to delegitimate the conservative-national project with which Kohl had become synonymous. He not only attacked what he saw as the apologetic tendencies in Nolte's argument; he also combined this with a claim that there was a national-conservative cabal of historians and politicians aiming to renationalize German historical consciousness. There were, of course, the history museums, and their promoter, Michael Stürmer, whom Habermas took to task for attempting to belittle the importance of the National Socialist past in German historical consciousness. Habermas also singled out another historian, whose work, he argued, contributed to the relativization of National Socialist crimes. Andreas Hillgruber's book *Two Downfalls*, published in 1986, described in two separate chapters the destruction of European Jewry and the destruction of the German East. Comparing these two events, according to Habermas, amounted to a relativization of the Holocaust. Furthermore, Hillgruber had depicted the Wehrmacht as a heroic force trying its best to defend German civilians and give them time to flee from the advancing Red Army. This, Habermas argued, completely ignored the involvement of the Wehrmacht in the Holocaust and the fact that the National Socialist regime expressly forbade civilians from leaving East Prussia and ordered every town and city to be defended.[27]

Habermas's article was the starting point of a whole series of articles, largely by left-liberal historians who published in left-liberal newspapers, such as *Die Zeit*, *Süddeutsche Zeitung* or *Frankfurter Rundschau*, and who aimed at the same target as Habermas. They wanted to defeat an alleged national-conservative turn in West Germany's history

---

[26] Nolte, "Vergangenheit, die nicht vergehen will. Eine Rede, die geschrieben, aber nicht gehalten werden konnte."
[27] Habermas, "Eine Art Schadensabwicklung: die apologetischen Tendenzen in der deutschen Zeitgeschichtsschreibung."

politics and rally to the cause of the history politics of the 1970s which had put an engagement with National Socialism center stage. They also saw themselves as defending "critical" history—i.e., a history that would not be apologetic or legitimatory, but which would be oppositional and pose critical and uncomfortable questions to the past. To this end they set up a number of positions which, they argued, needed to be defended. First, that the Holocaust was unique in world history. The systematic and industrial murder of an entire people based on ideologies of race could not be compared with any other genocide or atrocity. Second, that the National Socialist period prevented Germans from developing positive national consciousness. Therefore they would be better off to endorse the notion of postnationalism and develop what Habermas described as "constitutional patriotism." Taking this idea from the political scientist Dolf Sternberger, Habermas gave "constitutional patriotism" a postnational twist in that he associated it with a commitment to constitutional values of freedom and democracy that were potentially universal. He held up the USA and France as two nation-states where constitutional patriotism had successfully replaced ethnic definitions of nationalism and had been much more benign than an ethnically-based German nationalism during the first half of the twentieth century.[28]

The Historians' Controversy ended in 1987 with the alleged victory of this left-liberal position. Its representatives, above all the political social historians associated with the Bielefeld school, patted themselves on the back, safe in the knowledge that the public debate had prevented plans to renationalize German historical consciousness. And it is true, they had dominated the debate. Some more center-right historians, such as Kurt Hildebrandt or Horst Möller, and some publicists, such as Joachim Fest, had spoken up in defence of the accused troika of Stürmer, Nolte and Hillgruber and, in turn, attacked their critics for suffering from a persecution complex. Rather than portraying the work of these three historians as a political cabal to restore positive national consciousness, they argued that the three had very different motivations, that their arguments were primarily scholarly rather than

---

[28] On the career (or rise and fall) of the concepts of postnationalism and constitutional patriotism see Beyme, "Deutsche Identität zwischen Nationalismus und Verfassungspatriotismus."

political and they accused the left-liberal juste milieu to make them scapegoats in order to pursue their own history politics.[29]

On the left, a handful of West German Marxist historians, such as Reinhard Kühnl or Georg Fülberth depicted the Historians' Controversy as a sign that deeply problematical continuities in the interpretation of German history were about to surface again. In line with a number of GDR historians, such as Kurt Pätzold, who also commented on the controversy, they pointed to long-term nationalist continuities and drew a direct line between traditional historiographical nationalism and the positions of the West-German center-right in the mid-1980s. Yet they were also critical of the clear Western orientation of the left-liberal historians and instead emphasised that the revolutionary traditions of the German working class was the only sound basis for the development of positive forms of national identity. Like the center-right they were deeply sceptical of ideas of postnationalism and constitutional patriotism. The East German historians and the handful of their West-German allies took a position that was entirely in line with the GDR's history politics of the 1980s. The other Germany had its own "tradition and heritage" debate in this decade, that witnessed sustained efforts to rehabilitate national figures who had previously been banned from the Communist national pantheon, including Martin Luther and Otto von Bismarck. This East German historical revisionism was meant as a contribution to build the socialist nation of the GDR, which had become official policy of the ruling SED in the 1980s. Arguably, this national turn in the GDR only prepared the road to reunification, as it familiarized East Germans with many traditional national paradigms and heroes.

Yet, in the public, newspaper-based controversy, the opinions of the left-liberal critics of "spiritual-moral renewal" weighed more heavily than those of its defenders, perhaps not the least because many center-right historians viewed the controversy as a political event without any scholarly merits and therefore refused to take part in it. In the spirit of German historicism, they upheld the values of scholarliness against the demands of history politics. They refused to accept the

---

[29] Hildebrandt, "Wer dem Abgrund entkommen will, muss ihn aufs genaueste ausloten"; Möller, "Es kann nicht sein, was nicht sein darf"; Fest, "Die geschuldete Erinnerung."

degree to which this debate was shapend by politics and was aligned to clear party-political positions with Habermas and his allies practically speaking on behalf of the SPD and their opponents defending the actions of the Christian-Democratic government. However, by coincidence, Hillgruber died in 1989, Stürmer withdrew increasingly from his highly visible political role, and Nolte, partly through his own, ever more right-wing public utterances, manoeuvred himself into scholarly and social isolation. All of this seemed to demonstrate very visibly that the center-right had "lost" the debate. And the resignation of Jenninger, discussed at the beginning of this article, just confirmed the view that it had become impossible in the FRG to talk about National Socialism and the Holocaust in any other way than in the language of contrition.

Contrary to the intentions of Stürmer and the center-right history politics, initiated by the Kohl government, the 1980s saw the strengthening of a critical historical consciousness anchored in the National Socialist past. The popular history workshop movement made the National Socialist period the centre of its activities in many localities.[30] Villages, towns and cities commemorated their Jewish citizens persecuted and murdered under National Socialism. Leading historians of the history workshop movement in West Germany, such as Alf Lüdtke, Michael Wildt and Peter Schöttler, had been critical of attempts to renationalize German historical consciousness, but they also rejected the strong Western orientation of both main camps in the Historians' Controversy. Rejecting both master narratives of a positive and a negative Sonderweg in German history, they opted for a more radical decentering of national perspectives in history writing by paying greater attention to the everyday in which the national discourse was often not so prominent.[31] Films, such as Michael Verhoeven's *The Nasty Girl (Das schreckliche Mädchen)* celebrated attempts by the younger generation to explore the National Socialist past of their home towns and their inhabitants. By the end of the 1980s, then, West Germany seemed well on its way to endorsing a history politics that made National Socialism the anchor point of German historical

---

[30] On the German history workshop movement, see Lüdtke, *The History of Everday Life*.
[31] Gerstenberger and Schmidt, *Normalität oder Normalisierung*.

consciousness and drew lessons from that past which pointed in the direction of the acceptance of two German states. Postnationalism and constitutional patriotism appeared to many on the center-left as the only reasonable identitarian concepts open to the Germans. As Heinrich August Winkler famously put it in his article on the Historians' Controversy, a unified German nation state that had come into being in 1871 and lasted until 1945, had been disastrous not just for Germans but for Europeans more generally. Hence, it might be best to regard it as an historical abberration, an experiment proven not to work.[32]

The Historikerstreit as Seen from a Post-Unification Perspective

Reunification significantly changed the parameters of history politics. Suddenly and rather unexpectedly, a reunited Germany was confronted with the question whether it was not necessary to promote national identity as a means to bringing about inner unity. Between 1990 and 1995 a number of far right-wing historians and publicists, most of whom did not have a position at the universities, attempted to move German historical consciousness decisively to the right. With the help of the right-wing flagship weekly *Junge Freiheit* and a string of high-profile book publications, they sought to promote a new perspective on the National Socialist past. While they did not deny the Holocaust, they marginalized it in their writings on National Socialism which, instead, were dominated by ideas about the National Socialist modernization of Germany. Given that modernization was widely positively connotated in normative terms, they were hoping to rehabilitate the National Socialist past from its alleged one-sided fixation with the Holocaust. Equating the "brown" with the "red" dictatorship in the GDR was also a means to relativize the importance of the Third Reich for German historical consciousness. However, the "New Right" remained marginalized in the wider intellectual discourse of the FRG, and by 1995, one of its foremost representatives, Rainer Zitelmann,

---

[32] Winkler, "Auf ewig in Hitlers Schatten? Zum Streit über das Geschichtsbild der Deutschen."

admitted that they had been unsuccessful in shifting the terms of the history politics debate.³³ They failed, in particular, to take with them the national-conservative mainstream amongst established historians, who shared certain ideas with the "New Right," e.g., the need to renationalize German historical consciousness, the desire to highlight the criminal energies of the Communist regime in the GDR, the dislike of 1968 and the left-of-center juste milieu of the old FRG. However, this national-conservative mainstream had come to share the belief in the importance of National Socialism for German historical consciousness and were unwilling to condone and go along with the apologetic tendencies in the writings of the New Right. Even more, they were opposed to the New Right's anti-liberal and anti-democratic overtones, which found expression in their toying with ideas connected to the thinkers of the Conservative Revolution in the Weimar Republic.

Were the 1990s then much ado about nothing in terms of German history politics? Hardly. Reunification had led to a fundamental rethinking of the left-liberal position from the 1980s. For a start, many left liberals were now embarrassed about their previous contacts with Communist East Germany. A retrospective anti-Communism took hold of German politics and historiography, which led to the vilification of the post-Communist Party of Democratic Socialism (PDS) and to statements of historians devaluing practically all scholarship that GDR historians had carried out over the past 40 years.³⁴ The national sentiment displayed by the 1989 revolutionaries and parts of West Germany and the unexpected task of forging a new and greater Germany again also led to the abandonment of ideas of postnationalism and constitutional patriotism that had previous been championed by many left liberals. Finally, the argument about the uniqueness of the Holocaust was dropped, as more and more research comparing genocides across the globe was being published. At the beginning of the 21st century it was no longer taboo to compare the Holocaust to other genocides, even if we still encounter provisos that comparing is different from equating.

---

[33] For the rise and fall of the "new right," see Wiegel, *Die Zukunft der Vergangenheit*.
[34] Berger, "Anticommunism after the Fall of Communism?"; also ibid., "The Search for Normality."

In terms of German history politics, the 1990s were characterized by a re-alignment of historical-political positions in the reunified Germany. The center-right and the center-left, which had still done battle in the Historians' Controversy during the 1980s, now came together in a quasi-consensus on history politics. This involved recognition on all sides that German historical consciousness was in need of some renationalization, that National Socialism had to remain the anchor point of German historical consciousness, and that the achievements of the FRG after 1949 had to be celebrated as the long-delayed and successful westernization of the German mindset. It had already been clear during the Historians' Controversy that representatives from both sides of the controversy shared a strong attachment to "the West" and westernization: they were all committed Europeans and Atlanticists and admirers of Western forms of democracy, be they French, British or American. The new consensus found its expression in the inauguration of the Holocaust memorial in the center of Germany's new and old capital, Berlin, the Norman Foster cupola on top of the Reichstag, and the redesigned national history museum also in Berlin. The key historical narrative has been provided by Heinrich August Winkler's two-volume *The Long Way West (Der lange Weg nach Westen)*, which precisely described both the difficulties of Germans with westernization before 1945, culminating in the twelve darkest years of German history, and the successful westernization after 1945 which, alas, were combined with yet another Sonderweg—that of postnationalism. Only the revolution of 1989 opened the way towards "normal" post-national historical consciousness which combined with westernization would ensure the peaceful and harmonious integration of Germany into the European Union. The language of "normality" and the search for normality was *the* most significant parameter change in German history politics since the mid-1980s and amounted to a coda to the Historians' Controversy.

It was arguably on the basis of this new consensus on history politics that had been forged during the 1990s that the so-called New Victims' Discourse rose to prominence in the 2000s. The novelist W.G. Sebald was one of the first who argued, already in the 1990s, that it had become a taboo in German public discourse to talk about German victimhood surrounding the events of the Second World War. But, he maintained, Germans had been victims too: they had suffered tremendously from the bombing war against German cities, the ethnic cleansing of millions of Germans from East-Central and Eastern Europe and the atrocities committed by the Red Army as it advanced through German territories. One of the most prominent left-of-center intellectuals, Günter Grass, was to agree with him. His novel *Crabwalk (Im Krebsgang, 2002)* described the sinking of the Wilhelm Gustloff interweaving descriptions of the event with the story of right-wing attempts in contemporary Germany to gain political advantage from the tabooing of German victimhood in the Second World War. Grass argued that any such taboos would just work in favor of the political right which made it all the more urgent to bring private memories of victimhood in line with public memories of perpetratorship. This seemed all the more necessary, as research on the private memories of the National Socialist period seemed to show the inability of Germans to conceive of close family members as perpetrators in the crimes committed by the National Socialist regime.[35] The partial rediscovery of the "German East," noticeable in the popularity of books and television documentaries on East Prussia and the attention lavished by the German media on the 750th anniversary of Kaliningrad in 2005, was part and parcel of this recovery of stories of German victimhood.

Of course, as several historians have pointed out, the idea of the tabooing of German victimhood after 1945 is a myth.[36] As indicated above, the history politics of West Germany in the 1950s was all about victimhood and even the GDR's emphasis on anti-Fascism meant that the stories were about German Communist victims of National Socialism. It was arguably only with the fundamental change in the public memory culture of West Germany during the 1960s and 1970s that the memory of victimhood was privatized and left to far-right wing groups and the German expellee organizations. However, does such a timeline not indicate that the reunified Germany is returning to the deeply problematical sanitized memory of the 1950s?

I think the answer to this question has to be a resounding no. Why? Because West Germany has gone through a prolonged period in which it focused on German perpetratorship. Because Germans have become almost world champions in successful efforts of coming-to-terms with a deeply troubling past. And because what is returning is

---

[35] Welzer et al., *Opia war kein Nazi*.
[36] Berger, "On Taboos, Traumas and Other Myths."

substantially different from the history politics of the 1950s precisely because it is based on a very widespread consensus in German public debates that National Socialism and the memory of German responsibility for the holocaust and the cruelties of the Second World War should remain an essential ingredient of German historical consciousness. Germans can remember the German victims of the bombing war, because it comes with a realization that citizens of other nationalities had been victims of German aerial bombardment before. They can talk about mass rape committed by members of the Red Army because they at the same time remember the deliberate policy of scorched earth pursued by the Wehrmacht as they retreated through the Soviet Union. And they can mourn the loss of German culture in East Central and Eastern Europe, because it comes with a realization that the National Socialist reordering of Europe already involved ethnic cleansing on a massive scale. In this sense the debate on German victimhood introduces much-needed shades of grey into a very black and white debate surrounding perpetrators and victims. But, and one should not underestimate this, it remains a very difficult tightrope to walk, as it is so easy to hit the wrong tone and be misunderstood in this debate.

Conclusion

This all-too-brief survey of German history politics between 1949 and the present, that has focused on the National Socialist years in German historical consciousness, underlines the importance of wider political frameworks. The Communists in East Germany prescribed a history politics that was based on the GDR's self-understanding as anti-Fascist, representing all the positive traditions in German national history. The liberal-democratic framework in West Germany meant that the debate was more contested with many more open debates about history politics ranging from the widespread critique of Friedrich Meinecke's early attempt to learn lessons from the National Socialist past to the Historians' Controversy of the 1980s. The major political caesuras of the FRG impacted strongly on dominant forms of history politics. Thus an earlier forgetfulness about German perpetratorship and responsibility for National Socialist war and genocide gave way in the 1960s and 1970s to impressive attempts to make the National Socialist period the anchor point of German historical consciousness. The Historians' Controversy was an attempt by the left-liberal mainstream to prevent any alleged changes to the prominence of National Socialism for German historical consciousness, which had important repercussions on German national identity which was increasingly discussed in terms of postnationalism and constitutional patriotism—at least in the left liberal intellectual milieu of the FRG.

Reunification saw another decisive shift in German history politics—following on from a defeated challenge by an intellectual New Right, representatives of the center-right and center-left, which had found themselves on opposing sides during the Historians' Controversy, now came together in a more or less unified search for national normality. German history politics consequently became focussed on helping Germans to develop national normality, and the flag waving during the football World Cup in 2006 was widely seen as a sign that Germans were indeed on their way to becoming a normal "Western" nation. The discourse of normalcy is, of course, primarily re-assuring Germans and the world that Germans can wave national flags, sing national anthems and feel proud of being German without immediately feeling the urge to invade other countries. And, it has to be said, so far they have been doing quite a convincing job.

BIBLIOGRAPHY

Art, D. *The Politics of the Nazi Past in Germany and Austria.* Cambridge: Cambridge University Press, 2006.

Baldwin, P. *Reworking the Past: Hitler, the Holocaust and the Historians' Dispute.* Boston, MA: Beacon Press, 1990.

Berg, N. *Der Holocaust und die westdeutschen Historiker: Erforschung und Erinnerung.* Göttingen: Wallstein, 2003

Bergen, D.L. "Controversies About the Holocaust: Goldhagen, Arendt and the Historians' Conflict," in ed. Lehmann, H., *Historikerkontroveren.* Göttingen: Vandenhoeck and Ruprecht, 2000, 141–174.

Berger, S. "Anticommunism After the Fall of Communism? The Anti-Left Syndrome of the SPD and its Impact on Contemporary German Politics" in *Debatte* vol. 3, no. 1 (1995): 66–97.

———. "On Taboos, Traumas and Other Myths: Why the Debate about the German Victims of the Second World War is not a Historians' Controversy" in *Germans as Victims: Remembering the Past in Contemporary Germany.* Edited by Bill Niven, Basingstoke: Palgrave MacMillan, 2006, 210–224.

———. *The Search for Normality: National Identity and Historical Consciousness in Germany since 1800.* 2nd edition, Providence, R.I.: Bergham Books, 2003, Chapter 7.

Berthold, W. *Marxistisches Geschichtsbild – Volksfront und antifaschistisch-demokratische Revolution. Zur Vorgeschichte der Geschichtswissenschaft der DDR und zur Konzeption der Geschichte des deutschen Volkes.* Berlin: Akademie-Verlag, 1970.

Brinks, J.H. *Die DDR-Geschichtswissenschaft auf dem Weg zur deutschen Einheit.* Frankfurt/Main: Aufbau, 1992.

Cornelissen, C. *Gerhard Ritter: Geschichtswissenschaft und Politik im 20. Jahrhundert.* Düsseldorf: Droste, 2001

Dorpalen, A. *German History in Marxist Perspective. The East German Approach.* Detroit: Wayne State University Press, 1985.

Eckel, J. *Hans Rothfels: Eine intellektuelle Biographie im 20. Jahrhundert.* Göttingen: Vanderhoeck and Ruprecht, 2005.

Eley, G. "Nazism, Politics and the Image of the Past: Thoughts on the West-German Historikerstreit, 1986–1987," *Past and Present* vol. 121 (1988): 171–208.

Evans, R. *In Hitler's Shadow: West German Historians and the Attempt to Escape the Nazi Past.* New York: I. B. Tauris, 1989.

Fest, J. "Die geschuldete Erinnerung." *FAZ*, August 29, 1986.

Forever in the Shadow of Hitler? Original Documents of the Historikerstreit, the Controversy Concerning the Singularity of the Holocaust. Translated by James Knowlton and Truett Cates. Atlantic Highlands, N.J.: Humanities Press International, 1993.

Frei, N. *Vergangenheitspolitik: die Anfänge der Bundesrepublik und die NS-Vergangenheit.* Munich: C. H. Beck, 1996.

Frey, H. and S. Jordan. "Inside-Out: the Purposes of Form in Friedrich Meinecke's and Robert Aron's Explanations of National Disaster" in *Nationalizing the Past: Historians as Nation-Builders in Modern Europe.* Edited by Berger, S. and C. Lorenz. Basingstoke: Palgrave MacMillen, 2010, 282–297.

Gerstenberger, H. and Schmidt, D. eds. *Normalität oder Normalisierung: Geschichtswerkstätten und Faschismusanalyse.* Münster: Westfaelisches Dampfboot, 1987.

Groehler, O. "Der Holocaust in der Geschichtsschreibung der DDR" in *Zweierlei Bewältigung.* Edited by Herbert, U. and O. Groehler. Hamburg: Ergebnisse Verlag, 1992.

Habermas, J. "Eine Art Schadensabwicklung: die apologetischen Tendenzen in der deutschen Zeitgeschichtsschreibung." *Die Zeit*, July 11, 1986.

Hartmann, G.H. ed. *Bitburg in Moral and Political Perspective.* Indianapolis: Indiana University Press, 1986.

Heer, H. and Naumann, K. eds. *Vernichtungskrieg: die Verbrechen der Wehrmacht, 1941–1944.* Hamburg: Zweitauendeins, 1995.

Herf, J. *Divided Memory: The Nazi Past in the Two Germanies.* Cambridge, M.A.: Harvard University Press, 1997).

Hildebrandt, K. "'Wer dem Abgrund entkommen will, muss ihn aufs genaueste ausloten." *Die Welt*, Nov. 22 ,1986
Kruse, C. *Der Kniefall von 1970—ein symbolischer Durchbruch?* Norderstedt: Grin-Verlag, 2008.
Lüdtke, A. "Coming to Terms with the Past Illusions of Remembering, Ways of Forgetting Nazism in West Germany." *Journal of Modern History* vol. 65 (1993): 542–572.
Lüdtke, A. ed. *The History of Everday Life: Reconstructing Historical Experiences and Ways of Life.* Princeton, N.Y.: Princeton University Press, 1995.
Maier, C. *The Unmasterable Past: History, Holocaust and German National Identity.* Cambridge, MA: Harvard University Press, 1988.
Meinecke, F. *The German Catastrophe: Reflections and Recollections.* New York: Praeger, 1966.
Merseburger, P. *Willy Brandt, 1913–1992: Visionär und Realist.* Stuttgart: DVA, 2002.
Moeller, R. "War Stories: The Search for a Usable Past in the Federal Republic of Germany" *American Historical Review* vol. 101 (1996): 1029.
Möller, H. "Es kann nicht sein, was nicht sein darf" *Beiträge zur Konfliktforschung* vol. 4 (1986): 146–151.
Möller, H. and U. Wengst, eds. *50 Jahre Institut für Zeitgeschichte: eine Bilanz.* Munich: C. H. Beck, 1999.
Nolte, E. "Vergangenheit, die nicht vergehen will. Eine Rede, die geschrieben, aber nicht gehalten werden konnte." *Frankfurter Allgemeine Zeitung*, June 6, 1986.
Ritter, G. "The German Opposition to Hitler." *Contemporary Review* vol. 177 (1950): 339– 345.
———. *German Refugee Historians and Friedrich Meinecke: Letter and Documents, 1910–1977.* Leiden: Brill, 2010.
Rothfels, H. *The German Opposition to Hitler.* Chicago: Chicago University Press, 1962.
Sabrow, M. ed. *Erinnerungsorte der DDR.* Munich: C. H. Beck, 2009.
Siever, H. *Kommunikation und Verstehen. Der Fall Jenninger als Beispiel einer semiotischen Kommunikationsanalyse.* Frankfurt/Main: Peter Lang, 2001.
Sontheimer, K. *Antidemokratisches Denken in der Weimarer Republik: die politischen Ideen des deutschen Nationalismus zwischen 1918 und 1933.* Stuttgart: DVA, 1964.
Stölzl, C. ed. *Deutsches Historisches Museum Berlin: Ideen—Pespektiven—Kontroversen.* Berlin: Propylaen, 1988.
Stürmer, M. "Geschichte in geschichtslosem Land." *Frankfurter Allgemeine Zeitung*, April 25, 1986.
Timm, A. *Hammer, Zirkel, Davidstern: das gestörte Verhältnis der DDR zu Zionismus und Staat Israel.* Bonn: Bouvier, 1997.
von Beyme, K. "Deutsche Identität zwischen Nationalismus und Verfassungspatriotismus" in *Nation und Gesellschaft in Deutschland: historische Essays.* Hettling, M. and Nolte, P. eds. Göttingen: Vandenhoeck and Ruprecht, 1996. 80–99.

Welzer, H., Möller, S., and Tschuggnall, K. *Opi war kein Nazi: Nationalsozialismus und Holocaust im Familiengedächtnis.* Frankfurt/Main: Fischer, 2008.

Wiegel, G. *Die Zukunft der Vergangenheit. Konservativer Geschichtsdiskurs und kulturelle Hegemonie.* Cologne: Papyrossa, 2001.

Winkler, H.A. "Auf ewig in Hitlers Schatten? Zum Streit über das Geschichtsbild der Deutschen," *Frankfurter Rundschau*, November 14 ,1986

Poland's Institute of National Remembrance: A Ministry of Memory?

DARIUSZ STOLA

Poland was late among the countries of Central and Eastern Europe to establish a public institution to deal with the legacy of its Communist past. As elsewhere, the main reason for its establishment, and the most burning issue the institution was to tackle, was the operation of the Communist secret police and the post-1989 careers of its former secret collaborators. It was only in 2000 that construction of such institution begun. Causes of the delay were complex but three of them played key roles at three stages of Poland's political history of the 1990s.[1]

First, in the early 1990s the negotiated and peaceful transition from the dictatorship of the Communist party, combined with a widespread consensus that economic reforms were the priority, pushed the questions of lustration (i.e. vetting or screening the past of public officials and revealing former Security collaborators) and of coming to terms with the Communist past to the margins of public debates. The

---

[1] The subject of the Communist past is regularly present in the media and there is plethora of publications on the so called history policy (polityka historyczna) or politics of memory in contemporary Poland. Major books include: P. Śpiewak, *Pamięć po komunizmie*. Gdańsk 2005; L. Cichocka, A. Panecka (eds), *Polityka historyczna: historycy – politycy – prasa*. Warsaw, 2005; M. Cichocki, P. Kosiewski, *Pamięć jako przedmiot władzy*. Warsaw: Fundacja im. Stefana Batorego, 2008; M. Cichocki, *Władza i pamięć: o politycznej funkcji historii*. Kraków 2005; P. Kosiewski, *Pamięć i polityka zagraniczna*. Warszawa 2006; L.M. Nijakowski, *Polska polityka pamięci: esej socjologiczny*. Warsaw, 2008; S.M. Nowinowski, et al., *Pamięć i polityka historyczna : doświadczenia Polski i jej sąsiadów*, Łódź, 2008; R. Stobiecki, *Historiografia PRL. Ani dobra, ani mądra, ani piękna... ale skomplikowana. Studia i szkice*. Warsaw, 2007; R. Traba, *Przeszłość w teraźniejszości: polskie spory o historię na początku XXI wieku*. Poznań, 2009.

first non-Communist minister of interior, Krzysztof Kozłowski, having dissolved the Security Service, argued that declassifying its archives would be impractical, harmful, and cruel for victims of the past regime. Many of the former Security officers who passed the screening procedure were taken in service of the new Office for State Protection, and their new colleagues somehow absorbed the idea to keep their archival assets secret.

Second, the issue came to the center of the political stage in 1992 but in a least promising way: with an ill-worded and ill-prepared report of the Minister of Interior Antoni Macierewicz on the Security files related to persons holding key public offices.[2] This proved counterproductive: most of the deputies rejected the report, which listed a few dozen names of ministers, deputies and the president himself, as an attempt to destroy opponents of the unstable government, a threat to new Polish democracy and to its political elite. They promptly dismissed its author and the whole cabinet in the atmosphere of a major scandal. The events of June 1992 contributed to suspicious or openly hostile attitudes of many political and opinion leaders of the center and left towards the idea of lustration and to the idea of opening of the Security archives in general.

Third, in 1993 the post-Communist Social Democrats won the elections and through the following four years they made their best to prevent or at least delay any legislation on the issue.[3]

Also later on, when the electoral defeat of the Social Democrats in 1997 brought a different composition of the Sejm, the birth of the institution to take charge of the Security archives was long and difficult. It was only in late 1998, after battles between its proponents on the parliamentary right and center, and adversaries on the left, after equally heated quarrels between leaders of the post-Solidarity camp, and against harsh criticism from a significant part of the media, including the major national daily *Gazeta Wyborcza*, that the Parliament finally voted the act on the Institute of National Remembrance (Instytut Pamięci Narodowej – IPN), which was immediately but

---

[2] See for example Dudek, *Historia polityczna Polski 1989–2005*. 201–211.
[3] For a systematic presentation of the early attempts see Grzelak, *Wojna o lustrację*. The Constitutional Tribunal declared that the bill which allowed Macierewicz to present his report was unlawful.

ineffectively vetoed by the (post-Communist) president Aleksander Kwaśniewski. The Sejm rejected the veto but this was not yet the end of troubles: 18 months had passed before the Sejm finally appointed the IPN president, which was prerequisite for any institution building to start. Eventually, professor Leon Kieres, the newly appointed president, began hiring his key staff in fall 2000.

The visible hostility of the post-Communist left towards the Institute motivated its proponents in the Sejm to give it a legal shield against possible future attacks. The increasingly assertive policies of the left in 1993–1997 made such a future appear likely. Thus the Sejm made IPN a unique institution, being a part of public administration and enjoying status equal to a ministry but independent from the government and any other political organ. The key component of the shield was the position of the IPN president: elected by the Sejm in a complicated procedure with a 60 percent majority required, for a five-year term when he reigns in his institution and practically cannot be removed from office. His impeachment is legally possible but difficult to effectively apply unless he is found guilty of committing a crime, falls into serious illness, gravely neglects his duties or acts against the interests of IPN in a specific way. He also cannot be arrested unless under specified conditions. No other public official, except the country's (directly elected) president enjoys such a protected status. Although the act gave IPN the Board (council or collegium), its powers were limited to advising the president who could but did not have to take the advice.[4]

The authors of the act on IPN followed a model that had passed the test of practice since 1991 and was widely perceived a success. The idea to establish a separate public institution for handling the Security files came from Germany. IPN was to follow the German Office of the Federal Commissioner for Preserving the Records of the State Security Service of the former GDR (*Bundesbeauftragte für die Unterlagen des Staatssicherheitsdienstes der ehemaligen Deutschen Demokratischen Republik*, or BStU), then known as the Gauck institute and now as Birthler institute,

---

[4] The act on IPN of December 28, 1998, with further amendments (Ustawa o Instytucie Pamięci Narodowej – Komisji Ścigania Zbrodni przeciwko Narodowi Polskiemu) available at http://www.ipn.gov.pl/portal/pl/32/4862/USTAWY.html.

after the names of the commissioners Joachim Gauck and Marianne Birthler.[5] However, Polish legislators did not just imitate the Germans. They gave IPN a shorter and more inspired name, gave it more powers and charged it with a much broader scope of responsibilities. In response to widespread beliefs that the coming to terms with Communist past is an important issue and that Poland was in these matters late and behind other Central European countries, they designed a kind of special ministry for the difficult past. One does not have to be Hayekian to note that rather they followed the etatist (statist) way of thinking: if you have a problem, create a government agency. Paradoxically, the leaders of this legislation were former members of the democratic opposition, people of impeccable anti-Communist record such as Janusz Pałubicki, Andrzej Rzepliński or Witold Kulesza, whom we hardly could suppose to share a predilection for big government.

IPN became a most important, visible and controversial institution of contemporary Poland. Virtually every day the national media writes and speaks about the Institute, its archives and activities. Hardly a month passes without major news from the IPN, and every year a discovery, publication or scandal by IPN or one of its employees stirs public debate.[6] To some extent this reflects the importance of questions that IPN deals with—clearly the past is still present. In part this is a consequence of its educational and PR efforts and not infrequently results from heated political conflicts about the Institute. IPN has many outspoken critics eager to blame it for various real and imaginary sins, including the most serious (or hysterical) ones: deliberate slander of national heroes and innocent ordinary men, cynical manipulation and distorting historical truth, sowing disunity and hatred, etc. Their opponents defend the Institute with equally heavyweight arguments. For them IPN does nothing but reveals the truth, restores the nation its past, shows who the real heroes were, etc., while its critics must be Security Service collaborators or their allies.

---

[5] The influence of the German model visible in the bill and confimed by the first director of IPN's Public Education Office at EurhistXX conference "The Legacy and Memory of Communism in Europe," see Machcewicz, "Poland's way of coming to terms."

[6] For the results of systematic media monitoring see http://www.ipn.gov.pl/portal/pl/18/Media_o_IPN.html.

The responsibilities of IPN include several diverse and largely separate tasks, which public opinion often confuses. There are four major tasks that correspond to the four departments of the Institute.

The preamble of the act stated that "no lawless acts of the state against citizens shall be protected by secret and they shall not be forgotten," and the main task given to IPN, similar to that of the Gauck Institute, was to gather, manage, preserve and make accessible the archives of Communist security services.[7] The services were broadly defined to include not only the civilian Security Service and its pre-1956 predecessor Ministry of Public Security but also the military intelligence and counterintelligence agencies. In addition to their records, IPN took over a few other archival collections relevant for Communist as well as Nazi repressions. Contrary to BStU, which took the Stasi files together with their archival infrastructure, IPN took the files alone and had to make its infrastructure from scratch. It was truly a challenge to build or adapt buildings for almost 90 kilometers of files and physically transfer them to new locations. This author does not know any comparable undertaking of this kind in the archival history of Europe. Moreover, the files came from several institutions with different filing systems and poor office cultures. They required a general re-ordering, reclassification and cataloging on a gigantic scale, which has not been completed ten years later. Today IPN archives are the largest in Poland. The central archive in Warsaw has some 30 kilometers of files and 11 regional archives contain more than 58 kilometers. The archival department (IPN's Office for Preservation and Dissemination of Archival Records) with its 890 employees is the largest of IPN departments.[8]

A function of IPN, which its German model never had, is investigation and prosecution of a set of major crimes of the past. The act gave IPN the tasks, staff and archives of the former Main Commission

---

[7] See footnote 3.
[8] The data on IPN's staff, collections and activities come from its annual reports, available at http://www.ipn.gov.pl/portal/pl/31/Informacje_o_dzialalnosci_IPN.html, and from recent public presentations by Dr. Władysław Bułhak and Dr. Krzysztof Persak from the Public Education Office, who kindly extended their copies to this author: "The Institute of National Remembrance and the challenges of the past in Poland" and "IPN and the Poles confront the Communist past."

for the Investigation of Crimes against the Polish Nation, which became a separate IPN department. The Commission, established as the Main Commission for the Investigation of German Crimes in Poland, had operated under changing names since 1945.[9] At the incorporation into the Institute its powers were upgraded from investigation to prosecution and its responsibilities enlarged. Now they cover prosecution of the Nazi crimes and newly defined Communist crimes (those committed by the Security and police officers: killing, torture, unlawful incarceration, etc., and the grave abuses by the Communist judiciary—the "juridical murders") as well as crimes against peace, humanity or war crimes committed between September 1939 and July 1990 on Polish soil or against Polish citizens. Some 70 percent of cases under investigation have been Communist crimes, 20 percent Nazi crimes, and five percent crimes against peace, humanity and war crimes (the third group consists mostly of killings by Ukrainian nationalists in 1943–1944).

The prosecutors enjoy the highest legal position and salaries a public prosecutor in Poland may have. The director of the Main Commission is the deputy Prosecutor General and the 104 prosecutors in his staff have the rank of national prosecutors. This status makes them largely independent from both IPN's president and the minister of justice, and their dismissal is most complicated even if they underperform. Such was the claim of some of their critics, but effects of their work are difficult to measure. Since the incorporation of the Main Commission into the Institute, they have conducted more than 9,200 investigations, of which more than 8,000 they completed. Consequently they brought to justice more than 400 defendants, of whom 148 were found guilty, i.e. an average IPN prosecutor indicted effectively less than two criminals in ten years. Such a result is far from impressive, yet partially justified by special obstacles they face: IPN deals with crimes that took place many years ago and often under extraordinary conditions. A side effect of the investigations is a growing

---

[9] In 1949–1990 it was the Main Commission for the Investigation of Nazi Crimes in Poland, then the Main Commission for the Investigation of Crimes against the Polish Nation—Institute of National Remembrance. In a sense the new Institute of National Remembrance is the expansion of the Commission of the 1990s.

collection of testimonies, more than 65,000 at present, made during official interrogations. They may serve as a valuable source for historians, albeit their quality remains to be tested.

The third main task of IPN is education and research. Its chronological scope of interest covers the Communist period and the years of war and German and Soviet occupation. Initially the Institute was expected to research and educate on matters related to the crimes and operations of the Communist security services, similarly to what BStU was doing. However, it had to respond to demands articulated by media and politicians who believed IPN is the office for all difficult matters of the past. Also historians at IPN were happy to enlarge their field of interest beyond the narrow topics. Gradually the scope expanded to various other topics of Poland's history in five decades 1939–1989, although the crimes and secret services remain its main focus. Not only the timeframe and thematic scope but also the scale of IPN's educational projects is bigger than those of BStU. The Public Education Office has more than 280 employees (13 percent of the total staff) in Warsaw and 18 regional branch offices. Its activities are the most visible for the wider public and most often attract media attention.

By its budget, staff size and the nation-wide structure, the Public Education Office is Poland's largest institute of contemporary history. It conducts extensive archival research, publishes annually dozens of document collections, monographs, dictionaries, conference volumes and albums (more than 450 volumes so far), as well as three history journals, organizes conferences, seminars and a doctoral summer school. In addition to the planned activities it occasionally gets involved in extraordinary actions in response to urgent public demand, such as the project on the mass murder of Jews in Jedwabne. Thanks to these efforts, our knowledge of Communist Poland has dramatically increased. Educational activities are equally impressive and truly massive. They are decentralized, diverse and dispersed, thus less visible, but probably more influential than IPN best-known books. They include a few hundred exhibitions moving around the country, a monthly magazine sent to every public library, several IPN-run websites, training programs for teachers and competitions for students, printed and electronic educational materials, posters and billboards, public lectures and film screenings. They seem especially attractive and effective when reaching towns with less cultural events than Warsaw or Cracow or when they address issues of local importance, such as exhibitions on "Faces of the Security" in a given region.[10] To this part of IPN's operation and its consequences we will come back again.

Until 2006 IPN was not in charge of lustration. The 1997 act on lustration put this function elsewhere and IPN played just a secondary role in providing relevant documents to the office of Public Interest Advocate. Unfortunately, in 2006 the Sejm substantially changed the lustration principles, expanded the catalogue of offices requiring lustration and made IPN responsible for a major part of the lustration process. This had several adverse effects on the IPN. First, the highly controversial changes made the Institute the target of one more intense media campaign, which resulted in a kind of PR crisis. Second, the new functions meant many labor-consuming (and sometime not most reasonable) tasks. They were given to a new department— the Lustration Office, which makes at present some 10 percent of the IPN staff (215 employees, including 26 prosecutors). Since 2007, the department has processed almost 150 thousand "vetting declarations" and prepared (but not completed) four publicly accessible internet catalogues: of senior officials in the Communist governments and the party, of Security officers, of people who were target of the Security operations and of persons currently holding higher public posts.

IPN is therefore Poland's largest archive, biggest contemporary history research institute and publisher, a major educational institution, an independent part of public administration and a privileged part of the judiciary system, and the body responsible for the lustration. It is not clear why the legislators put all these functions into one institution. The four departments do not pay attention to one another; insiders confirm that interdepartmental cooperation is weak. We rather may hear of tensions between the archivists and the research historians; what unites them is the common dislike for the allegedly ineffective but demanding and much better paid prosecutors. Moreover, there are good reasons to strengthen some in-house divisions. Close ties between the Lustration Office and the Office for Education and Research should be prevented, to avoid any blurring of the border and difference

---

[10] Piekarska, A. ed. *Przewodnik po Instytucie Pamięci Narodowej.*

between the semi-criminal and politically sensitive investigation related to lustration and academic research. Similarly, the Institute's historians should have no privileged access to IPN archives. The access should be equal for all researchers. In the past some, not all of IPN historians enjoyed privileges which stirred irritation and suspicions of academic dishonesty. In general, there are no good reasons to make a history research institute part of the government. There are much better institutional solutions to carry out such tasks (university departments, research institutes and centers) and the status of civil servant does not help in scholarly work: it either constraints the academic freedom or makes the office appear liable for personal opinions of its staff.

To fulfill all the above tasks the Institute had to grow. Today it consists of the large headquarters in Warsaw, eleven branch offices in major provincial capitals (seats of courts of appeal) and seven smaller offices in other cities. Its staff, which initially numbered 800 people, grew to 2,170, while its budget rose from 84 million to 213 million zloty, i.e. to some €55 million ($75 million). Notably, most of the growth in spending took place in 2004–2008 when the major investments in infrastructure mentioned above were already over and the archival collections were accumulating much slower than before, just a few percent per year. This was clearly related to the offensive of history policy by the governing Law and Justice Party of the Kaczyński brothers. A major component of the increase resulted from the establishment of the Lustration Office yet it was impressive also when we exclude the allocations for the Office. Its main factor has been raising salaries of the growing staff. IPN has offered salaries higher than in academia and much better prospects for young employees for upward mobility within the expanding organization (this however has strengthen bad feelings that some outsiders have about IPN). MPs of the left have tried repeatedly to reduce its allocation in the state budget, but usually with very limited success. They met with staunch opposition of the deputies of the right and center, eager to label such motions as hostile to national memory and intended to hide a dark past.

It is difficult to establish how cost effective has been the Institute along this dynamic growth. With its young and well-educated staff (85 percent have a university degree, including 145 doctors and professors) it is likely to work better than many other government agencies. However, it seems that while it spends 50 percent more than few years before it does not deliver proportionally. Some observers, including insiders, have noted a tendency for bureaucratic elephantiasis and inward orientation. Like many large organizations free from external challenge, the Institute increasingly serves itself. IPN's second largest department is its inner administration: the sections of accounting, human resources, legal counseling, building maintenance, security, etc. These sections make some 28 percent of the total personnel. If we add administrative assistants in other departments we may see a third of the staff doing no archival work, research or lustration but taking care of the Institute itself.

A striking example of the inwardness is the size of IPN archival reading rooms. The reading room of the main archive in Warsaw, located in an impressive ten-floor office building, has just 20 seats at small tables, and is permanently crowded. Researchers have to book seats several days in advance to get in. They must wait much longer, from several weeks to several months, for the files they have requested. Clearly, serving them well is not the priority of the Institute. Another example comes from IPN extensive publications. Many of them are thick volumes of archival documents, sometimes dealing with marginal topics and most unlikely to find more than a couple of readers. It is difficult to find a rationale for their costly publication other than their editors' desire to show up with concrete, measurable results in the annual report.

In the midst of heated exchanges between IPN critics and supporters, such trivial deficiencies as a small reading room, publications of dubious usefulness or impractical computer catalogue pass unnoticed. Thus the secret of IPN this paper may reveal is the following: this is indeed a Ministry of Memory, but not of the Orwellian type. It is a regular continental European bureaucracy, with usual deficiencies of its kind, and a part of Polish government administration, which is not famous for its effectiveness. Relatively safe from major threats, be it a hostile political takeover, budget cuts or competition, it is increasingly self-centered and cost inefficient. In this aspect IPN paradoxically resembles the institutions of the Communist period it is to deal with: bureaucratic, centralist, heavy, inclined to extensive growth and quantity rather than quality of production, and decreasingly effective.

These socialist qualities, together with the multi-functionality discussed allow us to see IPN as a distant cousin of the socialist *kombinat* (state-owned, vertically integrated large industrial corporation), or *zjednoczenie* (conglomerate or cartel of several state-owned companies), which combines the mines of raw materials (the archives), a large processing plant (by research and editing) and distribution of the final product (knowledge and information in various forms). IPN is not monopolist, there are other institutions that provide similar products, yet its privileged, dominant position in the market of recent history is unquestionable; its subsidized products (books, exhibitions, etc.) flood the market. Would anyone buy your book if a publisher offers three other books on a similar topic at half the price?

This deserves attention as the last but not least difference from the German model. The research department of the Gauck/Birthler institute is an important but by no means the dominant point in the rich and varied landscape of German institutions dealing with the history of the Communist past. There are many institutes and university centers working in the field, as well as several funding bodies, public and private, which offer grants and scholarships for relevant research. In Poland, IPN towers above the much poorer academic landscape by its size, budget, number of publications, official status and focus of the media. It dominates the research on contemporary history of Poland stronger than the Royal Navy once dominated the seas: its research budget is most likely bigger than the budgets of all the other research centers combined.

This is not good news for those who share this author's belief in the benefits of a plurality of perspectives and methodologies, of their competition and cross-fertilization. An academic environment heavily dominated by one institution, which is not itself famous for inner diversity, excellence and innovation (unlikely in most government offices), does not provide the best conditions for progress in research. Such a situation may be particularly dangerous when the dominant institution shows a tendency for a questionable vision of interpretations of the past.

There were moments when the Institute or its senior officials were justifiably blamed for insufficient neutrality towards party politics or for highly controversial public statements. Oversensitivity of some of IPN critics does not invalidate the argument that misconduct in the delicate and highly emotional matters of the recent past may have dangerous consequences. The risk of such abuse is not negligible as various actors on the public scene, especially those of the right, tend to exploit certain representations of the past to confront their political competitors: they use emotions-loaded narratives or images of the past as instruments of mobilization and weapons for attack. Among these abusers of the past are politicians, senior officials, journalists and, most unfortunately, historians. A particular figure of militant historian has emerged out of my profession. The kind of symbolic politics they engage in has proved at several occasions effective. Producing *dissensus* around memory is a cheap means of attracting media attention, sharpening ones ideological profile and strengthening position on the partisan scene.[11] In the long term however, it is devastating for the consensual and communitarian narratives, which means erosion of the common past as a common good.

Besides the shortsighted political abuse, there is another threat we need to note. We do not yet have systematic research on IPN's historiographic output, yet this author has the strong impression, based on reading a part its publications, that IPN has a tendency to polarize the Communist past of Poland. Who are the main actors of narratives coming out of the Institute? One is the Soviet-imposed totalitarian regime, alien, illegitimate and cruel, personified by the security officers or party apparatchiks, sometimes impersonal. The other is "the society," the people or the nation: as a rule patriotic, freedom-loving and God-fearing, represented by freedom fighters, civilian resisters, innocent victims or embodied in collective actors such as the workers, rebellious youth or indomitable clergy. In the mind-mapping of the Communist past, these are the opposite Poles so to speak, that give an orientation to the authors and the readers, probably a moral orientation they desire.

Such people existed, of course, they significantly contributed to the way Communist Poland's history went on and they deserve an adequate place in historiography. The wrong tendency is that contrary to available evidence, advanced scholarship in Poland and in other post-Communist countries, and to common sense, not much is left in between the poles. Polarized narratives pay greatly insufficient attention to support for and adaptation to the regime (willing or not), which evidently dominated; to strategies of evasion rather than resistance; and to mass participation in various institutions of the regime, beginning with the

---

[11] Mink, "Between reconciliation and the reactivation of past conflicts in Europe."

Communist Party itself. They overemphasize conflict (hence they tend to go from one political crisis to another) and underestimate the size and role of the gray zone in-between the poles, the attituteds that do not fit with the polarized image of "the regime vs. the people." Last but not least, they largely neglect the fields that are far from political history and their respective perspectives and methodologies.

To some extent this tendency was a consequence of the Institute's official mission. The mission, given in the act on IPN, is to inform about the Communist institutions of oppression, educate about the resistance against the regime and commemorate its martyrs and heroes. Giving IPN such a mission was a legitimate reaction to the opposite policies of the Communists, their efforts to erase the memory the resistance and repression, put victims into oblivion and prove the unity or even identity of the Communist rulers and those under their rule. In early years of IPN such tendency compensated for the past manipulations but since a moment it has increasingly mystified the nature of the regime, especially in the post-1956 period, i.e. during most of the Communist times. We cannot criticize IPN for the tendency because this is what the Sejm established IPN for, and reasons for such a mission were legitimate. The problem is rather in the combination of such tendency with the dominant position IPN has taken.

2011 may mark the beginning of a new chapter of IPN history. In March the Sejm amended again the act on the Institute. The changes weaken the position of the president in relation to IPN's Board and make the Board more a group of scholars than a set of appointees of major political parties it has been so far. This author sees them as a step in the right direction, but they are not going to alter the key deficiencies of IPN outlined above. Just a few weeks later, Janusz Kurtyka, the IPN president for the previous three years, died in the plane crash in Smolensk together with the president of Poland and 95 other members of delegation for the commemoration of the Katyń massacre of 1940. This opened a legal crisis and split within the Board, as controversies erupted as to which rules of the appointment of new president apply. Eventually, the procedure by the newly amended rules begun yet it proved longer and more complicated than expected. Seven months after the crash it remains far from completed. IPN has only an acting president (former vice-president) and nobody knows how much time more it will wait for a new Board and president.

BIBLIOGRAPHY

Dudek, A. *Historia polityczna Polski 1989–2005*. Cracow: Arkana, 2007.
Grzelak, P. *Wojna o lustrację*. Warsaw: Trio, 2005.
Machcewicz, P. "Poland's way of coming to terms with the legacy of Communism," *IHTP* Paris, Dec. 17, 2007.
Mink, G. "Between Reconciliation and the Reactivation of Past Conflicts in Europe: Rethinking Social Memory Paradigms." *Czech Sociological Review* vol. 69, no. 3 (2008).
Piekarska, A., ed. *Przewodnik po Instytucie Pamięci Narodowej*. Warsaw: IPN, 2009.

Jedwabne, July 10, 1941: Debating the History of a Single Day

MACIEJ JANOWSKI

I.

On July 10, 1941, in the small town of Jedwabne some 150 kilometers northeast of Warsaw, a mass murder was committed. Most of the local Jewish population was led to a barn on the outskirts of the town and burned alive. Jedwabne, in the territory of Poland before 1939 and again after 1945, was occupied by the Soviet Union in September 1939 as a consequence of the dual Nazi-Soviet invasion on Poland and accompanying stipulations of the Ribentropp-Molotov pact. Just after the German assault on the Soviet Union on June 22, 1941, the town was occupied by the German troops (June 23). The slaughter in Jedwabne was forgotten and seemed to be lost among the enormous mass of atrocities committed during the Second World War. The case was uncovered by Jan Tomasz Gross, a Polish historian living in the U.S. who published in 2000 a small book in Polish, entitled *Sąsiedzi* (The Neighbors).[1] The debate on the Polish-Jewish relations, started by his book, was considered by some of its participants as the most important memory debate in Poland after the war. It would be hard to measure whether it is really so; undoubtedly, however, among all the debates on Poland's past after the collapse of Communism in 1989, this one has generated the most emotions both among the participants and the general public.

Jan Tomasz Gross has been working for a long time on the history of the Poles under the Soviet occupation between the Soviet invasion of September 17, 1939 and the start of the German-Soviet war on

---

[1] Gross, *Sąsiedzi. Historia zagłady żydowskiego miasteczka*.

June 22, 1941. Among others, he has published a source collection of relations of the Polish children deported to Siberia and other distant regions of the Soviet Union. He also published a book on mutual Polish-German-Jewish stereotypes during the war and immediately after. Written in a lively, essayistic style, constantly aiming at understanding and interpretation rather than mere description, the books by Gross were read, applauded, contested and discussed; no one, however, had influence comparable with the storm that started with the publication of *The Neighbors*. Because the Jews of Jedwabne, wrote Gross, were not murdered by the Germans, but by their Polish neighbors. The murderers were not recruited from any marginal group; they were typical people. In a footnote, Gross hints at the title of well-known book by Christopher Browning *Ordinary Men*, dealing with German policemen who participated in the Holocaust.

Gross' book is not voluminous; it leans on witness' testimonies from the post-war penal proceedings on the Jedwabne case, on relations of some Jewish survivors, notably of Szmul Wasersztejn, as well as on interviews with a few witnesses, still alive at the time of writing of the book. Very well written, not hiding the emotions of the author, the book had a high chance to reach the broader circles of public, who would not read a lengthy professional monograph.

The problem of the Polish-Jewish relations during the Second World War was obviously debated for years before the book by Gross. Under Communist rule, however, such debate, as other debates on recent history, could not be conducted without various limitations caused by politics and censorship. Communist propaganda at some moments produced openly anti-Semitic texts; generally, however, what dominated was not anti-Semitism in open or allusive form, but tendency to marginalize or even annihilate all more complicated problems that would demand serious reflection; the highly tangled field of Polish-Jewish relations was obviously high on the list. Clear liberalization of censorship during the "first Solidarity" movement (September 1980–December 1981) brought to the surface various hitherto forbidden to discuss problems, including the Polish-Jewish issue, which, however, did not occupy a prominent place in the multi-sided, highly emotional and highly politicized public debate of 1980–1981. Worth remembering is the essay by a well-known essayist, literary historian and supporter of non-Communist democratic socialism, Jan Józef

Lipski, entitled "Two Homelands, Two Patriotisms." The essay contrasted the xenophobic nationalism with open, liberal patriotism, but it touched upon the Jewish question only marginally.

It was the last decade of Communist rule, the 1980s, that brought renewed interest in Jewish and Polish-Jewish matters. Since about mid-1980s, the liberalized censorship concentrated on controlling openly political texts, thus leaving much more field for all cultural and historical debates. The Catholic weekly *Tygodnik Powszechny*, very important outlet for voicing criticism of all forms of anti-Semitism, published in 1987 an article by an eminent literary historian Jan Błoński, entitled "A Poor Christian looks at the Ghetto." The article, referring to two poems of Czesław Miłosz, discussed the problem of Poles' passivity towards the Holocaust during the war.

In 1994 an article by Michał Cichy appeared in *Gazeta Wyborcza*, exposing the cases of killing of the Jews during the Warsaw uprising in 1944.[2] It started a lively debate, as did the text by a Jesuit priest Stanisław Musiał "Czarne jest czarne," published in *Tygodnik Powszechny* and bitterly exposing the tolerance for anti-Semitism within the Roman Catholic Church. No one of these debates, however, can be compared to the one that was stirred by Gross' book.

The storm was gathering even before the publication. A few months earlier a volume of studies appeared, entitled *Europa nieprowincjonalna. Przemiany na ziemiach wschodnich dawnej Rzeczypospolitej*, a collection of studies in honour of a distinguished scholar of Polish conspiracies during World War Two, Tomasz Strzembosz, for his 70th birthday. In this volume Jan Tomasz Gross published a short paper entitled "Summer 1941 in Jedwabne," summarizing the main points of his future book. Agnieszka Arnold prepared a documentary film on the problem, and journalist Andrzej Kaczyński visited Jedwabne and published articles about it. All this happened still before the turmoil caused by the book by Gross, and Jedwabne inhabitants talked with Kaczyński more or less openly. "After what happened here during the Soviet occupation, you should not be surprised at the Polish rage that was directed against the Jews—one Jedwabne resident told me."[3]

---

[2] http://www.żydziwpolsce.edu.pl/biblioteka/czytelnia/h_pw/001.pdf (visited 8 December 2010)

[3] Kaczyński, "Całopalenie."

Later Kaczyński commented: "It is a paradox that as long as the circumstances of the massacre of the Jews in Jedwabne were not generally known, it was a public secret. The townspeople kept the truth to themselves and repeated it among themselves, but as soon as the truth came out into the open, many people became determined to deny it."[4]

Such were the circumstances in which Jan Tomasz Gross' book appeared in the Polish bookshops, in late May 2000.[5]

II.

The book gave rise to an enormous debate,[6] with thousands of articles in the press and a number of books. Among the most important is one in two thick volumes, edited by Paweł Machcewicz and Krzysztof Persak, entitled *Wokół Jedwabnego*, published by the Institute of National Memory (a state institution charged with pursuing Nazi and Communist crimes in Poland and collecting documentation on Polish history between 1939 and 1989, especially the files of the secret police). It consisted of a series of studies by the best Polish specialists together with selection of documents. Another important book is a lengthy essay by Anna Bikont, a journalist with *Gazeta Wyborcza*, entitled "My z Jedwabnego" (2004), which meticulously reconstructs the details of the crime and the fates both of survivors and of perpetrators. Both books will be often invoked in this text: they are fundamental readings for everybody interested in the Jedwabne problem.

If we look at the content of the debate about *The Neighbors*, we notice that it was centered on the following questions:

---

[4] Polonsky, Michlic, *Jedwabne, 10 lipca 1941*, 258.
[5] Szarota, *Mord w Jedwabnem*, a chronicle of events and publications related to the crime in Jedwabne untill the publication of the Gross' book.
[6] Forecki, *Spór o Jedwabne* is the most important book on the subject, valuable through the gathered information and interesting interpretatively; it is, however, written from a different perspective than the present text, as it is focused on the discourse analysis rather than on ideas. See also Polonsky, Michlic, with the analysis of the debate in the editors' introduction; Paczkowski, "Debata wokół 'Sąsiadów.'" (Typology of reactions towards the book by Gross: affirmative, defensive-open, defensive-closed, rejecting.)

Jedwabne, July 10, 1941: Debating the History of a Single Day

- Polish-Jewish relations in the periods preceding the massacre (both in independent Poland before 1939 and during the Soviet occupation of 1939–1941), and their importance for the events of July 1941, with special reference to the attitude of the Jews towards the Soviet occupier.
- the role of the Germans
- the number of casualties
- the number of perpetrators (majority of the Polish population, or only a small group)?
- their social status (elites of the town or marginal groups)?

The disputants were also interested in two theoretical problems: the possibility of understanding through contextualization and the problem of the new attitude towards the sources, as explained by Gross.

It is no wonder that all these questions vibrate with emotions, but for analytical reasons I will try first to deal with rational arguments, and turn to emotions later.

Let us start with the problem of the genesis of the crime, which is integrally connected with the above mentioned theoretical problem of possibility of understanding. It seems that Gross himself very emphatically dismissed the possibility of any contextualization of the Jedwabne massacre. A crime on this scale is not, in his eyes, susceptible to any attempts at understanding. "Are there any parameters... that would make the Jedwabne murder carried out by the Poles against the Jews 'comprehensible?' Can we imagine a sequence of events leading up to the murder in Jedwabne that would permit us to say in conclusion something like 'Aha, I understand'?"[7]

Among the polemics touching upon this problem, sociologist Antoni Sułek approached it in most interesting way in a deep and penetrating review essay on Gross' book.[8] Sułek granted that every explanation leaves something unclear, some space for surprise and impossibility of understanding. This, however, does not change the fact that a researcher should strive at understanding, and that this understanding, up to a certain degree, is possible. He stressed his allegiance to the German tradition of *verstehende Soziologie* as a methodological device

---

[7] Gross, "Mord 'zrozumiały?'" 103–104.
[8] Sułek, "'Sąsiedzi.' Zwykła recenzja."

that can help us approach the complicated truth. Gross remained unconvinced. Every contextualization, he claimed, skips over the fact that similar factors were active on the whole of Poland's territory occupied in 1939 by the Soviet Union, whereas slaughters on such a great scale happened only in Jedwabne and two neighboring towns, Radziłów and Wąsosz. So long as nobody succeeded in presenting the specificity of Jedwabne and convincingly present, what actually makes Jedwabne different from all other towns under the Soviet occupation, no attempts at contextualization can succeed.[9]

It is worth mentioning that even before the publication of the above text by Gross, Dariusz Stola tried to fulfill the postulate of Gross (in an important text that will be analysed in more detail further on). The feature that made the region of Jedwabne different from all other parts of Poland under Soviet occupation was that it is part of a more or less ethnically Polish (or rather Polish-Jewish) territory, without a strong presence of other nationalities (Belarusians or Ukrainians or Lithuanians). According to Stola, on the territories with strong Ukrainian or Lithuanian presence the Lithuanian or Ukrainian anti-Semitism made itself known immediately after the German entrance. The reason was not that these nationalities were more anti-Semitic than the Poles, there is no ground to suppose it: it happened because the Ukrainian and Lithuanian politicians, contrary to the Poles, hoped for a space for common political action with the Germans and believed that anti-Semitism offered such a space. In this situation the local Poles, in conflict with the Ukrainians and Lithiuanians, did not join the anti-Semitic actions which they perceived as alien and potentially dangerous to the Poles as well. In the region of Jedwabne, there were no other nationalities but Poles and Jews; thus, the Poles felt free to express their anti-Semitic attitudes.

Analyzing the genesis of the crime, the most controversial problem was what Tomasz Strzembosz in the title of one of his texts called "Collaboration passed over in silence," the question of degree and character of co-operation of the Jews with the Soviets after September 17, 1939. This problem is touched in various ways and with some authors the reader has the impression that in their opinion the Jewish collaboration

---

[9] Gross, "Antoniemu Sułkowi w odpowiedzi," 104.

in certain sense justifies the murderers or at least diminishes their guilt. However, the authors who are generally close to Gross in general terms of world-view, as Antoni Sułek or Andrzej Żbikowski, also stress the importance of this factor. Both the above mentioned suppose that a mental mechanism was present, which made the small minority of Jews, actively collaborating with the Soviets most visible and best memorized by the Poles which renovated the old stereotype of "Jewish Communism." Żbikowski and some other authors stress also that the Soviet system was not guided by the racist criteria in its repression, and the Jews were up to a certain degree admitted to the administrative functions which by itself caused surprise and outrage among many Poles. As Jan M. Milewski has put it, "the Polish community was offended by the unthinkable exchange of the social roles."[10] The authors dealing with this problem try to ascertain the nature of various instances of Jewish collaboration with the Soviets, as well as the voluntary or forced character of this collaboration. The additional element is that in the Polish language, more than in English, the very term "collaboration" is emotionally loaded as it means only collaboration with enemy occupying power (other words are used for all other types for collaboration). In this context it is quite amazing that almost nobody put the question whether the term "collaboration" at all fits the situation of the Jews (or Ukrainians or Belarusians) in Poland in 1939: the national minorities did not considered Poland "their" state, therefore it is difficult to reproach them with disloyalty or with treason. The only authors, as far as I know, who stressed this were historian from Warsaw University Marcin Kula and German historian Klaus Bachman.[11]

As if marginally, in one of his numerous texts, Tomasz Strzembosz turned our attention to one more circumstance of the crime: cruelty in the Polish countryside. "Cruelty, that one can observe with the children, tormenting a cat; cruel treatment of village dogs; cruelty towards elderly people," e.g., towards disabled parents, towards the disabled in general and towards the mentally handicapped. Strzembosz saw the cruelty towards the Jews in the context of this overwhelming cruelty.[12] This thread, to my knowledge, was not developed in further discussions.

---

[10] Milewski, "Polacy i Żydzi w Jedwabnem," 129–158.
[11] Both authors quoted by Bikont, *My z Jedwabnego*, 113.
[12] Strzembosz, "Szubienica i huśtawka,"

The next question is that of the role of the Germans. Numerous critics presented Gross as claiming that the Germans did not have any role in the massacre. Gross, however, is very clear here: "The overall undisputed bosses over life and death in Jedwabne were the Germans.... They were the only ones who could decide the fate of the Jews.... Had Jedwabne not been occupied by the Germans, the Jews of Jedwabne would not have been murdered by their neighbors.... The tragedy of Jedwabne Jewry is but an episode in the murderous war that Hitler waged against all Jews. As to the Germans' *direct* [my stress – MJ] participation in the mass murder in Jedwabne on July 10, 1941, however, one must admit that it was limited, pretty much, to taking pictures."[13]

Radical opponents of Gross claim that the whole crime was committed by the German hands, with possible marginal activity of the Poles. Most of those who claimed it were radical rightist publicists, among the historians Tomasz Strzembosz seemed to be close to this opinion in some of his publications. The majority of historians, however, acknowledged that the crime was committed physically by the Poles, although they acted under German pressure or perhaps even compulsion. Andrzej Żbikowski analyzed analogous crimes in Radziłów and Wąsosz.[14] Numerous researchers (A.Żbikowski, T.Strzembosz, T.Szarota,[15] D.Stola, and following him, Marek Wierzbicki) stress a repeating pattern of massacres. Especially important is here the work of Dariusz Stola, which indicates a degree of organization of the Jedwabne massacre, by far exceeding what we could have expected from the spontaneous initiative of the inhabitants. The Jedwabne massacre, claims Stola, is not a "classical" pogrom. He stresses that in the pogroms in the Ukraine in 1918–1919, analyzed by various historians, at least 80 percent of the Jews survived. A "normal" pogrom causes some deaths and more injuries, and then dissolves itself into robbery and drinking. The very idea to kill all the Jews remains beyond the horizon of imagination of the perpetrators of a "normal" pogrom. This idea must have been suggested by the Germans, most probably during a meeting at the city hall at the eve of the massacre—a meeting,

---

[13] *Neighbors*, 78.
[14] Żbikowski, "Pogromy i mordy ludności żydowskiej."
[15] Szarota, "Mord w Jedwabnem. Udział ludności miejscowej w Holokauscie," 175.

described by Gross as a "council," although in fact, writes Stola, it was rather "clearance." The local authorities, either organized spontaneously after the Soviet retreat, or nominated by the Germans after their advance, were no real partners with the German authorities; they could only receive the German orders. What is more, the internal organization of the pogrom was such as was absolutely unattainable by the local population by themselves; it must have been imposed from outside. There was, writes Stola, a certain "order of killing" with some people staying and watching, some other being "willing executioners" and between these two groups there was a whole spectrum of intermediary behavior.

According to Stola, Gross correctly hints at the role of individual acts of ordinary men in totalitarian systems, stressing that not everything can be explained by state activities. This time, however, "Gross has gone too far in marginalizing the role of the state institutions in the analyzed events." Stola writes: "In the events of July 10, I perceive.... a certain order.... This order comes from the state, we may even say that this order is the state. In the events of the 10th of July there appears a very singular, even grotesque, state—territorially very small Jedwabne state, existing by the will of the occupying power and (co-) administered by its local collaborators. We cannot treat it just as a form of self-organization of society, as an emanation of the civil society.... This state... possesses... a key property of a state: it has the means of compulsion at its disposal and it decides who can use force and on what principles. On these grounds it allows for the day of 10th of July the use of force by everybody, provided that it is used against the Jews and only against the Jews."

Stola notices that no sources mention any "specific murder that would have been committed on that day by a German," and he notices a fascinating thing: "What is missing in the descriptions of events is... the sound of shooting. In testimonies this silence is striking, silence in which people who work in fields outside of the town hear the voices of the victims.... And obviously some tens of people have been killed outside of the barn. This silence indicates that they have not been killed with firearms," as the Germans would have done.[16]

---

[16] Stola, "Pomnik ze słów."

Stola's text belongs to the most penetrating attempts at detailed analysis in the whole Jedwabne debate. In a similar vein, Edward Dmitrów, Andrzej Żakowski and Tomasz Szarota[17] analyzed in detail the attitudes and decisions of the high-level German officials, who, although not present at Jedwabne, obviously very much influenced the situation there through their orders. Especially important was the analysis of orders issued by chief of the Main Office of State Security (Reichssicherheitsamt), Reinhardt Heydrich, from the turn of June and July 1941, which stress the importance of encouraging the local population of occupied territories to anti-Jewish activities.

One of the central threads of the polemics around *The Neighbors* was a postulate of "affirmative attitude towards the sources," as presented by Gross. By and large, Gross' idea is that when studying the Holocaust period we should start with temporarily assuming the trustworthiness of the relations of Holocaust survivors, and reject them only in cases where find strong arguments against them. In other words, the burden of the proof should lie on those researchers who tend to disbelieve the testimonies of the survivors. Gross' argument is twofold: first he invokes the pragmatic motive, claiming that the danger of a mistake is smaller than in the opposite case. The second argument is more complicated. What we know from the eyewitness' reports "by the very fact that it was actually told, is not a representative sample of the Jewish fate," as it comes from the people who survived and even if they made their notes during the war and did not live to see its end, still they were alive up to the moment in which they were writing. "For what has reached us was written only while the authors were still alive. About the 'heart of darkness' that was also the very essence of their experience, about their last betrayal, about the Calvary of 90 percent of the prewar Polish Jewry—we will never know. And that is why we must take literally all fragments of information at our disposal, fully aware that what actually happened to the Jewish community during the Holocaust, can only be more tragic than the existing representation of events based

---

[17] Szarota, *U progu zagłady*. (Szarota's study, published at the same time as Gross' book, does not mention the case of Jedwabne, but it provides very broad and important comparative material about the anti-Semiic activities in the Nazi-occupied Europe on the eve of the Holocaust); Dmitrów, "Oddziały operacyjne niemieckiej Policji"; Żbikowski, *U genezy*, 167–211.

on surviving evidence."[18] Whether we agree with this heuristic proposal or not, it seems to me a serious proposal worthy of reflection, whereas many of Gross' opponents reduced it ad absurdum, claiming that according to Gross we should "prejudge in advance that the accounts of Holocaust survivors are true."[19] I do not know any of Gross' statements that would warrant such an interpretation of his position.

A lengthy and very critical review by Bogdan Musiał of *The Neighbours* concentrates precisely on the issue of the trustworthiness of witnesses. Musiał attempts to prove some are unreliable, showing internal contradictions in some accounts that he argues proves that the authors could not have been present in Jedwabne on July 10, 1940, so they cannot claim first-hand knowledge.[20] In turn, Gross responded by questioning many of Musiał's arguments, and reproaching the author with inaccuracies and in some cases clear polemical ill will.

The problem of the degree of involvement of Polish inhabitants of Jedwabne in the massacre is almost as central to the debate as the problem of the German presence and responsibility. Were they only insolated individuals, "scum of the earth," or decent people, in no way different from the rest of the society? Antoni Sułek had doubts whether they were really "ordinary men," assuming they may have been "dispensable people in the service of violence." Sułek invoked here a classical essay by Stefan Czarnowski from 1935, analyzing the role of the social margins in building support for Hitlerism. It is one of the founding texts of Polish sociology. After Gross in his answer quoted additional data on family background of the perpetrators, Sułek withdrew his assumption.

On the other hand, Dariusz Stola, in the text quoted above, stressed that the active perpetrators of the Jedwabne massacre, however typical or exceptional their family situation, were not exactly "ordinary people," like the heroes of Browning's book, because they were selected in a different way. The policemen described by Browning were simply mobilized into compulsory military service, whereas the murderers in Jedwabne appeared through the process of self-selection, so by definition they were different, through their mental qualities if

---

[18] Gross, *Neighbors*, 142.
[19] Gontarczyk, "Po pierwsze warsztat."
[20] Musiał, "Tezy dotyczące pogromu w Jedwabnem." 252–280.

not through their social stance, from the remaining population of Jedwabne. They were "willing executioners" rather than "ordinary men": the title of Daniel Goldhagen's book fits them better than Browning's.

Gross himself in a sense nuanced his radical opinion about the Polish half of the town that murdered the Jewish half. "Everyone, who on that day has torn out a Jew who was hidding behind a bush, who has exposed one hiding round the corner, who has caught one running away through the field, who has kicked one hurried in the crowd, who has thrown a stone at the Jews led towards death, who was cursing them, laughing at them, spitting—took part in the crime of genocide. Such is the essence of the events in Jedwabne."[21] It is clearly visible that Gross understands the participation in crime in a broad, inclusive sense, treating passive sympathy as a form of participation. The exact number of Poles who took part in catching Jews, guarding them, and escorting to the barn, however, remains unknown.

As the number of perpetrators, so the number of victims is fervently debated. Gross wrote of about 1,600 victims, a number he took from one of his sources, and this number was popularized among general public. Gross himself explained later that he meant only to quote the number, without taking position as regards its trustworthiness. It appears that the exact number of Jews living in Jedwabne in June 1941, at the moment of German entrance, is not known.[22] Of course this number is not tantamount to the number of Jews in the town on the tragic July 10, 1941, because some of permanent inhabitants could have escaped, whereas some of the refugees from other places could have been present in Jedwabne. Radosław Ignatiew, state attorney investigating the Jedwabne crime on behalf of the IPN, told Anna Bikont during an interview, with detailed justification of his words, that on July 10, 1941 in Jedwabne "no more that a few hundred" persons were killed, and the murderers "were the Polish inhabitants of Jedwabne and environs, men in number of at least forty."[23]

The debate did not lead to universally accepted conclusions about the events. One can suppose, however, that in its effect a majority of historians would most probably agree that Gross' book is more an essay

---

[21] Wokół, "Sąsiadów," 114–115.
[22] See Urynowicz, "Ludność żydowska w Jedwabnem," 129–158.
[23] Bikont, *My z Jedwabnego*, 334–335.

than serious research work, with mistakes in details, overhasty conclusions and methodically doubtful points. Probably less people than assumed by Gross were killed on the fatal day; probably fewer Poles than suggested in *The Neighbors* took part in the crime; and most probably the behind-the-scene German inspiration was stronger than Gross' book would suggest. At the same time most historians would most probably agree as regards the fact itself: as Marek Wierzbicki wrote "there can be no doubt... as regards the participation of part of Polish population of the Białystok region in murders and pogroms of the Jews."[24] Wierzbicki quotes approvingly very cautious words of Radosław Ignatiew, which can be considered a sort of "minimum" of what is confirmed (although they would be surely rejected by radical opponents of Gross): "The most probable hypothesis is one about the crime in Jedwabne being committed by the local Poles, by instigation of the Germans."[25]

III.

In the above analysis the professional argumentation related to the factual problems has been purposely presented as if it existed outside of any emotional, political or contemporary context of the Jedwabne debate. My aim was to show that the Jedwabne debate is interesting not only as an instance of a contemporary political and cultural conflict but also as professional discussion of researchers. At the same time, given the subject matter of the debate, it is obvious that all statements of researchers appear in an emotional atmosphere that is often more important for the general tone of the statements than their factual content. This emotionality, very much connected with professed general world-view, is present on both sides of the debate, but its character on each side is different.

Jan Tomasz Gross often appeals in a very emotional way to the moral feelings of the reader, to his compassion, indignation, empathy: "for the most important thing is not to accept from the start every word in *The Neighbors* as the final truth, but to think with compassion

---

[24] Wierzbicki, *Polacy i Żydzi w zaborze sowieckim*, 275.
[25] Ibid., 29.

about the victims of the Jedwabne crime."[26] With Anna Bikont similar emotions are discernible, with one important addition: In her book, written some time after *Neighbors*, a feeling of bitterness is clearly visible, caused by the fact that a big part of the Polish society refuses to acknowledge the role played by the Polish population in the massacre. These emotions are in no way hidden: Gross, Bikont and authors of similar way of thinking do not conceal that their aim is not to write purely rational scientific texts. Of course they do validate their reasoning by factual arguments and analysis of historical sources, nevertheless they believe that in studying such a tragic story it is natural and desirable to have emotions and to share them; that emotional attitude permits readers to better understand the case of Jedwabne.

The role of appeals to emotions and values with the opponents of Gross is different. As a rule, their texts appeal to the ideal of objective researcher, studying the documents and on their basis learning the truth about the past. "The task of a researcher is not 'affirmative attitude' but professional scepticism and careful analysis of every source. The application of Gross' methodological postulates causes the personal prejudices and dislikes of the witnesses to infiltrate, without verification, the scientific discourse," wrote Bogdan Musiał.[27] "The historians' duty is to investigate as many documents as possible, in order to answer the questions: what? who? how? where? why.... The task of a historian is to discern the truth from fiction," stressed Marek Jan Chodakiewicz.[28]

At the same time, in the very same texts we often encounter very sharp value-ridden and emotionally charged statements, in poetics that is radically different from the remaining parts of the same texts. There is, if we may say so, a clearly visible surplus of emotions over the theoretical declarations and over the presented facts. Thus for example, Chodakiewicz, stressing all the time the necessity of meticulous research without which it is impossible to judge, at a certain point changes his tone and states that in Poland, where liberal media are in majority and most of intelligentsia is liberal too, one does not need any courage to voice opinions about Polish anti-Semitism.[29] In a similar

---

[26] Gross, "Wstęp," 5.
[27] Musiał, "Historiografia mityczna."
[28] Chodakiewicz, "Kłopoty z kuracją szokową."
[29] Ibid.

way Piotr Gontarczyk, after turning the reader's attention to detailed mistakes in *Neighbors*, proceeds to summarize the main argument of the Gross' book in a following way: "The Poles are Nazi collaborators who struck with the Germans a deal about killing the Jews; the Germans wish to save somebody, but the Poles do not agree and murder in a cruel way almost all Jews—their neighbours.... The only place that gave the Jews a relatively safe shelter against the bloodthirsty Polish rabble was the Nazi police station. In general, we should not be puzzled by the criminal nature of the Poles, if their spiritual care was administered by the Roman Catholic clergy. Gross mentions only two of them and both are simple criminals."

After this summary, a scientific conclusion follows: "the problem is not whether somebody likes such a view of the past or not, but whether this picture is more or less true, and therefore—translating into the language of science—whether it was created according to the rules of the historical craft. I claim that it wasn't. The author of *Neighbors* has used a very narrow and tendentiously chosen source basis, he did not apply appropriate source criticism to it... he passes over and distorts whatever does not fit his theses, he does not follow the rules of logical reasoning and scientific objectivism, finally he utters ungrounded metaphysical-ideological judgments without scientific basis. Due to the above faults, the book by Jan Tomasz Gross cannot serve as basis for a serious discussion about our past, and especially about the crime in Jedwabne."[30]

It is rather obvious that the general picture that according to Gontarczyk appears from *Neighbors* is—to put it mildly—the fruit of a very unsympathetic reading of the text; a sort of reading directed at pinpointing errors in details rather than at understanding the way of thinking and the line of argumentation. We often encounter a similar strategy of reading, according to which each fragment in Gross book is interpreted in such a way that it may sound as absurd as possible. This, obviously, is very helpful in conducting a devastating criticism of the book.

Surely, the texts by Musiał, Gontarczyk, Chodakiewicz and other opponents of Gross who stress his factual and technical mistakes, do really correct some errors, do turn our attention to some real

---

[30] Gontarczyk, "Gross kontra fakty." Very similar stylistically and kept in analogous "professorial" tone is the conclusion of Musiał's review: "Tezy dotyczące pogromu w Jedwabnem," ibid.

contradictions in the source material, and in this sense they augment our knowledge of the Jedwabne crime. At the same time, no especially deep hermeneutic devices are needed to notice the ideological engagement of their authors. This engagement stays in obvious contradiction with their declared attachment to the objectivist model of history, free from any emotions or personal partiality of the researcher. (It can be added that the above authors profess very radical version of the model of history as exact science, reducing in fact the work of historian to the so called "craft": few people believed this even in the times of 19th century positivism, and since the anti-positivist turn of the 1890s this model has been universally questioned.)

Contrary to the above quoted authors, Tomasz Strzembosz openly presented the role of emotional factor in his attitude to the problem of Jedwabne crime. "I started to be interested in this case—he told in one of his interviews—only because I had a feeling of obligation towards the inhabitants of Jedwabne and its vicinity. Exactly because those very people, in the Communist period, when I was working on the Soviet occupation of north eastern territories of Poland, have shown me great courage and sympathy. They invited me to their homes, they talked about things, even about things which were threatened with the most severe repressions. I could not remain silent.... How could I turn my back on those people? I was walking there, I was talking with them, I was questioning them: were I to declare now that they mean nothing to me? I decided to check, how it really was, because I was and I am ready to accept every evil that happened and that was made with the Polish hands, but under one condition—that it really happened!"[31] Strzembosz for years collected materials for his book about anti-Soviet Polish conspiracy in the region of Jedwabne in 1939–1941, and one can understand (which does not mean accept) his reaction on Gross' book which he perceived as unjust accusation towards his heroes.

In the texts analyzed until now the emotional attitude of their authors does not annul their argumentation in factual matters. There exists, however, separate group of texts, whose radical opposition towards the book of Jan Tomasz Gross is expressed in highly emotional aggression. Whatever (marginal) informational value these texts may

---

[31] *Gross kłamie – nie mogłem milczeć.*

have, it is subordinated to aggressive expression. Their reasoning (if we make the authors a favour, using this term) is boringly monotonous. Usually they do not enter too deeply into factual questions. They stress that Gross' book and statements of his supporters are the result of an international conspiracy, based on the Jewish anti-Polonism, as well as an attempt to squeeze out from Poland as much money as possible in reparations for the Jewish property. The publications of Gross' supporters are referred to as "Polish-language," that is, not really Polish in spirit, but only using the language as a medium of communication. The whole debate is seen as a conflict of "Polish" and "cosmopolitan," or "Jewish" (which accounts for the same) points of view. Apart from the Polish historians opposing Gross, the often invoked authority is Norman Finkelstein, author of *The Holocaust Industry*. He is usually quoted in the context that, "even the Jews themselves admit that.." etc.

What is especially interesting, Poland and Polishness in this sort of reasoning are generally seen as object of mass attack, directed at once against Poland and the Catholic Church (under this optic both are almost identical). Some of the authors identify cosmopolitanism and liberalism as their main enemies, some however use the classical anti-Semitic argument, not essentially different from the one that was created by the European right in the second half of the 19th century. By and large, one can guess that more than half of the texts available on the internet at the time of writing of this essay (autumn 2010) belong to this genre. As usually in public life, the frontiers are blurred. Often it is difficult to decide whether a given text "still" can be counted as rational polemic with ideas of Jan Tomasz Gross or whether it is "already" just a manifestation of radical rightist political views. The most classical representative of the thread analyzed here, whose works do not leave any doubts as to where they should be ascribed, is Jerzy Robert Nowak, who publishes mainly in the ultra-rightist nationalist-Catholic daily *Nasz Dziennik*. There are no reasons to analyze this thread any further.

IV.

Moral debate in connection with the case of Jedwabne deals with one central problem and a few side questions. The central problem is how we—we the Poles, or rather we, the members of the Polish intelligentsia—react to the news of this old crime, or, to quote Jerzy Jedlicki, "how to deal with it."[32] Answer of those authors who look at Jedwabne first of all from the moral point of view was expressed in various forms and may be probably summarized like this: accept as fact, not try to deny, and live on with consciousness that one's own nation, like all others, has in its history pages that are better and worse, noble and mean.

If we look at the attitude of various authors towards the moral aspect of the Jedwabne problem, we may perhaps risk an opinion that the central debate here is not about facts but about criteria of their importance. One of important reactions to the book by Gross was a talk of well known journalist Jacek Żakowski with historian Tomasz Szarota in *Gazeta Wyborcza*. Szarota did not question the general picture of Gross; he said that we have to accept that we have to do with a murder that was committed by the Poles, and that is a part of the Holocaust. At the same time, he stressed that Gross' book is not trustworthy in its details, that one needs much more detailed investigation. "What Gross has written in *Neighbors* is enough to rattle our consciences. But it is necessary to know the details to understand the whole situation. Every historian knows that a multiplicity of details can often be the devil's workshop."[33] Jerzy Jedlicki during a public debate about the *Neighbors* in the Institute of History of the Polish Academy of Sciences polemically commented: "In Jedwabne and in Radziłów the devil remains not in details but in the most general matters."[34] This formulation, in turn, has been criticized by the polemists of Gross, Piotr Gontarczyk and Bogdan Musiał.[35]

It appears that for Jedlicki, for Hanna Świda-Zięba,[36] and many others who think in a similar vein, (probably also for Gross himself) in the last resort it is not so extremely important whether the number of fatalities in the tragic day was 1,600, or half or one-third of that number; whether there were five or fifty-five German soldiers in the town then;

---

[32] Jedlicki, "Jak się z tym uporać," 233–243.
[33] Żakowski, "Diabelskie szczegóły," 69.
[34] Jedlicki's contribution to this discussion was not published. His words are quoted by Anna Bikont, *My z Jedwabnego*, 21.
[35] Musiał, "Historiografia mityczna;" Gontarczyk, "Gross przemilczeń."
[36] Świda-Ziemba, "Krótkowzroczność 'kulturalnych.'"

whether every non-Jewish adult male, or every second, or only one-fifth of them actively participated in pulling the Jews out of their houses, in robbing them, dragging them to the place of murder and finally murdering them. What is important, is the moral problem and it is independent from the exact numbers. Too great a concentration on the technical problems of historical research threatens with pushing aside those questions that are really important. Jedlicki wrote: "We may, of course, continue to sidestep the issue. We may say it is too early, that reports are unclear, that there is no exact count of the murderers and the victims, that one set of archives or another still needs to be investigated. Investigation is always worthwhile, it should have been done many years ago, but it will not change a thing. The truth will not become any more pleasant than it is now and sooner or later we are going to have to deal with it" [p. 242–243]. As far as I know, the opponents of Gross never answered this; they never explained why further detailed research (apart from factual knowledge as an aim in itself) should contribute somehow to the moral evaluation of the Jedwabne case.

It is very hard to find any open polemic with the authors who discuss the moral problems in context of Jedwabne massacre. The critics of Gross, who stress the importance of technical questions, often present the moralists as a radical group, symmetrical with the radical right. "First, there are deniers.... Second, there are the moralizers.... They are as irrational as their counterparts on the right,"[37] wrote Marek Jan Chodakiewicz, and Bogdan Musiał expressed a similar opinion: "Some people reject the accusations altogether as groundless.... Some other fully accept the theses of Gross, they publish highly emotional accusations, developing philosophical-moralistic reflections.... they call for *repentance*." Musiał sees the people who think like himself as middle of the road: "There exists a matter of fact attitude, too, that stresses the need for debate on the problem."

It is not explained why the matter-of-fact attitude should be incompatible with ethical reflection on history. Further words of Musiał may serve as partial answer: "I do not think that Poland needs an overcoming of the past in the German style.... What Poland now needs is the return of memory. The historical consciousness of the

---

[37] Chodakiewicz, *The Massacre in Jedwabne July 10, 1941*.

post-war generations of Poles has been deformed by the Communist state. Honest historical research is needed."[38] Musiał seems to equate honest historical research with the criticism of the Gross' theses. The reader can easily feel that in this and other similar texts we have to do, in spite of declared positivist self-limitation to empirical research, with an attitude that is no less value-ridden than it is in the case of Gross, only with opposite sign. Gross' opponents do not see any facts that would demand from Poles a self-critical attitude. They believe, therefore, that any attempt at reflection on the ignoble pages of Polish history must be superficial and insincere (because ungrounded in historical facts) and what is more, noxious for one's own nation. One could presume, that according to this line of reasoning, there is, in fact, no ground for moral reflection on Jedwabne at all: the massacre was surely regrettable, but is was committed by a small marginal group, induced and probably forced by the Germans, and it does not seriously change the picture of the Poles' behaviour under the Nazi occupation.

The Cracow historian Andrzej Nowak expressed a fear that calls for taking national responsibility for sins committed in the past weaken the internal cohesion of national community—for community cannot be based on fear. Nowak entitled his essay "Westerplatte or Jedwabne," contrasting two symbolic terms: Westerplatte, a Polish fortress in the Free City of Gdansk, which defended against the Germans through the first week of World War Two, is a symbol of patriotic heroism, whereas Jedwabne stands for crime and collaboration. Paweł Machcewicz, a historian then at the Institute of National Memory, answered Nowak in a text entitled "Both Westerplatte and Jedwabne," and summarised his arguments in an article that became an introduction to the two volume study of Jedwabne by IPN. He wrote: "Turning one's head back... leads us nowhere.... A nation proud of its history can face even the most difficult truth about its past."[39] Machcewicz alluded to an essay from more than a decade earlier by Jerzy Jedlicki, "Inheritance and Collective Responsibility," which did not deal with Jewish questions, but analysed the problems of responsibility of people who accept their belonging to a community (nation, religion, class) for crimes committed by other members of the same group, sometimes in long passed

---

[38] Musiał, "Historiografia mityczna."
[39] Machcewicz, "Wokół Jedwabnego," 16–17.

epochs. By analyzing this difficult problem, this thought-provoking text by Jedlicki prepared the ground, in a sense, for the Jedwabne debate.

Apart from this main question of responsibility, there were some other marginal threads in the debate that dealt with various moral aspects of the Jedwabne case. There was a debate about the definition of the Polish nation ("Both perpetrators and victims were citizens of the Polish Republic. Does it follow that both perpetrators and victims were Poles?") about the sense of collective apology for the faults of the ancestors, about the attitude of present-day Poles to the Jewish past and heritage in Poland, and in general about the role of collective memory in the social life. All these questions we have to leave aside.

A thread, that was not pushed further during the debate, although it certainly deserved to be, was the problem of attitudes of Roman Catholic clergy towards the pogrom wave in the summer 1941 in Jedwabne and its environs. In an obvious way this is connected with a broader problem of the attitude of the Roman Catholic church in Poland towards the Jews and the question of anti-Semitism. One of the few authors who studied the case of Jedwabne carefully in this context is Dariusz Libionka, who quoted in his paper very clear testimonies of radical anti-Semitism reigning in the 1930s among the Polish clergy in general, and the clergy of archbishopric of Łomża (where Jedwabne is located) in particular.[40] We should also mention a text that does not deal specifically with the Jedwabne massacre but which provides an important element of contextualization, as regards the relation of the Catholic clergy towards the Jews. Tomasz Szarota analysed the image of Polish-Jewish relations as presented in an anonymous study written in Catholic circles in 1941, of course in conspiracy. The document, meant as a report to the Polish authorities in exile, commends Nazi politics towards the Jews as an ideal of the Christian attitude (of course the period is still before the "final solution"). Szarota meant his text as contributing to a broader explanation for the context of Jedwabne, and so, as a part of debate started by the book by Gross.[41]

---

[40] Libionka, "Duchowieństwo archidiecezji łomżyńskiej wobec antysemityzmu i zagłady Żydów," 105–128.

[41] Szarota, "Sprawozdanie kościelne z Polski za czerwiec i połowę lipca 1941go roku," 198–216.

The historical questions are connected with the contemporary problem of today's Church attitude towards the problem of Jedwabne. Unfortunately, we cannot but describe this attitude as passive and hesitating, avoiding as far as possible any activity. The Primate of Poland, Cardinal Józef Glemp, has said publicly that the fact of Poles as perpetrators of the crime is obvious—and the importance of this declaration should not be left unnoticed. The words of the Primate go together well with the ideas of those who do not think that any further detailed research can change the moral meaning of Jedwabne:

"From the moral point of view it is not of decisive importance... whether the results of the investigation... show the Poles in better or in worse light. The central fact will remain—there were people in Jedwabne who contributed to the death of their fellow-citizens." He stressed very strongly the necessity of expiation in face of God for the crimes in Jedwabne and its vicinity. In the same interview, however, Cardinal Glemp talked also about Jewish guilt towards Poles, about the Jewish collaboration with the Soviets, and he stated: in the Polish Church "I do not notice any prejudice against the Jewish religion and I never noticed such a phenomenon as anti-Judaism. This belongs to the past. We should, however, mention anti-Polonism [of the Jews. ed.]."[42]

On May 27, 2001 a festive expiatory service was celebrated in Warsaw in the Church of All the Saints, which stays in the part of the town formerly inhabited by the Jews. Father Adam Boniecki, the editor-in-chief of *Tygodnik Powszechny*, wrote, "what happened on Sunday, May 27 in the biggest of the Warsaw churches, close to the place where the frontier of the Ghetto run 60 years ago [during the German occupation—*ed.*], was a religious event that will forever be written into the history of Poland.... The primate, dressed in a violet ornate as a sign of repentance was presiding," and almost 50 bishops were participating, without mitres and without liturgical robes, in black cassocks without red or violet belts." At the same time, Father Boniecki noticed bitterly that Radio Maryja was the only Polish broadcasting company

---

[42] Polonsky-Michlic eds., *Wywiad Prymasa Polski ks. kardynała Józefa Glempa dla KAI*. 166–172.

on that day which failed to mention the celebration in its newsreel. Boniecki remarked that it was a "voice crying out in the desert."[43]

And so it is: the bishop of Łomża, and the parish priest from Jedwabne decisively took the side of the town inhabitants who reject all accusations,[44] and Radio Maryja was and is, together with the rightist daily *Nasz Dziennik*, the main channel for disseminating the thesis about anti-Polish conspiracy and attack against the nation and the Catholic faith. No bishop took part in the state celebrations in Jedwabne on July 10, 2001, led by President Aleksander Kwaśniewski. In order that the picture does not appear too one-sided, let us not forget about the role played by Cracow Catholic weekly *Tygodnik Powszechny* and Warsaw Catholic monthly *Więź*. Both periodicals have engaged very strongly in an honest discussion of the Jedwabne case, with published texts by Gross and other researchers and were among the most serious forums for discussion.

V.

Numerous books have appeared as additions or polemics with Gross' book, some of them have been mentioned in this essay. A special place belongs to the two volumes from the IPN *Around Jedwabne*, mentioned here many times, as well as to the book, *We from Jedwabne* by a journalist at *Gazeta Wyborcza*, Anna Bikont. Bikont has done tremendously rich historical-journalistic research, finding families of Jews from Jedwabne scattered across the world, and finding Polish eye-witnesses too. The study enriches the understanding of Jedwabne with a meticulously reconstructed local dimension, which is missing from Gross' book and was criticized by many reviewers. One of the most moving elements of Bikont's book is a visual (as a bird-eye panorama) reconstruction of the view of the town of Jedwabne as it must have looked in summer 1939.

By the time Bikont's book was published the Jedwabne debate had already passed its height. Sometime in the second half of 2002, the debate began to slowly wane, although it was never totally extinguished.

---

[43] Boniecki, "Oto rozległ się głos," 26.
[44] Orłowski, "Proboszcz parafii Jedwabne."

What changes in Poland did the debate produce? Some people expressed the hope that it will help Poles to come to terms with their past; some other were afraid that helped the growth of anti-Semitic attitudes in Polish society.

For the majority of the Polish population, it is most likely that attitudes in the short run did not change much, although the debate certainly caused greater awareness of the problem of Polish-Jewish relations. Jerzy Jedlicki, in a bitter review essay of Bikont's book, stressed how she "observes the mental blocks that many of her interlocutors build for themselves in order to protect their minds from knowledge about facts, even such facts that happened before their eyes. It is really curious and saddening to observe what excuses we may use in order to reject proposals that are grounded beyond any doubt, but whose acceptance would have to destroy the order of our convictions systematized through inheritance and to plant in us moral and cognitive disorder."[45]

Such mental blocks are at work not only with Anna Bikont's interlocutors but with the society at large; popular invocations of stereotypical and superficial version of romantic national tradition (with the real philosophical thought of the Polish romanticism this tradition has very little to do) seem to strengthen rather than decline. The stereotype of Polishness had found its way to bypass the case of Jedwabne in the same way as it bypassed so many other debates and historical facts that could be potentially dangerous for its integrity. The hopes of some and the fears of others that this stereotype would decline or transform itself under the influence of the Jedwabne debate have proved unfounded.

In December 2010, when I was writing the first version of this essay, the question of Jedwabne was passed over in silence rather than openly avoided. The best example was the webpage of the city of Jedwabne (visited in autumn 2010), where the crime is passed in silence. (With one exception: a reader interested in tourism can click to read about the historical monuments of Jedwabne; here one can learn about the existence of a monument to the Jews of Jedwabne, murdered on July 10, 1941, but no mention is made of who did it.) The silence, however, is periodically disturbed: the publication in Polish of another

---

[45] Jerzy Jedlicki, "Podróż do jądra ciemności."

book by Gross, entitled *Fear*, in 2008 (the English version was published in 2006) restarted a discussion that repeated the debates on Jedwabne on a smaller scale.

One more thing deserves attention. Many opponents of Gross, not only the most radical ones, presented the discussion as conflict of "Polish" and "Jewish" points of view on the history of World War Two, with Gross representing the Jewish side. Perhaps such dividing lines did to a certain degree appear in the international debate on the same subject, started after the English publication of the *Neighbors* in 2001. There we may perhaps find some voices whose authors felt themselves as depositaries of one or another "national" point of view on the past. As regards the debate within Poland, however, there are no grounds for such interpretation. The debate was not between "Polish" and "Jewish" perspective on the past, but between two Polish perspectives. In the Polish historiographical debates there exists a strong tradition of critical attitude towards the national past, starting with the Enlightenment historian Adam Naruszewicz, through the so called Cracow Historical School of the second half of 19th century (Józef Szujski, Michał Bobrzyński), until the numerous 20th century debates, as e.g. those about the sense of national uprisings.

Gross' book excellently fits this tradition (how much it is a conscious decision of the author, I am not sure), and thus it can be seen as integral part of debates on national past that go on in Poland for centuries.

In December 2010, the weekly *Polityka* wrote about a village Gniewczyna in the Polish Subcarpathia, whose Polish inhabitants killed 18 Jews during the war; the headline ran, "Gniewczyna like Jedwabne."[46] A drama by Tadeusz Słobodzianek, "Our Class," based on books by Gross and Anna Bikont, has won the "Nike" literary prize in 2010 and was subject to various reviews and criticisms, which reflected some of the attitudes presented in this essay.

At the turn of 2010 and 2011 the discussion seemed to revive once again. The press wrote about a new book from Gross, soon to be published, which stirred emotions even before it reached bookshops. The book, co-written by Gross and Irena Grudzińska-Gross, entitled

---

[46] Łazarewicz, "Letnisko w domu śmierci," 32–35.

Golden Harvest, dealt with the stealing of Jewish property by the Polish population in the final months and after the war. The book was wildly criticized even before it was read; its publisher, the Cracow Catholic publishing house "Znak" was reproached with publishing a book that derides Poland and the Poles.

Most probably the earliest review written after reading of the full book was by the historian Paweł Machcewicz,[47] who eleven years earlier had positively evaluated *Neighbors* about which he wrote that in spite of its emotional tone and inaccuracies in some details, it played an important and pioneering role in breaking the taboo around the problem of Polish participation in murdering Jews. Now, Machcewicz wrote, with the taboo already broken, books like *Golden Harvest* with their unwarranted generalizations and lack of attention to details, only strengthen emotions. They do not explain anything and contribute nothing to the fight against anti-Semitic prejudices in the Polish society.

At exactly the same moment, in February 2011, two other books by Polish researchers appeared that deal with a similar subject, analyzing the tragic fate of the Jews who tried to escape the Holocaust by hiding in the Polish countryside. These books are the fruit of long and detailed research, and to a degree they have gained from the media interest in the Gross' book, as in other case they would have been probably passed unnoticed (as did third volume on the same subject, published some ten months later, in autumn 2011). One of the books in question, by Barbara Engelking, is an attempt to draw a synthetic picture of Jews in the Polish countryside during Nazi occupation; another, by Jan Grabowski, is a monograph of one specific county.[48] Both works present a picture of broad, although difficult to assess numerically, participation of the Polish peasantry in catching and killing the Jews who tried to escape the Germans.[49]

It seems that a new thread has appeared in this latest phase of discussion which was absent from the *Neighbors* debate of 2000–2001,

---

[47] Machcewicz, "Recenzja ostatecznej wersji 'Złotych Żniw.'"
[48] Engelking, "Jest taki piękny słoneczny dzień."
[49] See "Strach przed niedzielą," Koniec z mitem bohaterskiej polskiej wsi (Interview by Wojciech Tochman with Barbara Engelking and Jan Grabowski in radio TOK FM. Text on the Internet page http://www.tokfm.pl , visited February 28, 2011).

and began to emerge after the publication of *Fear* in Polish in 2008. The focus moved from the case of Jedwabne to the more general problem of Polish-Jewish relations, and sometimes perhaps to even broader problem of human attitudes in terminal situations. The reflection of two leading Holocaust specialists in Poland, Jacek Leociak and Dariusz Libionka,[50] seems to go in this direction. Of course the people who are against any sort of deeper researches into the history of Polish anti-Semitism did not change their mind and continue to see books by Gross and others as nothing but anti-Polish propaganda.

The polarization, brought to surface by the debate of 2000–2001, continues today. Now, as then, some think that to accept the dark side of the national past is a sign of collective maturity and moral duty, while others are convinced that to defend the good name of one's nation is the highest demand of patriotism. These attitudes grow from a general world-view, not from empirical findings, so we should not suppose that they can be changed through any historical research. The future will show whether this duality will remain, or one side—and which one—will gain the preponderance.

Postscript

I have attempted to provide a foreign reader with factual information about the Jedwabne debate in Poland. It is, however, pretty clear that with a subject like this it is difficult to remain perfectly impartial. I believe I should, therefore, present my own opinion in the matter, not because I consider it especially original or important—I am not a specialist in the history of World War Two—but out of loyalty towards the reader, so that he may be able to check if, and to what degree, my own opinions influenced the way of presenting the positions of debating sides.

I believe that Jan Tomasz Gross, despite the inaccuracies of some details in his book, is correct in his main argument. There is no doubt that the Jedwabne massacre was committed by the Poles. At the same time it seems to me that Gross dismisses too lightly the voices of those opponents who stress the necessity of including the historical

---

[50] Leociak, Libionka, "Sny o Bezgrzesznej."

context, of better knowing the preceding periods of Polish-Jewish relations, both in the interwar period and during the Soviet occupation of 1939–1941. It seems obvious that both the Polish anti-Semitism of the 1930s (and tremendous role of the Catholic Church as one of the main propagators) and the real or imagined collaboration of the Jews with the Soviet authorities must have influenced the behaviour of the inhabitants of Jedwabne on July 10, 1941 to a much higher degree than assumed by Gross. I was convinced by the reflections of Dariusz Stola about the impossibility of planning and conducting the crime without a stronger German presence than supposed by Gross. I was also convinced by Stola's hypothesis about the role of the "Jedwabne state"— a local ephemeral center of power, with monopoly for using force. At the same time I suppose that we should not underestimate the natural human propensity for cruelty. This propensity in the conditions of war can easily liberate itself from the corsets of civilization, morality, religion, and respect towards the order-preserving state authority.

Already after writing this essay, in early 2011 (and not in 2001–2002, when I was witnessing the debate around *Neighbors*) I started to wonder whether the meaning of Gross' book can be reduced simply to the criticism of the Polish anti-Semitism.

None of Gross' writing that I know of claims that Poles are worse anti-Semites than anyone else. After all, in the 20th century (and not only then) people belonging to very different nationalities were in various situations killing their neighbours who belonged to another ethnic group. So perhaps we should treat Gross' books not only as an instance of a critical attitude to the Polish history (see above) but also—perhaps first of all—as a philosophical reflection on poisoning of the entire European culture by anti-Semitism, or perhaps in an even broader sense—on flawed human nature and the spontaneous appearance for cruelty that is inscribed into it.

I believe therefore that the moral reflection on the case of Jedwabne is indispensable, although I am not sure in which direction it should lead. I think that the publication of the *Neighbors* and the ensuing debate were, all in all, a positive phenomenon which in the long run will contribute to better understanding of dramatic Polish history during the war. I am also utterly convinced that all those who believe that the disclosure of the past dishonours Poland in any way, are wrong. Exactly the reverse is true, and Jacek Kuroń was right when he wrote in the introduction to Anna Bikont's book that it is not the fact of a murder committed years ago but "hiding the murderers and negating the reality that constitutes great harm for the good name of Poland."[51]

Bibliography

Bikont, A. *My z Jedwabnego*, Warsaw: Proszynski I S-Ka, 2004.
Boniecki, A. "Oto rozległ się głos...," *Tygodnik Powszechny* no. 22 (2001). Reprinted in *Żydownik powszechny. Dodatek do Tygodnika Powszechnego na 65 lecie pisma*, edited by Mucharski, P. and M. Okoński. Cracow: Znak, 2010. (This suplement to *Tygodnik Powszechny* is an anthology of texts on the Jewish question, published weekly between 1946 and 2009.)
Chodakiewicz, M.J. "Kłopoty z kuracją szokową," *Rzeczpospolita*. Available at http://new-arch.rp.pl/artykul/317680_z_kuracja_szokowa.html, or: http://naszawitryna.pl/jedwabne_312.html, visited 22 December 2010.
———. *The Massacre in Jedwabne, July 10, 1941. Before, During and After*. Boulder, CO: Columbia University Press, 2005. (Series: East European Monographs).
Dmitrów, E. "Oddziały operacyjne niemieckiej Policji Bezpieczeństwa i Służby Bezpieczeństwa a początek zagłady Żydów w Łomżyńskiem i na Białostocczyźnie latem 1941 roku," in *Wokół Jedwabnego*, edited by Machcewicz, P. and K. Persak. Warsaw: IPN, 2002, vol. I, 273–352.
Engelking, B. *Jest taki piękny słoneczny dzień... Losy Żydów szukających ratunku na wsi polskiej 1942–1945*. Warsaw: Centrum Badań nad Zagładą Żydów, Instytut Filozofii i Socjologii PAN, 2011.
Forecki, P. *Spór o Jedwabne. Analiza debaty publicznej*. Poznań: Uniwersytet Adama Mickiewicza, 2008.
Gontarczyk, P. "Gross kontra fakty," *Życie*, January, 31, 2001. Available at http://www.naszawitryna.pl/jedwabne_253.html (Last visited December 21, 2010).
———. "Gross przemilczeń," *Życie*, March 31, 2001. Available at http://www.naszawitryna.pl/jedwabne_176.html (Last visited December 9, 2010).
———. "Po pierwsze warsztat," *Życie*, April 29, 2001. Available at http://www.naszawitryna.pl/jedwabne_87.html (Last visited December 22, 2010).
Grabowski, J. *Judenjagd. Polowanie na Żydów 1942–1945. Studium dziejów pewnego powiatu*. Warsaw: Centrum Badań nad Zagładą Żydów, Instytut Filozofii i Socjologii PAN, 2011.
Gross, J.T. "Antoniemu Sułkowi w odpowiedzi," *Więź*, April 2002. Reprinted in idem, *Wokół Sąsiadów. Polemiki i wyjaśnienia*. Sejny: Pogranicze, 2003, 104.
———. "Mord 'zrozumiały?'" *Gazeta Wyborcza*, November 25–26, 2000. Reprinted in *Wokół Sąsiadów. Polemiki i wyjaśnienia*. Sejny: Pogranicze, 2003,

---

[51] Bikont, *My z Jedwabnego*, 15.

18. In English *"Comprehensible" Murder*, in "Thou," 91–104, quotation 103–104.

———. *Sąsiedzi. Historia zagłady żydowskiego miasteczka*. Sejny: Pogranicze, 2000, 2nd ed. (Internet version: http://pogranicze.sejny.pl/archiwum/jedwabne/ksiazka.pdf, visited 9 December 2010). In English: Gross, *Neighbors: The Destruction of the Jewish Community in Jedwabne, Poland*. Princeton, Oxford: Princeton University Press, 2001.

———. "Gross kłamie—nie mogłem milczeć." prof. dr hab. Tomaszem Strzemboszem rozmawiają: Paweł Smogorzewski i Eugeniusz Zdanowicz, *Powściągliwość i Praca* no. 12 (December 2001). Available at http:/www.naszawitryna.pl/jedwabne_659.html (Last visited December 23, 2010.

Jedlicki, J. "Jak się z tym uporać" [How to deal with this], *Polityka* no. 6 (February 10, 2001).

———, "Podróż do jądra ciemności," *Zeszyty Literackie* vol. 89, no. 1 (2005). Available at http:/czytelnia.onet.pl/0,33811,1,5840,recenzje.html (Last visited December 4, 2010).

Kaczyński, A. "Całopalenie," *Rzeczpospolita*, May 5, 2000. Available at http//:niniwa2.cba.pl/calo.htm. In English: *Burning Alive: Thou shalt not kill. Poles on Jedwabne*. Warsaw: Więź, 2001. 29–40.

Łazarewicz, C. "Letnisko w domu śmierci," *Polityka* no. 49 (December 4, 2010).

Leociak, J. and D. Libionka. "Sny o Bezgrzesznej," *Tygodnik Powszechny*, January 11, 2011. Available at http://tygodnik.onet.pl (Last visited February 28, 2011).

Libionka, D. "Duchowieństwo archidiecezji łomżyńskiej wobec antysemityzmu i zagłady Żydów." In *Wokół Jedwabnego*, edited by P.Machcewicz and K. Persak. Warsaw: IPN, 2002, vol. I, 105–128.

Machcewicz, "Recenzja ostatecznej wersji, 'Złotych Żniw': historia zaangażowana," *Gazeta Wyborcza*. Febrary 14, 2011. Available at http://wyborcza.pl (Last visited February 28, 2011).

———. "Wokół Jedwabnego." In *Wokół Jedwabnego*, edited by P.Machcewicz and K. Persak. Warsaw: IPN, 2002, vol. I, 16–17.

Milewski, J.J. "Polacy i Żydzi w Jedwabnem i okolicy przed 22 czerwca 1941 roku," in *Wokół Jedwabnego*. Edited by P.Machcewicz and K. Persak., Warsaw: IPN, 2002, 75.

Musiał, B. "Historiografia mityczna," *Rzeczpospolita*, Feb. 24, 2001. Available at http://niniwa2.cba.pl/historiografia_mityczna.htm (Last visited December 21, 2010).

———. "Tezy dotyczące pogromu w Jedwabnem. Uwagi krytyczne do książki 'Sąsiedzi' autorstwa Jana Tomasza Grossa," *Dzieje Najnowsze* no. 3 (2001): 252–280.

Orłowski, E., Proboszcz Parafii Jedwabne. "Celebracja kłamstwa" (December 12, 2002). Available at http://www.naszawitryna.pl/jedwabne_889.html (Last visited December 22, 2010).

Paczkowski, A. "Debata wokół 'Sąsiadów'. Próba wstępnej typologii." *Rzeczpospolita*, March 24, 2001, No. 73. Available at http:/www.rzeczpospolita.

pl/dodatki/plus_minus_010324/plus_minus_a_9. (Last visited December 23, 2010).

Polonsky, A. and J. B. Michlic. "Jedwabne, 10 lipca 1941—zbrodnia i pamięć" [A Roundtable discussion: Jedwabne – Crime and Memory]. A discussion organized by the editors of *Rzeczpospolita*, March 3, 2001, with J.T. Gross, T. Strzembosz, A. Żbikowski, P. Machcewicz, and R. Ignatiew], in Gross, *Wokół Sąsiadów*, 61. In English: *The Neighbors Respond: The Controversy over the Jedwabne Massacre in Poland*, Princeton: Princeton University Press, 2004.

Stola, D. "Pomnik ze słów," *Rzeczpospolita* June 1–2, 2001; in English: "A Monument of Worlds," *Yad Vashem Studies* vol. XXX, 2002.

Strzembosz, T. "Szubienica i huśtawka," *Gazeta Polska*, January 17, 2001. Available at http://pogranicze.sejny.pl/archiwum/jedwabne/strzembo.html (Last visited December 23, 2010).

Sułek, A. "'Sąsiedzi'. Zwykła recenzja," *Więź* no. 12 (2001). Available at http:/pogranicze.sejny.pl/archiwum/jedwabne/wiez/12.html (Last visited December 4, 2010).

Świda-Ziemba, H. "Krótkowzroczność 'kulturalnych,'" *Gazeta Wyborcza*, April 7, 2001. Available at http://polish-jewish-heritage.org/pol/krotko.htm (Last visited December 23, 2010. (Also in English: "The Shortsightendness of the 'Cultured,'" in Polonsky and Michlic, 103–113.)

Szarota, T. "Mord w Jedwabnem. Dokumenty, publikacje i interpretacje z lat 1941–2000. Kalendarium." In *Wokół Jedwabnego*, edited by P. Machcewicz and K. Persak, vol. I–II. Warsaw: IPN, 2002, vol. I, "Studia."

———. "Sprawozdanie kościelne z Polski za czerwiec i połowę lipca 1941go roku, Próba analizy dokumentu." In *Karuzela na placu Krasińskich. Studia i szkice z lat wojny i okupacji*. Warsaw: Rytm, 2007, 175.

———. *U progu zagłady. Zajścia antyżydowskie i pogromy w okupowanej Europie. Warszawa, Paryż, Amsterdam, Antwerpia, Kowno*. Warsaw: Sic!, 2000.

Urynowicz, M. "Ludność żydowska w Jedwabnem. Zmiany demograficzne od końca XIX wieku do 1941 roku na tle regionu łomżyńskiego." In *Wokół Jedwabnego*, edited by P. Machcewicz and K. Persak, vol. I, 129–158.

Wierzbicki, M. *Polacy i Żydzi w zaborze sowieckim. Stosunki polsko-żydowskie na ziemiach północno-wschodnich II Rzeczypospolitej pod okupacją sowiecką (1939–1941)*. Warsaw: Fronda, 2007. 2nd augmented edition.

Żakowski, J. "Diabelskie szczegóły [rozmowa z Tomaszem Szarotą]," *Gazeta Wyborcza*, November, 18–19, 2000. Available at http://pogranicze.sejny.pl/archiwum/jedwabne/szavzak.html (Last visited Dcember 17, 2010). In English as "Tomasz Szarota interviewed by Jacek Żakowski, 'The Devil is in the Details.'" In *Thou*, 65–75.

Żbikowski, A. "Pogromy i mordy ludności żydowskiej w Łomżyńskiem i na Białostocczyźnie latem 1941 roku w świetle relacji ocalałych Żydów i dokumentów sądowych." In *Wokół Jedwabnego*, edited by P. Machcewicz and K. Persak, vol. I.

———. *U genezy Jedwabnego. Żydzi na Kresach Północno-Wschodnich II Rzeczypospolitej wrzesień 1939-lipiec 1941*. Warsaw: Żydowski Instytut Historyczny, 2006.

The Memory of Trianon as a Political Instrument in Hungary Today

GÁBOR GYÁNI

Following the political change of 1989, history came to attract more and more attention in Hungary and every other post-Communist country in Central and Eastern Europe. The emerging cult of the national past created by politicians derived not just from the negative, Communist attitude which prevailed during the decades of their rule, as has often been accused. The discourse—called at the time a "return to history"—was as much a reaction to the demands of the new democracies established amidst the circumstances of national sovereignty. The revival of historically tried methods, and the emergent discovery or invention of traditions, served in many post-Communist countries to preserve or gain vitally important mass political support, or at least an assurance of the passive loyalty of people, the voters, who started then to experience in ever larger numbers the heavy economic price of political change (mass unemployment, drastic decrease either in the wages and the occupational position of many and not the least increase in material inequality among the members of society).

The preoccupation with the national past was necessary for creating and strengthening the democratic national community which thus could replace the forces of political loyalty in a situation where the former mechanisms of legitimacy (the fear of terror or of its remembrance, discrimination, and the gentler forms of suppression, political apathy, and, last but not least, the involvement of many in maintaining the old system, which also rewarded this active role) had suddenly ceased to operate.[1]

---

[1] Gyáni, "Political Uses of Tradition in Postcommuniust East Central Europe," especially 902–903.

This argument advanced in the first years of the post-Communist transition may easily be adapted to succeeding developments. But it is true, however, that the use of history for clearly political purposes, the political instrumentalization of the national image of the past, was always preferred by conservative or right-wing governments rather than socialist or liberal ones. This was already the case with the first (conservative) government led by József Antall, and was perpetuated and further deepened by the first Fidesz government which came to power in 1998. The pattern is much the same now, when after the Parliamentary elections in spring 2010, another conservative, right-wing government came to power.

Let's see now how the past has been instrumentalized both by politics and society during the last two decades. In describing the main features of the public use of history at that time, I am going to point to specific political aims sought and found in the various ways of accommodating the past images to the changing political discourses. Three historical issues seem to have been the most important reference points: the memory of the Holocaust, the memory of the 1956 revolution, and the mental legacy of the former Communist past.

Coming to Terms with the Past after 1989

Unlike Germany, Western Europe, and the United States—but similar to many other Eastern European countries—public memory of the Jewish Holocaust does not play a great role in shaping the present-day historical consciousness in Hungary. This is true even though the country, which was occupied by Nazi Germany in March 1944, took an active part in carrying out the terrible project of Jewish genocide. Coming to terms with that particular past was, and is even more today, an urgent part of creating a stable national identity. The more or less total obliviousness of Hungarian society of their own complicity in committing the Holocaust (beyond the role of state authorities of the Horthy regime) was followed after 1989 by officially initiated, forceful commemorative practices about the Jewish tragedy of 1944 and 1945. Just a few weeks after the new, democratically-elected government led by József Antall entered office in 1990, the president of the republic and the Prime Minister attended the unveiling of a monument dedicated to the victims of the Holocaust located on the territory of the former Great Pest Ghetto. Also, the Minister of the Interior spoke at another commemorative ceremony that year, organized for the inauguration of a monument dedicated to Jewish Hungarian martyrs on the enbankment of the Danube River.

The message delivered at these official commemorative events was, however, not to wholly acknowledge the past misdeeds of the "Hungarian nation" with a belated official apology. Antall argued in one of his commemorative speeches that while it is true that "serious tribulations, violations of law occurred, or rather laws [were passed] contrary to the concept of human rights and humanism.... But nobody should forget that until March 19, 1944, Europe's largest Jewish community was still alive."[2] There was no reference to the responsibility of the Hungarian state bureaucracy (including local administrations) as perpetrators and the people as bystanders to the genocide committed in Hungary later in 1944.

Still, as a plain indication of the changed attitude to the Holocaust the Hungarian Parliament passed several laws on restitution concerning the "unfairly" committed damages to Hungarian citizens between 1939 and 1949. This was to replace the official apology offered for the victims of the genocidal anti-Semitism of a former Hungarian political authority (more or less supported by the majority of the Hungarian society) which thus expressed the obvious recognition of the Hungarian state's responsibility for the sinful acts of the past.

The next step was taken again by another conservative government, the Fidesz one (in power between 1998 and 2002) by declaring (in 2000) April 16 as the day to commemorate the Holocaust; besides it established the House of Terror for commemmorating twentieth century state horrors. The latter, however, laid more emphasis on displaying the atrocities committed by the Communist regime, rather than on the Horthy regime for discriminating against Jewish citizens in the prelude to the Holocaust. The establishment of the Budapest Holocaust Museum and Education Center, which opened in 2004 in a former Orthodox Synagogue under the patronage of a Socialist-Liberal coalition government, was devised to counterbalance this one-sidedness.

---

[2] Cited in Pók, "Why was there no *Historikerstreit* in Hungary after 1989–1990?" 148.

The division of labour between the two memorial sites reproduced and further strengthened the long tradition of a divided memory of the brutalities featured in the twentieth century in Hungary. The main issue looming behind all this has been the insecure definition of who may truly be considered to embody the victim and the perpetrator in the past. The obvious lack of a coherent culture of memory in Hungary also follows from the common, but still contradictory traumatic experiences of the twentieth century.

Very few attempts have been made after 1989 to transcend this duality of how past experiences are remembered now. One of the positive endeavors was the dialogue proposed by the Abbey of Pannonhalma, a prominent institution of the Hungarian Catholic Church. Using the circular letter of Pope John Paul II, issued in September 1996 on the memory of Shoah (*We remember: considerations on Shoah*) as a starting point, Asztrik Várszegi, abbot of Pannonhalma, organized a conference in 1998 with the aim of confronting on a scholarly basis the main problems of history of the Jews in Hungary. He stressed: "We did not want only to tear the wounds open by this dialogue and remain only at the rigorous analysis of the various topics. We wanted that everything brought forward should become memory and the ground for dialogue. We would be remedied through remembering only. The scholarly conference and the volume produced as a result thus serve the reconciliation and the social calming down, or a conscious beginning of such a reconciliation."[3] The project, however, was not continued and the effort of drawing closer to each other the two realms of memory, the Jewish and the Gentile one, seems not to have been successful.

The statement has been wholly justified by the scholarly and intellectual discourse pursued in today's Hungary on the so-called Jewish problem. Tamás Ungvári, to name one of the few scholars contributing to this discussion, has expressed his dissatisfaction with the present state of affairs concerning the common Jewish-Hungarian *cultural national memory*. However, Ungvári has argued the "memory of the non-Jewish Hungarians would be complete only together with the memory of the Hungarian Jews."[4] Ungvári holds the view that the time has only now

---

[3] Várszegi, "Magyar megfontolások a soáról," 12–13.
[4] Ungvári, "Csalódások kora," 29. An earlier version of the book is available in English: Idem., *The 'Jewish Question' in Europe*.

come to reconstruct a *commonly shared history* incorporating the past of the assimilated Jews. This seems for him to be the only way of transforming memory into history, made possible now by the fading of the experience of the tragedy of the Holocaust (experience of the dissimilation *per se*). In trying to return to the true historical experience of assimilation, which has fallen into oblivion due in part to the Holocaust and in part to the subsequent events of Communist rule, a radical change of the scholarly recognition is also needed. History-writing—both the history of literature and social history—is entitled to create the kind of memory in which the assessment of various historical experiences on both sides may finally be brought together.[5]

Apart from the public discourse referred to, actual historical inquiries in the field have increased since 1989. As a reaction to the monumental monograph on the history of the Jewish question in Hungary,[6] there arose an interesting debate on how the notion of the Jew may be defined at all both in the past and the present; it also included the question of to what extent the term "Jewish question" may be used in reference to assimilation, national and Jewish identity.[7] Parallel to and somewhat independent of all this, a separate mode of collective memory on Jewish side has also gained legitimacy during the last few years; these include the ambition of some young people to invent or re-invent the lost traditions of a past Jewishness.[8]

The memory of 1956 was shaped first and foremost, and even determined, by the harsh terror that came in its aftermath and the permanent presence of the Soviet army in the country. These related circumstances stood behind both the forced amnesia—the attempt of the Kádárite authorities to contain the still vivid social memory of

---

[5] Ibid., 30.
[6] Gyurgyák, *A zsidókérdés Magyarországon*.
[7] Horváth, "A szimmetriakövetelés" [The demand of symmetry], 3–13; Spiró, "Zsidógyártás" [Production of Jew], 19–23; Veres, "Egy elhibázott könyvről" [On a faulted book], 24–28; Trencsényi, "Megtalálni az angyalok hangját – és a részletekben lakozó ördögöket" [In finding the voice of the angels – and the devils residing in the details], 9–19.
[8] The monthly *Szombat* [Saturday] plays great role both in reviving and articulating a modern and not denominationally bound Jewish identity in today's Hungary.

1956—and the ultimate failure of that attempt. The public oblivion surrounding 1956 seemed to be deep and irreversible.

The latent collective memory, instead of a publicly articulated one,[9] remained in force from 1956 to 1989. In assessing the weight and the meaning of 1956 both in the past and in today's collective memory in Hungary, the double notion of the "cold" and "hot" memory seems to be a useful analytical tool.[10] Hot memory renders the past worth remembering by suggesting that *it is still with us*. Any account of the past influenced by hot memory thereby immediately becomes a "grounding narrative," a sort of myth embracing facts and fictions, history and mythology alike: the grounding narrative is a myth that is at once fictitious and factual.

The memory of the 1956 revolution has always been a myth of that kind. It became a grounding narrative as soon as the Kádár regime had established itself, and this seems to be confirmed by Kádárite memory politics itself.[11] The revolution for the Kádárite political elite was much more a negative than a positive grounding narrative or myth, and so the memory politics of the day tended more to obscure it than to reconstruct the actual story of a notable event. The most common method was to impose silence about 1956 and rigorously restrict the knowledge available for any public discussion. The propaganda material produced and manipulated by the Kádárite political police was the only material from retaliatory documents available as a source for school curricula, historical textbooks or the mass media.

This legacy of the Kádár regime's memory of the revolution faced a reversal with the political change of 1989, which transformed it into a positive grounding narrative. The way was opened by the ceremony to rebury Imre Nagy and his fellow martyrs, held in June 1989 on

---

[9] As Maciej Janowski describes in his chapter in the volume, a similar phenomenon was identified in the case of the Polish villagers, Jedwabne as for their amnesia concerning the Jewish genocide committed by themselves in the war years. Wolentarska-Ocman, "Collective remembrance in Jedwabne," 174–175. The argument has been criticized by Kapralski, "The Jedwabne village green?" 181.

[10] Assmann, "Collective memory and cultural identity," 125–133. More broadly, Assmann, *Das kulturelle Gedächtnis*.

[11] Ripp, "1956 emlékezete és az MSZMP," 233–238.

Heroes' Square in Budapest. But the initial great hopes for this process were not to be fulfilled.[12] The reburial ceremony itself revealed that there had not been a consensus on what 1956 should mean for the present. It emerged again that modern memory is born from what Gillis calls "an intense awareness of the conflicting representations of the past and the effort of each group to make its version the basis" of commemoration.[13]

Does this mean that 1956 finally lost all of its mythic importance and meaning? Not at all, but in trying to create a nuanced picture, it is important to place it into a conceptual framework that assumes there has always been a big difference between the notions of ritual and myth. The mythic material contains a wide range of possible meanings and interpretations, so that selection among them derives from the function the myth performs in a specific context, as a grounding narrative. As Paul Connerton has pointed out, "By comparison with myths, the structure of rituals has significantly less potential for *variance*."[14] Because ritual is both performing language and formalized language, it is a series of speech acts that always takes canonical form. Myth, on the other hand, is often subject to continual reshaping until it eventually achieves a relatively stable form and meaning.

Several efforts have been made to establish a canon for assessing the revolution and its main heroes. In this effort not just the professional masters of creating a collective cultural memory, the historians, but many social agents were deeply involved. They all sought to submit themselves to the power of anarchy or freedom of interpretation, as a consequence of the way the memory of 1956 was (and still is) more closely connected to a grounding narrative myth than to a ritual form that does not imply a fixed and stable meaning. In such cases, any allusions to a past occurence, 1956 in particular, necessarily has a vital function in perpetuating some present-day political and ideological

---

[12] An abundant literature is available on the failure to accord 1956 a true Hungarian *lieu de memoire*, see Litván, ,"Politikai beszéd 1956-ról – 1989 után" (Political Speech on 1956 – after 1989.; Kende, "Megmarad-e 1956 nemzeti hagyománynak?" [Does 1956 remain to be a national tradition?]; Rainer, "Ötvenhat után" [After Fifty-six]; György, "Az emlékezet szétesése – az olvashatatlan város" [Disintegrating of memory – The unreadable city].
[13] Gillis, "Memory and identity: the history of a relationship," 8.
[14] Connerton, *How Societies Remember*, 58.

ends. As a result, on the day to commemorate the revolution (October 23) there are usually many different political gatherings (including quasi-demonstrations on the right-wing side) held, under the auspices of political parties—parliamentary and non-parliamentary—each intent on remembering the revolution in its own way and according to its own taste. In addition, on the occasion of the fiftieth anniversary of the revolution, in 2006, violence broke out at some demonstrations in the streets and squares of Budapest, which show the mobilizing force inherent in the commemoration of 1956.

If we turn now our attention to the political instrumentalization of 1956 following 1989, one can easily discern the close relationship between the political (the party) sympathy and the meaning customarily attached to commemorating 1956. The Socialists, inheriting the burdensome heritage of the Kádárite ruling party, endeavoured to create an image of 1956 to embody a past socialist undertaking, led by the original Bolshevik apparatchik, Imre Nagy. This effort culminated between 1994 and 1998 during the government of a Socialist-Liberal coalition, when they tried to create a cult of Imre Nagy. This, however, was not entirely successful.[15] The Fidesz government (1998–2002) also made an attempt to create a special image of 1956 by stressing that the specific sense and the real significance of 1956 lay only in its anticipation of the day when Fidesz would eventually come to power. This view followed logically from their firm belief that they alone could continue and restore the legacy of 1956, which had been neglected even after 1989. By assuming the role of the present true mouthpiece of an exclusive historical truth about 1956, the storyteller (in this case a specific politician actor), dubbed the 1956 revolution as distinctively bourgeois and turned an image of the past into a mere reflection of the future. The label that 1956 actually was a bourgeois revolt against the Communist (and Soviet) despotism wholly coincided with the then actual self-designation of the governing party: Fidesz Bourgeois Party.

Both the rhetoric and the meanings of the discourse on 1956 greatly depend on the various political affiliations and shared public sentiments. In examining Parliamentary and other political speeches

---

[15] On the role of the Prime Minister's daughter and her family in the cultic reverence toward the memory Imre Nagy see, Gyáni, "Memory and discourse on the 1956 Hungarian Revolution," 13–15.

delivered since 1989 on the day of commemoration of the revolution, there may be observed a close relationship between the political attitude and the way 1956 has been interpreted. The measure of this correlation cannot, however, be exaggerated. The present-day vision of 1956 looks to have been shaped and defined by the still extant communicative (live) memory of the event as it is guided by the demands of current political discourse.[16] The great weight that living memory may play even today in terms of the revolution urges historians to reconstruct or at least document the past experiences of 1956. This led during the last couple of years to the publication of an increasing number of oral histories of 1956,[17] which give a detailed account of the lived history of revolutionary events.[18]

The unending rivalry among opposing political parties, through their various ways of commemorating the revolution of 1956, may also have a role in that "apparently not a single easily identifiable social strata holds as truly important an issue to link his or her identity to as the heritage of 1956."[19] It is symptomatic that a majority of people asked considered János Kádár more a victim than a traitor, and only a few believed Kádár betrayed the cause of the Hungarian revolution.[20] That the vitality of the memory of the Kádár era persists in present-day Hungarian historical consciousness is thus beyond any dispute.

Now let's look at the image of the Communist past as presented in today's politics and collective or social memory. János Kádár and the period named after him have now gained a clear, widespread popularity. It is associated with a stable social existence, the unambiguous mobility perspectives and the sense of social solidarity, "social facts" scantily available amidst the circumstances of the market economy. The memory of the dictatorship, however, fades away. Any evaluation

---

[16] See Bazsalya, *Az 1956-os forradalom társadalmi reprezentációja* [Social representation of the 1956 revolution].

[17] Molnár et al, *A forradalom emlékezete. Személyes történelem* [Memory of the revolution. A personal history].

[18] Standeisky, *Népuralom ötvenhatban* [Rule of the people in fifty-six].

[19] Vásárhelyi, *Csalóka emlékezet. A 20. század történelme a magyar közgondolkodásban* [Misleading memory. The twentieth-century history in Hungarian public thinking], 133. The statement is based on the findings of an opinion poll.

[20] Ibid., 135.

of the Kádár regime is, however, extremely polarised: there are many who show loyalty to the memory of the Kádár regime, but some others look back with anger and contempt.[21]

The many contradictions that characterize the public attitude (memory work) toward the Communist (Kádárite) past may be demonstrated by the telling example of the so-called informer's cases. Tens of thousands—about 40,000—civilian informers were employed before 1989 by state security to regularly watch over and denounce their fellow citizens.[22] The first democratically elected government was already confronted with the fact that a great number of MPs and other active politicians of the day—on the right and left —were previously employed as informers. The government refused to make available the files of the secret police, and established a practice that has continued more or less through today. When Péter Medgyessy, the Socialist prime minister, was unmasked in 2002 as having worked for the secret police during the Kádár era, changes appeared likely to come. From that time onwards, scholars were allowed to study secret police documents, but did not have a free hand in making public the findings of their own research carried out in the Historical Office, which was renamed in 2003 as the Historical Archive of the State Security. Informers who are identified threaten defamation suits against the historians and journalists who expose them, creating a significant problem. The courts regularly give special consideration to the unmasked former informers on the principle that negative information should only be published about a public figure. The big question, however, is how to define who is or isn't a public figure.

The views present-day public opinion holds about past wrongdoings by informers can be seen in cases where the exposed is among the country's most famous and respected politicians, church leaders, sports broadcasters, rock musicians, actors, journalists, artists or other professionals.

One of the most notable scandals to erupt, concerned István Szabó, the internationally famous, Oscar-winning film director. He worked for the State Security as a civilian informer between 1957 and

---

[21] Ibid., 146.
[22] For more about it see, Rainer, "Fragments on State Security," 5.

1961, giving 48 reports on 72 "target persons" in which he sometimes (not always) denounced some of his colleagues.

The customary public reaction to such cases had always been to engage in hot debates about the unambiguous responsibility (or more rather, the irresponsibility) of the politicians who held back the documents of the secret police. The reactions given to István Szabó's affair, however, clearly showed a shift in this attitude. The change was already anticipated by how Szabó himself first reacted to the announcement that he had been an informer. The film director said, "to agree to work for State Security was the bravest, the most daring act of my life," because he could thus save the life of one of his classmates who participated in the armed action in 1956, the one that took place at the Köztársaság square. Not much later it turned out, however, that the story was not true. But even this was not enough for Szabó to show repentance. He admitted only that, "I had to act to protect myself." He would have been expelled from the College of the Film and Theater Arts, Szabó claimed, if he had refused an offer to cooperate with State Security.

His changing excuses to explain his past misdeed proved, however, plausible for many. A great number of colleagues who were also informed on by Szabó, and almost the entire filmmaking profession in Hungary, and even a considerable part of the intelligentsia, declared solidarity with him. Well over a hundred prominent intellectuals published a manifesto in which they expressed their love and admiration for the man, "who has been making superb and important films for the last forty-five years. And he did it not only for us Hungarians, but has extended our fame to all parts of the world." The main message of the manifesto has been to claim that instead of blaming such a great talent for past misbehaviour (which is indeed worth forgetting), one rather has to endorse him in trying to explain it. It was striking that the manifesto was also signed by several of the "target persons" whom Szabó denounced in his secret reports.[23]

The events described offer deep insight into Hungarian society's emotional and intellectual process of coming to terms with its own past. The striking absence of a critical—or self-critical—confrontation

---

[23] The case was described from an American perspective by Deák, "Scandal in Budapest."

with this past on the part not just of the political elite, but even the wider public, most probably derives from the common experience of general collaboration with the Kádár regime. That is what makes the memory of that particular past so uneasy for everybody concerned. The plain moral condemnation of the past implying the misbehaviour of our own, cannot be fulfilled amid such conditions without threatening personal identity. The case of civilian police informers, collaborating in this way with the dictatorship, is not an exception, but rather an extreme manifestation of the attitude of every citizen who to some extent was involved in sustaining the imposed tyranny.

The moral problem of judging the past has been known more or less in almost every post-Communist country of Eastern and Central Europe. In explaining the positive public attitude towards the Communist past, one may refer to the notion of the "solidarity of the culpable" formulated by Jirina Šiklová, the well-known, once dissident Czech sociologist. She has argued that the fall of socialism "did not mean just the fall of the bearers of Communist power... but was also the fall of ordinary people who lived under this system and had, to a greater or lesser degree, adapted to it." Since everyone "who lived here inevitably achieved his secondary acquired social status... [demanding] to conform to this system to some degree."[24] In any discussion of everybody's own role in the many ways of sustaining the former dictatorship the sentiment of shame seems hard to avoid. The growing readiness of the public, at least in Hungary, for tolerance and even empathy towards the unmasked informers and collaborators underlines the invisible force of the so called "solidarity of the culpable," one shaping or even defining the moral and spiritual remembrance of Communism. We will return to this problem later.

A Return to the Cult of Trianon

Trianon's psychological shock to twentieth- and twenty-first-century Hungarian historical awareness and national identity was acute during the interwar period, and now seems to have revived. Trianon is

---

[24] Šiklová, "The solidarity of the culpable," 767.

a metaphor to express the discontinuity of the "natural" trajectory of modern Hungary's history. By redrawing Hungary's borders, the 1920 Treaty of Trianon caused the country to lose 71 percent of her former territory, with a corresponding loss of 64 percent of her population. More than three million ethnic Hungarians, compared to the eight million remaining within the new state's borders, became citizens of the successor countries around Hungary. This truly traumatic experience and permanent source of collective grievance manifested itself in various ways during the last nearly hundred years. The irredentism dominating the official politics and the public discourse of the Horthy-period (1920–1944) was followed by a long, deep silence on Trianon imposed by the Communists.

The political shift of 1989 brought, however, fundamental change by allowing talk about past grievances, particularly Trianon. However, the generality of such a discourse allows diverse meanings to become attached to a past event, and leads to various ways it can be politically instrumentalized. This diversity of meanings can be discerned in the rhetorics of the Trianon discourse as articulated in present-day Hungarian party politics.

One could begin by looking at the many ways of mentioning Trianon in Parliamentary speeches delivered between 1990 and 2002 and thereafter. A study written on the topic has revealed that no more than 443 Parliamentary speeches out of nearly twelve thousand included direct references to Trianon at that time; this looks not to be a great number, indeed.[25] The issue of Trianon was brought forward almost exclusively by the right-wing MPs and was mentioned much less by any left-wing politicians. In addition, the connotation added to it differed in each case. The analyst Gergely Romsics set up various analytical categories into which he tried to classify the various discussions of Trianon. Accordingly, MPs of the right-wing parties tended to apply a so-called "historical," "plebeian historical," or "historical

---

[25] Romsics, "Trianon a Házban. A Trianon-fogalom megjelenése és funkciói a pártok diskurzusaiban az első három parlamenti ciklus idején (1990–2002) [Trianon in the House. Appearance and the functions of the notion of Trianon in discourses of the parties during the first three parliamentary cycles, 1990–2002], 35–52; Ablonczy, *Trianon-legendák* [Trianon legends], 31–32.

plebeian" dominant poetics in their speeches delivered at the House in connection with Trianon. By adapting a historical rhetoric, the speaker expressed his unconditional identification with the tragic Hungarian past eloquently symbolized by Trianon. In applying the so called "historical plebeian" rhetorics, the speaker showed the sign of his conscious identification with the national heritage, and his firm belief that the trauma caused by Trianon might finally be successfully dissolved. Application of the third trope as a dominant one in the talk about Trianon, emphasizes the speaker's insistance on his strong commitment to the trauma engendered by the unending memory of Trianon. On the basis of the latter, the injustice caused by that particular historical event, did not lose at all its present-day actual political meaning and significance; it is thus a guideline even today for any truly national political strategy. Apart from the terminology constructed and the analytical tools used by the analyst, one may argue that more than one option would have been in currency even within the right-wing political camp of the possible meanings and the ways of intrumentalization of Trianon.

The obvious propensity of right-wing political forces to revive the memory of Trianon is clearly shown by the second Fidesz government, which came to power in April 2010. The first law that the newly elected Parliament passed concerned the idea of extending Hungarian citizenship to every ethnic Magyar living in neighbouring countries. The second step the Fidesz government took was to release a declaration, the Nemzeti Együttműködés Nyilatkozata (National Cooperation Proclamation) which announced the introduction of the so-called System of National Cooperation. It was a plan devised to integrate, at least in principle, every Hungarian living either within or outside the borders of the country. Finally, the new government declared June 4, the day of signing the Peace Treaty in Trianon in 1920, to be a national day of commemoration, one comparable to March 15 or October 23, the commemorative days of the 1848 and the 1956 revolutions.

These new developments within the sphere of state politics were preceded however by a great number of civil society endeavours in the same direction. The mass demonstrations, which sometimes became violent in 2006, were usually intertwined with public articulation of a forceful anti-Trianon sentiment. It is no accident that several of the riots organized and managed by an extreme right-wing social association, Sixty-four Counties,[26] were at least tacitly supported by the then oppositional Fidesz. The tactic followed by the latter both as an oppositional and a governing party in the aftermath has always been to denounce the liberal and especially the socialist political forces. This was done by suggesting and even arguing that they do not belong to the authentic national political community of the country. Following 2002, at a time when Fidesz had lost the parliamentary elections and became for eight years an oppositional party, Viktor Orbán, president of the party and the former Prime Minister, asserted again and again that, "the nation could not be in opposition," and that "the socialists have always attacked the nation both in the past and the present," or that "the liberals represent an alien-hearted component of the country's population," etc.

Trianon politics, however, soon became a double-edged sword in the hands of Fidesz, as it has also been used to counterbalance the overt revisionist ideology of the extreme right-wing forces, represented now by the parliamentary party, Jobbik (Better). The growing nationalism of today's Hungarian right-wing government was and remains a reaction to the xenophobic and aggressively nationalist state politics of some of neighboring countries, where a considerable Hungarian minority is to be found. This caused recurring conflicts during the last couple of years between Hungary and Slovakia. The latter country's dominant anti-Hungarian nationalist line of politics, "playing the Hungarian card," fed the militant Hungarian nationalism in the last Parliamentary elections. The whole problem cannot be reconciled by the guiding ideals and politics of the European Union, of which both countries are members. The EU, however, is reluctant to intervene in these international disputes between member countries, and deals much less with the internal political issues concerning the measure and form of nationalism.

The sort of political populism described before was accompanied and further strengthened by a parallel development in public discourse. With the explicit aim of producing and disseminating a plainly nationalist image of history, focusing on Trianon, the public history getting out of the control practised by academic history writing, started to take

---

[26] The name refers to the territorial subdivision of the Hungarian Kingdom before 1918 (and/or 1920).

institutional forms. As a clear sign of this more recent development a Trianon Museum was founded in a provincial city, Várpalota, and a Trianon Research Institute was set up in 2007 led by, among others, Ernő Raffay, a one-time academic historian (who also held a post as under-secretary of state at the Ministry of Military Affairs in the Antall government). Raffay has been a key figure in the whole story by becoming, in the aftermath of 1989, the most well-known spokesman of the group of historians declaring themselves to represent "national history writing" as opposed to mainstream (academic) historical scholarship. "National" in this case means mostly a Trianon-focused account of Hungary's twentieth-century history. In order to achieve greater public influence, Raffay and his close colleagues set up in 2009 a historical journal, *Trianoni Szemle* (Trianon Review) dedicated solely to discussion of the Trianon question. The journal focuses on criticism of the internal enemy of Hungary, both in the past and the present. These enemies allegedly contributed greatly to the tragedy of Hungary at the end of World War I, and are now engaged in diminishing the great importance of the border changes accomplished at the Treaty of Paris. The way of reasoning pursued by these historians to explain Trianon revolves around identifying scapegoats to bear the primary responsibility for Hungary's suffering.[27] They, alongside the Entente Powers (France in particuar) and the new states created as a result of the dissolution of the Austro-Hungarian Monarchy (the later Little Entente) are Mihály Károlyi, Oszkár Jászi, leaders and representatives of the 1918 Revolution and the first Bourgeois Republic afterwards, and last but not least the Freemasons. This argument certainly contains a latent anti-Semitism and the whole historical construct is actually a mere replica of the historical image produced and propagated as early as the 1920s. The approach outlined stands not too far from the historical vision cherished and propagated by the present-day Fidesz government. This may also explain the many ties connecting these historians and their efforts to some of the leading politicians of the governing party. Sándor Lezsák, to cite a few examples only, the Fidesz appointed deputy chair of the Parliament from the beginning took an active part in

---

[27] The great role of scapegoating in conceptualizing twentieth-century Hungary's history is discussed in detail in Pók, "Why was there no *Historikerstreit* in Hungary after 1989–1990?"

popoularizing the journal. Géza Szőcs, the then would-be Minister of Culture of the new Fidesz government also showed his unambiguous sympathy to the endeavors of the historians mentioned above, by stressing that they alone are able to sweep away the historical falsehoods and distortions advanced by the "official history writing."[28]

Some further similar developments are also to be registered within the realm of public history in terms of the growing cult of Trianon. The journal, *Nagy Magyarország* (Greater Hungary), was established in 2009 by a group of second-rate historians, not holding academic status, with the aim of discussing Trianon and other vital events of the 20th century on the basis of the *single national truth*. The group, many without any professional qualifications or credentials, have established their own institutional base, the Emlékpont Múzeum (Memory-point Museum) located in a provincial town, Hódmezővásárhely. The Museum was maintained by the local municipal authorities and founded in cooperation with the House of Terror a few years ago.

The House of Terror, already mentioned, was actually founded under the patronage of Fidesz in 2002 for political propaganda purposes, specifically to create and deepen an explicit anti-Communist historical image. The building that houses the museum serves as a commemorative place,[29] while the exhibitions feature the telos of representing the national suffering caused by the Communist rule.[30] It is also located on one of the most important thoroughfares in Budapest, Andrássy út, which gives room for diverse commemorative public rituals and ceremonies organized by Fidesz. The head of the Museum, Mária Schmidt, also manages other Fidesz-founded historical institutes, and has been assigned to incorporate other history research

---

[28] On the active role that Géza Szőcs, the Transylvanian poet, has played for several years in organizing the "conservative intellectual discourse" with the aim of backing the FIDESZ road to power, see: Laki, *A nemzeti diskurzus* [The national discourse], 24–31.

[29] This building served for several years as headquarters for the ÁVH (State Security Office), the Communist Secret Police. True, however, that the same building was previously the headquarters of the Arrow-Cross Movement (the Hungarian Fascists) and also gave room in 1944 to the terror tribunal of the Arrow-Cross Party (Nyilas Számonkérőszék).

[30] For more about the Museum and the debates around it see, Pittaway: "The 'House of Terror' and Hungary's politics of memory," 16–17.

institutes, whose maintenance is not provided by the new Fidesz government. The most notable of them is the Institute of the 1956 Revolution, an internationally known and respected research center which, however, is doomed to die by the present-day government.

In returning for a moment to the recent emergence of conservative national historians, who are trying to establish themselves in the realm of public history, it is worth noting the declaration made when they founded their own organization in September 2010. The aim of the foundation, the text says, is to support and publicize periodicals concerned with the history of the Carpathian Basin, to help young historians by making available the findings of their research, to support the publication of books on Hungarian history in the Carpathian Basin, and to maintain Internet forums. One prominent end is to improve and neutralize the negative influences of Marxist history writing, which is felt even today.[31]

The openly revisionist image of modern Hungarian history constructed by the aforementioned historians, coupled with an explicit anti-Communist thrust makes them akin to the extreme right-wing political forces, embodied now by Jobbik. The unambiguous personal relationsips connecting the National Conservative History Research Foundation to Jobbik are quite obvious. The question of funding, however, is hardly known. Some reporting appeared in the conservative press, like the weekly *Heti Válasz* (Weekly response), that tried to guess who could be the businessmen who finance these alternative historical undertakings, but nothing certain can be said about them. The close proximity of the Fidesz—and the Jobbik—supported nationalist and anti-Communist interpretation of Hungary's modern history is also a striking fact.

The differences between them are also obvious. One of the being the presence (or the absence) of the racist approach to history with inherent antisemitism, which does not play a visible role in the historical vision advocated by Fidesz-run history forums. And, of course, the openly revisionist interpretation of the Trianon problematic is also alien to the latter, which is an integral part of the historical imagery offered by the "conservative historians."

---

[31] http://tortenelemportal.hu/2010/09/megalakult-a-nemzeti-konzervativ-tortenetkutato-alapitvany

In placing the whole process of institutionalization into a wider, international context, an analogy may be observed between the Hungarian developments and those of the so-called Holocaust denial industry. Such organizations like the Institute for Historical Review, located in California, which declares itself to be a respectable academic body, even publishing a quasi-academic magazine, *The Journal of Historical Review*, are to legitimize the scientific basis of Holocaust denial. This has also been emphasized by David Irving, the well-known Holocaust denier, in his court proceedings before the High Court in London in the late 1990s: "the Institute, Irving claimed, was a respectable and nonextremist institution whose board members held established academic qualifications."[32]

The new public forums of the Hungarian alternative public history, devised to produce "true national, but still scholarly based" knowledge about Hungary's history in modern times, are assisted by "national publishers" specialized in publicizing the products only of the "national corpus of knowledge" of our history. The books published by these special publishers are sold at special bookstores named Szkíta, but some of the books classified here also find their way even into the commercially based big bookstore chains, like Alexandra, one of the biggest of that kind in Hungary. Sales of these books are much higher than true academic scholarship. This also has a lot to do with the ever broadening social (civil society) network encircling and backing the intellectual pursuit channelled by the national publishing industry, and the new "alternative" historical magazines, like *Trianoni Szemle* and *Nagy Magyarország*. The Trianon Societies, as the core of this civil society movement, consider their main task to revive and maintain the social memory of Trianon. In doing this they strive for setting up an increasing number of local Trianon monuments, which are often supported by local authorities.

This unique historical subculture is further enriched by adopting so-called national pop music (whose lyrics include nationalist messages), and not least by incorporating certain leisure activites such as historical military games. This is supplemented by the reading of alternative historical accounts either on Trianon or of the ancient history

---

[32] More about all this see Evans, *Lying about Hitler*, 140–142.

of the Hungarians, with their pre-Christian tribal social and political frameworks. The number and the extent of membership in these societies, however, is not known at this moment.

Mainstream history writing about Trianon is indeed a well-established field, which also existed before 1989. Way before the fall of the Communist regime several academic historians made a huge and successful effort to research archives (not just in Budapest, but in Paris and elsewhere, too) on the history of the Trianon question (the late Zsuzsa L. Nagy and Mária Ormos in particular). More recently, Ignác Romsics, one of the most prominent historians of the day,[33] and several of his students have been busily engaged in dealing with the problem of Trianon, approaching it from very diverse angles.[34]

Not even mainstream historiography has missed the opportunity to try to shape the public history image of Trianon. The occasion of commemorating the ninetieth anniversary of Trianon in 2010 was used by academic-based popular historical magazines, such as *Rubicon* and *História*, which sold at several tens of thousand copies, to discuss Trianon on a rigorously scholarly base.[35] Furthermore, Ignác Romsics and some others publish articles in national dailies (*Népszabadság*) with the aim of popularizing the concept of a non-nationalist (non-revisionist) approach to the issue.[36] Romsics tends to give a detailed description and explanation of the specific historical road leading to the fall of the

---

[33] Romsics, I., *A trianoni békeszerződés* [The Peace Treaty of Trianon].

[34] Zeidler, *A revíziós gondolat* [The revisionist thought], and Idem., *A magyar irredenta kultusz a két világháború között* [The Hungarian cult of irredentism between the two world wars]. These two books were published in one volume in English in the United States. See further, Romsics, *Mítosz és emlékezet. A Habsburg Birodalom felbomlása az osztrák és a magyar politikai elit emlékirat-irodalmában* [Myth and remembrance. The dissolution of the Habsburg Empire in the memoir literature of the Austro-Hungarian political elite], also published in English in the United States. Finally, see Bertényi, *Trianon és a magyar politikai gondolkodás 1920–1953* [Trianon and the Hungarian political thinking].

[35] The magazine *Rubicon* dedicated two complete issues to Trianon this year. The other magazine, *História*, which is closely linked to the Institute of Historical Sciences of the Hungarian Academy of Sciences, has also dealt abundantly with Trianon in one its 2010 issues.

[36] Romsics, Ignác, "Trianon okai," and "A második bécsi döntés. Erdély és a magyar revíziós tervek."

Austro-Hungarian dual system. In this process, the clearly subjective factors so much emphasized by the scapegoating historical approach, are rendered by him to play an inferior role, if any role at all. Finally, mainstream historians insist on considering Trianon as already belonging to the closed past, which may or should be viewed as history, without any direct implications for our present-day world.

A telling example for the latter argument can be the message of the article made public in the left-wing daily *Népszava*. The historian author described the absurd consequences of what would happen if the territories lost in 1920 were returned. "What could be the result, if all the territories lost in Trianon were returned by a fairy? The gain is: every Hungarian living in the Carpathian basin would come together again. National unity obviously means that both in the culture, and maybe in the economy, some positive impulses would occur. The downside is as follows: it is hard to envisage a bigger disaster than that. We would live in a country where around 40 percent of the population is Hungarian only. The option accessible amidst such circumstances is either establishing a national dictatorship, accompanied by fear and anxiety, constant conflict, and the giving up of democratic ideals resulted from all this, or insisting on a democracy in which Hungary might not have a Hungarian prime minister for decades." So, he concludes, Trianon is really an extreme injustice that cannot be remedied now. "This is not only a military and political impossibility, but something not worth trying." True, however, that it is hard to realize.[37] Another, also striking contribution to the present-day Trianon discourse written by a liberal-minded historian, has stressed the necessity of adapting the diverse national viewpoints for a much better understanding both of the precedents leading to and the results following from Trianon.[38] An obvious indication of the possibly divergent attitudes towards the memory of Trianon even among the liberal-minded historians, Krisztián Ungváry engaged in a heated debate over the last argument, advanced by Éva Kovács.[39]

---

[37] Újlaki, "Trianon patologikus gyásza."
[38] Kovács, "Jeder Nachkrieg ist ein Vorkrieg? Trianon traumatikus emlékezetéről."
[39] Ungváry, "A meg nem értett Trianon."

The gradual emergence and the recent triumphant expansion of the Trianon industry was linked initially to the political opposition movements, when Fidesz was in opposition to the Socialist-Liberal government. Still, it was not simply an ingredient element of the political strategy applied by the Fidesz, but something created more or less independently of its political guidance. The historical subculture manifesting itself through the spreading cult of Trianon was thus an autonomous form of public history which, however, could easily be appropriated by any right-wing political propaganda.

What are the social factors giving birth to this entity? The basic socio-mental preconditions that may be held responsible for facilitating these processes are among others the democratization of the creation (and dissemination) of more than one possible image of a historical past, independent of the history taught at school. A further factor to be mentioned in this context is the sudden return of some of the old corpuses of historical knowledge and conceptual approaches. This closely relates to viewing the national historical cause through the prism of the so called "fate issues," which has been an extensive and highly popular sort of discourse both in the interwar Hungary and elsewhere.[40] And, lastly, one is tempted to refer to the urgent need of many young men and women for a newly (re)established community identity to replace the former one invalidated by the political change of 1989. The obvious absence of a feasible group identity due to the subversive forces of a strongly individualist new social order, may easily bring back some of the older and apparently outdated group commitments like the national one. That alone can explain the evolvement of such a unique, but not wholly unprecented alternative historical consciousness, which looks to take the form of a public history domain.

Epilogue

To what extent can the Trianon cult be integrated into the state-formed public history supervised from this day by the Fidesz cultural (educational and science) policy? Or to put it another way, will the

---

[40] See Sanders, "Post-Trianon searching: the early career of László Németh."

influence of the state on public history be so powerful it will become uncontested? This seems to be the decisive and strategic question with regard to the politically dangerous implications of the extremely nationalist image of Trianon. The incalculable geopolitical consequences of the whole-hearted embrace of memorial practice of that kind actually always restricts the range of options available to any Hungarian government, including the present one. The first steps taken by the new Fidesz government in this direction in the form of passing a law on citizenship, or designating June 4 to be "The Day of the National Belonging Together," the Nemzeti Összetartozás Napja, devised as a permanent Trianon-based commemoration, predict a future in which the cult of Trianon will finally be nationalized in the same way as it was appropriated and controlled from above in the Horthy era.

BIBLIOGRAPHY

Ablonczy, B. *Trianon-legendák* [Trianon legends]. Budapest: Jaffa, 2010.
Assmann, J. "Collective memory and cultural identity." *New German Critique* vol. 65 (Spring–Summer, 1995): 125–133.
———. *Das kulturelle Gedächtnis. Shrift, Erinnerung und politische Identität in frühen Hochkulturen*. Munich: Verlag V. H. Beck, 1992.
Bazsalya, B. *Az 1956-os forradalom társadalmi reprezentációja* [Social representation of the 1956 revolution]. MA Thesis, 2009. Eötvös Loránd University, Budapest, Social Science Faculty.
Bertényi, I. and I. Romsics, eds. *Trianon és a magyar politikai gondolkodás 1920–1953* [Trianon and the Hungarian political thinking]. Budapest: Osiris, 1998.
Connerton, P. *How Societies Remember*. Cambridge: Cambridge University Press, 1989.
Deák, I. "Scandal in Budapest." *New York Review of Books* vol. 53, no. 16 (October 19, 2006).
Evans, R.J. *Lying about Hitler. History, Holocaust, and the David Irving Trial*. New York: Basic Books, 2002.
Gillis, J.R. "Memory and Identity: The History of a Relationship." In *Commemorations. The Politics of National Identity* edited by Gillies. Princeton, N.J.: Princeton University Press, 1996.
Gyáni, G. "Memory and Discourse on the 1956 Hungarian Revolution." In *Challenging Communism in Eastern Europe. 1956 and its Legacy* edited by T. Cox. London: Routledge, 2008.
———. "Political Uses of Tradition in Postcommuniust East Central Europe." *Social Research* vol. 60, no. 4 (Winter 1993).

György, P. "Az emlékezet szétesése – az olvashatatlan város" [Disintegrating of space – the city not being readable]. *2000* (October 2006): 3–12.

Gyurgyák, J. *A zsidókérdés Magyarországon. Politikai eszmetörténet* [The Jewish Question in Hungary. A History of Political Ideology]. Budapest: Osiris, 2001.

Horváth, I. "A szimmetriakövetelés." [The demand of symmetry] *2000* (October 2001): 3–13.

Kapralski, S. "The Jedwabne village green? The memory and counter-memory of the crime." *History & Memory* vol. 18, no. 1 (Spring/Summer 2006): 181.

Kende, P: "Megmarad-e 1956 nemzeti hagyománynak?" [Does 1956 remain a national tradition?]. In *Évkönyv II*. Budapest: 1956-os Intézet, 1993. 7–19.

Kovács, E. "Jeder Nachkrieg ist ein Vorkrieg? Trianon traumatikus emlékezetéről" [Jeder Nachkrieg ist ein Vorkrieg? On the traumatic memory of Trianon]. *Élet és Irodalom*, October 1, 2010. 4.

Laki, M. "A nemzeti diskurzus" [The national discourse], *Buksz* vol. 22, no. 1 (Spring 2010): 24–31.

Litván, Gy. "Politikai beszéd 1956-ról – 1989 után" [Political speech on 1956 – after 1989]. In *Évkönyv 2002. Magyarország a jelenkorban*. Budapest: 1956-os Intézet, 2002. 258–263.

Molnár, A., Z. Kőrösi, and M. Keller, eds. *A forradalom emlékezete. Személyes történelem* [Memory of the revolution. A personal history]. Budapest: 1956-os Intézet, 2006.

Pittaway, M. "The 'House of Terror' and Hungary's politics of memory." *Austrian Studies Newsletter* vol. 15, no. 1 (Winter 2003): 16–17.

Pók, A. "Why was there no *Historikerstreit* in Hungary after 1989–1990?" In Pók, *The Politics of Hatred in the Middle of Europe. Scapegoating in Twentieth Century Hungary. History and Historiography*. Szombathely: Savaria University Press, 2009.

Rainer, M.J. "Fragments on State Security and Middle Class Values in Kádárist Hungary." *Trondheim Studies on East European Cultures & Societies* no. 22. (2007): 5.

———. *Ötvenhat után* [After Fifty-six]. Budapest: 1956-os Intézet, 2003.

Ripp, Z. "1956 emlékezete és az MSZMP" [Memory of 1956 and the MSZMP]. In *Évkönyv 2002. X. Magyarország a jelenkorban*. Budapest: 1956-os Intézet, 2002.

Romsics, G. *Mítosz és emlékezet. A Habsburg Birodalom felbomlása az osztrák és a magyar politikai elit emlékirat-irodalmában* [Myth and remembrance. The dissolution of the Habsburg Empire in the memoir literature of the Austro-Hungarian political elite]. Budapest: L'Harmattan, 2004.

———. "Trianon a Házban. A Trianon-fogalom megjelenése és funkciói a pártok diskurzusaiban az első három parlamenti ciklus idején (1990–2002)" [Trianon in the house. Appearance and the functions of the notion of Trianon in discourses of the parties during the first three Parliamentary cycles, 1990–2002]. In Czoch, G., C. Fedinecz, eds. *Az emlékezet konstrukciói. Példák a 19–20. századi magyar és közép-európai történelemből* [Constructions of memory. Examples from the 19th- and 20th-century Hungarian and Central-European history]. Budapest: Teleki László Alapítvány, 2006.

Romsics. I. *A trianoni békeszerződés* [The peace treaty of Trianon]. Budapest: Osiris, 2001.

———. "Trianon okai [The causes of Trianon]" *Népszabadság*, June, 5, 2010.

———. "A második bécsi döntés. Erdély és a magyar revíziós tervek" [The second decision in Vienna. Transylvania and the Hungarian plans for revision]. *Népszabadság*, August, 21, 2010. Hétvége 2–4.1

Sanders, I. "Post-Trianon searching: the early career of László Németh." In Király, B.K., P. Pastor, and I. Sanders, eds. *War and Society in East Central Europe. Vol. VI. Essays on World War I: Total War and Peacemaking, A Case Study on Trianon*. Social Science Monographs, Brooklyn College Press, distributed by New York: Columbia University Press, 1982. 347–359.

Šiklová, J. "The solidarity of the culpable." *Social Research* vol. 58, nov. 4 (Winter 1991): 767.

Spiró, Gy. "Zsidógyártás" [Production of Jews]. *2000* (November 2001): 19–23.

Standeisky, É. *Népuralom ötvenhatban* [Rule of the people in fifty-six]. Budapest: Pesti Kalligram, 2010.

Trencsényi, B., "Megtalálni az angyalok hangját – és a részletekben lakozó ördögöket" [Finding the voice of the angels—and the devils residing in the details]. *2000* (January 2002): 9–19.

Újlaki, I. "Trianon patologikus gyásza" [Pathological mourning of Trianon]. *Népszava*, August 7, 2010, Szép Szó Melléklet 7.

Ungváry, K. "A meg nem értett Trianon" [Trianon not understood]. *Élet és Irodalom*, December 10, 2010. 12.

Ungvári, T. "Csalódások kora. A 'zsidókérdés' magyarországi története" [Age of disillusionments. History of the "Jewish Question" in Hungary]. Budapest: Scolar, 2010.

———. *The 'Jewish Question' in Europe—The Case of Hungary*. New York: Columbia University Press, 2000.

Várszegi, A, "Magyar megfontolások a soáról" [Hungarian considerations on Shoa]. In *Magyar megfontolások a soáról* [Hungarian considerations on Shoa] edited by Hamp, G., Ö. Horányi, and L. Rábai. Budapest–Pannonhalma, 1999, 12–13.

Vásárhelyi, M. *Csalóka emlékezet. A 20. század történelme a magyar közgondolkodásban* [Misleading memory. The twentieth-century history in the Hungarian public thinking]. Bratislava/Pozsony: Kalligram, 2007. 133.

Veres, A. "Egy elhibázott könyvről" [On a faulted book]. *2000* (November 2001): 24–28.

Wolentarska-Ocman, E. "Collective Remembrance in Jedwabne. Unsettled Memory of World War II in PostCommunist Poland." *History & Memory* vol. 18, no. 1 (Spring/Summer 2006): 174–175.

Zeidler, M. *A revíziós gondolat* [The revisionist thought]. Budapest: Osiris, 2001.

———. "A magyar irredenta kultusz a két világháború között" [The Hungarian cult of irredentism between the two wars]. Teleki László Alapítvány, 2002.

The "Politics of History" as a Case of Foreign-Policy Making

ALEXANDER ASTROV

Changes in the configurations of political power are often accompanied by shifts in the priorities of specific policies, which in turn acquire catchy marketing labels. The Russian *Perestroika* or "sovereign democracy," the Estonian "tiger leap," or the British "big society," while never exhausting the whole of the state's politics, sometimes succeed in fastening short-term public attention on one specific aspect. Something similar is happening in world politics, even though here there was no "transitions of power" through regular elections and successful changes of priorities are more difficult to achieve. At some point the "politics of history," for example, clearly tends to dominate the agenda alongside "energy security" and "colored revolutions." Still, there is something about the "politics of history" which seems to distinguish it from, say, "war on terror" or *détente*.

To begin with, the fascination with the "politics of history" erupted almost simultaneously in a number of states in Central Europe who employed similar techniques in their pursuit of this kind of politics. And then it ebbed almost as simultaneously. Second, political fashion, if that is what it was, in this case, was dictated by small states, rather than "great powers." For some, these two aspects alone serve as a justification for seeking the causes of the "politics of history" at the established centers of global political power: more likely than not, the "politics of history" was nothing but a tool through which Washington and Brussels used small states in their increasingly problematic relations with Russia.

Yet, a closer look at the substance of the "politics of history" in different European states suggests that Russia was not the sole object of this politics, sometimes it was not even the most important one.

Rather, the concrete shape was given to the "politics of history" by the process of international socialization of small post-Communist states that was taking place in the context of European and transatlantic integration. This socialization, in turn, was driven by the accelerated adoption of "best practices" for the sake of successful accession to the EU and NATO. It is quite possible to expect that specific procedural solutions learned in the social, economic and military spheres were then applied to the "politics of history." Hence certain synchronicity and similarity across various national contexts.

Still, even if joint socialization promises to explain procedural similarities, they leave open the question of substance: why history? More specifically: Why indisputable political interest in history took shape in the first decade of the new millennium? How exactly this interest was different from the routine references to history invariably made in any politics?

My answer to these questions comes down to an attempt to discern a specific conceptual language in which history was discussed by Estonian politicians right after the state's accession to the EU and NATO. Needless to say, this language has its specific Estonian dialect and its own vocabulary. For example, the "Bronze soldier" monument, once in the center of Tallinn, points directly to Russian-Estonian relations as well as interethnic relations within Estonia. However, this language also has a certain grammar, which, I believe, is shared across a number of Central European states and is shaped by even broader European and transatlantic contexts. Once reconstructed, this general grammar together with a more coherent vocabulary, allows for an understanding of the "politics of history" in its relation with foreign policy.

Changes of Emphasis

During the "singing revolution" at the end of the 1980s, Mart Laar, who was subsequently to head the government of Estonia more than once, came up with the slogan "Give the nation back its history!" Since then, the past has invariably been an important argument in Estonian politics; nor has there been a lack of reflection on this theme. At the start of the new century, an intensification of the politics of history may be clearly observed. By intensification I mean not only that the emotional level of discussions has risen or that they have become more frequent but also there has been an obvious shift in emphasis. Whereas in the past, events used for political purposes were mostly restricted to the interwar period or the Communist past of certain elite politicians, the concepts of "totalitarianism," "genocide," and "crimes against humanity" now occupy an increasingly prominent place in such rhetoric. This shift in emphasis signifies the intensification of the politics of history, as long as "totalitarianism" and the crimes associated with it are, more and more often, treated not as historical events open to different interpretations but as the unshakable foundation for understanding both politics and political history themselves. The experience of totalitarianism is put beyond the pale of legitimate pluralism as a "measure of all things political" itself exempt from any measurement.

Such "fundamentalization" of totalitarianism makes it easier for a state like Russia, for instance, to counteract the alleged "rewriting of history." But it also, and more generally, structures contemporary political discourse in a certain way, opening up new opportunities for the active participation of small states that were traditionally viewed—and treated—as objects of political actions taken by the "great powers." Such structural change is the focus of my article. In other words, for the communities that Hegel once called "peoples without history," "the politics of history" is becoming a weapon in the political struggle for a place in history.[1]

Here I must immediately dissociate myself from certain interpretations that, at first glance, resemble my own position. For example, from the interpretation proposed by the activist of Russian "politics of history" Aleksandr Dyukov: "After the disintegration of the Soviet Union, Estonia, like the other Baltic slates, faced the necessity of constructing a new, non-Soviet national identity that would correspond to set parameters of independence, to anti-Russian strivings, and so on. Although Estonia is a splendid country, it has not accumulated

---

[1] On how the system of international relations and political systems in general are structured by the exclusion of certain elements—be they "peoples without history," "outlaw states," "stateless persons," or "the lumpenproletariat"—see, for example, Simpson, *Great Powers and Outlaw States* and Laclau, *On Populist Reason*.

much experience of its own statehood and, unfortunately, has found no national heroes apart from the members of police battalions and of the Estonian Legion of the Waffen-SS who fought the Soviet Union. It is precisely for this reason that they try to make new national heroes of them."[2]

This view is consistent with the opinion of the Russian journalist Galina Sapozhnikova, who has worked for many years in Estonia. Sapozhnikova believes that the change in official Estonian rhetoric took place almost instantaneously, immediately after the country joined the European Union. The implication is that once the political elite of Estonia felt safe from its eastern neighbor it finally gave free rein to old phobias that until then it had to conceal.[3]

At first glance, there is justification for such an approach. The most striking evidence in its favor may be the monument erected in the summer of 2004 to Estonians who fought in Waffen-SS units during World War II, or an article by the well-known journalist Kaarel Tarand, published a week before Estonia's official accession to the EU, which appeared in one of the leading dailies, *Eesti Päevaleht*. There Tarand wrote openly that what was unthinkable immediately after the restoration of independence is now possible: all those who are dissatisfied with the policy for integrating "foreigners" can now be assembled in a small camp on the border with Russia.[4]

Yet, if we examine these two cases more closely by placing them in the appropriate context, we will see that the issue is less straightforward than deliberate striving to fulfill long-held aspirations buttressed by newly-acquired self-assuredness. Rather, the opposite may be the case: after accession to NATO and the EU, a certain political anxiety in Estonia increased. In the final analysis, this anxiety led to a succession of domestic political crises, and "anti-totalitarian" rhetoric was a response to these crises. It is important to understand what motivated this response and why its roots are to be found in the state's foreign, rather than domestic, policy.

---

[2] Kapov, "Rossiiskii istorik nadeetsia na diskussiiu s estonskimi kollegami."
[3] R. Troshkina, "Obratnyi kod: razgovor s vragom naroda," *Subbota* (Riga), 14 May 2009.
[4] Tarand, "Eesti keel on venelastele parim."

My hypothesis goes as follows. For over ten years after the restoration of independence, the foreign policy guidelines set at the beginning of the 1990s largely determined the basic parameters of the Estonian public sphere. The effort to join NATO and the EU and the high degree of consensus regarding this goal among the country's political elite relegated the painful and potentially divisive circumstances of the past to the back burner and kept them from becoming a topic for public discussion. Meanwhile, to accelerate transatlantic integration as much as possible, itself a clearly stated foreign-policy objective at that time, a restricted community of technocratic experts, concentrated around the executive branch of government in general and the Ministry of Foreign Affairs in particular, decided key issues of national development.[5]

As soon as Estonia joined NATO and then the EU, society found itself in an unfamiliar situation: the single consolidating narrative that had long displaced an open public sphere suddenly lost its relevance, and with it, its hold on public discourse. Moreover, it became obvious that the country lacked social institutions that could provide a forum to discuss painful conflicts. Thus the mass media increasingly began to tout the need for a new national goal, while politicians tinkered with the idea of a formal "social contract."

Put differently, the situation that took shape around 2004–2007 may be described as "ontological anxiety."[6] As a theoretical concept, "ontological anxiety" suggests that amid an uncertainty that threatens not so much the physical survival of the subject as his or her very identity, people often fall back on a familiar social routine, in search of "ontological security," even if it entails obvious risks and sometimes even physical insecurity. The very familiarity of such risks and insecurities make them preferable to uncertainty. At moments of abrupt change in the world order, states, too, prefer familiar conflicts to new, untried models of behavior.[7]

Small states, however, cannot always adopt such a strategy. If one of the routines of international relations is Realpolitik with its "security

---

[5] Raik, "Bureaucratisation or Strengthening," 137–56; Raik, "EU Accession of Central and Eastern European Countries," 567–94.
[6] The term was proposed in Giddens, *Modernity and Self-Identity*.
[7] Mitzen, "Ontological Security in World Politics," 341–70.

dilemmas," it supposedly rests exclusively on objective national interests and for this very reason is sometimes declared an extra-historical constant of the world order. Yet, participation in this game may prove unacceptably dangerous for small states—not least because this sort of political realism cannot guarantee reliable support from the great powers, which within the framework of the given paradigm of international relations must be guided solely by their own interests.

Furthermore, by the time of the outbreak of what I take to be the "ontological crisis" of 2004–2007, the small states of Central and Eastern Europe generally, had pieced together a foreign-policy stance which seemed successful to them. It centered on the possibility of appealing not to the interests but to the identity of powerful Western partners. This is not surprising, given that to formulate their interests, especially in an unstable environment, states both "great" and small must first resolve the question of their identity. And so smaller states of the region made successful use of the discourse of transatlantic solidarity to put a check on the egoistic impulses of the great powers through "rhetorical action" of their own.[8]

This strategy, however, reached its limits (not without the help of the small states themselves) when the beginning of the war in Iraq split the transatlantic community. In the new circumstances, which coincided with the onset of the "ontological crisis" in the small states' domestic politics, these small states had to cope with the disagreement between the United States and their influential allies in Western Europe. The division into "new" and "old" Europe proposed at that time by Donald Rumsfeld impeded the attainment of this goal, as did Russian foreign policy efforts emphasizing bilateral relations with the great powers to the detriment of any forms of multilateral cooperation. The small states, in turn, tried their best to avoid a categorical choice between the Americans and the Europeans, which, by bringing an end

---

[8] Schimmelfennig, "The Community Trap" 47–80. "Identity" in this context means the social role assigned to the subject within the framework of the world order. After the cold war ended, Western powers conceptualized their identity mainly around liberal values, to convince their Western partners that such traditional interests as protecting domestic markets from an influx of cheap labor from the east or maintaining a partnership with Russia despite the constraints that relationship placed on NATO expansion were of secondary importance or even ethically unacceptable.

to the idea of a liberal transatlantic community, would have deprived the "junior partners" of their chief rhetorical means of restraining the egoistic interests of the great powers.[9] But that now required a reformulation of the transatlantic identity.

In other words, at the turn of the century the small states of Central and Eastern Europe needed, both in their domestic and foreign policies, a new discourse of unity or community that would guarantee their own inclusion into this entity. In Estonia, the foreign policy elite was better prepared than other political actors to articulate (or at least to participate in) such a discourse. In 2003, even before the formal accession of Estonia to the EU, one of its undisputed leaders, Toomas Hendrik Ilves issued a sharp critique both of Rumsfeld and of a joint letter published by Jacques Derrida and Jürgen Habermas in which prominent continental philosophers offered their critique of U.S. foreign policy. In his opinion, the anti-Americanism of Derrida and Habermas, or any split with the U.S. generally, threatened Europe with an error of historical dimensions.[10]

The transition from criticism to something like a positive program required time. The first serious document of this kind appeared about a year after the publication of the Derrida-Habermas letter. Its initiators included two U.S. senators, John McCain and Joseph Biden, who at that time were presenting a united front against the foreign policy course of Bush, Vaclav Havel, and one of the leading European Atlanticists, the Swedish diplomat and politician Carl Bildt, who had made an important contribution to the formation of Estonia's political identity after 1991. Estonia was again represented by Ilves, now acting in the capacity of a deputy of the European Parliament. This document,

---

[9] The most striking expression of this conflict was the declaration of the so-called "Vilnius ten," new NATO member-states, in support of intervention in Iraq at a time when France and Germany were actively opposing the idea of intervention in the United Nations.

[10] T.H. Lives, "Taassunni ajalooline valu." The letter of Derrida and Habermas, rather unexpected in light of the long-established philosophical disagreements between them, was published simultaneously in France and Germany. Its essence was that certain methods of "promoting democracy" are a threat to democracy. See Derrida and Habermas, "Unsere Emeuerung. Nach dem Krieg: Die Wiedergeburt Europas," and "Europe: plaidoyer pour une politique extérieure commune."

known as the "letter of the 115," was written in response to the tragedy in Beslan but devoted mainly to a critical analysis of Russia's politics.

Among the signatories was the well-known French essayist André Glucksmann, one of the founders of the group of "new philosophers," whose interpretation of "totalitarianism" and understanding of contemporary international relations based on this interpretation played, in my view, a significant role in bringing about the aforementioned shift of emphasis in Estonian "politics of history." It did so because it contained a nucleus of the idea of a redefined transatlantic unity with a special place assigned within it to the small European states.

If we examine how and why the "new philosophers" redefine totalitarianism, the quoted position of Dyukov, for instance, seems unjustifiably egocentric. Estonian politicians, in quite deliberately rewriting history, were least of all interested in Russia.[11] As in the economic field, the basic interests of Estonian "politics of history" lay in the West, where a peculiar confrontation was developing, defined by Glucksmann as "West against West."[12] For Estonia this meant, apart from anything else, moving beyond the limits of the other, the earlier historical-political discourse, which in its time largely defined the parameters of the restoration of independence.

Dual Depoliticization

The discourse in question was the so-called "Historians' Controversy" (*Historikerstret*). Originally it designated a debate that unfolded at the end of the cold war and concerned Germany's attitudes toward its own history, identity in general and the Holocaust in particular. The German Right interpreted the Holocaust as a response forced on Germany by the essentially equivalent Stalinist purges, whereas the German Left regarded it as a uniquely inhuman crime of Nazism, rooted in the "special path" of Germany's development. In politics, the

---

[11] See "'We Want to Re-Write History': Interview with Estonian President Tomas Hendrik Ilves," *Spiegel Online*, 26 June 2007.
[12] Glucksmann, *Ouest contre ouest*.

Historikerstreit ended in the victory of the Left.[13] This victory not only strengthened the postwar consensus in Germany itself but also largely determined the general European attitude toward history during the EU expansion that began soon after the debate.

When, after the fall of the Berlin Wall, debates similar to the *Historikerstreit* flared up one after another throughout Central and Eastern Europe, the EU, through various initiatives, imposed an implicit condition: candidates for EU membership had to adopt not so much a specific European consensus on history as an orientation toward the creation of a single, consensual, communicative space; the central idea behind Habermas' interventions in the *Historikerstreit*. Theoretically, this space implied a division into "private" and "public" spheres. Participants in European integration were expected to form a pan-European public sphere on the basis of consensus, deliberately excluding from this process more controversial issues of their own "private" identity.

Whereas for the "old" members of the EU this confirmed at a new level a set of previously established foreign-policy practices, the proposed consensus meant something quite different to the candidate states. Many of them had yet to form their own domestic public sphere—often by coming to terms with the past, among other things. Because in Central and Eastern Europe the interpretation of history had rarely been a purely internal matter for individual states, the EU tried to regulate this process, especially as it pertained to border disputes or to the status of ethnic minorities.

In the case of Estonia, external regulation entailed the presence of an Organization for Security and Cooperation in Europe (OSCE) mission, whose mandate pertained to interethnic relations inside the country, and the requirement of settling border disputes with Russia. As NATO and EU membership became a practical task to be implemented in accordance with a rigid timetable imposed from without, relations with Russia and policies toward local ethnic Russians shifted from the sphere of public debate and legislative initiative to that of

---

[13] In the discipline of history the polemic continued much longer. One of its most interesting documents is the correspondence between Francois Furet and Ernst Nolte, which again bears—to use Nolte's expression—the imprint of "a Western civil war." Furet and Nolte, *Fascisme et Communisme*.

routine administrative decision making, mostly by those responsible for the implementation of the accession process.

This shift was not always caused by direct NATO or EU pressure. Rather, Estonian politicians themselves understood and interpreted the sometimes tacit rules of the new game and tried to follow them the best they could so as to achieve their chief political goal: entry into both international organizations. A former minister of foreign affairs, Trivimi Velliste, is representative of this development. Although actively opposed to the amendments to the Language Law that international organizations were pushing on the eve of EU expansion, Velliste eventually agreed that they would have to be adopted. Explaining his position in parliament, he spoke of a "conflict between the experience of Estonia and the experience acquired by the international community in a different historical context."[14]

However, by that time, the tension between the experience of Estonia and that of "old Europe" extended beyond the attitude toward history and national identity, to include the very procedures, established already in the years of restored independence, through which this attitude was clarified. Whereas in "old Europe" the new consensus was the result of intense, prolonged, and above all open debate like the *Historikerstreit*, in Estonia a dual depoliticization of the public sphere took place. Issues that lay at the foundation of state identity were reduced to matters of technocratic administration on the one hand and security policy on the other.

The culmination of this tendency was the Lihula crisis. In August 2004 a monument was erected in the small town of Lihula in honor of Estonians who fought in World War II on the side of Germany. The occasion for the crisis was not the erection of the monument but its demolition, carried out less than two weeks later, in the dead of night, without any public discussion. The prime minister then in office, speaking after the monument had already been demolished, explained the government's decision in terms of national security considerations.

---

[14] The controversial amendments recommended by international organizations were designed to change legislation that restricted the use of foreign languages (including Russian) not only in government offices but also, for instance, in private business. In addition, there were a number of specific language-based restrictions on participation in municipal elections.

By that he meant the embarrassment with which influential allies of Estonia—above all, the United States—might react to the sight of the soldier in Nazi uniform portrayed on the bas-relief. Such explanations, however, merely increased public irritation, as did the circumstances of the monument's demolition. Shortly afterwards, the resignation of the government followed.[15]

The Lihula crisis revealed not so much the decline of an initially popular government but a crisis of the public sphere generally. The executive branch, it turned out, had only two instruments at its disposal: heavy technical equipment and an appeal to equally irresistible foreign policy requirements. These could still be employed against a relatively remote monument, but were of little help in dealing with the debates that, at that time, threatened to split Estonian society into two groups. This split, in turn, had nothing to do with ethnic relations and was taking place mostly within the ethnically Estonian part, where the position of one of the emerging poles was expressed in the winged phrase *JOKK* (expanded as "legally everything is correct") and maintained that ethical demands that go beyond formal conformity with the law have no place in political life. Others formulated their position with the phrase *Kommarid ahju!* which may be rendered as "Commies into the oven!" This group deliberately shocked public opinion by demanding the resignation of government officials who had belonged to the Communist Party.

Leading Estonian public figures defined the crisis afflicting society as "decivilization" or "delegitimization" and noted that its sources must be sought in Estonians' attitudes toward their history. History, they declared, releases us only when we gather the courage to look it in the face. This, in turn, requires recognition of the ambiguity both of the Soviet period and of collaboration with the Nazis. Otherwise, monuments like those in Lihula and Tallinn will continue to tear society apart.

In practice, however, the historical theme was usurped by the right wing of Estonian politics. Right-wing politicians made active use of it during the debate in 2005 concerning whether President Rüütel should travel to Moscow for the celebration of the sixtieth anniversary of the end of the Great Patriotic War of 1941–45, as well as in subsequent

---

[15] Brüggemann and Kasekamp, "The Politics of History and the 'War of Monuments' in Estonia," 425–448.

debates about the border agreement with Russia. The most radically inclined Estonian nationalists also became noticeably more active. In April 2005, they created the Estonian Nationalist Movement, whose activists published a letter demanding immediate removal of the monument to the Soviet soldier on Tõnismägi hill in Tallinn, while expressing doubt in the ability of a state controlled from "Washington, Brussels, Tel Aviv, and Moscow" to take such a step. The movement's favorite targets were not only former Communists in the Estonian government and the Tõnismägi monument but also the EU and integration policy within the country.

Thus, when in May 2006 activists of the Estonian Nationalist Movement were among the main participants in the events on Tõnismägi hill, the government then in office felt not the slightest sympathy for them. In a statement that played a crucial role in the subsequent escalation of the conflict Estonian Prime Minister Andrus Ansip clearly referred to both Estonian nationalists and ethnic Russian activists while saying that he did not wish to "talk with marginal elements" and would not "allow an arbitrarily self-constituted community to control part of Estonian territory".

The only major Estonian politician to have declared his wish to meet openly with Russian activists was Mart Laar. Characteristically, however, he set one condition for such a meeting: the meeting would have to be devoted to a discussion of history, not politics. Such an approach reflected a position that even now remains dominant in Estonian society: political problems in relations between communities grow out of differences in the interpretation of history. This approach views history as a set of objective facts that are open to impartial discussion. "Politics of history" then comes down to the questions that Enn Soosaar, the doyen of Estonian political commentators, formulated as follows: "Is it at all possible to educate those tens and tens of thousands of people who have more faith in Russian propaganda than in historical facts and historical documents so that they will be loyal citizens of the Estonian republic? And if it is possible, then how exactly can it be done?"[16]

But there also exists another view—one that implies a more complex relationship between history and politics. One of the most striking

---

[16] Soosaar, "Muulaste loimurnise rajad."

formulations of this position belongs to Jüri Luik, who at various times has occupied the posts of minister of foreign affairs, minister of defense, and ambassador to the United States and to NATO.

The Need for a New Discourse

Luik's position, as formulated in the February 2008 issue of *Diplomaatia*, differed significantly from that of the other authors of the publication.[17] In 2008, Estonia commemorated the ninetieth anniversary of the independent state established in 1918. The issue of *Diplomaatia* contributed to the celebrations. The authors discussed the usual set of topics: the legal aspects of the loss of independence at the end of the 1930s, the prerequisites for its restoration in the early 1990s, and so on. The leitmotif of the issue as a whole was also hardly original: Estonia's main distinction in terms of world history and international relations is its smallness and the associated need to rely on resources different from those that "great powers" have in their arsenal. This way or another, all publications were devoted to the most important of these resources—international law.

Unlike his coauthors, Luik from the outset decisively distances himself from legalistic arguments. Estonians, he declares, often talk about Estonia's rights as a member of the international community when they should talk more about its duties. In considering the specific duties of states that have liberated themselves from the Communist yoke, Estonians should indeed draw lessons from the past. In this context, however, the past has only an indirect connection with history as an academic pursuit. Its significance is purely practical, and "practice" here is squarely political and thus conceptually separate from the legal issues. The article, in other words, was devoted to something that precedes law and is a precondition of its functioning—politics.

Luik's basic thesis boils down to the following. The seventeen years that have passed since the collapse of Communism in Eastern and Central Europe are no reason for forgetting the crimes of Communism. On the contrary, in this period many Central and East Euro-

---

[17] Luik, "Meie kohustus."

pean states have finally been able to build legal institutions sufficiently strong to investigate these crimes. The basis for such investigation is not the "rewriting of history," not a revision of the results of the Nuremberg Tribunal, but adherence to their letter and spirit insofar as they concern the definition of "crimes against humanity." The task is not to alter the definitions, let alone the facts on which they were based. It is a question of extending their rigorous application to the actions that *The Black Book of Communism*, which was published in 1997 and evoked very mixed reactions in Europe, classified provisionally as "crimes of Communism."[18]

At first glance, the reference to a book that provoked much controversy in its time may seem to be a weak spot in Luik's argument. But on closer examination it is clear that Luik is not inclined to agree unreservedly with the assertions of the editor of *The Black Book*, Stéphane Courtois. In particular, while Courtois has been accused—justifiably or not—of anti-Semitism for his assertion that the current meaning of the Holocaust is a result of the activity of "international Jewish organizations," Luik, on the contrary, presents the activity of these organizations as a model to emulate. To the extent that Luik does discuss lessons of the past in his article, they are, above all, lessons connected with the activity of nongovernmental Jewish organizations. The main lesson worth learning from them, in his opinion, is the skill of creating an international political consensus by means of specific, clearly formulated, and effectively realized initiatives.

In Luik's opinion, the most important task of post-Communist societies is to develop a consensus regarding the crimes of Communism. He insists that the institutions created to accomplish this task, whether national or international, should not be of legal nature. Their primary mission should be to initiate the broadest possible public discussion of events that are well known to historians. The need is not for alternative historical or legal investigations but for a new public sphere—and this is the chief purpose of politics.

---

[18] Courtois, ed., *Le Livre noir du Communisme*. The chief disagreement concerns whether, as some authors of the edited volume argue, the crimes of Communism should be regarded as phenomena of the same order as the crimes of Nazism. An intensive debate on this topic has been in progress for many years in the West.

Luik concludes his article by explaining why exactly it is so important to create a new public sphere. Post-Communist societies "will begin to function normally only if their pain is openly discussed and universally recognized." States "experiencing difficulties more easily fall victim to illusions about an ideal society"; young people wearing T-shirts with portraits of Che Guevara show that even nowadays such illusions are popular. "Only a new international consensus will enable us to avoid these dangers."

This declaration is interesting from several points of view. First, four years after the accession of Estonia to the EU, it acknowledges the existence of "difficulties of social growth." It states that Estonian society, like many others in Central and Eastern Europe, cannot be said to function normally. In itself, such an admission was hardly big news in Estonian domestic politics. But it was clearly out of tune with the general tone of the anniversary celebrations that constitute its context and contrasted even more strongly with the way in which foreign affairs were customarily discussed in Estonia; as a rule, such discussions resembled reports on the successes of respected government experts.

Yet, no sooner had Luik's article appeared in print than approving references to it became virtually obligatory in any public discussion with a claim to being serious. This is indirect evidence in favor of my initial hypothesis: the intensification of the "politics of history" in Estonia did not result from a strengthening of state positions following accession to NATO and the EU but, on the contrary, it reflected an "ontological crisis," one of the reasons for which was the successful completion of this foreign policy project.

But why does Luik think that the strategy for overcoming the crisis depends on the "politics of history," primarily on overcoming the Communist past? If he sees illusory dreams of an ideal society as the chief danger, it only seems reasonable to acknowledge that the idea of restitution—that is, of restoring in Estonia an idealized version of the ethnonational state of the interwar period—was a dream of the same kind, especially given that such acknowledgment would not require titanic efforts to form a new international consensus but, on the contrary, could rest on the post-World War II consensus generally, and, in particular, on the post-*Historikerstreit* European consensus concerning the problematic character of the ethnonational state as such.

It seems to me that the main spring of Luik's intervention was the perceived absence of international consensus *of any kind whatsoever*, be it intra-European or transatlantic, at the time of his writing. This absence is what mainly prompts Luik's argument and numerous similar statements far beyond the borders of Central And Eastern Europe. It is for this reason that Habermas, whose "civic patriotism" was perceived as the European response to the questions raised in the course of the *Historikerstreit*, has ended up at the center of the aforementioned transatlantic discord of the time. The sources of this discord, however, can be detected long before the end of the cold war, at its very height in the social upheavals of the late 1960s and the early 1970s.

The inner tension present in Luik's article also points in this direction. On the one hand, consistently drawing the distinction between purely political questions and all others, Luik emphasizes that the current status of the Holocaust was not—and, indeed, could not have been—predetermined by the legal rulings of the Nuremberg Tribunal or by the professional research of historians. It was the result of a long, intense political struggle. This struggle, as Luik himself acknowledges, could succeed only in the 1960s, when an initial desire to leave behind the tragedy of the two world wars as quickly as possible was replaced by a striving to assess the past anew. Once again, this shift occurred not by itself but under pressure from a radically inclined young generation. On the other hand, Luik is clearly worried by the predilection of today's young people for political radicalism.

Perhaps the reasons for this tension lie in the fact that the "young people" who arouse Luik's concern are not as abstract and anonymous as may appear at first glance. Among the admirers of Che was the young medical student Bernard Kouchner, who dedicated his dissertation to "Doctor Ernesto Che Guevara." In 2007, not long before the publication of Luik's article, he became the French minister of foreign affairs. In various anthologies devoted to the 1960s, his name is often listed alongside not only Joschka Fischer or Daniel Cohn-Bendit but also, for example, Bill Ayers, founder of the radical American organization Weather Underground (during the presidential race of 2008 attempts were made to expose ties between Ayers and Barack Obama).[19]

---

[19] Here it should be noted that the Estonian political elite took a guarded attitude toward the rise of Obama in American politics. During the presidential

To be sure, these names and associations cannot in themselves explain why Luik is so concerned to form a new international consensus. But it is impossible to deny that behind these names lie concrete changes in world politics—and, not least, those associated with the appearance on the political arena of the "1960s generation." By the time representatives of this generation started to come to power, they already had a number of ontological crises behind them, one being the crisis caused by the exposure of the crimes of Communism.

According to the testimony of Paul Berman, an American sympathizer with what was once the "new" European Left, the chief issue not only for the political stance but also for the general identity of future politicians like Fischer or Kouchner has always been the choice between collaboration and resistance.[20] After the storms of the 1960s had abated, however, it became increasingly difficult to make—or even to formulate—this choice. By the mid-1970s, to a large extent under the influence of the works of Solzhenitsyn, there had emerged in France a group of "new philosophers" that included intellectuals who had once—as had, by the way, Courtois, the editor of *The Black Book*—belonged to radical Maoist organizations. Now "totalitarianism" and the struggle against totalitarianism had become their response to the questions generated by ontological crises.

A New Discourse Taking Place

The "new philosophers" redefine totalitarianism as an "absolute evil" and an indisputable historical fact. The unbreakable connection between totalitarianism and genocide makes this fact indisputable.

---

race, most Estonian politicians did not conceal the fact that they would have preferred to see McCain in the White House. None of the Estonian newspapers devoted any serious attention to Obama's pre-electoral speech in Berlin or—after his election as president—his speeches in Cairo and Moscow. In contrast, the Center for Strategic Research attached to the Ministry of Defense of Estonia was one of organizers of the letter of retired Central and East European politicians expressing concern at the possible weakening of NATO's role in the region and of transatlantic ties in general (*New York Times*, July 20, 2009).

[20] Berman, *Power and the Idealists*.

Opposition to unconditional evil becomes the basis for the choice between collaboration and resistance; the absolute nature of evil enables the "new philosopher" not only to guard his identity from fits of "ontological anxiety" but also to position himself in relation to several significant political forces, including anti-Americanism, Islamic fundamentalism, and "European nihilism," which indirectly panders to all kinds of tyrants. In the words of Glucksmann, one of the founders of the group, the world is divided into those "for whom facts do not exist, only pure symbols of faith," and those for whom "free discussion, aimed at separating truth from invention, has meaning; for whom politics, science, and the power of judgment are based on facts, which do not depend on questionable or acquired biases."[21] From the point of view of the "new philosophers," totalitarianism in its various manifestations is just such an indisputable fact.

For all the importance that the "new philosophers" attach to indisputable facts, however, they have an unusual adversary—"political realism." Berman accurately conveys the essence of the conflict: "Realism never confronts genocide. Nowadays genocide is always perpetrated on the periphery of great events and never at the epicenter; and political realism is concerned with power calculations at the center, with—to use the expression of [Alain] Finkielkraut—calculations of Big History. Genocide attacks the weak; realism defends the strong."[22]

As a result, the new European identity is also emerging at the periphery of big European politics—or, in Glucksmann's formulation, "on the winds blowing between Tbilisi and Kiev." It is taking form despite "antiliberalism, anti-Americanism, and fears of migrants from the South and, above all, from the East."[23] So it is hardly surprising that in the opening days of the Russian-Georgian war of 2008, Glucksmann and his colleague Bernard-Henri Lévy, even before the circumstances of what was happening in the Caucasus were clear, rushed to defend Mikheil Saakashvili—and not only from "Russian imperialism" but also from the "realism" of the American foreign policy veterans George Shultz and Henry Kissinger. Nor is it surprising that their

---

[21] Glucksmann, "Mohammed und die Gaskammern."
[22] Berman, *Power and the Idealists*, 84.
[23] Glucksmann, "Das Land der Europa-Nihilisten."

attack on "cold realism" was taken up on the pages of *Die Welt* by Mart Laar and Andres Herkel, leaders of the Estonian Fatherland Union.[24]

My point here is not that Laar and Herkel borrowed directly from Glucksmann and Lévy. Rather, the conceptual language of the "new philosophers" came in handy for Estonian politicians going through a crisis of political identity—for those who created this language had found themselves in a similar situation. Whereas Glucksrnann, Lévy, and Finkielkraut faced the crisis of overcoming their own Maoist past, politicians in Estonia were reacting to the split within the transatlantic community. But in both cases the need arose for a new foundation—and as firm a foundation as possible—for collective identity. Totalitarianism, newly reinterpreted, was well suited to accomplish this task—both as an attribute of large collectivistic projects, Big History, and great-power ambitions and as an unforeseen but inevitably tragic consequence of the dreams of an ideal society that Luik mentions.

On the one hand, totalitarianism thus understood served to justify U.S. foreign policy, which was causing increasing discontent in "old Europe;" on the other hand, it enabled Estonians to distance themselves from the American neocons, whose position in one way or another intersected with the theoretical assumptions of "realism." As Glucksmann expressed it, the "new philosophers," with their specific reading of history, offered the small states of Eastern and Central Europe a special entry into world politics (and into world history), an entry for "all these 'small fry' for whom 'realists' have never given a damn."[25]

Thus, it is impossible to miss the similarity between the arguments of the "new philosophers" and the recent speech of Estonian President Ilves at the University of Turku. Like Luik in his article, Ilves spoke of the possibility (and necessity) of constructing new, consensus-based identities that would not, as has happened in the past, "be imposed on us by history and by others."[26] By others who now—in the new historical role assigned to them as "peoples without democracy"—also find themselves outside history, like Hegel's "peoples without history,"

---

[24] Herkel and Laar, "Russland ausschließen!"
[25] Glucksmann, "Beslan. Ja moral y la polftica."
[26] Ilves, "Kes me oleme? Kus me oleme? Rahvuslik identiteet ja vaimne geograafia."

before them. The "politics of history" in this version, in other words, does not tinker with history politically, but sees the substance of politics in redrawing the boundaries of History and thus redefining its meaning.

Repeating in this speech the critique he made of Habermas six years before, Ilves reproduces—perhaps without being aware of it—not only Habermas's idea of a constructed "civic patriotism" but also the underlying Durkheimian division into "traditional" and "industrial" societies. This one-dimensional and essentially eschatological model of history once enabled Habermas to propose specific historical content for the abstract Kantian critique of "traditional" metaphysical consciousness: the "will to reason" finds concrete form in modernization, which Kant could only foresee and which we, according to Habermas, are obliged to complete. This, in turn, requires the repudiation of all forms of "fundamentalism." Being a theoretical model, however, Habermas's construction relieves us of the necessity of paying heed to the real historical diversity of all sorts of traditionalist communities within Europe (or communities that try to preserve their traditionalism). Habermas's model, like any other implies that "in principle we already know everything that we need to know about the religious Muslims of Europe, while completely ignoring the real concerns and strivings of specific communities, each of which may enter democratic society along its own special historical trajectory."[27] In the case of the "new philosophers," this model becomes the justification for "a self-satisfied secularism that is no less hostage to indisputable truths than the most 'fundamentalist' of Muslim discourses."

But this kind of essentialism, problematic as it may be theoretically, is precisely what any state seeking "ontological security" is looking for. In particular, it is urgently needed in small states who cannot unprolematically fall back on other versions of essentialism, such as political realism. In the specific case of Estonian "politics of history," the not-so-veiled fundamentalism of this position was clearly formulated in an article by Tunne Kelam, a European parliamentarian, about relations between the EU and Russia: "The mission of a united Europe

---

[27] Henkel, "'The Journalists of Jyllands-Posten Are a Bunch of Reactionary Provocateurs': The Danish Cartoon Controversy and the Self-Image of Europe."

must be to tell the truth and establish boundaries, emphasizing that our principles and values are not subject to negotiation."[28]

Ironically, Kelam presents his own vision of relations between the EU and Russia as "realpolitik," quoting Churchill, for whom the key to the riddle of Russia was its national interests. Obviously, the non-negotiable principles and values of which Kelam speaks are as compatible with "realpolitik" as Churchill's understanding of Russian national interests at the end of World War II was compatible with the independence of Estonia. Taking into account the national interests of Russia "required" the sacrifice of the independence of the Baltic States. But I would not hasten to expose Kelam as ignorant. Like any shrewd practitioner, he works with the rhetorical material at hand, without worrying overmuch about the academic irreproachability of his arguments. The material at hand here is the obvious shift of emphasis in European-Russian relations toward "realpolitik" after the Georgian war. Instead of swimming against the burgeoning European current, Kelam tries to direct it into the necessary channel, appealing for this purpose to the dominant discourse. With a certain persistence and a certain skill in seeking out allies, such a strategy is within the capacity of even the smallest states.

A Policy for 'Small Fry'

So it should not come as a surprise that my story of the rise of the "politics of history" in Estonia follows the fluctuations of the dominant discourses outside Estonia. The first of such discourses is the "Historians' Controversy" which in Estonia led to the temporary freezing of the potentially conflict-laden debates about the essence (and comparability) of the two totalitarian regimes of the past, which is so important for the formation of Estonia's state identity. The practical justification for freezing the debate was the idea of European stability, which in its turn was inextricably linked with the transatlantic consensus and with the assumption of friendly support for Russian reforms from the West. At the start of the new century both these pillars of foreign policy got

---

[28] Kelam, "An EU Realpolitik to Unravel the Riddle of Unruly Russia."

somewhat shaky, while Estonian domestic policy was in a state of crisis. The need arose for a new consolidating discourse that would correspond both to internal and to external political priorities. And, as President Ilves said in one interview: "Until we write ourselves, we shall translate."[29]

There was no lack of texts which could be translated. Let us recall, for instance, the correspondence (see note 13) between François Furet and Ernst Nolte or the publications of Robert Kagan, a commentator close to the neoconservatives, one of whose numerous works provided the basis for an international conference held in Tallinn.[30] But if European comparative analysis of the two totalitarian regimes, with its conservative critique of "modernity," could not serve as the source of the sought-after certainty, American neoconservatism dangerously hovered on the edge of the "realist" fixation on Big History and its powerful dramatic personae.

The "new philosophers," by contrast, deliberately positioned themselves as European partners of the American neocons; they willingly relied on American might, but to solve their own political tasks (and to resolve their own "ontological anxieties") they cited the lessons of European history, the chief of those being totalitarianism. Whatever the theoretical costs of this position might be, in the case of Estonia, they were more than recompensed by the practical advantages of a "policy for small fry." It would be worth trying to rebuild the lost international consensus around such a policy, so that we can again use it as an effective foreign policy instrument against the interests of those who, in Luik's words, "declare that we are destroying consensus and creating a parallel universe of our own." Moreover, this goes well beyond the attitude to be taken toward totalitarianism. In the structure of world order, small states—all these "small fry"—have invariably found themselves in a parallel universe, beyond the limits of the Big History created by the great powers. Retroactively recalibrating World History through the discourse initially found in the "new philosophers" Estonian "politics of history" not only attempts to re-create a bounded we-community, but moves small states from its ever-contested boundary to the center.

---

[29] Ilves, "Kuni me ise ei kirjuta, peame tõlkima."
[30] Kagan, *The Return of History and the End of Dreams.*

Bibliography

Berman, P. *Power and the Idealists: Or, The Passion of Joschka Fischer and Its Aftermath.* New York: WW Norton, 2007.
Brügemann, K. and A. Kasekamp. "The Politics of History and the 'War of Monuments' in Estonia." *Nationalities Papers* vol. 36, no. 3 (2008), 425–448.
Courtois, S. ed. *Le Livre noir du Communisme: Crimes, terreur; repression.* Paris: Robert Laffont, 2000.
Derrida, J. and J. Habermas. "Unsere Emeuerung. Nach dem Krieg: Die Wiedergeburt Europas," *Frankfurter Allgemeine Zeitung*, May 31, 2003.
———. "Europe: plaidoyer pour une politique extérieure commune," *Liberation*, May 31, 2003.
Furet and Nolte. *Fascisme et Communisme: echange epistolaire avec l'historien allemand Ernst Nolte prolongeant la Historikerstreit.* Paris: Plon, 1998.
Giddens, A. *Modernity and Self-Identity.* New York: Polity Press, 1991.
Glucksmann, A. "Beslan.Ja moral y la polftica," *El Pais*. June 15, 2009.
———. "Das Land der Europa-Nihilisten," *Die Welt*, June 1, 2005.
———. "Mohammed und die Gaskammern," *Die Welt*, March 6, 2006.
———, *Ouest contre ouest.* Paris: Plon, 2003.
Henkel, H. "'The Journalists of Jyllands-Posten Are a Bunch of Reactionary Provocateurs': The Danish Cartoon Controversy and the Self-Image of Europe." *Radical Philosophy*, no. 137 (May/June 2006).
Herkel, A. and Laar, M. "Russland ausschließen!" *Die Welt.* September 14, 2008.
Ilves, T.H. "Kes me oleme? Kus me oleme? Rahvuslik identiteet ja vaimne geograafia." *Akadeemia* no. 6 (2009). 1067–1074.
———. "Kuni me ise ei kirjuta, peame tõlkima." *Sirp*, January 26, 2007.
———. "Taassunni ajalooline valu." *Eesti Ptievaleht*, July 17, 2003.
Kagan, R. *The Return of History and the End of Dreams.* New York: Knopf, 2008.
Kapov, E. "Rossiiskii istorik nadeetsia na diskussiiu s estonskimi kollegami." *DELFI* (Tallinn). March 28, 2009.
Kelam, T. "An EU Realpolitik to Unravel the Riddle of Unruly Russia," *Europe's World* no. 11 (Spring 2009).
Laclau, E. *On Populist Reason.* London: Verso, 2005.
Luik, J. "Meie kohustus." *Diplomaatia*, no. 54 (February 2008).
Mitzen, J. "Ontological Security in World Politics: State Identity and the Security Dilemma." *European Journal of International Relations* vol. 12, no. 3 (2006): 341–370.
Raik, K. "Bureaucratisation or Strengthening of the Political? Estonian Institutions and Integration into the European Union." *Cooperation and Conflict* vol. 37, no. 2 (2002): 137–156.
———. "EU Accession of Central and Eastern European Countries: Democracy and Integration as Conflicting Logics." *East European Politics and Societies* vol. 18, no. 4 (2004): 567–594.

Schimmelfennig, F. "The Community Trap: Liberal Norms, Rhetorical Action, and the Eastern Enlargcment of the European Union." *International Organization* vol. 55, no. I (2001): 47–80.

Simpson, G. J. *Great Powers and Outlaw States: Unequal Sovereignties in the International Order.* Cambridge: Cambridge University Press, 2004.

Soosaar, E. "Muulaste loimurnise rajad." *Postimees,* October 22, 2007.

Tarand, K. "Eesti keel on venelastele parim." *Eesti Piievaleht,* April 24, 2004.

Troshkina, R. "Obratnyi kod: razgovor s vragom naroda." *Subbota* (Riga), 14.05.2009 DATE.

The 'Nationalization" of History in Ukraine[1]

GEORGIY KASIANOV

Developments marking the "nationalization" of history/historiography in Ukraine in the late 1980s and early 1990s unfolded in a way that was basically quite similar to analogous processes in other post-Soviet republics.[2] Historians initially focused their attention on historical "blank spots" that were found mainly in the Soviet period. Revising the Soviet version of the history of that period also provided the basis for its rejection. The subject under discussion was, of course, the crimes of Stalinism, banned or persecuted individuals, and national tragedies.

It was the attitude to the Soviet (Communist) historical legacy that became the point of departure for the revision of all other history. The "Soviet" version of Soviet history, based on a single ideology, left no room for other versions of the recent past; hence its revision led inevitably to a search for alternatives. The construction of a "fuller" version of Soviet history (without "blank spots") led inevitably to the development of a new, "fuller" account of "one's own" history as a whole. The

---

[1] Some of the material in this article has been published in Bomsdorf and Bordiugov, *Natsional'nye istorii na postsovetskom prostranstve*—II, and in Kasianov and Ther, *A Laboratory of Transnational History: Ukraine and Recent Ukrainian Historiography*.

[2] The 1990s are covered in considerable detail in a substantial collection of articles published twice in Moscow, in 1999 and 2003. See Aimermakher and Bordiugov, *Natsional'nye istorii v sovetskom i postsovetskom prostranstve*,. It should be noted that the articles about Ukraine in this collection manifest two different approaches to the understanding and treatment of historiographic processes on the part of Russian colleagues: T. Guzenkova basically maintains a neutral attitude, while S. Konstantinov and A. Ushakov sometimes evince a most lamentable tendentiousness. The later period is covered in a second collection, *Natsional'nye istorii na postsovetskom prostranstve*—II.

logic of creating a holistic version of national history prompted historians to extend their revisions, go beyond a critique of the Soviet period proper, and continue into the "deep past." In practice, this amounted to the replacement of the "Soviet" version of history with a "national" one; the reestablishment of a national master narrative to supplant the Soviet one.

This history in reverse developed according to its own artless logic: a selective review of the Soviet period (in the manner of the Nuremberg tribunal) was followed by a return to the experience of national statehood in the period after World War I. In Ukraine, this mainly involved the history of the Central Rada and the Ukrainian People's Republic (UNR), the Western Ukrainian People's Republic, and the Hetman State (1918–1920).

As with the examination of Stalinism, the motives here were wholly determined by the "instrumentalization of history": the political reasons for going back to the brief period of national sovereignty were quite obvious. There was even an attempt to establish a symbolic connection between current sovereignty and the above-mentioned historical episodes. In 1993 the first president of Ukraine, Leonid Kravchuk, who had earlier made a highly successful career in the Communist establishment, accepted symbols of sovereignty preserved since the 1920s from a representative of the "Government-in-Exile of the Ukrainian People's Republic," Mykola Plawiuk, who simultaneously headed the Organization of Ukrainian Nationalists (Melnyk faction). Some historians even spoke of the present-day Ukrainian state as a successor to the UNR. The symbols of statehood used in 1918–1920 were legitimized in Ukraine.[3]

Historians engaged in the creation of a national mythology[4] then devoted special attention to the late medieval and early modern

---

[3] In 1992, the yellow and blue flag and trident, the display of which might have carried a prison sentence a couple of years earlier, were employed as symbols of statehood. They were finally legalized in that capacity by the Constitution of 1996.

[4] The terms "national mythology" and "national myth" carry no negative or moralizing connotations. These are analytical categories encompassing a relatively stable complex of mutually related and complementary historical representations, symbols, stereotypes, and standard treatments possessing socially significant ideological and cultural meaning and functioning as cultural markers.

periods, which offered unrivaled opportunities for fashioning an image of a "historic" nation with its own "golden age." The Cossack era, including the Hetmanate, became that "golden age" of Ukrainian history. In a manner completely befitting reflexive history, this campaign proceeded under the motto "Forward into the past" to investigate early feudal sovereignty and ethnogenesis, with a further excursus into ancient history antedating written records. In Ukraine, Kyivan Rus' was "nationalized" as a model of early sovereignty. This was followed by an investigation of the deep past that ultimately turned up early tribal forms of social organization on "native" grounds, presented as a locus of autochthonous habitation over centuries and millennia. The result was the development of a "complete" or "standard" account of national history extending from the depths of the past to the "triumph of historical justice"—the establishment of an independent state.[5]

In its most general, "genetic" forms, so to speak, the basic contemporary narrative of "nationalized" history took shape (or, more precisely, was revived) in Ukraine in the early 1990s. Inevitably, it took the form of a teleological construction in which "one's own" "nationalized" history is fulfilled by the appearance of "one's own" unique nation and its corresponding state. History is represented as ontologically predetermined progress toward a higher goal—the rise of a nation-state that constitutes the supreme embodiment of national purpose. The goal (or result) is directly or implicitly identified with the raison d'être; consequently, the notion of the necessary, natural, organic character of the nation and the nation-state is taken to be self-evident. The nation and the nation state cannot fail to come into existence; hence the task of the historian is not to justify the fact of their presence in general human history but to find a sufficient explanation for their absence in certain periods of that history. Accordingly, the "genetic" trait of "nationalized" history is determinism (in any and all hypostases, from economic to cultural).

This gives rise to a corresponding cognitive strategy in which the nation is considered a transcendent phenomenon of some kind that does not require the labor of historians to secure its existence. The task of historiography then comes down to adequately describing that

---

[5] Of course, every national history is actually written "in reverse," proceeding from the present to the past: the present situation is projected into the past.

history, properly identifying the essence of the nation, explaining its innate characteristics, and finding confirmation of those characteristics with the aid of theoretical tools and facts. Such an approach naturally substantiates (and only then goes on to explain) the historical *necessity* and inevitability of the existence of the nation, whose essential characteristics are discerned in "historical reality" or, better, in "historical truth." This may explain why categories of ideological and political practice in "nationalized" history/historiography so readily take on the status of scholarly and analytical verities. In that capacity they return to ideological currency and, in their turn, legitimize political terminology with their "scholarly" character. The notion of "national renaissance," employed with equal intensity in both ideological and scholarly linguistic space, may serve as an ideal example of this.

Teleology and essentialism are most strikingly expressed in the ethnocentrism of the canon. The principal subject of history is the (Ukrainian) people, which is identified with a genetically related ethnos or subethnos (or a group of them). The content of "nationalized" history in its scholarly version is the transformation of that people (or ethnoses) into a nation. Such a method of explanation and explication requires that the concepts of "people" and "nation" be identified with each other.

Indissolubly associated with this is yet another component of the canon—cultural exclusivity, which runs the gamut from ignoring the presence of other ethnoses and nations in "one's own" space and time, or the denial of a whole complex of mutual influences and interactions with the Other, to acknowledging the Other's existence primarily as background to one's own national exclusivity or uniqueness. This comes in a variety of gradations: the Other may serve as a positive or neutral background, remaining in "his own" territory or going beyond it. One of the Others will of course play the role of the enemy interfering with the objective course of history—the normal development of "one's own" nation.

All the basic methodological characteristics of "nationalized" history/historiography mentioned above are manifested in such professionally conditioned elements of the canon as linearity and absolutization of continuity in the history of the "ethnos-people-nation." The most revealing feature is the account of "continuity" in national history. In the Ukrainian case, this "continuity" is established as follows:

the presence of autochthonous tribes and tribal associations (going back, needless to say, to Trypilian culture) on the territory of present-day Ukraine in the first millennia before and after the beginning of the Common Era; the beginnings of sovereignty, its development and ethnic consolidation in the times of Kyivan Rus'; the passing of the baton to the Principality of Galicia-Volhynia; the "Polish-Lithuanian era," with ethnoconfessional and cultural "distinctiveness;" the Cossack era and statehood (already identified as national); the Hetmanate and its autonomy, however limited; the fall of the Hetmanate and the "compensating" presence of cultural/territorial patriotism; then the "national renaissance" with its apogee in the (national, Ukrainian) Revolution of 1917–1921 and Ukrainian sovereignty in the various forms of that period.

The account then bifurcates: for some, Soviet statehood is a "failure," a "black spot" in national existence; for others it is an entirely legitimate episode of national history. For the first group, the "break" is compensated by the existence of a national-liberation movement (encompassing all forms of resistance to "foreign" regimes, from cultural frondes to partisan movements). For the second group, there is no break. And, finally, the year 1991 becomes the culmination of a "thousand-year history." It is here that the "historic" nation finally becomes a full-fledged subject of history. Breaks in the history of statehood are compensated by the idea of cultural and folk tradition, with the autochthonous Ukrainian ethnos/people naturally taking on the role of continuator.[6]

The "genetic" features of the canon of "nationalized" history/historiography presented here conform entirely to the standard European account of national history that took shape in the second half of the nineteenth century and survived into our own time in the pages of school textbooks in many European lands. Paradoxically, however, in a certain sense a return to the canon of "nationalized" history also made possible something of a return to "Europe," only *prewar* Europe.

---

[6] The traditional account of "continuity" in Ukrainian history, appealing to the people as the bearer of historical succession, took final shape in the times of Volodymyr Antonovych and Mykhailo Hrushevsky. After World War II it was modified by the eminent "diaspora" historian and essayist Ivan Lysiak-Rudnytsky.

It should be noted that these features determine the interpretative and cognitive attitude of "nationalized" historiography not only in the self-definition of the collective national "I" but also in the process of confronting that "I" with the Other. This self-evidently affects the task of explaining the status and mission of one's nation between "East" and "West." Here the problem is solved by means of teleological and essentialist constructions and a monochrome vision of one's nation, leading directly to oppositions, confrontations, polar opposites, and exclusions.

No less important, the intellectual hermeticism of "nationalized" historiography, along with the methodological vacuum that appeared when the Soviet version of Marxist historical methodology was intellectually and morally discredited, prompted a search for a greater variety of interpretative and cognitive models.

Practically from the end of the 1980s, the "national" (or nationalized) version of the history of the homeland gained dominance in social discourse, overriding the "Soviet" model, to which the ruling party adhered,[7] and in the early 1990s it actually became an inalienable part of the official model of Ukrainian history, and even an element of the state's "nation-building" ideology. It became central to the teaching of history and to scholarly elaborations, and it enjoyed the moral and material support of the state and the governing bureaucracy.

At an official function in 1993, President Leonid Kravchuk of Ukraine expressed his disappointment that "the Ukrainian people do not have a history of their own." In response, the National Academy of Sciences of Ukraine immediately came up with the prospectus of a fifteen-volume history of the Ukrainian people. The conceptual essence of the prospectus was set forth in a brochure written by Rem Symonenko, a staff member of the Institute of Ukrainian History at the Academy: "the restoration of national history per se to its rightful place; its restoration as the past of the Ukrainian ethnos on its own autochthonous territory. The subject here is Ukrainian history as a unique, uninterrupted process whose principal object is the Ukrainian people—from its primal origins to its present-day sovereign

---

[7] For a more detailed account, see Kasianov, "Ukraina-1990: 'boi za istoriiu.'" I trust that this and other references to my own articles are justified by the need to save space.

statehood."[8] The same year witnessed a rather curious attempt to introduce a course in Ukrainian political science, or "scientific nationalism,"[9] in higher educational institutions, which met with a critical reaction on the part of some members of the scholarly community.

From the early 1990s, political and social groups representing the "Soviet" version of Ukrainian history (Communists, Soviet army veterans, some members of the regional state bureaucracy) lost influence on the "politics of history" and educational policy, which did not prevent them from expressing very active opposition to the "nationalization" of history in public discourse, but not in practical politics.

It should be noted that in the 1990s concern with history in official policy was mainly a concession to a specific political conjuncture. On the one hand, introducing the canonical version of nationalized history into the curricula of schools and higher educational institutions was supposed to promote the civic education of new citizens of a new country. On the other hand, the supreme governing institutions concerned themselves with historical symbols and commemorative practices pro forma, just enough to meet the needs of the moment. Moreover, those in the highest (especially presidential) offices avoided radical declarations at all costs, except for instances when historical concerns were essential for their own legitimation (for example, refuting the view that those holding power at the time were successors to a criminal Communist *nomenklatura*) or for ideological discreditation of political opponents (in the given instance, these were the Communists, who were assigned the role of "official opposition").

Historical debates had no great social resonance, both because of the lack of any systematic historical policy[10] and because of other, more pressing problems (a major socioeconomic crisis).

It cannot be said that the return of the canonical account of nationalized history to sociopolitical and cognitive practice was

---

[8] Symonenko. *Do kontseptsiï bahatotomnoï "Istoriï ukraïns'koho narodu,"* 7.

[9] The essence of the innovation and criticism of it are presented in Bystryts'kyi, "Chomu natsionalizm ne mozhe buty naukoiu."

[10] This does not mean the absence of such a policy: in the 1990s a system of historically based state awards was created; a national currency was introduced, featuring a visual representation of the national pantheon; monuments were erected to eminent national figures belonging to that pantheon; and national commemorative practices were established.

wholly unproblematic: in the early 1990s there were already discussions between those Ukrainian historians who supported the "classical" version of national history and those dissatisfied with its cognitive and explanatory canons.[11] In 1995 the American historian Mark von Hagen placed the first clear accents for a critique of "nationalized" historiography in his highly provocative article "Does Ukraine Have a History?"[12] The scenario he proposed was subsequently played out by Ukrainian historians, even those who had not read his article. By the late 1990s there was already a small but fairly stable community of historians in Ukraine capable of presenting both a revision of the dominant scheme of national history and alternative interpretations.[13] Those historians "reunited" with their Western colleagues, who saw broader scope in Ukrainian history for making theoretical generalizations and for researching particular subjects.[14]

In the Ukrainian case, the 1990s witnessed a certain "division of labor": those supporting the basic canon of "nationalized history" (representing a physical majority) firmly established themselves in the sphere of historical policy, as well as affirmative and didactic history, while their opponents concentrated on the sphere of analytical historiography.[15]

Until the early 2000s, discussions between them took place in parallel intellectual spaces, with each side successfully cultivating its own specialty and very rarely straying into the neutral zone, but from the middle of the first decade of the 2000s one sees the activization of open intellectual opposition between them—as in the sphere of

---

[11] For more detail on this discussion, see Kasianov, "Rewriting and Rethinking: Contemporary Historiography and Nation Building in Ukraine," 29–46.

[12] von Hagen, "Does Ukraine Have a History?"

[13] It is worth referring to the substantial work of the Polish historian Tomasz Stryjek, which contains a detailed description of the views and discussions of Ukrainian "revisionist" historians of nationalized history. See Stryjek, *Jakiej przeszłości potrzebuje przyszłość*.

[14] A collection attesting to the existence of such an international community is Kasianov and Ther, *A Laboratory of Transnational History: Ukraine and Recent Ukrainian Historiography*.

[15] This classification is proposed in A. Megill, with contributions by Steven Shephard and Phillip Honenberger, *Historical Knowledge, Historical Error: A Contemporary Guide to Practice* (Chicago, 2007).

academic discussion, so in that of historical policy.[16] This is probably due to two main factors. In the first place, there has been a considerable broadening of intellectual horizons among Ukrainian historians themselves, both those who already sought to go beyond the basic discourse of "nationalized" history in the 1990s and the new generation of scholars whose intellectual formation took place in the late 1990s and early 2000s under the influence of the above-mentioned "older" colleagues and by way of various exchange programs with Western universities.

Secondly, between 2005 and 2010 there was a considerable activization of state policy with regard to history, based precisely on the fundamental canon of "nationalized" history. This was associated in part with the person of President Viktor Yushchenko and the presence in his entourage of ideologically active members of the Ukrainian diaspora and radically inclined representatives of the national-democratic intelligentsia who were dissatisfied with the status of the titular nation and the provisions for its cultural rights in independent Ukraine. Both the president himself and these elements of his entourage were convinced that the lack of a nationally oriented, systematic policy with regard to the humanities was the cause of the moral decline of Ukrainian society and its lack of moral and political unity. Active concern with problems of culture in general and history in particular was dictated by a desire to exert moral and political pressure on political opponents: it can hardly be considered an accident that active concern with problems of historical memory and activization of the discussion of such problems in society coincided with moments of acute internal political crisis.

---

[16] I shall cite only two examples: Natalia Yakovenko's sharply polemical review of a book by Valerii Smolii and Valerii Stepankov, *Ukraïns'ka natsional'na revoliutsiia XVII st.*, and the discussion of an article by Wilfried Jilge in *Krytyka* (Kyiv). In the first instance, the critical remarks came down to a protest against anachronisms, as well as irony with reference to the unconscious use of Soviet schemata in national discourse. In the second instance, the discussion concerned the instrumentalization of history and distortions associated with it. See Iakovenko, "U kol'orakh proletars'koï revoliutsiï,," Il'ge, "Zmahannia zhertv," Hyrych, "Triumf syl'nykh,"; Mokrousov, "Perekaz z 'soviets'koï." Hrynevych, "Zmahannia peremozhtsiv." H. Kasianov, "Déjà vu!"

From mid-2005, ever more systematic[17] and goal-oriented (but by no means always well-considered) policies took shape in the president's office with regard to the politics of history and memory. As already noted, they were based on a strategy[18] of ethnosymbolism characteristic of the standard cultural nationalism and romanticism of so-called "non-historic" (stateless) peoples of the nineteenth century. The main element here was the revival or strengthening of the myth of the exclusive historical path of one's own nation, with particular stress on its heroism and suffering. To that end, two historical phenomena of the greatest significance were chosen—the Ukrainian Insurgent Army (UPA) as an example of the heroic pages of history and the Holodomor[19] as an example of a national tragedy on an extraordinary scale.

---

[17] Up to and including the erection of new memorial complexes and institutions. Among the latter, the most significant was the Institute of National Memory, established by Yushchenko's decree on May 31, 2006. The institute was established on the Polish model. Unlike its Polish counterpart, the Ukrainian Institute of National Memory did not obtain real status or substantial financing. For some time it coordinated the work of state institutions with regard to compiling the Book of Remembrance of the Holodomor; its other functions were public education and scholarly research, but it proved unable to compete with existing research institutions. Moreover, some of its projects were clearly at variance with Yushchenko's historical policy: it suffices to mention the work of a group of historians under the aegis of the institute whose task was to carry out a critical analysis of school courses and textbooks on Ukrainian history. They produced a concept of historical education that was clearly at odds with the ideology of Yushchenko's ethnosymbolism. See *Kontseptsiia ta prohramy vykladannia istoriï v shkolakh (proekt)* (Kyiv, 2009), posted on the institute's website: http://www.memory.gov.ua/ua/publication/content/1461.htm.

[18] The word "strategy" means the presence of a certain sufficiently elaborated goal and an understanding of the resources required to attain it; however, given that a whole society is involved, it does not exclude many instances of spontaneous reactions, unexpected actions, and emotional motives for those actions.

[19] I propose that the word *Holodomor* be italicized when it does not refer to the official name of a historical phenomenon employed in official state and international documents and papers but to certain dominant stereotypical representations and canonical discursive practices representing a specific historical phenomenon—the famine of 1932–33. See H. Kasianov, *Danse macabre*. It is worth noting that the word "Holodomor" is already being used in the works of some Russian historians (with reference to the famine

Since both were presented in extremely exclusive form, as constituents of Ukrainian ethnic history alone (the UPA as representing the Ukrainian struggle for independence and the Holodomor as genocide of the Ukrainian nation/people),[20] they aroused not only quite acute social and political discussion that rose to the level of international and interstate relations but also active countermeasures on the part of opponents.[21]

If in the discussions of the 1990s and the social and political actions provoked by them it was left-wing elements that figured as the main opponents of those in power, the 2000s saw a broadening of the political and social base of those opposed to historical policy. The Communists, traditionally opposed to the "nationalization" of history, and their supporters among those nostalgic for Soviet times were joined by political forces representing the eastern and southeastern parts of the country.

From 2006 to 2010, in the course of acute political rivalry resulting from the struggle for power between the president and his supporters in parliament on the one hand and the party of large capital (the Party of Regions), representing the parts of the country just mentioned, on the other, problems of historical policy turned out to be among the

---

of 1932–33 in the RSFSR and the USSR) and in Moldavia with regard to the famine of 1946–47.

[20] In the Ukrainian intellectual and, in a narrower sense, historiographic tradition up to the turn of the twentieth century, "people" and "nation" were identical concepts; the Ukrainian nation meant ethnic Ukrainians. The concept of a civic nation is usually conveyed by the term "people of Ukraine."

[21] Yushchenko did not, of course, limit himself to these subjects. His enthusiasm for archaeology, which took the form of a public expression of his dedication to the idea of Trypilian culture as Ukrainian, was generally known. The president was an active promoter of a number of commemorative actions that had significant (and highly contradictory) resonance in society. Noteworthy among them were the restoration of Hetman Ivan Mazepa's capital of Baturyn (Chernihiv *oblast*) and the tercentenary of the destruction of Baturyn by the troops of Aleksandr Menshikov (1708); the celebration of the "Constitution of Pylyp Orlyk;" the "jubilee" of the Battle of Konotop (1659); the ninetieth anniversary of the Battle of Kruty (1918); and the tercentenary of the Battle of Poltava (1709). It is quite apparent that all these anniversaries took on a particular context in relations with Russia, whose senior leadership and diplomatic services were not sparing with very harsh comments, declarations, and actions.

most pressing, as was only to be expected. The politicization of history reached a level comparable to that of the late 1980s and early 1990s, when discussions about historical revision were directly associated with the struggle for power. Furthermore, both sides exploited contested historical questions to discredit opponents politically and morally and to exert pressure on them with regard to problems quite remote from history but most palpably related to the division of power.

In 2005, in connection with a round anniversary of the end of the Second World War, a heated discussion broke out concerning the evaluation of that period of Ukrainian history in schoolbooks. The discussion, initiated by organizations of veterans of the Great Patriotic War, was taken up by certain "talking heads" from the Party of Regions who came out, like the veterans, against what they considered the inadequate elucidation of the role of the Organization of Ukrainian Nationalists and the Ukrainian Insurgent Army (OUN-UPA) in school textbooks and against the replacement of the term "Great Patriotic War" with the broader "Second World War." Those nostalgic for the Soviet past were also annoyed by the change in the conceptualization of the warring parties: in the official conception of history, Ukraine figured as a victim in the clash of two totalitarian regimes. If for veterans this was in some measure a question of moral priority and inability to overcome ideological stereotypes, then for the left-wing parties, above all the Communist Party of Ukraine (CPU) and its allies in the Party of Regions, it was a matter of presenting the political incumbents (presidential and governmental) as nationalists twisting history and dividing the country.

The discussions did not end with the traditional appeals and demands to the authorities to replace "incorrect" textbooks with "correct" ones: it came to physical skirmishes in the central squares of the national capital.[22] In the same year of 2005, there was a scandal in connection with the publication of a new grade five textbook of Ukrainian history. One of the texts approved by the Ministry of Education

---

[22] In 2005–6, when the October anniversary of the formation of the UPA was again being commemorated, UPA veterans and their supporters gathered in the central square of the capital, as did veterans of the Great Patriotic War, "stirred up" by leftists. Fisticuffs between them became something of a tradition. Since 2007 there has been a practice of holding public actions representing the hostile parties in different places.

and Science for use in schools contained a chapter on the Orange Revolution written in the most apologetic tones.

The following years saw a notable strengthening of the tendency toward acute confrontation on problems of historical policy, which became part of a broader political struggle.

That tendency may be illustrated with the example of the Holodomor, which, owing to the efforts of the authorities, turned into a specific form of cultural reality and a significant symbol of national historical mythology, as well as an object of extremely polarized political speculation and heated discussions in society at large.

President Yushchenko took a number of steps infringing on the tacit and rather shaky consensus attained in that sphere in the days of President Leonid Kuchma. At his initiative, an unprecedented ideological and political campaign was undertaken to turn the famine of 1932–1933 into the central mobilizing symbol of Ukrainian history—the symbol of the greatest human catastrophe of the twentieth century, surpassing the Holocaust and other instances of genocide.

Let us enumerate the basic elements of that campaign.

First, the creation of a national Book of Remembrance. In all regions of the Ukraine that suffered from the famine, coordinating groups were formed under the aegis of *oblast* and *raion* state administrations to collect data about those who suffered and died in the famine of 1932–1933. These makeshift staffs coordinated the activity of hundreds of local groups that collected data on the ground, mainly in villages. The local groups included teachers, students, elementary-school pupils, librarians, museum staff, local historians, club presidents, and so on. The collection of data for the Book of Remembrance often turned into chasing after numbers in order to fill quotas, which aroused dissatisfaction even among those positively disposed to the idea of turning the Holodomor into a defining national symbol. In March 2008, at a "round table" on the famine of 1932–1933 in Dnipropetrovsk, students and young teachers complained that efforts to perpetuate the memory of the victims were turning into quota fulfillment.[23] The dean of the department of history at the Kharkiv National University, Serhii Posokhov, who attended Yushchenko's meeting with

---

[23] Kul'chyts'kyi, "Ne mozhna peretvoriuvaty pam'iat' pro Holodomor na 'kampaniishchynu.'"

oblast governors in Kharkiv concerning preparations for marking the seventy-fifth anniversary of the tragedy, was shaken by the conduct of the president, who "lambasted" governors presenting inadequate results with regard to the collection of names for the Book of Remembrance. In the historian's opinion, the famine itself had been organized in the very same way, as a race for quotas.[24] The oppressive "chasing after numbers" found its most striking expression in the actions of President Yushchenko himself, who ignored the calculations of demographers, historians, and sociologists, citing the figure of 7–10 million victims of the famine in Ukraine in all his public appearances.[25]

Second, the organization of mass commemorative actions ("Light a Candle," "The Inextinguishable Candle," and the like);[26] meetings

---

[24] Gessen, "The Orange and the Blue."

[25] The results of a special research project undertaken by the Institute of Demography, National Academy of Sciences of Ukraine, were published in November 2008. According to the scholars' calculations, direct losses from the famine of 1932–33 in Ukraine were estimated at 3.4 million. To these, the demographers added losses of 1.1 million from the decrease in births. The cumulative effect of the famine (unborn children and grandchildren of the dead) was estimated at 6 million. The presidential press center treated these data as corroboration of the figure of 10 million (http://www.president.gov.ua/news/16407.html).

[26] "Light a Candle" is an annual action conceived as involving the whole nation. It was first carried out as early as 2003. On the day of commemoration of the victims of the famine of 1932–33 (the fourth Saturday of November), those wishing to take part place a lighted candle in their window. In Kyiv, icon lights with lighted candles are placed near the monument to victims of the famine of 1932–33 on that day. The "Inextinguishable Candle" is a sheaf of grain approximately 1.5 meters high, weighing about 200 kg, made of high-quality beeswax collected from all *oblasts* of Ukraine. In the course of 2008 it was passed from one country to another (33 countries, the number chosen to coincide with the date of the tragedy), where memorial services and meetings were held upon its arrival. By the autumn of 2008, the symbol had also been taken through every *oblast* of Ukraine. The "Inextinguishable Candle" ended its journey at the Memorial of Remembrance, opened in Kyiv in November 2008, where it became one of the first exhibits. "Thirty-Three Minutes" was a public action held from June to November 2008 in public places (in squares or near surviving monuments or memorial plaques to "figures of the totalitarian regime") on every non-working day: for thirty-three minutes, the full names of those who died of hunger in 1932–33 were read aloud.

and concerts to mourn the victims; contests of artistic and literary works, as well as student papers; the laying of wreaths, ears and sheaves of wheat or rye; commemorative lessons in schools; and the creation of places of memory (exhibits in museums, schools, and libraries; the erection of crosses, memorial plaques, and gravemounds of mourning; the planting of red viburnum groves;[27] the establishment of memorial complexes). Such actions had taken place earlier as well, mainly on the basis of initiatives "from below," and some of them had been supported by the authorities, but it was under Yushchenko that they took on a pan-national character and enjoyed the complete support of state institutions, first and foremost those subject to the president (governors; municipal and *raion* state administrations).

Third, the juridical legitimation of the Holodomor through the adoption of laws characterizing it as genocide and forbidding any other public interpretation of the tragedy,[28] or by holding official investigations and delivering judicial verdicts. In May 2009 the Security Service of Ukraine (SBU) even undertook a criminal investigation into the "act of genocide of 1932–33." Investigative squads worked in Kyiv and seventeen *oblasts* of Ukraine; according to the SBU authorities at the time, two hundred volumes of evidence were compiled. At the beginning of 2010 the case was submitted to the Kyiv court of appeal, which

---

[27] Viburnum groves: in 2007, under Yushchenko's leadership, parliamentary deputies planted more than two hundred viburnum bushes on the banks of the Dnipro River near the Kyivan Cave Monastery. A memorial complex, the Memorial of Remembrance of Victims of Holodomors, was also opened there in November 2008. Its central element is a chapel in the form of a twenty-six-meter candle rising above the memorial museum.

[28] In 2008, owing to support from the presidential factions, the Ukrainian parliament adopted a law on the Holodomor that defined the famine of 1932–1933 as genocide. Public denial of the *Holodomor* was termed amoral and illegal. On the basis of that law, at the end of 2006 Yushchenko submitted a bill proposing criminal responsibility for denial of the *Holodomor* and the *Holocaust* as acts of genocide. A similar bill was also submitted by deputies from the pro-presidential faction: true, it referred only to denial of the *Holodomor* as genocide. The sanctions proposed in the bills began with fines and ended with imprisonment up to three years. Subsequently Yushchenko included this bill as an "urgent" element of all packages of bills negotiated with his opponents in order to resolve the political crisis—a very striking fact indicating the seriousness of his attitude to the problem.

considered it for all of one day, whereupon it "acknowledged the fact of genocide," identified the guilty parties (the party and state authorities of the Ukrainian SSR and the USSR as a whole), and closed the case, since the defendants were already deceased.

Fourth, sponsoring the publication of scholarly research on subjects related to the famine of 1932 through the system of state grants to publishers. In this case, since scholars were filling a specific order from the authorities, all the publications either extended the factual basis of the subject at best or served as "scholarly" substantiation of ideological slogans at worst.

Finally, the campaign to have the famine of 1932–33 recognized at the international level by parliaments of other countries and international organizations. Here the president's efforts produced the greatest international resonance concerning the famine: on the one hand, the world truly learned of the tragedy; on the other, the way in which the "genocide" version of the famine was promoted often produced bewilderment and rejection among thoughtful addressees, as well as acute counteraction on the part of countries with competing versions of "historical truth."

Yushchenko himself headed the international committee to organize the commemoration of the seventy-fifth anniversary of the famine of 1932–1933, which included representatives of the largest community organizations of the Ukrainian diaspora (such committees had usually been headed by the deputy prime minister in charge of humanitarian issues). Under Yushchenko's patronage, an international campaign was initiated under the motto "Ukraine remembers, the world acknowledges." In practically all his "benefit" appearances of 2005 at the international level (the U.S. Congress, the European Parliament, and the like), Yushchenko made a point of mentioning the famine of 1932–33, and, in the years 2006–8, meeting with leaders of the most influential international organizations, he requested their cooperation in promoting international awareness of the famine.[29]

---

[29] Between 1993 and 2008, the parliaments of thirteen countries recognized the famine of 1932–33 as an act of genocide against the Ukrainian people. The efforts of Ukrainian diplomacy to have such decisions adopted at the level of international organizations ended in failure. In 2007–8 the Parliamentary Assembly of the Council of Europe, the European Parliament, and UNESCO adopted special resolutions on the famine of 1932–1933, but,

Yushchenko's efforts to "intensify" national history not only produced a very stormy reaction and protests from the above-mentioned political forces but also provoked counteraction on the part of the top Russian political authorities, who by then had also become active in the sphere of historical policy and memory. Their version of history was based on imperial ambitions and glorification of the Soviet past. For the top Russian political leadership and most historians studying the subject, the famine of 1932–33 was a tragedy of all-Union scale. Furthermore, the specifically national aspects of what took place in Ukraine at the time were denied for obvious reasons: if they were recognized, there would be a particular victim of "Moscow," with all the resulting undesirable moral and political consequences for the latter.

In his turn, the Ukrainian head of state clearly insisted that the famine of 1932–33 was a Holodomor—an act of genocide directed against the Ukrainian people. In the course of the years 2005–7, exchanges of notes between ministries of foreign affairs, statements by politicians in the parliaments of both countries, and even acts of vandalism[30] became routine. Russia took unprecedented measures at the level of international organizations (the European Parliament, UNESCO, the UN) intended to block Ukrainian diplomatic efforts to have the Holodomor recognized as an act of genocide against Ukrainians. The refusal of President Dmitry Medvedev of the Russian Federation to take part in the official ceremony marking the seventy-fifth anniversary of the famine of 1932–33 may be considered the peak of the conflict. The refusal was not conveyed through diplomatic channels but as a demonstrative action: on November 14, 2008 Medvedev sent Yushchenko an open message. It is worth noting that less thunderous but no less effective counter-measures were taken by Israel against the promotion of the "genocidal" version of the Holodomor in international organizations.[31]

---

    despite the efforts of Ukrainian diplomatic services, the word "genocide" did not appear in them.

[30] Reference here is to an outrage upon the state symbols of Ukraine on Mount Hoverla and to a violent attack on an exhibition about the *Holodomor* at the Ukrainian House in Moscow, both carried out by activists of a Russian organization, the Eurasian Youth Association, in 2007.

[31] Here, to all appearances, one may speak of a certain competition between two projects, the Holodomor and the Holocaust. The actions of the

The dispute between senior Russian and Ukrainian state authorities over the representation of the Holodomor was not the only zone of conflict to open up in historical policy in the early 2000s. No less passion was aroused by the decision of Yushchenko and his parliamentary supporters to give UPA veterans rights equal to those of veterans of the Great Patriotic War, as well as concurrent official measures to turn the OUN and UPA into positive features of national mythology. Particular displeasure, accompanied by critical public statements on the part of leaders of the Russian Federation, was provoked by Yushchenko's decision to award the title of Hero of Ukraine[32] posthumously to the commander in chief of the UPA, Roman Shukhevych. Russia raised this question at the highest levels, including a resolution "pushed through" at the UN in November 2008 condemning the glorification of collaborators with the Nazis.[33] As the curtain was falling on his presidency, Yushchenko awarded the title of Hero of Ukraine to another OUN leader, Stepan Bandera. This demonstrative action aroused protests not only from a considerable part of the population and politicians in Ukraine but also abroad: it was condemned by President Lech Kaczyński of Poland and by a number of Jewish organizations

---

Ukrainian side, which clearly followed the example of the formation of rhetoric about and representations of the Holocaust, reveal an intention to "surpass" their predecessors with regard to the principal indicator—the number of victims. This could not fail to prompt counteraction on the part of Israel and those who consider the Holocaust unique. It is worth noting that anti-Semitic motifs are not infrequently to be found in the rhetoric of the Holodomor, both on the part of known anti-Semitic organizations (such as the Interregional Academy of Personnel Management) and of state structures, especially in the form of "unobtrusive" but insistent repetition of the true full names of "Holodomor organizers"—to take a random example, the list published by the SBU.

[32] The title and the chest decoration pertaining to it are basically copied from the title of Hero of the Soviet Union.

[33] The draft of such a resolution was adopted by the UN General Assembly. The United States voted against it; all countries of the European Union, including Estonia and Latvia, abstained, as did Ukraine. The adoption of the draft resolution was prompted by the actions of Baltic authorities that, in Russia's opinion, condoned the "rehabilitation" of the soldiers and officers of national Waffen SS military formations (the Latvian Legion and the 40th Estonian Division). The reference was, of course, to the UPA, Shukhevych, and Bandera.

in Ukraine and elsewhere. On February 25, 2010 the European Parliament adopted a resolution expressing "regret" with regard to Yushchenko's decree and affirming the hope that the new leadership would "review those decisions and maintain its dedication to European values."[34]

It is worth noting that over the last five years a "monument war" has become common practice in Ukraine. It suffices to recall the public controversy concerning the erection of a monument to Bandera[35] in Lviv in 2006–7 (the Polish community of Lviv treated it as a provocation) or the demonstrations of national democrats and Ukrainian nationalists in Odesa, where a group sculpture dedicated to the city's founders, featuring Catherine II as the central figure, was installed in October 2007.[36] In 2005 passions were aroused in the Crimea concerning a monument to Joseph Stalin (on the sixtieth anniversary of the Yalta Conference), leading to open conflict with the Crimean Tatar Mejlis. In May 2010, Communists and an organization of veterans of the Soviet army placed a monument to Stalin in Zaporizhia, provoking sharp debate both at home and abroad. The human-rights commissioner of the Council of Europe, Thomas Hammarberg, expressed "regret" concerning the Communists' intention to erect the monument. It was installed in a wing of the Zaporizhia *oblast* committee of the CPU: the local authorities forbade a public meeting to mark the unveiling, but it took place nevertheless in the guise of a meeting with a parliamentary deputy. In protest, representatives of the nationalist organization Svoboda (Liberty) organized a march to the municipal council, where Communists pelted them with eggs. On December 27, 2010 a "mobile detachment" of the All-Ukrainian Stepan Bandera Tryzub (Trident) Organization decapitated the monument with

---

[34] European Parliament resolution on the situation in Ukraine 22.2.2010 RC-B7-0116/2010. Cf. http://www.Europarl.europa.eu.

[35] The first monument to Bandera was erected in his native village in western Ukraine in 1990. It became an object of repeated vandalism and was even blown up.

[36] In early February 2010, when emotions were running high in Ukraine over the award of the title of Hero of Ukraine to Bandera, the Odesa monument was defaced by representatives of some organization called "Unknown Patriots" who declared that a "monument to Bandera" should stand there.

a power saw.[37] In a few days the chief's visage reappeared, but on the eve of January 1, 2011 the monument was blown up by persons unknown.[38]

By the mid-1990s, the "nationalization" of history was basically complete in Ukraine. The discourse of "nationalized" historiography merged completely with official state ideological discourse in the same period. Something of a tacit consensus took shape with regard to the general account of national history. At the level of state institutions, at least, there was unanimity on the content of the national narrative.

In Ukraine, the top level of the state bureaucracy and the political elites adopted a strategy[39] of employing standard accounts of national history to legitimize their social, cultural, and political status. Consequently, as "nationalized history" took form, it was integrated into the rather amorphous state ideology (constituting its most structured element), educational policy, and civics.

In some sense that process took place of its own accord: in the early 1990s the state simply lacked the resources to give it full support, but moral support was perfectly apparent. This was the period in which the basic standard account of the "history of the homeland" was established, both in scholarship and in the educational system. The basic national narrative on the nineteenth-century model was adopted in public-school and university-level courses of Ukrainian history. Indeed, high schools and, in part, higher educational institutions became the main channels for promoting the model of national history that, according to its creators, was to ensure the civic loyalty of new generations. The "History of Ukraine" was introduced as a subject in middle schools (from grades 4 to 10, and, in 2005, from grades 5 to 12), and an obligatory one-semester course under the same title was introduced in all educational institutions regardless of profile. Teaching was conducted according to a standard program that postulated

---

[37] "V Zaporozh'e 'trizubovtsy' otrezali golovu pamiatniku 'mezhdunarodnomu terroristu' Stalinu." See the video at http://www.rus.newsru.ua/ukraine/28dec2010/mol_trysub.html.

[38] "Pam'iatnyk Stalinu v Zaporizhzhi znyshcheno povnistiu," *Dzerkalo tyzhnia* (novyny), January 1, 2011 (http://news.dt.ua/news/83700).

[39] The term "strategy" is used here only as a descriptive and analytical category. The reference is essentially to means of adapting to ideological and political conjunctures.

indoctrination according to standard forms. Unfortunately, history textbooks turned out to be full of xenophobic motifs, whether directly or contextually expressed.[40] Public discussions over history issues were mostly focused either on overcoming the Soviet legacy (in this case Communists acted as a main opponents of "nationalization" of history), or on "ideological ambivalence"[41] of state policies—the national democrats were the major

This situation changed after the Orange Revolution. President Yushchenko's evident desire to enhance the national component of Ukrainian history, with particular stress on those subjects where consensus was lacking or could easily be infringed, led to the headlong actualization of subjects that aroused extreme irritation among certain segments of politically active society. Accordingly, the second half of the first decade of the twenty-first century witnessed exceptionally heated public discussions of the past that involved not only Ukrainian citizens but entire states.

The year 2010 saw Yushchenko's opponents, the Party of Regions, come into power. Viktor Yanukovych won the presidential elections of February 2010, and over several weeks after his victory a parliamentary majority was formed that made it possible to adopt laws and establish a government obedient to the president. The Party of Regions itself never had a clear ideological platform, being a conglomerate of representatives of big business and associated bureaucratic elements, as well as local political elites. As the political struggle continued, becoming more acute after the Orange Revolution, a group appeared within the party that sought to develop an ideological orientation for that political force in order to define it more sharply.

The basic elements of that ideological platform were the status of the Russian language in Ukraine and, accordingly, the defense of the rights of the "Russian-speaking population," as well as a "struggle

---

[40] Discussions on that problem started at the very beginning of the 2000s and continue to the present day. For the first publications on the subject, see Honcharenko and Kushnar'ova, "Shkola inshuvannia," and *Ukraïns'ka istorychna dydaktyka*.

[41] For instance, the commemorative campaign on the Great Famine 1932–1933 was followed by official celebrations of the 85th anniversary of Volodymyr Shcherbytsky (2003) as well as of the 85th anniversary of the Ukrainian Young Communist League *Komsomol* (2004).

against nationalism," above all in the sphere of historical policy. Both elements were closely associated with the political struggle against Yushchenko and were part of the acute confrontation with him. They were used to create a repulsive image of Ukrainian nationalism and, accordingly, to discredit Yushchenko and the "Orange" elements morally and politically. As something of a side effect of this struggle, ideological motifs became more prominent in the public actions of the Party of Regions.

During the presidential campaign of winter 2010, questions of historical policy were part of the intrigue. All the top candidates addressed the subject: Viktor Yushchenko, unanimously considered by observers to have no hope of victory, took a defensive traditionalist position, and Yulia Tymoshenko did likewise, while Viktor Yanukovych exploited the above-mentioned motifs—the status of the Russian language and the "threat of nationalism"—in habitual fashion.

After Yanukovych's electoral victory, the ideological element in his activity and that of the Party of Regions took on new significance. On the one hand, it was necessary to conform to established ideological schemata associated with the moral and political legitimacy of any authority claiming to speak on behalf of the Ukrainian state. On the other hand, there began a "cleanup"[42] of problem areas creating tension in relations with Russia and causing dissatisfaction among parliamentary allies (the Communists) or among citizens nostalgic for the Soviet past.

The tactic remained basically the same as under Yushchenko:[43] the president himself spoke and acted in rather neutral fashion (except for asserting that the Holodomor was not genocide). Yanukovych returned to the line of conduct tested in Kuchma's time, which consisted of avoiding acutely ideological subjects and, when necessary,

---

[42] A term that I heard twice in personal conversations in 2010 from an activist of the Party of Regions who was also a "talking head" on ideological questions and a deputy to the Verkhovna Rada, and from a highly placed official of the Cabinet of Ministers of Ukraine responsible for humanities policy.

[43] Yushchenko, for example, while president, never personally said that Russia should bear responsibility for the Holodomor, apologize to Ukraine, or pay compensation. In his entourage, however, especially in the presidential faction of parliament, there was no shortage of such statements, often quite radical ones.

calling for pluralism of ideas. For Yanukovych, as for the technocrat Kuchma, questions of historical policy are of secondary importance,[44] and his approach to them is determined by raison d'état.

At the same time, the statements and actions of certain members of the Party of Regions representing its "ideological bloc," such as the Sevastopol deputy Vadim Kolesnichenko and the newly appointed minister of education and science, Dmytro Tabachnyk, provoked tremendous indignation among Ukrainian national democrats and nationalists who went over from government to opposition. Something of a buffer role was assigned to Anna Herman,[45] the former press secretary of the newly appointed president. Taking up the post of deputy head of the presidential administration, she began to offer a running commentary on all of Yanukovych's undertakings in the "humanitarian" sphere.

A mere two days after Yanukovych's inauguration (February 28, 2010), headings pertaining to the Holodomor vanished from the president's official Internet site. Subsequent reproaches from the opposition were brief in duration, as the corresponding pages were restored in abridged form.[46] Yanukovych's next significant remark, made during the traditional commemoration ceremony at the grave of Taras Shevchenko in Kaniv on March 9, 2010, was that Ukrainian alone could be the official language in Ukraine.

Suspense remained for some time with regard to the annulment of Yushchenko's decrees on awarding the title of Hero of Ukraine to Shukhevych and Bandera (during the election campaign, Yanukovych had promised to review or annul the decrees). On March 5,

---

[44] By all accounts, Yanukovych generally dislikes "subjects pertaining to the humanities" and quite often finds himself in embarrassing situations when required to address such questions. The best-known "pearls" of his public appearances are associated with just such subjects: it was from him that Ukraine learned of the poetess Anna "Akhmetova" and of Anton Chekhov, the famous Ukrainian poet, while western Ukrainians were flabbergasted to hear that they were the "genocide of the nation" (Yanukovych meant *henofond*, "gene pool").

[45] Herman is the only representative of western Ukraine in the president's immediate entourage. Before going over to Yanukovych, she was the director of the Ukrainian service of Radio Liberty in Kyiv, which found itself in opposition to the "Kuchma regime."

[46] http://www.president.gov.ua/content/golodomor_75.html.

2010, during a joint press conference with Medvedev, Yanukovych said that by Victory Day he would "make a decision."[47] In April 2010 the Donetsk regional administrative court declared that Yushchenko's decree awarding the title to Bandera was illegal and subject to annulment (on the grounds that Bandera had never been a citizen of Ukraine). The same procedure was followed with regard to Shukhevych on April 21. (At almost the same time, the city councils of Ivano-Frankivsk, Lviv, Ternopil, and Lutsk awarded honorary citizenship to Bandera and Shukhevych.)[48] Soon after Victory Day, Yanukovych did indeed make a decision, but not the one expected of him. On May 14, 2010, speaking at a meeting of the Civic Humanitarian Council attached to the office of President of Ukraine, he said that it was necessary to attain mutual understanding with regard to historical figures that aroused public controversy and declared himself in favor of "gradualism and delicacy" in resolving such problems.[49]

On April 27, 2010, speaking at a session of the Parliamentary Assembly of the Council of Europe in Strasbourg, Yanukovych asserted that "declaring the Holodomor an act of genocide against one nation or another would be incorrect and unjust."[50] He made the statement on the day before the session was to consider a report on the famine of 1932–33 and adopt a resolution concerning which Ukrainian participants in the session were waging a rearguard action against their Russian opponents in an effort to secure the use of the term "genocide." Yanukovych's declaration was agreeable to most delegations (especially that of Russia) but aroused the ire of Ukrainian parliamentarians representing the Ukrainian national-democratic opposition.

In June 2010 the 68-year old Volodymyr Volosiuk, a Ukrainian citizen and a former lawyer belonging to the People's Movement of

---

[47] http://www. unian.net/ukr/news-366084.html.

[48] According to a survey by the Reiting sociological group, 53 percent of respondents supported the annulment of the decree, 28 percent did not support it, and 19 percent expressed no definite opinion. Every tenth resident of western Ukraine surveyed was prepared to take part in protest actions against the annulment of Yushchenko's decree.

[49] "Ianukovich nazval 'naibol'shyi destruktiv' v Ukraine" (www.unian.net/rus/news/news-376684.html).

[50] "Ianukovych skazav deputatam PASE, shcho Holodomor—ne henotsyd" (http://eunews.unian.net/ukr/detail/193461).

Ukraine, filed a lawsuit against Viktor Yanukovych pertaining to the article on "insults to honor and dignity." The lawsuit claimed that besides infringing the article, Yanukovych had violated the Law of Ukraine (November 2006) on the Holodomor of 1932–33, in which the famine was deemed a genocide, and public denial of the Holodomor as genocide was declared illegal.[51] The Pechersk district court of Kyiv found against the plaintiff, whereafter an appeal was made to the Kyiv court of appeal, which rejected it on December 8, 2010. Curiously enough, on January 13, 2010 the same court had found Joseph Stalin (Dzhugashvili), Viacheslav Molotov (Skriabin), Lazar Kaganovich, Pavel Postyshev, Stanislav Kosior, Vlas Chubar, and Mendel Khataevich guilty of the crime of genocide under Art. 442, par. 1 (genocide) of the Criminal Code of Ukraine, closing the criminal case on the same day in connection with the decease of the defendants.[52]

Unwillingness to characterize the Holodomor as genocide did not mean rejection of the ideological symbol. Over the past twenty years the "Holodomor" has become firmly established as one of the basic symbols of the constitutive Ukrainian historical myth. Commemorative practices associated with it have become habitual, and stereotypical notions and public representations of it have become part of constructed "historical memory" and official ceremonies. The very word "Holodomor" has entered the language of official documents, legislative acts, and international relations.

Rejection of the "genocidal" version of the Holodomor was an essential symbolic gesture for Yanukovych that eliminated tension in one aspect of relations with Russia. All other components of the corresponding historical myth and the ideological practices associated with it (as well as the very term "Holodomor") remained untouched. A visit to the Memorial of Remembrance of Victims of Holodomors in Ukraine[53] erected in Yushchenko's day has become a standard protocol item for visiting leaders of foreign countries on par with the laying

---

[51] "Volodymyr Volosiuk sudyt'sia z Viktorom Ianukovychem" (http://gazeta.ua/index.php?id=343385).
[52] "Holodomor 1932–33 rokiv na Ukraïni vyznano henotsydom chastyny ukraïns'koï natsional'noï hrupy." See the court's official website: http://apcourtkiev.gov.ua/control/uk/publish/article?art_id=41962&cat_id=35857.
[53] The official name.

of wreaths at the Eternal Flame and the monument to the Unknown Soldier on the Avenue of Glory (a symbol of Soviet commemorative practices). In that sense, the visit to Kyiv on May 17, 2010 by President Dmitry Medvedev of the Russian Federation was symbolically telling: he visited the Memorial of Remembrance of Victims of Holodomors in Ukraine, whose dedication he had demonstratively refused to attend two years earlier.

On November 26, 2010, the Day of Memory of victims of the Holodomor, an appeal was posted on the presidential website in which Yanukovych called the famine of 1932–33 an "Armageddon," came out against speculation with regard to the number of dead (having in mind the "chase after numbers"), and called for speaking "the truth and nothing but the truth."[54] On the following day, in the company of Prime Minister Nikolai Azarov, he took part in commemorative mourning at the Memorial of Remembrance of the Victims of Holodomors in Ukraine.

Yanukovych's political declarations and ritual symbolic gestures were accompanied by a number of changes to infrastructure, the most significant of which was a change in the status of the Institute of National Memory. Under Yushchenko, the institute was granted the de facto status and powers of a state agency. In the course of an administrative reform announced as an "optimization" of the state apparatus, the Institute of National Memory was abolished by Yanukovych's decree of December 9, 2010[55] and reestablished the same day, this time as a scholarly research institution attached to and funded by the Cabinet of Ministers. Its functions remain quite murky.

It may be said that Yanukovych has personally made a de facto return to the "ambivalent" historical policy practiced in Kuchma's time. That policy combines ethnosymbolism (to the extent required for the authorities' national legitimation) with elements of Soviet nostalgia (as a necessary gesture to that part of the citizenry attached to the corresponding collective experiences).

---

[54] http://www.president.gov.ua/news/18809.html.
[55] Decree no. 1085/2010 of the President of Ukraine "Pro optymizatsiiu systemy tsentral'nykh orhaniv vykonavchoï vlady" (http://www.president.gov.ua/documents/12584.html).

While Yanukovych himself plays the role of a president standing above the battle and "uniting the nation," representatives of the Party of Regions' "ideocracy" periodically create public disturbances with actions and declarations that on the one hand are hypothetically intended to overcome "Yushchenko's legacy" and "resist nationalism" and, on the other, to affirm something of their own ideological standard. That standard combines elements of Soviet nostalgia, a rhetoric of reunion (vis-à-vis Russia), and rather vague observations and slogans pertaining to "internal unity" in Ukraine.

In some cases the actions of official agencies and certain significant figures of the new establishment take the form of demonstrative provocations. On September 8, 2010 officials of the Security Service of Ukraine (SBU) detained the director of the Łącki Prison Memorial Museum (formerly a KGB strict-regime prison and a Polish jail), Ruslan Zabily, on the pretext of his intention to provide secret information to certain third parties. Zabily's computer and electronic data devices were confiscated; he was interrogated (by his account) for fourteen hours and then released.

Subsequently the SBU undertook a criminal investigation, whose object became for a week perhaps the most popular figure on news programs and political talk shows. The opposition immediately began a campaign against "witch-hunting," a return to the "times of the KGB," and the persecution of dissidents and "independent historians."[56] The former director of the SBU archives, Volodymyr Viatrovych, who had been dismissed immediately after Yanukovych's inauguration, even asserted that the "Zabily case" was a "Kremlin action" intended to wipe out the memory of the UPA.[57] More moderate explanations (which were not, however, voiced openly) came down

---

[56] Zabily was an active promoter of the version of national history that was in accord with Yushchenko's policy. Zabily was a de facto staff member of the SBU and an active participant in the declassification of SBU documents while Yushchenko was in power. The files confiscated from him may indeed have been officially restricted at the time, but in Yushchenko's day such documents (dealing mainly with the history of the OUN and the UPA) were openly accessible and saw print in generally available publications.

[57] "V'iatrovych: sprava Zabiloho—spets operatsiia Kremlia," http://ua.glavred.info/archive/2010/09/09/140047-14.html.

to a banal attempt to divide property in central Lviv or to "clean up" the composition of cadres in institutions subordinate to the SBU (the senior staff of the SBU archival service was of course replaced immediately after Yanukovych's accession to power). These explanations find some measure of corroboration in the fact that Yanukovych intervened in the situation as supreme arbiter: by his decree, the memorial museum was placed under the supervision of the Institute of National Memory, and the "Zabily case" somehow blew over of its own accord.

No less resounding, but more consequential, were the actions of the minister of education and science, Dmytro Tabachnyk, concerning the "normalization" of the school curriculum in Ukrainian history and of the language situation in the educational sector. As a member of the opposition during the "Orange" period, Tabachnyk emerged as one of the most radical critics of Yushchenko's historical policy, distinguishing himself with very harsh comments about the president and his entourage, especially the "Galicians." The national-democratic intelligentsia and the opposition took Tabachnyk's appointment as minister of education and science to be an anti-Ukrainian measure. An "anti-Tabachnyk campaign" developed in the western Ukrainian *oblasts*, and opposition deputies submitted a bill to dismiss the minister, calling him "virulently anti-Ukrainian" (*ukraïnozher*).

In a BBC interview given in April 2010, Tabachnyk said that Ukrainian history textbooks were written from an ethnocentric viewpoint: they should be revised and written from an anthropocentric viewpoint. In this connection, he made an indirect reference to results of the activity of a working group of historians at the Institute of National Memory.[58] In June 2010 he posted a programmatic article on the official site of the Party of Regions, repeating his thesis about an "anthropocentric approach" to history in schools and declaring that "the treatment of the history of the homeland and the world cannot vary with changes of presidents or ministers of education; it cannot and should not depend on the personal tastes, complexes, and phobias of any official." This was promptly followed by a declaration of his personal treatment, wholly conditioned by politics, of the history of the

---

[58] "Tabachnik khochet sdelat' uchebniki po istorii 'gumannymi,'" (http://news.liga.net/news/N1010709.html).

Second World War and of such individuals as Stalin, Shukhevych, and Bandera.

Further steps pertaining to the "review of national history" had no particular resonance and developed according to the laws of bureaucratic hierarchy: some authors of textbooks received behind-the-scenes directives to make corrections. An image of the "Orange" Independence Square disappeared from the cover of a textbook. In its text, the formula "artificial [i.e., man-made] holodomor" was removed (the term "holodomor" remained); the description of UPA activity was abridged; a photo of Shukhevych was deleted; and the book ended with the year 2004. Material on the UPA was also abridged in another textbook, which said that the army fought against the Germans and the Bolsheviks (not a word about the Poles). According to the authors, they received directives by telephone from the ministry about correcting their textbooks: the directives came down to reducing anti-Russian motifs and abridging material on the UPA.[59]

In August 2010 there was another controversy associated with the preparation of a joint Ukrainian-Russian textbook for teachers of history (the decision of a subcommittee of an intergovernmental commission on humanitarian cooperation between Ukraine and Russia, rendered on October 27, 2010). The opposition promptly labeled the work a "joint textbook," while nationalists and journalists commented that Russia would dictate to Ukraine how history was to be written. Historians, for their part, reacted very cautiously to the idea, although the working group formed to prepare the textbook included some highly respectable historians.[60] In the following year no further action in preparation of a "joint textbook" was undertaken (apart from some meetings devoted to general academic issues).

It is worth noting some more radical public actions that go beyond official declarations on historical subjects, but which enjoy the de facto, behind-the-scenes sponsorship of elements of the Party of Regions that align with the Communists on ideological questions. Their actions are usually directed toward those who are nostalgic for Soviet times and

---

[59] "Perepysana istoriia Ukraïny. Versiia epokhy Dmytra Tabachnyka," (http://www.pravda.com.ua/articles/2010/08/26/5332444/).

[60] "Oleksandr Udod: Spil'noho pidruchnyka buty ne mozhe," *Den'*, December 30, 2010.

live by the stereotypes of Soviet propaganda. Such actions included, first and foremost, the erection of monuments to victims of the OUN-UPA in Luhansk, Rivne, and Odesa and in *raion* centers and villages of Luhansk and Sumy *oblasts* in 2010,[61] as well as a highly tendentious exhibition entitled "The Volhynian Slaughter: Polish and Jewish Victims of the OUN-UPA," which was displayed in Kyiv and major cities of eastern and southern Ukraine. Paradoxically, the exhibition repeated the actions of the Yushchenko period, copying the techniques and methods of representing the past that were used in the traveling exhibition "Ukraine Remembers! The Holodomor of 1932–33—The Genocide of the Ukrainian People."

It is still too early draw even provisional conclusions about the historical policy of the "Yanukovych era." The era itself is only beginning, and the actions of politicians and official figures representing the ideological face of the "new" authorities still include too many elements attesting to certain post-election syndromes and a desire for revenge and final victory, especially on the "ideological front." At the same time, one cannot help noting the usual tendency of Ukrainian politicians going over from opposition to government: they readily accept established political practices, commemorative rituals, and historical myths and symbols that promote their legitimation as representatives of authority and bearers of national sovereignty. The basic canon of nationalized history is not subject to radical revision.

Between "East" and "West": A "Local Orientation"[62]

The central problem involved in "subjectivizing" Ukrainian national history, that is, turning Ukraine from an object into a subject of history, was how to fit "one's own" emancipated history into a system of

---

[61] "Pamiatniki zhertvam OUN-UPA," (http://dragonmoonbird.livejournal.com/759184.html).

[62] The popular contemporary Ukrainian author Yurii Andrukhovych made a clever play on words, titling an essay collection of his *Dezoriientatsiia na mistsevosti* (Disorientation on Location). Among the many possible readings of the term "disorientation" is liberation from the "Orient" and abandonment of the "East."

historical and geographic coordinates. In full conformity with the logic of the construction of national history, the central question became how to define Ukraine's place in the "East–West" dichotomy—a question that many continental European nations, from the Atlantic to the Urals and the Caucasus, have had to answer.

The integration of history into the formation of national identity; the legitimation of new states and their political elites; the use of history for developing some general form of civic consciousness and for the large-scale indoctrination and formation of loyal citizens: all this inevitably requires the clarification of an image of one's own collectivity—in this case, a national "I"—and confronting it with an imagined "Other."

In the system of spatial coordinates, this meant identifying the place of one's nation[63] within systems of civilization—in the broadest terms, within the metaphorical "East–West" dichotomy—taking the former to represent the cultural, political, economic, and sociopsychological forms associated with cultural and economic backwardness; the subjection of the individual to the collective and the state; despotism and authoritarianism, and the latter to represent individualism, democracy, the free market, a variety of cultural forms, ideological pluralism, and freedom of the individual.

Since separation took place in the form of alienation from empires in both "West" and "East," "separated" national history was inevitably counterposed to a previously common space and accompanied by efforts to achieve integration (often understood as reintegration) into another common space represented as a desirable and optimal alternative. In the conventional, standard East European national project it was of course the "East," or Russia,[64] that figured as the historically imagined space to be abandoned, while the imagined "West," or "Europe," was the space to be entered/reentered.

Defining the place of "one's own" nation in a system of historical, geographic, cultural, and political coordinates within the framework of a "nationalized" history/historiography postulated the creation of national mythologies that would not only make it possible to "delimit"

---

[63] In this case it is immaterial which nation is meant, "ethnic" ("cultural") or "political" ("civic").

[64] This series of associations may be continued: the "socialist camp," Communism, and so on.

or "detach" one's history from cognitive structures, accounts, and narratives earlier represented as held in common, but also to demonstrate the historical rationale for such delimitation. It should be noted that the main goal, articulated directly or indirectly, but very intensely in every instance, was separation from "all-Russian" history and "reunion with all-European history."[65] Such a vector of "departure" and "entrance" may be rationaled quite sufficiently by the standard practice of nationalism: the attainment of real and imagined (spiritual, intellectual, ideological, cultural, political) autonomy (independence) for the nations of the Soviet Union (or, more broadly, of the "socialist camp") postulated, aside from everything else, entrance into the community of European nations in the capacity of culturally (and thus politically) self-sufficient entities.

Since it was held that in the framework of the earlier Soviet, Communist historical, cultural, and political experience such self-sufficiency was not permitted, that experience was quite logically rejected, cast aside, and condemned as negative. The logic of "nationalized" history postulated that the first step would be transformation into a standard "historic" nation, and the second would see the nation, having "regained" its history and historical status, enter the family of European nations. The question of belonging to a particular civilization was basically resolved in one of two ways. The first was a radical break with the "East" (Russia, the Soviet Union, the empire) and a no less radical imagined entrance (treated as a "return") into Europe, that is, into the "West." The second is more of a compromise, but at times no less radical from the viewpoint of forming negative/idealized stereotypes of the "Other." It takes the form of self-representation as a cultural or civilizational bridge, a mixed cultural zone or, to express it in more current scholarly argot, a "borderland" between "East" and "West." As a rule,

---

[65] Using Ukraine and Ukrainian historiography as an example, Natalia Yakovenko set forth a brief intellectual and ideological genealogy of the "reunion syndrome" in an essay that is short but substantial with regard to contexts: Iakovenko, "Kil'ka sposterezhen' nad modyfikatsiiamy ukraïns'koho natsional'noho mifu v istoriohrafiï." In light of her discussion, one cannot help thinking that the numerous and importunate treatments of Ukraine's "Europeanness" and its "return" to Europe in contemporary "nationalized" historiography are a mirror image of the schemata of "reunion" in Soviet historiography, which proposed reunion with Russia.

the "Western" elements in this account are represented as positive and the "Eastern" ones as negative aspects of the national ego. Variations may be observed here: in some cases, one's own nation is represented as a bearer of "Western," "progressive" cultural values and priorities to the "backward East;" in others, the mission of "barrier between East and West" is stressed; in still other cases, there is a notion of combining certain cultural characteristics of "East" and "West" in national history and culture as evidence of its uniqueness, mutability, and strength. The idea that "Western" elements take priority over "Eastern" ones appears in all these variants.

Conclusions

The "nationalization of history" was completed in Ukraine by the end of the 1990s. The history of Ukraine in the form of a basic national narrative, a canonical version of national history, became an inalienable part of society's self-representation; of ways of representing the state and the nation both at home and abroad. The canonical version of national history is reflected in educational standards, curricula, and textbooks. It would seem that all preconditions are in place for its "normal functioning" as the basis of civic education. Nevertheless, in recent years that version of Ukrainian history has aroused ever more complaints and criticisms, sometimes generated by political conjunctures and political intrigue or speculation, at other times by genuinely humanitarian motives and the concern of professional historians and social activists for the moral condition of a society in which a unified version of ethnically exclusive history gives rise to cultural intolerance, xenophobia, confrontational instincts and political manipulations. Certain tendencies toward a retreat from ethnocentrism in historical policy that became apparent after the coming to power of the ideologically amorphous Party of Regions have a compensatory character on the one hand but (not to mention instrumentalization of history for political needs), on the other, lead to conflict with that part of society for which the version of national history developed in previous years, and taken to an extreme by Yushchenko's policy, has become part of national consciousness and a basic element of identity. This in turn makes the prospect of a general national consensus rather cloudy.

Bibliography

Aimermakher, K. and G. Bordiugov, eds. *Natsional'nye istorii v sovetskom i postsovetskom prostranstve*. Moscow: AIRO-XX, 2003.
Bomsdorf, F. and G. Bordiugov, eds. *Natsional'nye istorii na postsovetskom prostranstve—II*. Moscow: AIRO-XX, 2009.
Bystryts'kyi, S. "Chomu natsionalizm ne mozhe buty naukoiu." *Politychna dumka* no. 2, (1994) 30–35.
Gessen, K. "The Orange and the Blue." *New Yorker*, March 1, 2010, 34.
Honcharenko, N. and Kushnar'ova, M. "Shkola inshuvannia." *Krytyka* no. 4 (2001).
Hrynevych, V. "Zmahannia peremozhtsiv," *Krytyka* nos. 1–2 (2007).
Hyrych, I. "Triumf syl'nykh," *Krytyka* no. 12 (2006).
Iakovenko, N. "Kil'ka sposterezhen' nad modyfikatsiiamy ukraïns'koho natsional'noho mifu v istoriohrafiï," *Dukh i Litera* nos. 3–4 (1998) 118–21.
Iakovenko, N. "U kol'orakh proletars'koï revoliutsiï," *Ukraïns'kyi humanitarnyi ohliad* vol. 3 (2000).
Jilge, "Zmahannia zhertv," *Krytyka* no. 5 (2006).
Kasianov, G. "Rewriting and Rethinking: Contemporary Historiography and Nation Building in Ukraine." In *Dilemmas of State-Led Nation Building in Ukraine*, edited by Kuzio, T. and P. D'Anieri. Westport, CT: Praeger Publishers, 2002, 29–46.
Kasianov, G. and P. Ther, eds. *A Laboratory of Transnational History: Ukraine and Recent Ukrainian Historiography*. Budapest–New York: CEU Press, 2009.
Kasianov, H. "Ukraina-1990: 'boi za istoriiu.'" *Novoe literaturnoe obozrenie*, nos. 1–2 (2007).
———. *Danse macabre: Holod 1932–1933 rokiv u politytsi, masovii svidomosti ta istoriohrafiï (1980-ti — pochatok 2000-kh)*. Kyiv: Nash chas, 2010.
———. "Déjà vu!" *Krytyka*, no. 3 (2007).
Kul'chyts'kyi, S. "Ne mozhna peretvoriuvaty pam'iat' pro Holodomor na 'kampaniishchynu,'" *Den'* (Kyiv), March 22, 2008.
Megill, A., P. Honenberger, and S. Shepard, eds. *Historical Knowledge, Historical Error: A Contemporary Guide to Historical Practice*. Chicago: University of Chicago Press, 2007.
Mokrousov, A. "Perekaz z 'soviets'koï," *Krytyka* no. 12 (2006).
Stryjek, T. *Jakiej przeszłości potrzebuje przyszłość? Interpretacje dziejów narodowych w historiografii i debacie publicznej na Ukrainie 1991–2004*. Warsaw: Instytut Studiów Politycznych PAN, 2007.
Symonenko, R. H. *Do kontseptsiï bahatotomnoï "Istoriï ukraïns'koho narodu" (mizhnatsional'nyi ta mizhnarodnyi aspekty)*. Kyiv: Instytut istoriï Ukraïny 1993.
Telus, M. and Iu. Shapoval, eds. *Ukraïns'ka istorychna dydaktyka: mizhnarodnyi dialoh (fakhivtsi riznykh kraïn pro suchasni ukraïns'ki pidruchnyky z istoriï). Zbirnyk naukovykh statei*, Kyiv: Heneza, 2000.
von Hagen, M. "Does Ukraine Have a History?" *Slavic Review* no. 3 (1995).

The "Politics of Memory" and "Historical Policy" in Post-Soviet Moldova

ANDREI CUSCO

The connection between history, politics and "collective memory" in Eastern Europe is particularly complex, multi-layered and fragmented. This state of affairs led, among other things, to the active involvement of professional historians in various nation-building projects and, more broadly, in the politicization of the past. The latter tendency serves as a legitimizing strategy for the intellectual and political elites within the post-Soviet space. The case of the Republic of Moldova confirms this general assessment, but is further complicated by the endless debates concerning the national identity of the country's majority ethnic group. There is no consensus within Moldovan society on the issue of defining the essence, boundaries, or basic values of the nation as an "imagined community." After the disintegration of the USSR, followed by the proclamation of independence in August 1991, the majority of Moldovan historians uncritically accepted a simplified version of the Romanian national historiography, which replaced the discredited "Soviet model" while preserving a number of the Soviet-style essentialist and outdated methodological tenets.[1] At the same time, most of the post-Soviet political elite aimed at strengthening the newly acquired Moldovan "statehood." This also presupposed the pursuit of a special kind of "politics of memory," which distanced itself both from the Romanian national narrative and (although to a lesser extent) from the Soviet past.

---

[1] For a more detailed discussion of the subject, see Taki, Cusco, "Kto my? Istoriograficheskii vybor: Rumynskaia natsiia ili moldavskaia gosudarstvennost'" *Ab Imperio* 1, 2003 485–495.

To put it differently, an antagonism between two mutually exclusive variants of local nationalism—and of associated memorial practices—emerged in the Moldovan case. The advocates of "pan-Romanian nationalism," who claim that the Moldovans are a part of the "greater Romanian nation," had a staunchly negative view of the Soviet period, dismissing it as an era of foreign domination and "occupation." They accordingly idealized the epoch of Bessarabia's inclusion into "Greater Romania" (1918–1940). The supporters of the opposite ideological current—"Moldovanism"—were in many ways recycling the Soviet-era conceptual legacy, attempting to use certain categories of ethnic nationalism as well. They strove to prove the existence of an uninterrupted tradition of Moldovan statehood, finding its purported roots in the Middle Ages and emphasizing the (mythical) continuity between the medieval Moldavian Principality and the contemporary political entities which emerged on the territory of Bessarabia. A sort of fine balance between these two visions of Moldovan identity prevailed for much of the post-1991 period: the "Romanianists" dominated the academic circles and the university milieu, while the moderate "Moldovanists" enjoyed the support of the government, but ultimately failed to significantly undermine the strong positions of their adversaries in the educational system. Thus, the "politics of memory" in the Moldovan context was often reducible to the symbolic competition and conflict between the two antagonistic projects of the local national identity. Within the framework of this "zero-sum game," the 20th century was the most contested period, while the interpretation of the events of 1917–1918, the years of Romanian administration, World War II, the Holocaust on the territory of Bessarabia, and the Soviet legacy represented as many objects of heated and ideologically charged debates and of political manipulation.

Moldovan historians were far from adopting the position of "neutral observers" or non-involved scholars. On the contrary, they became direct participants of these "memory wars." The dilemma of professional ethics versus political bias was at best secondary for the protagonists, and quite often this question was not posed at all. The professional historians assumed the mantle of militant intellectuals and openly promoted a certain version of the "politics of memory." At the same time, any significant initiatives in this sphere coming from "below" (e.g., from civil society) were conspicuously lacking.

The relevance of the public "memory discourse" can be examined at least from two points of view. On the one hand, the "politics of memory" in post-Soviet Moldova is linked to the fundamental significance of the nation—and, consequently, of "national memory"—for the competing identity projects of the Moldovan intellectual and political elites. This observation is just as valid in the case of the "Romanianists" as in that of their ideological foes—the "Moldovanists." Collective memory is, in this case, clearly subordinate to the national narrative, which employs and manipulates certain key elements of the latter for the purpose of self-legitimization and in order to discern certain features purportedly defining the "national character" of the given community. In this form, collective memory only has an indirect and mediated influence on historical representations. The "memory of the nation" becomes tangible through symbols or ritual memorial ceremonies, but is generally not complicated by the personal (sometimes "uncomfortable") reminiscences of the direct participants or witnesses. In this case, collective memory functions as a device for symbolic stylization, the consolidation of social ties and the creation of a unified national historical "tradition." Such mechanisms are still functional, at the level of everyday life, even at present, although they are less effective than in the past.

On the other hand, "collective memory" is not a given, nor an unchanging phenomenon, but an evolving social construct, which always depends on the concrete circumstances of a society's political culture and on the (subjective) temporal factor. The "politics of memory" is especially important for those societies, which are still struggling with their own difficult past and were not able to overcome it either through the strategy of *reconciliation* or through the *mourning* for the victims of repressions, genocide etc.[2]

The "politics of memory" in Central and Eastern Europe (including in the Moldovan case) is in many ways different from the familiar Western European models of "overcoming" or "dealing with" the past (*Vergangenheitsbewältigung*). Even in those cases when the official "politics of memory" presupposed a complete break with the Communist past and a radical "de-Communization" of the public sphere, including

---

[2] Winter and Sivan, eds. *War and Remembrance in the Twentieth Century*, 32.

on the level of state legislation (e.g., in the former GDR or the Czech Republic), these measures, as a rule, amounted neither to an effective and lasting "national reconciliation" nor to a decrease of nostalgia throughout those societies. The attempts to explain such outcomes by using the notion of "transition" (or even by building a discipline of "transitology"), by invoking the peculiarities of political culture or by emphasizing the continuity of the former *nomenklatura* in government are only partially justified.[3] According to Tony Judt, the complexity and multiple layers of the "memory of Communism" in Eastern Europe are perfectly comparable to the "memory of Nazism" in the West. This disparity leads to the emergence of an "asymmetry of memory" between the two parts of the continent.[4]

The process of "overcoming the past" in the Republic of Moldova was, until quite recently, in an embryonic stage. This was due not only to the particular local context, but also to the overall structure of "collective memory" in Eastern Europe, which is constantly confronted by the dilemma of simultaneously dealing with the "problematic" or traumatic memory of Communism and Nazism (and/or the Holocaust). In this sense, the reflections of the American historian Charles S. Maier on the profound difference between the "hot" memory of Nazism and the "cold" memory of Communism are revealing.[5] The first part of this dichotomy has a deeper psychological nature and impact, provoking a much more vivid and heated emotional response in the process of "remembering," while the Communist past is generally perceived in less dramatic terms, not the least because of the relative "normalization" of the Soviet regime after Stalin's death. This psychological difference is highlighted by the author through the concept of *shame*, which presumably has deeper roots in the case of Nazism. Thus, the "memory wars" raging recently in the Ukraine and (although to a lesser extent) in the Republic of Moldova have far wider implications for the societies involved and cannot be reduced to academic debates. They are directly related to the problem of national identity and to the state policies pursued in this field. The connection between the political agendas and

---

[3] Gonzalez-Enriquez, "De-Communization and Political Justice in Central and Eastern Europe," 218–247.
[4] Judt, "From the House of the Dead," 803–831.
[5] Maier, "Hot Memory... Cold Memory."

projects of the post-Soviet elites, the manipulation of history for political purposes and the existence of certain elements of "historical policy" is clearly discernible in the Moldovan context.

"Symbolic Competition" and the Uses of History in Moldovan Political Discourse (1991–2009)

In the first years following the dissolution of the USSR, coherent attempts have been made in newly independent Moldova to radically revise the attitude toward the Soviet past and to rethink the country's history through the prism of a "national paradigm." The sphere of official symbols and the public space were mostly "nationalized" relatively quickly and without significant resistance.

These tendencies were expressed in several concrete forms, including: 1) the removal of most Soviet-era monuments or their transfer to special depositories, out of the public eye (this was applied, first of all, to statues of V. I. Lenin and of other Soviet leaders). However, this process did not uniformly affect all Moldova's regions (e.g., the Soviet monuments were preserved in the Gagauz autonomous region in the south of the country). At the same time, some monuments associated to the Soviet past were left standing even in the republic's capital (e.g., the monument to the "Komsomol heroes" or the statues commemorating the "revolutionary fighters" Sergei Lazo and Grigorii Kotovskii); 2) the "de-communization" of the public space, which found its expression in the mass renaming of streets and institutions and the gradual displacement of Soviet "places of memory" from the broader public sphere. In contrast to the Ukrainian case, the symbolic "nationalization" of space did not result in a wave of protests and public discontent, partly because the new nomenclature, heavily borrowed from the Romanian national "canon," simply did not resonate with a large part of Moldova's population. This was especially true of the national minorities, who perceived the new names as "foreign" and were unable to decipher their symbolic "weight of meaning." A concrete example concerns the elements of the purported continuity of the Romanian ethnicity on Moldova's current territory symbolized by the use of ancient Roman names and notions referring to the time of Dacia's conquest by the Romans while renaming streets, schools, public institutions etc. The same applied to the "symbolic rehabilitation" of little-known militants of the Moldovan national movement from the late 19th and early 20th century. The majority of the population perceived these innovations either neutrally or with outright indifference; 3) the radical revision of educational programs and curricula, particularly in the field of the humanities and social sciences.

However, at the level of political practice and debate the situation was far from unambiguous. The Declaration of Independence, passed by the Moldovan Parliament on August 27, 1991, referred to the "liquidation of the political and legal consequences" of the Soviet-German "conspiracy" of August 23, 1939[6] and to the "illegal state of occupation" of the Republic of Moldova by the Soviet Union, starting from 1940–1944 (the parallels with the context of the Baltic countries are obvious).[7] However, these radical tendencies did not lead to any corresponding sweeping political decisions. Moldova's "transition" can be best described in terms of a gradual movement towards a compromise between the moderate elements of the "Old Regime" and the moderates within the nationalist "opposition."

In the midst of growing tensions in the second half of 1991, fueled both by the increasingly radical nationalism of the "Popular Front" and by the Moscow-supported separatist movements in Transnistria and the Gagauz districts, the moderate wing of the former Soviet *nomenklatura* regrouped to form the Agrarian Democratic Party of Moldova (PDAM), registered in November 1991. On the one hand, the political leadership of the PDAM squarely rejected the "pan-Romanian" nation-building project and supported the consolidation of "Moldovan statehood." On the other hand, they advocated a strategy of "public amnesia" and a lenient attitude regarding the Soviet legacy and the Communist past. Thus, after an initial surge throughout 1991 and 1992, the fledgling elements of "historical policy" and strategies for "overcoming the past" were quickly shelved. The factors influencing this outcome included the consequences of the Transnistrian conflict,

---

[6] Here the Declaration implies the provisions of the secret Soviet-German protocol dividing the spheres of influence in Eastern Europe, annexed to the "Molotov-Ribbentrop" pact signed on August 23, 1939.

[7] Declaration of Independence of the Republic of Moldova. Available at: www.europa.md

the fragmentation of the nationalist political parties and the growing apathy of the electorate with regard to an active "politics of memory."

Another important event occurring in this period (with long-term political impact) was the rebirth of a recreated "Party of Communists," on a platform of Communist "re-foundation." As a sign of a general "swing to the left" of the political spectrum, a constituent conference of the Party of Communists of the Republic of Moldova (PCRM) was convened in late 1993. The new party was led by Vladimir Voronin, a former Minister of the Interior under the last Soviet-era government. The PCRM proclaimed itself the legal and ideological successor of the CPSU and the CPM. The appearance of a political organization, whose initial aims included "the restoration of the USSR," although without immediate impact on the political scene, pointed to an important change in the position of the state authorities toward the Soviet past. Throughout the rest of the 1990s, the symbolic competition in the public sphere and on the political arena was basically expressed in the endless debates on the subject of the Moldovans' "true" national identity.

The "national question" became a political watershed and an indicator of political preferences in the local context, displacing other criteria of ideological difference. This became clear during the 1994 parliamentary electoral campaign, when a full-fledged "Moldovan national project" was formulated at the level of the governing political elites. It was explicitly directed against "pan-Romanianism," which dominated the symbolic and cultural sphere during the first post-independence years. In contrast to the previous Soviet version of "Moldovanism," the new Moldovan nationalism represented a peculiar reaction to the Romanian national interpretation of Moldova's history and of the nature of the post-1991 Moldovan state. A defining moment in the development of "New Moldovanism" was marked by the so-called "national congress," "Our House—the Republic of Moldova," organized on February 5, 1994, under the patronage of the authorities. The Moldovan president at the time, Mircea Snegur, who earlier refrained from directly supporting the most radical "Moldovanist" tendencies, rapidly increasing during the previous year,[8] gave a speech

---

[8] The most well-known example in this sense was undoubtedly the brochure authored by one of the most outspoken "ideologues" of the Moldovanist current: Petre P. Moldovan [Vasile Stati]. *Moldovenii în istorie* (Chişinău, 1993).

to the participants of the Congress. In this speech, he strongly condemned the pan-Romanian national project as a "treason" of Moldova's national interest. He also directly accused most Moldovan writers and historians of harboring unwarranted doubts concerning the "legitimacy and historical foundations of our right to be an independent state [and] to be called the Moldovan people."[9] Snegur did not stop at the claim of the existence of a separate Moldovan nation as a potential foundation for building the post-Soviet state. He also advanced the questionable thesis about certain peculiarities of the "Moldovan language," which was meant to emphasize the anti-Romanian thrust of his political agenda. In this speech the president also reminded his audience of "the historical continuity of the Moldovan nation," which invoked the short-lived period of Bessarabia's notional "independence" in late 1917 and early 1918, before its unification with Romania. Thus, a purported basis for the legitimacy of the new state was created *ex nihilo*, but the earlier Soviet version of "Moldavian statehood," intimately linked to the creation of the MASSR in 1924, was clearly rejected. Aside from the charged rhetoric and the open manipulation of historical references for political purposes, this moment signified "the initial stage of the Moldovan state's official ideology."[10] The core of this ideology remained essentially stable during the second half of the 1990s and acquired a more radical bent during the PCRM's stint in government (2001–2009).

In order to better grasp the policy of the Moldovan state in the symbolic sphere, a closer look at the crucial period of the mid-1990s is necessary. Following the 1994 elections, when the nationalist forces suffered a heavy defeat, many of the earlier decisions directed at the gradual "Romanianization" of the state symbols were reversed or revised. Thus, the new Moldovan constitution, adopted in July 1994, decreed that the designation for the official language of the republic was to be "Moldovan" (whereas in the Declaration of Independence the national language was called "Romanian"). The same year, the Moldovan parliament replaced the country's national anthem. Instead of the Romanian anthem *Deșteaptă-te, române!* (Awaken, Romanian!), which had been common for Romania and Moldova since 1991,

---

[9] King, *Moldovenii: România, Rusia și politica culturală*, 160.
[10] Ibid. 160.

Parliament opted for a more "neutral" text —*Limba noastră* (Our Language), a poem written by the early-20th century Bessarabian poet A. Mateevici.

Still, it would be wrong to conclude that a wholesale and complete revision of the "politics of the past" initiated during the early 1990s took place. There were no attempts at a total rehabilitation of the Soviet past. One could more plausibly talk about a number of efforts to elaborate a viable core of a "Moldovan national mythology." The latter should have contributed to the consolidation of Moldovan "statehood," a loose concept mostly understood in negative terms, as a rejection of the Romanian national project. The main problem besetting the Moldovan political elites was the acute lack of legitimacy that the newly established polity had to face. Without abandoning the nationalist rhetoric in principle, the "Moldovanist" ideology was based on the supposed existence of an unchanging and stable "Moldovan ethnic essence" on the territory situated between the Dniester and Prut rivers (or, in a modified version, between the Dniester and the Carpathians) at least starting from the Middle Ages (if not from times immemorial).[11] The "Moldovanist" vision of the origins and development of the Moldovan national community shares with its counterpart—Romanian nationalism—espoused by the majority of Moldovan intellectuals, the same ethnocentric and primordialist features and presuppositions. Thus, only the presumable "vector" of historical development is different for the two sides, while the essential ingredients of their nationalist world-view are quite similar. Here is only one among many examples of this kind of nation-centered logic. Moldova's second president and a prominent representative of the former Soviet *nomenklatura*, P. Lucinschi, declared in 1999: "The Republic of Moldova, proclaimed as a sovereign and independent state on August 27, 1991, is at the same time the homeland of a people with traditions dating back thousands of years, with deep roots in history. An unassailable proof of this is [the celebration] of the 640th anniversary from the day of the creation of the Moldavian State."[12]

---

[11] Gheorghe Cojocaru, "Simboluri şi mituri: Mitul politic părtaş la guvernare," in *Arena Politică*, cited in Fruntaşu, *O istorie etnopolitică a Basarabiei*, 375.

[12] Fruntaşu, *O istorie etnopolitică a Basarabiei*, 375. Lucinschi is a historian by training.

However, this type of ideological constructs had a rather limited impact on the Moldovan society at large. Especially after 2001, the attitude toward the Soviet past became an increasingly relevant and "burning" topic of the political debates and a central factor in the polarization of antagonistic social and ideological positions.[13] The previously disparate and fragmented elements of "historical policy" acquire a systematic and coherent character in this period.

Similarly to the situation prevailing in the late 1990s, the "national question" became a priority of the version of "historical policy" initiated and promoted by the PCRM after it came to power in April 2001. The PCRM gradually distanced itself from its initial negative attitude toward the independent Moldovan state as a temporary and transitory phenomenon. Somewhat ironically, it became the main proponent of the idea of "Moldovan statehood." To achieve their goals, the Communists actively used the works of the consecrated ideologues of the "Moldovanist" current—Vasile Stati and Victor Stepaniuc (the latter was an important member of the PCRM leadership until 2009).[14] The ideological platform of "Moldovanism" was officially sanctioned and endorsed in the so-called "Conception of the Nationality Policy of the Republic of Moldova" (*Concepția politicii naționale a Republicii Moldova*), approved by Parliament on December 19, 2003. The importance of this document consists not only in that it asserts a relatively coherent (if simplistic) vision of nation-building in post-Soviet Moldova, but also in its formulation of a concrete strategy for the direct interference of the state authorities into the struggle against the "adversaries of Moldovan statehood."

The state attempted to monopolize and control the debate on the national identity of Moldova's Romanian-speaking population and to impose strict limits on the discussion of this issue in the public sphere. The language and rhetoric of the document owed much to the vocabulary and principles of the Soviet "nationalities policy," though it also took into account the post-Soviet context and the reality on the

---

[13] An interesting (and interdisciplinary) approach to the dilemmas and challenges of Moldovan post-Soviet state- and nation-building can be found in Heintz, *Stat slab, cetățenie incertă*.

[14] Stati, *Istoriia Moldovy* and Stepaniuk, *Gosudarstvennost' moldavskogo naroda: istoricheskie, politicheskie i pravovye aspekty*.

ground in Moldova. Certain passages of the text strangely combine the nation-building pathos typical for 19th century "national activists" with phraseology reminiscent of Soviet rhetorical devices. Here is a concrete example of this combination:

> The Republic of Moldova represents the political and legal continuation of the centuries-old process of the Moldovan people's uninterrupted statehood... The Conception proceeds from the historically developed truth confirmed by the general literary thesaurus: the Moldovan and Romanian peoples use a common literary form, "based on the living source of the folk speech of Moldova"—a reality which gives to the Moldovan national language a distinctive specific peculiarity, a certain charm (! – *ed.*), widely known and valued. Having a common origin and a common basic lexical fund, both the Moldovan national language and the Romanian national language preserve their linguonym / glottonym as an identification feature of each nation: the Moldovan and Romanian [one].[15]

Moreover, the Moldovan authorities ingeniously attempted to combine the most unlikely elements. Thus, the references to the foundational character of the 1917–18 events for the creation of a purported Moldovan tradition of statehood merged with the basic symbolically charged moments pertaining to the development of "Soviet Moldavian statehood." The second set of references essentially annihilated the symbolic validity of the first: the two schemes are mutually exclusive. Nevertheless, one can read the following assertions in this official document-cum-manifesto:

> The main principles of the Conception are based upon the centuries-old past of the Moldovan people and on its uninterrupted statehood within the historical and ethnic space of its national becoming [the terminology used here in fact directly refers to the vocabulary of the Declaration of Independence. – *ed.*]. Emerging

---

[15] Conception of the Nationality Policy of the Republic of Moldova (Law Nr. 546-XV of 19 December 2003). Available at http://interethnicmoldova.wordpress.com/law-conception/

in 1359 and surviving for centuries as an independent country, [despite] being territorially split and [finding itself] under foreign domination for a long period of time, Moldova restored its statehood through the constitutive act of 2 December 1917, when the Sfatul Țării (Assembly of the Land), "relying on the historical past of the Moldovan people," proclaimed in Chisinau the creation of the Moldovan Democratic Republic. The legitimate right of the Moldovan people to statehood was confirmed also by the creation of the Autonomous Moldovan Republic on the left bank of Dniester River on 12 October 1924. The statehood of Moldova within its new borders was decisively confirmed by the political and legal acts adopted in August 1940 and August 1991, and strengthened subsequently its legality in 1994, when the Constitution of the Republic of Moldova was adopted.

The Soviet period is thus surreptitiously included into the national narrative along with the 1917 and 1991 events, which directly undermined and contested the Soviet version of "Moldovan statehood." From the ideological point of view, Moldovan statehood thus appears as a rather paradoxical phenomenon, based on mutually exclusive principles of political legitimacy. However, the elements of "historical policy" proper are to be found in a different sphere. The document contains a set of explicit recommendations suggesting the adoption of concrete measures directed against the forces and individuals which presumably aim at "undermining Moldovan statehood." The conception recommended, among other things, to "neutralize, according to the current legislation on human rights and constitutional requirements (? – *ed.*), the unceasing attempts to promote de-Moldovanization, to deny the existence of the Moldovan nation and Moldovan statehood, to discredit the history of Moldova, to ignore the ethnonym "Moldovans" and the glottonym "Moldovan language."[16] In another context, the authors of the Conception proposed to create the necessary conditions in order to ensure the promotion "by the State of a personnel policy based on the criteria of professionalism and devotion to

---

[16] Conception of the Nationality Policy of the Republic of Moldova (Law Nr. 546-XV of 19 December 2003). Available at http://interethnicmoldova.wordpress.com/law-conception/

the fatherland,"[17] while at the same time proclaiming their adherence to the principle of non-discrimination based on ethnic, religious and/or social criteria. Such measures primarily targeted the potentially "undesirable elements" from the academic milieu and the educational system. The interpretation of this kind of initiatives as instances of "historical policy" is not in any way linked to the internal logic of the symbolic competition between the "Moldovanists" and the "Romanianists" in the public sphere. It is the *official* character of these documents and projects and their open endorsement by the state which allows them to be categorized as examples of "historical policy." The discriminatory nature of such measures uncovers the direction and aims of the PCRM's "politics of memory," combining an ambiguous attitude toward the Soviet past with the use of a number of Soviet-inspired ideological devices and political practices.

The educational sphere represented the main space for the deployment of "historical policy" in post-Soviet Moldova. After 1991, the majority of the Moldovan "intelligentsia," who shifted to a "pro-Romanian" position, held a starkly negative view of "Moldovanism" as a whole and persistently resisted the penetration of its advocates into the academic and university milieu. The first intimations of an open conflict between the state authorities and the academic circles emerged immediately following the events of February 1994 (i.e., the convocation of the Congress "Our House—the Republic of Moldova"). On February 24, 1994, a group of prominent Moldovan historians published an open letter to President M. Snegur in which they accused the president, among other things, of pursuing an agenda amounting to the "falsification of history" and of interference into the scholarly activity of the professional historians. Casting themselves as open supporters of the "Romanian" historical model, they directly blamed the authorities for promoting a policy of "primitive Moldovanism," which presupposed a return to the discredited Soviet scheme of "historical development." After the 1994 elections, which fundamentally changed the political picture by marginalizing the "pro-Romanian" nationalist parties, the debate on the inculcation of "Moldovan national identity"

---

[17] Conception of the Nationality Policy of the Republic of Moldova (Law Nr. 546-XV of 19 December 2003). Available at http://interethnicmoldova.wordpress.com/law-conception/

through the educational system was immediately reignited. A special government commission with the task of elaborating a comprehensive reform of history teaching was created. The core idea of this project was to replace the previously taught subject of *History of the Romanians* (introduced in the curricula in 1991) by the *History of Moldova*. The historians supporting the "Romanian" orientation immediately accused the government of "revanchist" and obscurantist tendencies, coupled with attempts to restore the Soviet historical paradigm.

However, in March 1995 the Ministry of Education issued a decision introducing the school subject of *History of Moldova* instead of the *History of the Romanians*. This attempt by the PDAM government to radically revise the educational policy was met by a fierce resistance from the Popular Front, which successfully organized a series of mass strikes of schoolteachers and students. The authorities were forced to retreat and make significant concessions. They declared the imposition of a "moratorium" on the discussion of the sensitive subjects linked to the Moldovans' national identity, the official designation of the state language and the school history curricula. The subject of *History of the Romanians* was reinstated, while its content remained essentially within the framework of the Romanian national model (with a more detailed study of Bessarabian specificity and local developments).

A new stage in the conflict between the "Romanianist" and "Moldovanist" visions of national history was reached in 1998, when a controversial didactic aid (in fact, a textbook) on *The History of the Republic of Moldova from Ancient Times to the Present* was published. This work was authored by a group of researchers who had earlier held privileged positions and had been part of the mainstream of "Soviet Moldavian historians," but were marginalized in the profession after the change of the historical paradigm in the early 1990s. These historians upheld a narrow vision of Moldovan history, limiting it exclusively to the boundaries of Moldova's current territory. This was partly due to the "Moldovanist" preferences of the authors and partly to their aspirations to restore their lost positions within the local academic circles. Their work was focused on the medieval Moldavian Principality (which they interpreted as the "forerunner" of the present Moldovan state) and further reduced its scope to the Prut-Dniester basin and Transnistria when discussing the modern and contemporary history of the area. This group of historians thus attempted to elaborate a coherent narrative of historical events within this territory, emphasizing the purported differences of Moldova's history from the broader Romanian context. In fact, this was an obvious case of retrospective historical analysis, based on the "transfer" of the current configuration of state borders to other historical epochs. The clichés and stereotypes of Soviet historiography figured prominently in this interpretation. One should note that the didactic aid was recommended by the Ministry of Education for school use, but was strongly rejected or boycotted by the historians of "Romanianist" persuasion and failed to effectively penetrate the school system.

The gap between the ideological tenets of the "pro-Romanian" current of Moldovan intellectuals and the political power became virtually unbridgeable after 2001, when the PCRM government forcefully attempted to undermine the influence of the "pro-Romanian" tendency on the educational system. Another "swing to the left" of the Moldovan electorate in the late 1990s and the ensuing landslide victory of the Communists in the 2001 parliamentary elections again strengthened the positions of the "Moldovanist" camp.

However, a new attempt of the government to introduce in the curricula a course on the *History of Moldova*, in 2002, led to the virtual reenactment of the 1995 scenario. If anything, the protests developed on an even larger scale. After their 2001 electoral victory, the new Communist authorities immediately initiated an all-out offensive on the "educational front." The declaration of PCRM's leader (and Moldova's president from April 2001) Vladimir Voronin that the first decade of Moldova's independence was a period of "a planned destruction of the future [of Moldovan statehood]" served as a signal for the implementation of new strategies aimed at changing the balance between "Romanianist" and "Moldovanist" elements in the scholarly and educational sphere. The official policy provoked stormy protests from the part of the majority of Moldovan historians. These protests were mainly voiced by the National Association of Historians, which had an NGO status, but in fact included a major part of history university professors and schoolteachers. On July 1, 2001, a "Congress of Historians of the Republic of Moldova" was convened. The Congress adopted a series of resolutions and memoranda basically confirming the historians' full support for the "Romanian" version of national history and condemning the authorities for the pressures exerted upon the scientific institutions and universities in order to achieve the suspension of the *History of Romanians* course.[18]

On February 1, 2002, the Association of Historians addressed a memorandum to the highest state dignitaries. This memorandum expressed serious concern about the "current situation in the Republic of Moldova in the sphere of constitutional liberties."[19] The signatories of the memorandum also put forward several demands, including: "the respect and promotion of scholarly truth in the questions concerning the national language, literature and history; an immediate end of the cultural genocide (! – *ed.*) against the native population; the cessation of the campaign of fomenting "Romanophobia" and discrediting the Romanian language and the history of the Romanians; the organization of a series of "round tables" involving specialists in the abovementioned fields; the suspension of the work on new school curricula and textbooks for the Romanian language, literature and history; the exclusion of the governing party's ideology from the economic, political, social and cultural life [of the country]."[20] This memorandum represents one of the most typical and interesting examples of the fullfledged "Romanianist" discourse and reveals the "sore points" of the unending debates in the public sphere, within Moldovan society and in the field of "historical policy."

After another round of mass demonstrations and protest movements in early 2002, provoked by a series of government initiatives, the PCRM changed its strategy and attempted to implement a new concept of historical education at the school level. This concept presupposed the merging of the courses of national and world history into an "integrated" subject and the elaboration of new textbooks of "integrated history." According to the new strategy for the study and teaching of history, approved in 2003, new textbooks for the primary and secondary cycles (4th-12th grades) were prepared for publication. They essentially replaced the previous "Romanian" historical paradigm with similarly biased "Moldovanist" tenets. However, one should

---

[18] In 2003, several booklets and brochures containing detailed reports on the Congress's proceedings and "resolutions" referring to every historical period were published.

[19] *Memoriu al Asociaţiei Istoricilor din Republica Moldova*, 39.

[20] Ibid., 41.

emphasize that the textbooks written in this period vastly differed from one another both in terms of quality and in the degree of politicization. Despite the repeated declarations of the Moldovan government regarding its respect for European educational principles and standards, the attempts at reforming the teaching of history became an instrument of "historical policy" in the hands of state authorities, who tried to eliminate the deeply politicized "Romanianist" vision of history by simply replacing it with the no less biased and tendentious "Moldovanist" model. The textbooks that did not fit the scheme imposed from above were rejected by a special commission of experts created under the aegis of the government. The former president V. Voronin became personally involved in the debate and openly supported the authors who displayed a clear "Moldovanist" agenda in their work. For example, the 11th-grade textbook was found wanting by the commission, while its authors were accused of promoting "anti-Moldovan" ideas.[21] However, the tone and argument of the textbook proved to be rather balanced (with a slight "Romanianist" bias), and the textbook was finally published, even though major difficulties had to be overcome.

In a letter from Deputy Prime Minister Victor Stepaniuc addressed to President V. Voronin, which was written in the context of the acute political tensions and crisis threatening the Communist government in late April 2009, a comprehensive program for combating "anti-state elements" in the Academy of Sciences and the establishments of higher education was outlined. The content of this document reveals, on the one hand, the inefficiency and incoherence of the PCRM's strategy in the sphere of "historical policy" and, on the other hand, the seriousness of the authorities' intentions to radically change the situation in this field. The letter's author emphasized, among other things:

> Today, the majority among the teaching staff in the historical departments of our Moldovan universities—70 percent—represent active adherents of the History of the Romanians. The same situation still prevails within the Institute of History, State and Law of the Academy of Sciences. As a result of the reorganization of this institute, [the pro-Romanian] aggressiveness of

---

[21] Letter of the Deputy Prime Minister Victor Stepaniuc to President V. Voronin, dated April 28, 2009, in Țurcanu, *Din poșta secretă a comuniștilor.*

the historians from the Academy somewhat decreased, but they continue to write anti-statist and anti-Moldovan dissertations and works. I constantly drew the attention of the President of the Academy of Sciences, Gh. Duca, to this fact. Taking into account this situation, I am absolutely convinced, that the state must create an educational institution in order to train specialists in the social sciences and humanities, namely in: history, Moldovan philology and literature, political science, international relations. Thus, the strict selection of cadres supporting our statehood for these very important departments in the field of educating and cultivating the [future] citizens of the Republic of Moldova could be coordinated and controlled by a serious government commission. The specialized departments from other universities could also be gradually reorganized. I am convinced, that such a decision would be radical, but less scandalous. In order to fight the anti-state ideology of Romanianism, which has penetrated, during the last 20 years, [our] culture, science, education, it is particularly important to strengthen the statist intellectual forces, which can conduct the ideological fight in a civilized manner, with competence and with a militant spirit and energy.[22]

In early 2009 the debates concerning the existence of a Moldovan "historical tradition" were refueled in connection with another attempt to celebrate the ancient "Moldovan statehood:" the 650th anniversary of the establishment of the medieval Moldavian Principality, considered by the "Moldovanists" to be the historical predecessor of the contemporary Republic of Moldova. The manipulation of historical discourse by politicians and certain militant historians alike is not surprising in this context. They were not deterred by the total lack of substance of such historical parallels and claims. However, soon enough the escalating tensions of the current political struggle pushed "historical policy" to the periphery of the public sphere.

Despite the considerable efforts of the PCRM government, the "Romanianist" paradigm remains dominant in most educational institutions, museums etc. The clearest and most revealing example is

---

[22] Ibid.

the version of the "politics of memory" displayed, in a synthetic and "concentrated" form, in the National Museum of History in Chisinau. The concept of the museum was radically revised in the early 1990s in order to correspond to the "nationalization" of historical discourse. The current version of the permanent exhibition was approved in 1997 and has not suffered significant alterations since then, even under the PCRM government. It is hardly surprising that the most radically reevaluated segments, in comparison with the Soviet era, were: the period of Bessarabia's inclusion into the Russian Empire (1812–1917), the epoch of Romanian administration (1918–1940), and the subsequent integration of the Moldavian SSR within the Soviet Union. In the hall reserved for Bessarabia's modern history ("the period of tsarist occupation"), the public is offered an unequivocally "national" interpretation of Russian policy in the region. A special emphasis is placed upon "Bessarabia's national specificity [in the general Romanian context] and the policy of national oppression pursued by the Russian Empire" in the area. The general evaluation of the entire 1812–1917 period leaves no doubt about the exhibition's message: "The impact of the policy of Russification and forcible isolation of Bessarabia [from Romania] during a whole century was deleterious in all the spheres of life, including in the educational, ecclesiastical and administrative fields." This desolate image of decline and calamities is contrasted with the 22-year period of Romanian administration, which is viewed as a "Golden Age" in the canonical version of the Romanian national narrative. The interwar period is described as a "new era" in the history of Bessarabia, marked by "important social-economic transformations and a large-scale flourishing of culture and education" in the framework of Greater Romania. The symbolic antagonism between the two epochs appears more than obvious. The subsequent description of World War II and Stalinist repressions is conceived along the lines of national victimization. For example, almost nothing is mentioned about the Holocaust on the territory of Bessarabia, while the national component of the repressions and deportations is especially emphasized. It is also revealing that the exhibition abruptly ends with the late Stalinist period. The next decades of the Soviet regime in Moldova are either totally ignored or barely reflected in the museum's collections. The basic elements of the "Romanian" interpretation of history figure prominently in the museum and are meant to construct a certain type of narrative and public perception of the region's tragic history under the domination of the Russian Empire and the USSR.

The "politics of memory" regarding the recent past—in other words, the attitude toward the Soviet legacy—was an important part of the PCRM's ideological baggage during its time in power (2001–2009). The symbolism, rituals and rhetoric of the Moldovan Communists continued to effectively employ the Soviet legacy as a foundation for legitimizing their own political identity. If the solemn commemoration of the Soviet founding moments and memorial dates (e.g., November 7) or Lenin's glorification had the character of "intra-party" rituals, other elements of the "politics of memory" promoted by the PCRM directly touched on the public sphere. Thus, a central motive for the symbolic space that the PCRM leadership strove to (re)construct was linked to the "Great Patriotic War." The war memorial complexes were perceived as especially significant "places of memory," and the war itself was to become a stimulus for "national reconciliation." On the other hand, the memory of the war was cultivated much more intensively than the memorial practices dedicated to the victims of the Communist regime. This emphasized the "asymmetry" and one-sidedness of the PCRM-supported version of the politics of memory.

On the whole, such a policy hardly contributed to the closing of the "memorial rupture" between various groups in Moldovan society, which continued to cultivate starkly opposed visions of the recent past.[23] The symbolism of the "Great Patriotic War" remains a key element of the image of the Soviet past shared by the PCRM and a major part of its electorate. The classification of the June 1940 and August 1944 events as a "liberation from the yoke of the Romanian invaders" or, alternatively, as "Soviet occupation" are still the subject of heated emotional outbursts and current political debates. An interesting parallelism can be observed in the mutual "rejection of the other's past" operating within the antagonistic groups in Moldovan society. Although several attempts to reach a compromise on this issue were successful (e.g., the granting of equal legal rights to the veterans of the Soviet and Romanian armies, projects for common war memorials

---

[23] A more detailed analysis of these questions is provided in Cojocari, "100 Grams for Victory!" or the Dilemmas of Collective Memory in the Republic of Moldova," *Caiete de Antropologie Istorică*, 2010, 51–58.

etc.), the perception of the war and the evaluation of its consequences for the local population still represents a sphere of controversy and a source of conflict in Moldovan society.

Another source of potential conflict is the "problem of the Holocaust" in Bessarabia. This subject was manipulated both by the state authorities and by their ideological opponents. During the first post-independence decade, local historians all but ignored the topic of the Holocaust on the territory of Bessarabia and Transnistria. This was due, first, to the previous Soviet historical tradition, which viewed the tragedy of the Jews in the framework of the "victims among the peaceful population" image and, second, to the ethnocentrism of the national paradigm, which only recognized and deplored the victimization of its own ethnic group. During the 1990s, an additional factor was the impact of the Romanian historiography, which tended at the time to idealize (or at least "rehabilitate") the Antonescu regime.

This situation witnessed a fundamental change after the PCRM came to power in 2001. First, the Communists, in contrast to the previous governments, began to display a significant interest in the topic of the Holocaust. This was due, on the one hand, to the focus of its policies on the protection of the ethnic minorities' interests and, on the other, to the peculiarities of the PCRM's "politics of memory" concerning World War II. Second, the policy in this sphere was directly influenced by the PCRM's sudden change of rhetoric and its shift to an ostensibly "pro-Western" foreign policy position in the second half of 2003. The Moldovan authorities started paying more and more attention to the "memorialization" of the Holocaust and of other tragic episodes in the history of Bessarabian Jewry. For example, in April 2003 memorial ceremonies dedicated to the commemoration of 100 years from the 1903 Chisinau pogrom were organized at the official level and attended by the country's leadership. Another important symbolic step, initiated by President V. Voronin, was the transfer of archival materials connected to the Holocaust on the territory of Bessarabia from the depositories of the Moldovan Intelligence and Security Service (SIS) to the Holocaust Memorial Museum in Washington, D. C. (in December 2003). Third, the changes in the position of the Romanian state authorities and historians towards the Holocaust on Romanian-controlled territories had long-term consequences for the Moldovan context as well. The results of the work conducted by the Commission for the Study of the Holocaust in Romania (the "Elie Wiesel Commission") also had its impact. The official recognition of the responsibility of the Romanian state for the crimes committed against the Jewish community by the Antonescu regime on its wartime territory (including Bessarabia) played an especially significant role in this respect.

At the same time, the majority among Moldovan historians refused to accept the new perspective on the Holocaust, mostly because this topic was obviously "uncomfortable" for the national narrative. As Vladimir Solonari, one of the first Moldovan authors dealing with this subject, astutely remarked, the experience of the Holocaust did not fit either the nationalist or the Communist historical "canon." However, for "Romanianist" historians the subject of the Holocaust was even more unpalatable, since they often based their judgments and conclusions on radical and marginal elements within the Romanian academic or even pseudo-scholarly circles. From another angle, the PCRM ideologists fully exploited this "vulnerability" of their political opponents and skillfully used the issue of the Holocaust in order to discredit their adversaries. One of the most active militants on this "ideological front" is the historian Sergiu Nazaria, closely associated with the PCRM. The problem of the Holocaust in Bessarabia thus became an object of the "memory wars" between the "Romanianists" and "Moldovanists." The politicization of the historical discourse and the historians' involvement into these antagonistic nation-building projects seriously undermines the scholarly investigations in this field. Any research results become, almost inevitably, targets of political controversy or ideological manipulation.[24]

Thus, between 1994 and 2009 a peculiar "duality of power" prevailed within the cultural and symbolic sphere of post-Soviet Moldova. In this sense, I fully endorse the conclusions of the German researcher Stefan Ihrig, the author of a recent monograph on the politics of identity, historiography and school textbooks in post-independence Moldova: "The 1994–2006 period can be described as a time, when the 'Romanianists' dominated the cultural institutions, although

---

[24] A detailed and balanced analysis of the "uses" and political manipulation of the Holocaust in post-Soviet Moldova can be found in Dumitru, "The Use and Abuse of the Holocaust," 49–73.

governmental power was practically concentrated in the hands of the 'Moldovanists.' During this period the 'Moldovanist' side repeatedly attempted to impose its ideological and political positions, but these attempts were met by a strong and, apparently, insurmountable resistance from the Romanian-oriented elites. Although the political power of the Romanianists, starting from 1994, was steadily declining, they nevertheless continued to further oppose and resist the policy of the government through the mobilization of the masses around the issue of national identity. They also continued to spread their own vision of the nation through the educational system."[25]

The "Ghimpu Commission" or the "Historical Policy" of Anti-Communism

A completely new stage in the development of "historical policy" in Moldova was inaugurated after the early parliamentary elections of July 2009, when the PCRM lost its majority and a four-party center-right coalition came to power. Following the PCRM's defeat, the former opposition political parties created a broad parliamentary coalition—the "Alliance for European Integration"—which controlled 53 out of the 101 parliamentary seats. The leader of the nationalist Liberal Party (LP), Mihai Ghimpu, was elected parliamentary chairman. His party was the second largest coalition partner (with 15 seats). Vlad Filat, the head of the largest party in the coalition—the Liberal Democrats (PLDM) (with 18 seats)—became Prime Minister, while Marian Lupu, the chairman of the third member of the coalition—the Democratic Party (PD)—was to become the new President of the Republic.

After Voronin's resignation in September, Ghimpu assumed the interim presidency, according to the constitution, while keeping his earlier position of Chairman of Parliament. It was assumed that this situation would be temporary and limited to a transitional period. However, following several attempts to elect a president in November and December 2009, the coalition failed to secure the necessary 61 votes for its presidential candidate. A political stalemate ensued,

---

[25] Ihrig, *Wer sind die Moldawier?* 63–64

allowing Ghimpu to continue as acting President for almost a year and a half.

Moldova was very slow to move towards confronting its Communist past since proclaiming its independence twenty years ago. Although some initial legal redress for the victims of Soviet-era "repressions" was undertaken during the early 1990s, when the interest for reclaiming the "suppressed" memory of the Communist regime was high on the public agenda, no political action followed. Politicians were either avoiding "sensitive issues" due to their association with the former regime or citing low public interest to justify their reluctance to effectively engage with the Communist past. The political stalemate was matched by a clear lack of interest and apathy of the public. Demand for open access to the files of the secret police was almost non-existent, aside from the occasional private initiatives and low-intensity lobbying promoted by victims' groups or professional associations (notably, the National Association of Historians). After the changes in the political balance of power, major shifts in the sphere of the "politics of memory" occurred. Some of the coalition partners (especially the right-wing nationalist Liberal Party, PL, led by Mihai Ghimpu and Chisinau Mayor Dorin Chirtoacă) were longtime advocates of an active and decisive "politics of memory," including a complete symbolic break with the Communist legacy.

However, the political landscape remained very fragmented. The coalition had a fragile parliamentary majority, which was divided over its attitude towards the former regime and the extent to which any "transitional justice" initiatives were at all desirable, given the tense political situation in Moldova. The centrist Democratic Party (PD), led by former parliamentary chairman Marian Lupu, who only left PCRM in June 2009, was particularly reluctant to support any initiatives in this regard, insisting on a policy of "national reconciliation" through "amnesia." Given the lack of political consensus, but with the open support of a part of the governing coalition, a group of Moldovan historians launched the initiative to create a "Commission for the Study and Evaluation of the Communist Totalitarian Regime in Moldova." The authors of this idea were inspired by the relative success of similar endeavors in other East European countries (e.g., Romania and the Baltic States) and suggested to apply this experience in the Moldovan context.

This initiative was supported by the PL leader and Moldova's acting president, Mihai Ghimpu, who agreed to place the new institution under the aegis of the Presidency (a clear analogy to the Romanian case). He also (rightly) anticipated that this project would not be endorsed if submitted to Parliament. The obvious interest of the Liberal Party leader in "historical policy" can also be explained by the fact that his status as Acting President inevitably undermined his political legitimacy. However, counting on the support of only 15 members of parliament, Ghimpu's party had a limited influence on effective government policy. As a result, a peculiar "division of labor" emerged within the coalition: M. Ghimpu began to actively promote radical initiatives in the sphere of the "politics of memory" and foreign policy (mostly on the rhetorical level), while the center-right Liberal-Democratic Party (PLDM), headed by Prime Minister Vlad Filat, and particularly the Democratic Party, assumed a more pragmatic stance within the governing alliance. In other words, Ghimpu aimed at using his limited "administrative resources" in the field of "historical policy," thus responding to the expectations of the nationalist-minded electorate who had supported the Liberal Party and attempting to formulate his independent, often openly anti-Russian, foreign policy agenda.

In this respect, the comparison between the policies pursued by Mihai Ghimpu and the former Ukrainian President Viktor Yushchenko is revealing. Although Ghimpu possessed a much weaker political legitimacy than Yushchenko (at least initially), having less space for effective political action, similar tendencies can be identified in the two cases. Both politicians concentrated their efforts in the sphere of the "politics of memory" and stood on a platform of radical anti-Communism. In Moldova the creation of the commission was, on the whole, supported by the largest party of the coalition—the Liberal Democrats. At the same time, the DP had a prudent, even skeptical, position with regard to this project. The PCRM, now in opposition, strongly criticized both the aims and the essence of the prospective Commission, viewing this idea as a tool of its ideological foes in the future political struggle.

The Commission was established by a special decree of President Ghimpu on January 14, 2010. Its mandate was initially limited to a six-month period, expiring on July 1, 2010. In its preamble, the decree referred to the founding acts of Moldovan statehood—the Declaration of Sovereignty, adopted on June 23, 1990, and the Declaration of Independence of August 27, 1991—which "signified for the Republic of Moldova not only the removal of the Communist totalitarian regime, but also a chance for the construction of a democratic society." The document strongly emphasized the need to establish "the truth concerning the totalitarian Communist regime" and to inform the public "objectively and multilaterally" about its essence. It appealed to two potential precedents in international law: Resolution 1096 (1996) of the Parliamentary Assembly of the Council of Europe on measures to dismantle the heritage of the former Communist totalitarian systems, and Resolution 1481 (2006) on the need for international condemnation of the crimes of totalitarian Communist regimes. No details were provided on the chronological framework and the concrete aspects of the former regime's "activities" to be investigated. This vagueness later resulted in controversies over the Commission's mandate, mission and recommendations. The institution was conceived as a "truth commission," but its relationship to the state authorities was loosely defined: the decree stated only that "the ministries and the other central and local administrative authorities will provide the Commission will all necessary assistance."

The Commission's mandate, as defined in the decree issued on January 14, 2010, was limited to "truth revelation." The new institution had the following goals: "to study the documents and materials concerning the activity of the main institutions involved in the establishment and perpetuation of the Communist totalitarian regime" while assessing its atrocities and human rights abuses; "to inform the public, periodically, on its activity" and results; to draft "a study, a collection of documents, and an analytical report regarding the historical and political-legal evaluation of the Communist totalitarian regime;" to submit "recommendations" to the President of the Republic until June 1, 2010. A general provision also allowed the creation of subcommittees ("working groups") within the institution. The Commission was supposed to formulate policy proposals that would eventually lead to political and legal consequences, but was not granted any effective instruments to promote their enforcement.

The Commission included thirty members, being one of the largest institutions of its kind in the region. Of its overall membership, two-thirds were academic historians; the other ten members were divided between three lawyers/legal scholars, two political scientists, a linguist, a sociologist, a philosopher, an economist, and a prominent writer (the only person without an academic background). The leadership of the Commission consisted exclusively of historians. It was headed by Gheorghe Cojocaru, an expert in 20th century history, who was close to the Liberal Party leadership by his political views and orientation. One should emphasize the uncertain institutional status of the Commission. This uncertainty was enhanced by the absence of a permanent headquarters and by the lack of state funding. While the latter feature increased the Commission's potential autonomy vis-à-vis the authorities, it also deprived it of an effective organizational framework. The work format of the Commission was based on monthly general ("plenary") sessions and on smaller working meetings, held in subcommittees twice a month.

Most of the Commission's members were not directly affiliated with political parties, but shared a broad political agenda and consensus on the necessity of a radical break with the Communist past. This often led to (partially justified) accusations that "anti-Communism" was the main driving force behind the whole project. The Commission's members were frequently accused of serving the interests of the governing "liberal" parties or of pursuing a "slander campaign" against the Communist opposition under the guise of academic objectivity. The Commission was vulnerable to criticism on two main grounds. First, its critics invoked a lack of transparency in the members' selection and appointment. Second, no representatives of the political opposition or of ethnic minorities were included in the Commission, which undermined the institution's claim of representing a broad segment of "civil society" and lent some substance to allegations of its role as a "political instrument." Another debatable point was the exclusively "national" composition of the institution: no international experts were invited to participate in its proceedings. Although the involvement of such experts in an advisory capacity was considered, it was rejected due to considerations of lack of time and political expediency. Some critics pointed to the biased and "narrow" nature of its historical perspective on Communism.

Public interest in the Commission ebbed and flowed according to the political situation and the immediate concerns of the local actors. The Commission's leadership (entitled to represent the institution in its dealings with the authorities and the public) launched a vigorous press and PR campaign, which reached its apex during the late winter and spring of 2010. This resulted in a series of regular press conferences, interviews, round tables and TV shows which increased the Commission's visibility and impact in the local media. The first press conference of the Commission on January 18 was immediately followed by a strongly worded reply from the Communist leader, Vladimir Voronin, who called the whole project a "stupidity" and a "heresy," viewing the intention of condemning the Communist regime as a "slap on the face of those who fought against Fascism." This was followed by a concerted attack in the PCRM-affiliated press (coordinated by the party's chief ideologist, Mark Tkachuk) against a number of the Commission's members (mostly senior historians, including the chairman, Gheorghe Cojocaru). They were accused of having actively collaborated with the former regime and of lacking any credibility as "moral judges" or neutral investigators of the Communist past. Finally, the PCRM attacks culminated with Voronin's demand (in May 2010) to abolish the Commission, as a first step towards future political negotiations with the authorities for solving the political crisis. Throughout, the Communists insisted that the real aim of the Commission was to "eliminate the PCRM from the political arena." This suspicion stemmed from the initial confusion regarding the period to be covered by the final report. Although initially the Commission's members insisted that the sphere of their interests would be limited to the 1917–1991 period, they later declared that the post-Soviet period will also be subjected to analysis from the point of view of the "legacy of the Communist regime." The results of this analysis were to be reflected in the Commission's final report.

Another attack came from a "fringe" party representing a part of the Russian-speaking population (the "Ravnopravie" movement). The leaders of this organization formed an alliance with several historians close to the PCRM and launched the initiative of creating an "alternative" Commission. This body would investigate the activities of both the Communist and Antonescu regimes in Moldova, positing itself as a reaction to the official Commission and including representatives of the ethnic minorities and (unnamed) international experts. Though nothing came of this, it is symptomatic for the initial mobilization of the public sphere. Also, certain publications of the "Ghimpu Commission's" ideological opponents (for example, of the historian and political scientist S. Nazaria) illustrate the rather intensive debates concerning the "correct" version of "historical policy" and of the depth of the antagonisms persisting within Moldovan society.

Finally, the Commission was also criticized "from the right." The most outspoken position belonged to the leader of the right-wing nationalist National Liberal Party (PNL), Vitalia Pavlicenco, who supports the total ban of Communist symbols from the public space. The PNL accused the Commission, in a series of articles, of harboring a "dissident faction" mostly consisting of "Western-educated" young researchers. This purported "faction" was accused of undermining the "national" and anti-Communist message of the project and of operating as a kind of "fifth column" subservient to (unidentified) "cosmopolitan interests" and corrupted by Western "revisionist" historical trends. This reflected, to an extent, the existence of internal debates and disagreements within the Commission, but also the unfulfilled expectations of a certain radically-inclined part of the public related to the outcomes of the institution's activity. These expectations concerned a series of decisive measures, including: 1) the immediate ban of all Communist-related symbols, including the elimination of the PCRM from the political scene as a legal successor of the Soviet regime; 2) a restrictive and sweeping "Lustration Law;" 3) the complete opening of the former KGB archives and of other archival holdings belonging to Soviet institutions, with the subsequent disclosure of the persons having collaborated with the KGB and their legal prosecution; 4) the discussion of the issue of "material compensation for the damages caused by the Soviet occupation" (analogous to similar debates taking place in the Baltic countries).

However, the direct political consequences of the Commission's work proved to be minimal and were generally not followed by concrete actions. This outcome was to be anticipated, given the unfavorable political conjuncture and the growing discord and controversy among the Moldovan political elite. Given the limited duration of the Commission's mandate and its scarce resources, its main achievements were related to the gradual broadening of the access to previously unavailable archival files (including those of the secret police). Its members benefited from some government assistance (e.g., through the special committee on de-classifying official documents), and they were granted access to previously restricted departmental archives (e.g., the Archive of the Ministry for Internal Affairs, the Archive of the Prosecutor General's Office and the former NKVD/KGB Archive, now hosted by the Intelligence and Security Service, SIS). The access to the relevant documentary collections of the specialized historical archives was significantly improved (although problems persisted). A second dimension of the Commission's activity concerned the organization of public events for the dissemination of its findings. Several symposia and scholarly conferences were organized (with the participation of international experts). The intermediary results of the Commission's research were made public on this occasion. Possibilities of institutional consolidation were also discussed with foreign colleagues.

Starting from late spring of 2010, the political climate in Moldova became less congenial for the Commission's activity, while the political pressures increased. This became obvious as the deadline for the submission of the "analytical report" and the related policy recommendations approached. The initial vagueness of the Commission's tasks (conflating the academic and policy dimensions, while depriving it of any effective legal tools and financial resources) led to serious limitations placed upon its effectiveness. These weaknesses were aggravated by the short period of its operation (barely four months).

In the closing stages of the preparation of the final report, serious internal disagreements emerged among its members. A group of younger academics with a "Western" educational background advocated a more "neutral" and scholarly-oriented report, without obvious value judgments and focusing on the concrete cases of the Soviet regime's human rights abuses. A more militant faction, supported by the majority of the Commission's members and its chairman, Gheorghe Cojocaru, insisted on a radical anti-Communist message and on wide-ranging and comprehensive policy proposals. This controversy resulted in the postponement of the publication of the full report and the drafting of a short (sixteen-page) "analytical report" summarizing the main "crimes, horrors, atrocities, abuses, and injustices" of the Communist regime and advancing several recommendations for the state authorities. This text amounted to a barely veiled accusatory act against the Soviet past. The Commission also elaborated several "policy recommendations" that are an excellent illustration of its version of "historical policy." These included the following points: 1) the condemnation of the "Communist totalitarian" regime in Moldova for crimes against humanity, followed by a "moral condemnation" of their perpetrators; 2) the ban on the use of the term "Communist" for political parties and institutions, as well as the elimination of all Communist and Nazi symbols from the public sphere; 3) the urgent drafting and adoption of the Lustration Law; 4) the complete legal, moral and material rehabilitation of the regime's victims and their descendants; 5) the creation of memorial complexes and museums for the commemoration of the regime's atrocities; 6) the introduction of special "days of mourning" commemorating the regime's victims and the traumatic pages of the country's history under Soviet rule (deportations etc.); 7) the creation of a special group of experts for the evaluation of the material damage caused by the former regime; 8) the transformation of the former Party Archive into the Archive of the Communist Totalitarian Regime in Moldova, with the transfer of all relevant funds from the departmental archives to the new depository; 9) the creation of an Institute for the Study of Totalitarianism and the elaboration of a school textbook and courses on the history of Communism; 10) the organization of special debates on the "inhuman essence of the totalitarian (Communist and Nazi) regimes" in the mass media etc.

This report was submitted to the acting President in late May 2010. It is deeply biased and bears the imprint of politically motivated urgency. Moreover, according to credible sources, the report was personally edited and approved by the President. This fact completely undermined both the political autonomy and the academic status of the Commission.

Despite the wide-ranging and radical nature of the proposals, no effective political action to implement them followed. By the early summer of 2010 the differences within the governing coalition regarding the best course of a state-sponsored "historical policy" reached their culmination. The PD openly expressed its dissatisfaction with the Commission's recommendations, stating that the latter would lead to "splits in society and growing political tension" and rejecting some of them as unfeasible. This concerned, first of all, the projected Lustration Law and the potential ban of the Communist-inspired symbols in the public sphere. The Commission's report was to be discussed in a special Parliament meeting in late June or early July of 2010. However, no consensus on a common position of the governing coalition could be reached. As a result of the stalemate, the two scheduled special parliamentary sessions were cancelled, and the vote on the

Commission's report was postponed "indefinitely." The Democratic Party proposed to renew the discussion and examination of this document after the next round of parliamentary elections, scheduled for November 28, 2010. The uncertain political situation and the unpredictable outcome of the November 2010 elections discouraged the political actors from addressing the issue of "transitional justice."

The same factors contributed to the ultimate failure of the Liberal Party's and Mihai Ghimpu's ambitious plans for the elaboration of a full-fledged "historical policy," founded on a radically anti-Communist platform. At the same time, Ghimpu did not abandon his intentions to actively use the "politics of memory" as a tool in the internal political struggle. In accord with one of the Commission's recommendations, on June 24, 2010, he issued a presidential decree proclaiming June 28 as "the day of [the commemoration of] Soviet occupation" and including this date in the "pantheon of national memory."[26] This decision not only provoked a painful and angry reaction from the part of the Russian officials and of certain Moldovan political forces (the PCRM, in particular), but was negatively perceived even by the other parties of the governing alliance. Mihai Ghimpu himself admitted that this decision was his personal political initiative and did not receive the support and endorsement of the other members of the coalition. As a result of the PCRM's official inquiry filed with the Constitutional Court, the decree was declared unconstitutional and abolished.

The only concrete consequence of this decree was represented by the "memorial stone" dedicated to the victims of the repressions of the Communist regime and the "Soviet occupation." This monument was erected on Chisinau's main square. Thus, the Liberal Party's attempts to "outmaneuver" its political opponents on the field of "historical policy" were far from successful.[27]

---

[26] On June 28, 1940, the Soviet troops entered Bessarabia according to the provisions of the ultimatum presented by the USSR to the Romanian government two days earlier.

[27] The results of the early parliamentary elections organized on November 28, 2010, showed that Ghimpu's activity in the sphere of "historical policy" did not bring him any political dividends. On the contrary, his party lost around five percent of its previous share of the vote and now has only 12 seats in the current Parliament (compared to 15 in the previous legislature).

However, the use and abuse of history for political purposes did not fade away or even decrease. Moldovan politicians (and most of the practicing historians) continue to perceive the historical discourse as a field for "symbolic competition." A vivid example of this tendency is another decree signed by acting President M. Ghimpu on December 21, 2010. This decree was issued after the November parliamentary elections, in circumstances of continuing political instability and crisis. According to the decree, a group of "historians" and "prominent scholarly figures" were awarded state decorations "as a sign of the high recognition of their special service in propagating historical truth and national values." The historians were also decorated for their "significant contribution to the development of the links between the academic and university communities and their fruitful didactic-methodical and scholarly activity."[28] The majority of the decorated historians are active supporters and advocates of the Romanian national version of Bessarabia's history and served as members of the Commission.[29] Thus, M. Ghimpu attempted to consolidate his role as the main promoter and initiator of a radical vision of "historical policy." However, according to a number of political commentators and even to some of the Liberal Party's partners in the governing coalition, such a course is self-defeating and has no realistic long-term prospects in the current Moldovan context.

Although the Decree of January 14, 2010 is still valid (meaning that the Commission's period of activity has not officially expired), in fact it suspended its activity as a coherent institution in the late summer of 2010. The initial interest in its work, displayed by the media and a part of Moldovan society has all but faded. The effectiveness of the Commission's work was limited by several factors, including: the vagueness of its mandate; the short time span of its operation; the lack of effective legal tools (subpoena powers) and the absence of a corresponding legal framework; the limited political support for its work and the tendency of certain political forces to make it instrumental for their own purposes; the under-representation of the civil society and

---

[28] "Gimpu nagradil bessarabskih istorikov-rumynounionistov za 'propagandu istoricheskoi pravdy'." Available at http://regnum.ru/news/fd-abroad/moldova/1359038.html#ixzz18pczK7YL

[29] Ibid.

of certain social groups (victims' associations) and ethnic minorities within the Commission; the contradiction between the scholarly and political components of its activity.

However, it achieved several important breakthroughs in the Moldovan context, notably through the opening of previously inaccessible archival (including secret police) files and the growing public awareness of the nature and consequences of the former regime. Despite all this, the social impact of the Commission's activity was, on the whole, rather low. Thus, the broader aim of reaching "national reconciliation" through a coherent "historical policy" remains, at best, unrealistic and utopian.

Conclusion

To summarize, four main stages can be identified in the dynamics of the "politics of memory" and "historical policy" in post-Soviet Moldova:

1) 1990/91–1993: the "nationalization" of the public sphere, official symbolism and the educational system, defined by the dominance of the Romanian national narrative and by a number of attempts at a complete "symbolic break" with the Soviet past;
2) 1994–2000: the strengthening of the elements of "Moldovan nationalism" and a movement toward a partial compromise in the field of the "politics of memory" through "amnesia" and the rhetoric of national harmony;
3) 2001–2009: the PCRM's attempts to formulate a full-fledged "national ideology" of Moldovan statehood, featuring a radical (ethno-centric) version of "Moldovanism," a partial symbolic rehabilitation of the Soviet past and a strategy for fighting the "undesirable elements," which targeted the supporters of "pan-Romanianism;"
4) 2009–2010: a tendency toward a radical revision of the "politics of memory" in the direction of state-sponsored anti-Communism and the first steps toward the institutional consolidation of the model of "transitional justice" (the creation of the "Ghimpu Commission").

Despite the crucial role of the initial stage in the "nationalization" of the public sphere, one can hardly talk about a coordinated and state-articulated "historical policy" before the year 2001. The polarization of Moldovan society—and the ensuing ambiguity and contradictory character of the "politics of memory"—reached a particular intensity after the Party of Communists of the Republic of Moldova came to power. In this sense, both the PCRM's policy and the "anti-Communism" displayed by a part of the present Moldovan authorities perfectly fit the general tendency of the politicization of historical discourse apparent in many other East European countries. The specificity of the Moldovan (not fully crystallized) version of "historical policy" points to the complex interaction between issues of identity, "collective memory" and lack of the post-Soviet state's legitimacy in the Moldovan case.

BIBLIOGRAPHY

Cojocari, L. "'100 Grams for Victory!' or the Dilemmas of Collective Memory in the Republic of Moldova," *Caiete de Antropologie Istorică*, 2010, 51–58.
Dumitru, D. "The Use and Abuse of the Holocaust: Historiography and Politics in Moldova" *Holocaust and Genocide Studies* vol. 22, no. 1 (Spring 2008): 49–73.
Fruntașu, Iu. *O istorie etnopolitică a Basarabiei (1812–2002)*. Chișinău: Cartier, 2002.
Gonzalez-Enriquez, C. "De-Communization and Political Justice in Central and Eastern Europe" in *The Politics of Memory: Transitional Justice in Democratizing Societies* Barahona de Brito, A., Gonzalez-Enriquez, C., and Aguilar, P. eds. (Oxford: Oxford University Press, 2001), 218–247.
Heintz, M. ed. *Stat slab, cetățenie incertă: Studii despre Republica Moldova*. București: Curtea Veche, 2007.
Ihrig, S. *Wer sind die Moldawier? Rumänismus versus Moldowanismus in Historiographie und Schulbüchern der Republik Moldova, 1991–2006*. Stuttgart: Ibidem-Verlag, 2008.
Judt, T. "From the House of the Dead: An Essay on Modern European Memory" in *Postwar: A History of Europe since 1945*. New York: The Penguin Press, 2005.
King, C. *Moldovenii: România, Rusia și politica culturală*. Chișinău: ARC, 2002.
Maier, C.S. "Hot Memory... Cold Memory: On the Political Half-Life of Fascist and Communist Memory" *Transit- Virtuelles Forum* no. 22 (2002).
Memoriu al Asociației Istoricilor din Republica Moldova. In *În apărarea istoriei și demnității naționale* [In defence of history and national dignity]. Chișinău, 2003.

Stati, V. *Istoriia Moldovy*. Kishinev: IPF "Tsentral'naia tipografiia," 2002.
Stepaniuk, V. *Gosudarstvennost' moldavskogo naroda: istoricheskie, politicheskie i pravovye aspekty*. Kishinev: IPF "Tsentral'naia tipografiia," 2006.
Taki, V. and A. Cusco. "Kto my? Istoriograficheskii vybor: Rumynskaia natsiia ili moldavskaia gosudarstvennost'," in *Ab Imperio*, No. 1, (2003) 485–495.
Țurcanu, A. *Din poșta secretă a comuniștilor: Stepaniuc și Voronin, combătând românismul*. Chisinau: Timpul, 2010.
Winter, J. and E. Sivan, eds. *War and Remembrance in the Twentieth Century*. Cambrigde: Cambridge University Press, 1999.

Interventions: Challenging the Myths of Twentieth-Century Ukrainian History

JOHN-PAUL HIMKA

I was asked to reflect on my experiences as a challenger of nationalist historical myths, in this case, Ukrainian myths about traumatic aspects of the twentieth-century.[1] By myths here I mean unexamined components of an ideologized version of history, articles of faith more than of reason. In this essay, I will first try to explain my motivations for challenging such myths, even though I realized it would cause considerable discomfort both to my targeted audience and to me. Then I will describe and evaluate the strategies I chose for my interventions. This will be followed by a description of the backlash to my interventions, and of my reactions to it. Finally, I will say what I think has been achieved so far by my efforts to change thinking in the Ukrainian discursive sphere. But before proceeding to the body of this article, it is necessary to explain what myths I have been challenging.

One of the areas of contention is the interpretation of the great famine that racked Ukraine in 1932–1933. In the mythicized version, Stalin unleashed the famine deliberately in order to kill Ukrainians in mass and prevent them from achieving their aspirations to establish a nation state. I, however, point out that the precondition for the famine was the reckless collectivization drive, which almost destroyed

---

[1] This article grows out of research supported by the Social Sciences and Humanities Research Council of Canada; the Pinchas and Mark Wisen Fellowship at the Center for Advanced Holocaust Studies, United States Holocaust Memorial Museum; and the University of Alberta. I am grateful for detailed comments on an earlier from Dominique Arel, Myrna Kostash, and Per Anders Rudling; I did not follow all their suggestions, but their input did much to improve this text.

Soviet agriculture as a whole. I do not deny that the famine in Soviet Ukraine and in the Ukrainian-inhabited Kuban region of Soviet Russia was more intense than elsewhere in the Soviet Union, that its intensity resulted from particularly severe measures applied to Ukraine and Kuban, and that the severity was connected with a major offensive against perceived nationalism in the Communist party of Ukraine.

My somewhat more nuanced view is a problem for the mythologists, who want the world to recognize that the famine, or as they call it—the Holodomor—was a genocide as defined by the United Nations in 1948. This campaign became Ukrainian state policy during the presidency of Viktor Yushchenko (2005–10). Although I do think that what happened in Ukraine in 1932–1933 could fit under the capacious UN definition ("deliberately inflicting on the group conditions of life, calculated to bring about its physical destruction in whole or in part"), I oppose the campaign for recognition as genocide for a number of reasons.

The genocide argument is used to buttress the campaign to glorify the anti-Communist resistance of the Ukrainian nationalists during World War II. I do not think that Ukrainians who embrace the heritage of the wartime nationalists should be calling on the world to empathize with the victims of the famine if they are not able to empathize with the victims of the nationalists. I think, further, that there is something wrong with a campaign that finds its greatest resonance in the area of Ukraine where there was no famine, and in the overseas diaspora deriving from that region. I have problems with all the anger at Russians and Jews that gets wrapped up in the genocide campaign. And I also have problems with the UN definition itself, which excludes victims of social and political mass murder and has become a category for political manipulation (witness the international repercussions of whether what happened in Armenia and Darfur constitute proper genocides).[2]

---

[2] I presented my views more fully in "Problems with the Category of Genocide and with Classifying the Ukrainian Famine of 1932–1933 as a Genocide," paper presented to the Department of History, University of Winnipeg; Oseredok Ukrainian Cultural and Educational Centre; Department of German and Slavic Studies, University of Manitoba, Winnipeg, September 16, 2008; also in a Ukrainian version at the International Scientific Conference "Holodomor of 1932–1933 in Ukraine: Reasons, Demographic Consequences, Legal Treatment," Ukrainian Institute of National Memory and

I also have been critical of the use of inflated numbers for the tally of the famine's victims: President Yushchenko and his Ukrainian Institute of National Memory insisted it was ten million; overseas diaspora organizations have been using seven to ten million; individuals have made claims of "at least" ten or fifteen million victims. None of these figures can be justified by demographic data, so I (as well as the Institute of Demography and Social Research of the National Academy of Sciences of Ukraine) use the figure of 3.5 million for excess mortality in Ukraine in 1932–33. What galls the mythologists is that this number is less than the number usually used for the Jewish Holocaust, and having a number bigger than six million is important to them. I have also been active in exposing how this kind of competing victimology is used to justify the violence of radical Ukrainian nationalists during World War II.

My interest in the famine flowed out of my work on another moment in Ukraine's traumatic history, the second large theme of my interventions and challenges—the Holocaust. Often when I consider the famine, I do so from the perspective of comparative genocide studies, which is a field that began to interest me in connection with the Holocaust. The fundamental point of contention between the adherents of the national myth and me is whether or not the Organization of Ukrainian Nationalists (OUN) and its armed force, the Ukrainian Insurgent Army (UPA from its Ukrainian initials) participated in the Holocaust. They deny this entirely. My research indicates, however, that the participation was significant.

In the summer of 1941, as the Germans invaded Ukraine, militias connected with the OUN organized several massive pogroms against the Jewish population, notably in Lviv. The militias arrested and beat Jews, abused Jewish women, and rounded up Jews for the Germans to shoot. In many other localities in the regions of Bukovina, Galicia and Volhynia, the militias did not organize pogrom-like public spectacles, but arrested Jews (and some Communists and Poles) and either shot them themselves or handed them over to the German or Romanian authorities to shoot. Altogether in this phase, OUN was implicated in the murder of tens of thousands of Jews.

National Academy of Sciences of Ukraine, Kyiv, September 25–26, 2008. Neither the English nor Ukrainian text has been published.

After this wave of mass violence subsided, and the Germans began a more systematic liquidation of the Jewish population, OUN sent many of its members into the Ukrainian auxiliary police force in German service or to various *Schutzmannschaften*.[3] OUN did not do this in order to kill Jews—it had other reasons, but these Ukrainian police served as important implements of the Final Solution in Ukraine and Belarus, particularly in rounding up Jews for execution. In this way OUN members became involved in hundreds of thousands of murders.

Then in spring 1943 thousands of these Ukrainian policemen deserted their posts with their weapons and formed the nucleus of the OUN-led UPA. The preparation of such an action was among the reasons why OUN had sent its men into the police in the first place. UPA launched a massive ethnic cleansing action against the Polish population of Volhynia and later Galicia, in which perhaps a hundred thousand Poles perished. (The slaughter of the Poles is well documented, but the national mythologizers downplay it.) While killing Poles, the soldiers of UPA also routinely killed any Jewish survivors that they encountered. As the Red Army approached Volhynia in the winter of 1944, UPA and separate OUN security forces lured Jews out of hiding in the woods, then enrolled them in labor camps, and later killed them systematically. Overall, UPA killed at least thousands of Jews. The myth maintains that Jews served as doctors in UPA, and therefore UPA rescued, rather than killed, Jews. Defenders of the mythical history often circulate fabricated memoirs of a non-existent Jewish woman who served in UPA.

When I first began to intervene on the Holocaust issue, I did not know all that I have just laid out. It was only in the course of intensive research conducted between August 2008 and May 2010 that I understood the extent of OUN-UPA collaboration in the Holocaust. Particularly important was the fall of 2009, which I spent on a three-month fellowship at the United States Holocaust Memorial Museum.

In speaking of the views I oppose as mythologies, I do not always mean to make truth claims. Whether OUN organized pogroms and how many people perished in the famine are indeed about questions of fact; but whether the famine constituted a genocide is a matter of

---

[3] I benefited from reading the excellent, essentially unpublished research on the *Schutzmannschaften* by Per Anders Rudling.

interpretation; and whether one should campaign for its recognition as a genocide is rather a political and moral issue.

One of my critics from the mythologizing camp has done a good job of summing up where I fall afoul. The author, writing under a pseudonym, posted his short piece on an *Ukrains'ka pravda*[4] forum under the title "The Canadian Ukrainophobe, the Falsifier of History John-Paul Himka":

> The main theses of this 'historian,' who dreams of the fame of the Ukrainophobe Wiktor Poliszczuk:[5]
> —The Holodomor of 1931-1933 in Ukraine—this was an agricultural experiment and not a planned genocide or simply a crime of the Soviet regime against the Ukrainian nation
> —The Ukrainian militia created by OUN took part in mass in pogroms of the Jewish population, OUN-UPA killed Poles, Ukrainian nationalism is Fascism, etc.[6]

This gets my position on the famine wrong, but it is certainly the one the mythologizers attribute to me.

Motivations of Intervention

In small part, my decision to intervene on these issues is simply a result of my training as a historian. I am always thinking of interesting projects to work on next. Even as I am entering the writing stage of my work on Ukrainian nationalists and the Holocaust, I am thinking about what to undertake after that. I had already considered working on

---

[4] *Ukrains'ka pravda* is one of the national democratic online periodicals. It was founded by Heorhii Gongadze, who was subsequenly beheaded in murky circumstances. It is strongly "Orange" in its perspective.
[5] A well informed critic of OUN and UPA, but not a professional historian, Poliszczuk died in Toronto in 2008. He is best known for his book *Bitter Truth*, which exists in several languages, including English.
[6] Slavw, "Kanads'kyi ukrainofob, fal'syfikator istorii Dzhon-Pol Khymka," http://forum.pravda.com.ua/read.php?10,209135993,209135993 (accessed October 6, 2010). The posting uses emoticons holding signs saying *Han'ba*, i.e., "shame on you."

the Holocaust in Ukraine in the mid-1990s, after I had finished three monographs on the history of Galicia in the nineteenth century, but instead I started work on a book about the Last Judgment in Ukrainian culture. When I rejected the Holocaust topic in the mid-1990s, I had thought that it was neither challenging nor particularly important. (My views have since, of course, changed.) But once chosen, the topic was submitted to the usual disciplinary procedures, which include researching in primary sources and rethinking in relation to existing research. The tremendous gulf between what the sources told me and the common wisdom in Ukrainian discourse was something I had never encountered before in my professional career. I was also struck by the complete absence of literature on the topic written from within the field of Ukrainian studies. As I worked, I more and more came to the conclusion that here was a moment where a revisionist treatment was not only appropriate, but obligatory.

As I worked, I released bits of my research, and became the object of criticism and even vilification. Upset, I kept returning in my mind to the same basic idea: that the truth is a value in and of itself. No matter what we would like to believe about something, we are obliged to uncover the truth. I could formulate this point in other ways. Perhaps following Pierre Nora and Tony Judt, I could write about how history is an important antidote to memory. But I will stick to the idea of getting at the truth. It has never ceased to astound me in the course of all the debates in which I have engaged, that so few people seem to be interested in that. My arguments are rejected out of hand, without a serious and honest confrontation with them or with the sources on which they rest. My opponents in debate seem to be interested in defending a certain position, not in figuring out what happened, as historians are supposed to do. When I took up this project seriously in 2008, I had no idea about the OUN militias in summer 1941 and I doubted that UPA killed Jews or thought that it did so only exceptionally.[7] I made my discoveries with very mixed feelings. I did not like what I was finding out. On the other hand, I had that satisfaction that a professional historian obtains when solving a difficult problem.

---

[7] See, for comparison, an earlier piece I wrote: Himka, "Ukrainian Collaboration in the Extermination of the Jews during the Second World War."

What actually provoked my quest to investigate what happened was my correspondence with a dear friend, the late Janusz Radziejowski.[8] In 1988 we had an argument by mail over UPA. At that time my research concentrated on the nineteenth century, and with regard to the twentieth century, I simply assimilated the basic view prevalent in my milieu. That milieu was the Ukrainian-Canadian anti-Soviet left associated with the journal *Diialoh* (its motto was "for socialism and democracy in an independent Ukraine"). Our position was that UPA started out as a narrowly nationalist force but very quickly, as a result of contacts with the Ukrainian masses, evolved into a democratic and anticolonialist army. We considered the murder of the Poles, which we condemned, both an aberration and a result of what was essentially a mutual rather than one-sided conflict. It pains me to recall how dogmatic we were, but this is the truth. For my part, I honestly believed that it was a great tragedy for the Jews that UPA became a formidable fighting force so late, i.e., mid-1943, by which time most Jews in Ukraine had already been murdered. If it had appeared earlier, UPA would have saved the Jews. As I say, it pains me to recall these views.

It was Radziejowski who began to point out all their problems. Although I marshaled my paltry counterarguments in response, I decided that I would look into the issue myself. The mid-1980s had already roused my curiosity; this was a time when Ukrainians in North America were fending off accusations of war criminals in their midst (this was the time of the John Demjanjuk trial and of the Deschênes Commission).[9] Though aware of them, I had not taken part in these disputes. But in the aftermath of the interchange with Radziejowski, I conducted original research. Almost immediately afterwards I began to explore the issue in the revealing archives of my late father-in-law, who had edited a Ukrainian newspaper during the German occupation. Later, in 1995, I worked in Yad Vashem in Jerusalem and YIVO in New York. I had not yet arrived at the knowledge that I was to acquire in 2008–10, but I had certainly abandoned the viewpoint I had

---

[8] On Radziejowski, see Himka, "In Memoriam: Janusz Radziejowski (1925–2002)."
[9] Officially known as the Commission of Inquiry on War Criminals in Canada, the Deschênes Commission was active in 1985 and 1986. Its terms of reference can be found in Boshyk, ed., *Ukraine during World War II*, 261–62.

held shortly before. Reading and reviewing Dieter Pohl's pathbreaking monograph on the Holocaust in Galicia[10] was also important in the development of my thinking.

Heightening my interest in the topic, because of the intellectual challenge it posed, was the extreme polarization of memory between Ukrainians and Jews. How could their views on what happened be so strikingly different? Protestations of total innocence on one side were contradicted by deep resentments for complicity on the other. Indeed, some Jews felt that the Ukrainians were simply "the worst."[11] It was a puzzle for me, one that I feel I eventually worked out in its essentials;[12] it whetted my curiosity and drove my quest to find out what actually happened and thus make sense of the disparities.

My research and thinking also awakened a moral sense about this topic, something that was not so prominent in my earlier studies. I wrote a piece in 2003 that raised the issue of how Ukrainian-diaspora discourse could be so complacent and reticent about UPA's murder of the Poles and the Ukrainian police's well documented role in the Holocaust.[13] To me, this nonchalance seemed wrong. Omer Bartov's work[14] and especially Sofia Grachova's powerful piece in *Krytyka*,[15] which strives to be the Ukrainian equivalent of the *New York Review of Books*, drew my attention to what was going on in Ukraine, and for that matter in the diaspora: on the one hand, OUN and UPA were being glorified, and on the other, the history of Ukrainian Jews in the Holocaust was being suppressed. This too, seemed to me very wrong. What crystallized my moral thinking was my reading early in 2008 of

---

[10] Pohl, *Nationalsozialistische Judenverfolgung in Ostgalizien 1941–1944*.
[11] Mendelsohn, *The Lost*, 100, 116. Mendelsohn himself handles the issue of Ukrainian behavior during the Holocaust with great sensitivity. See my discussion, "How to Think about Difficult Things: Daniel Mendelsohn's *The Lost*," forthcoming in *Harvard Ukrainian Studies*.
[12] Himka, *Ukrainians, Jews and the Holocaust*. This is the text of the 2009 Mohyla Lecture sponsored by the Prairie Centre for the Study of Ukrainian Heritage, St. Thomas More College, University of Saskatchewan. I am grateful to Bohdan Kordan for inviting me.
[13] Himka, "War Criminality: A Blank Spot in the Collective Memory of the Ukrainian Diaspora."
[14] See Bartov, *Erased: Vanishing Traces of Jewish Galicia in Present-Day Ukraine*.
[15] Hrachova, "Vony zhyly sered nas?" See also another very moving contribution to the discussion: Carynnyk, "Zolochiv movchyt'."

Eva Hoffman's *After Such Knowledge*.¹⁶ It clarified my thinking enough that I could formulate my position with precision: The crimes committed by Ukrainian nationalists against Jews and Poles during the Second World War were horrible. They cannot be undone, and all that later Ukrainians can do about them is to admit that they happened and to regret them. It is not enough, but it is all that is possible. Certainly they cannot glorify the people who committed them. The moral charge that developed in my interventions has irritated my colleagues in Ukrainian studies who support the nationalist mythologies.¹⁷

Another major spur to my activities as a gadfly was the *Geschichtspolitik* of President Yushchenko in Ukraine. In June 2007 he officially celebrated the centenary of the birth of UPA commander Roman Shukhevych. Shortly thereafter the Ukrainian post office issued a stamp in Shukhevych's honor that bore the emblems of both OUN and UPA. Not much later Yushchenko named Shukhevych a posthumous Hero of Ukraine. At the same time he was honoring Shukhevych, Yushchenko promoted the cult of Yaroslav Stetsko, who headed the shortlived and violent Ukrainian government proclaimed in summer 1941.¹⁸ Shortly before leaving office in early 2010, Yushchenko also made Stepan Bandera, the leader of the radical wing of OUN that was the chief Ukrainian perpetrator during the Holocaust and ethnic cleansing actions, a posthumous Hero of Ukraine. A few days later, he called on municipalities to name schools, streets, and squares after the heroes of OUN-UPA. Almost immediately afterwards, the Ukrainian Canadian Congress (UCC) appealed to the government of Canada to recognize veterans of OUN-UPA as members of the resistance during World War II and to pay them veterans' benefits. In these same years Yushchenko also pursued his campaign to have every country recognize the famine of 1932–33 as a genocide, while simultaneously suppressing the history of the other genocide, the Holocaust. He used the Security Service of Ukraine (SBU) to pur-

---

¹⁶ Hoffman, *After Such Knowledge*.
¹⁷ Zenon Kohut referred to my "partisan moralizing" and Roman Serbyn to my "flippant moralizing." *The Ukraine List (UKL)*, No. 441 (February 16, 2010). 15, 41.
¹⁸ The official decree was issued May 16, 2007 and is on the presidential website, http://www.president.gov.ua/documents/6145.html.

sue his historico-political agenda. The SBU produced two deceptions, one that whitewashed the history of OUN vis-à-vis the pogroms and another that blamed Jews disproportionately for the Holodomor.[19] Someone had to say something about this, and I felt well positioned to do so. The most heated debate came after Yushchenko made Bandera a Hero of Ukraine and the UCC effectively tried to put OUN-UPA at the base of Ukrainian identity in Canada. With regard to these matters I and some close colleagues at the University of Alberta, David Marples and Per Anders Rudling, began to protest more vociferously.

The last motivation that I will mention is also connected to Yushchenko and his historical policies. Ukraine has a divided memory about both the Holodomor and OUN-UPA. Simply put, the West of Ukraine puts OUN-UPA at the center of its heroic narrative of World War II, while the East and South put the Red Army at the center. Western Ukraine is also more convinced that the famine was a genocide than the rest of Ukraine, even though Western Ukraine was not part of the Soviet Union when the famine occurred. Ukraine's first president, Leonid Kravchuk (1991–94), deftly avoided alienating either regional perspective, while his successor, Leonid Kuchma (1994–2005), sometimes played one identity project off against the other. President Yushchenko, however, embraced entirely what one of my colleagues nicknamed the "OUN-UPA-Holodomor" identity and pushed it vigorously on the Ukrainian public. He was massively defeated in the 2010 presidential election and replaced by a man, Viktor Yanukovych, who pushes the opposite perspective. Yanukovych's government downplays the Holodomor (now identified as a tragedy, not a genocide) and excoriates OUN and UPA. In my view, this historical-identity war has been very harmful to Ukraine. Politicians find it all too attractive to mobilize the population with historical symbols, but they thereby drive the wedge in deeper between regions and between perspectives. It is always easier to deliver symbols than decent health care or affordable homes. I consider the desconstruction of the historical mythologies of both camps to be more than a healthy exercise; rather, it is the precribed medicine for Ukrainian political discourse.

---

[19] On these issues, see Rybakov, "Marko Tsarynnyk," and Himka, "The Holodomor in the Ukrainian-Jewish Encounter Initiative."

Strategies

I have made my interventions in forms appropriate to both a scholar (a monograph in progress, articles in scholarly journals, book reviews, conference presentations) and to a public intellectual (opinion pieces, letters to the editor, open letters). Here I will assess some of the pluses and minuses of these genres.

There are several problems with the scholarly forms. One is that they are very slow. It takes a long time to research and write a monograph, at least in my case. I started serious research on my first book in 1974, and my last book was published in 2009, so it took me thirty-five years to write four monographs. The pace of scholarly publication, not just production, is slow. A major article on the Holocaust I wrote in 2004 has still not been published, although it has been accepted for a long time. One way I have attempted to overcome this problem is to let some of my texts circulate in digital form.

The other major problem with scholarly forms is that they have a small readership. It is hard to make a dent on public opinion when one writes in the antiquated form of a twenty-five page, footnoted article in a professional journal that is purchased primarily by major research libraries. If the topic is of interest to a wider audience, however, pdfs of scholarly articles can circulate more widely. The third problem is that scholarly forms take effort and time to read. Today's reader prefers shorter, simpler pieces; op-eds are the perfect size and at the perfect level for addressing the public.

I discovered the power of short pieces delivered via internet in 2004, on the eve of the Orange Revolution in Ukraine. I reacted to what I thought was hysterical and sometimes xenophobic rhetoric on the part of the partisans of Yushchenko, then a presidential candidate, and sent around to various lists and colleagues an eleven-hundred-word text dissenting from the prevailing view.[20] Soon everyone I knew had read it, and many more whom I did not know, in Ukraine as well as in the overseas diaspora to whom I actually addressed my text. An open letter distributed by email and the internet proved to be an

---

[20] Himka, "Apocalypse Tomorrow."

extraordinarily effective way to communicate with a large audience in a timely fashion. No normal scholarly venue could have accomplished what a short text on the internet could.

After this lesson, I was able to intervene in a similar fashion when a diaspora filmmaker was making an offensive movie about the Holodomor,[21] when Yushchenko's SBU was deceiving the public about OUN and the pogroms,[22] and particularly when Yushchenko made Bandera and OUN-UPA into heroes, while the UCC endorsed this on behalf of a community of which I consider myself a member.[23]

But there are disadvantages to short, instant response. One is that instant is sloppier. For example, in one piece I accidentally referred to Taras Bulba-Borovets as the founder of OUN, although I know perfectly well that he was not; I meant to write that he was the original founder of UPA. One of my nationalists critics, a former president of the Ukrainian World Congress, Askold Lozynskyj, caught me out and accused me of incompetent scholarship.[24] I replied to him instantly, admitting to my error and pointing out that in his response to me he had confused the person of Mykhailo Kolodzinsky with an UPA unit named after him.[25] In this reply, I noticed too late, I had slightly misdescribed one photograph, but Lozynskyj did not catch it. He replied once again, however, and this time incorrectly dated the Lviv pogrom

---

[21] Himka, "How Many Perished in the Famine and Why Does It Matter?" Versions of this also appeared online in UNIAN (a Ukrainian news agency), *The Ukraine List*, and *Kyiv Post*; in Ukrainian translation in *Liva sprava* and *Ukrains'ka pravda*; and in Russian translation in *My – Mankurty*.

[22] Himka, "True and False Lessons from the Nachtigall Episode" and Himka, "Be Wary of Faulty Nachtigall Lessons."

[23] The most important text of mine was a debate I had with Zenon Kohut. I did not send it out for publication at all, but just emailed it to colleagues. It was then "virally" circulated. Soon it was picked up by *The Ukraine List*, a Ukrainian translation has appeared in *Krytyka*, another Ukrainian translation is to be published in a volume edited by Yaroslav Hrytsak and Tarik Cyril Amar, and a Russian translation is forthcoming in *Zhurnal rossiiskikh i vostochnoevropeiskikh istoricheskikh issledovanii* no. 2 (2010).

[24] Lozynskyj, "History Should Be Written by Objective and Competent Scholars."

[25] Himka, "The Lviv Pogrom."

to 1942 instead of to 1941.²⁶ I contrast this quick repartee, with its recurring errors, to the slow interchange in scholarship. That article that I have not published since 2004 has been rewritten three or four times, and a number of sets of careful eyes have gone over it. My last monograph took three years to go from my finished draft to publication. In that time, I had to respond twice to the comments of very careful reviewers. I did not like it that the appearance of my book was being delayed, but I must admit that it is a much better book as a result.

Short, like instant, is also problematic, because history is complex and a short text often has to oversimplify. Short texts are best at throwing monkey wrenches into the spokes of larger narratives or myths, but they are not good for articulating a sustained argument of any complexity. Something always has to give. In an article on the Lviv pogrom that I published as an opinion piece in *Kyiv Post*,²⁷ I distilled from my book in progress the main sources that document the role of OUN militiamen in the violence. Although I was able to show the variety of sources and what they indicated, I could not, given the genre, provide the archival or bibliographic citations or explain how to assess the veracity and usefulness of various kinds of sources. So ultimately, it will be the book that will make the full argument. Moreover, another problem with short and instant pieces is that they sharpen the debate too much, which can constitute an impediment to thoughtful work.

My former doctoral student Grzegorz Rossolinski-Liebe argued that it was premature to engage in polemics with nationalist myths. First, he said, we must publish all our research findings. I agree that this would have been the ideal way to proceed, although I have published some scholarly studies already²⁸ and other scholars have been coming to conclusions very similar to mine.²⁹ If we had left the myth-making unchallenged—Yushchenko's heroization of Shukhevych, Stetsko, Bandera, and OUN, seconded by the UCC; the promotion of

---

26 Lozynskyj, "Where's the Evidence of Ukrainian Wartime Atrocities against the Jews?"
27 Himka, "The Lviv Pogrom."
28 Notably Himka, *Ukrainians, Jews and the Holocaust*; Himka, "Dostovirnist' svidchennia;" and Himka and Kurylo, "Iak OUN stavylasia do ievreiv?"
29 For example, Bruder, *Den ukrainischen Staat erkämpfen oder sterben!* and Dietsch, *Making Sense of Suffering*.

the famine as a genocide; the falsifications regarding the Jews as perpetrators and OUN-UPA as innocents—then the nationalist viewpoint, already hegemonic in the overseas diaspora, in the Ukrainian studies community, and in Western Ukraine, would be even stronger and even harder to dislodge. No evidence, I am sure, will convince the nationalist true believers. But it seemed to me absolutely necessary to express a different view, to create a space for and possibility of intellectual dissent; hence the recourse to the short pieces on the internet.

An issue that comes up particularly in reference to the shorter, less scholarly interventions is tone. In my scholarship I try to avoid loaded terms or emotional flourishes and aim instead to express my thoughts in plain, straightforward language. In the pieces meant to influence public opinion, I adopt a less neutral language, but I do strive for restraint.[30] When I am replying, I am not usually much interested in showing that my opponent is in the wrong; rather, I try to seize the opportunity to address the public and explain to them what I am thinking. My most successful realization of this ideal was a reply to one of Lozynskyj's attacks on me. In his philippic, he called me "a notorious Soviet apologist" and "a Ukraine detractor" and my work "alleged scholarship that really is not scholarly at all."[31] I used the pretext of defending my work to lay out more evidence about OUN-UPA war crimes but then went on to argue that there are better strands in the Ukrainian tradition than that of these nationalists and that it is high time we rethink what Ukrainian identity should consist of. There is little direct polemic with Lozynskyj.[32]

---

[30] It has not always proved possible to meet this ideal. After reading my debate with the director of the Canadian Institute of Ukrainian Studies, Zenon Kohut, my friend and former student, the historian Mark Baker, sent me this message in an email on February 22, 2010: "Your prose is not as cool as is your wont, but I like it! You seem pissed off, and it is sometimes good to be pissed off." I wrote back: "The polemics have been rather draining and emotional. I guess that shone through in my responses to Zenon." Copies of all letters and emails cited in the text are in the author's possession.

[31] Lozynskyj, "Rewriting History."

[32] Himka, "Ukrainian Past and Ukrainian Future." This article was first published in *The Ukraine List (UKL)*, no. 442 (March 15, 2010): 11–15. It was only published in *Kyiv Post* after a long delay. The most liberal venue of the Ukrainian overseas diaspora, the news service Brama, declined to publish it after a vote of the editorial board.

Although one of my courses became the subject of rather intense controversy,[33] I have never considered the classroom to be the place for promoting one idea or another. I have given a number of undergraduate and graduate seminars on the Holocaust and one on the famine of 1932–33. I use these occasions to explore things for myself through collective reading and discussion. When an issue is controversial, I have tried to find the best presentations of the varying points of view. In my famine seminar, for example, I assigned what I consider to be the most intelligent case for genocide (Andrea Graziosi), the best case for the famine being a result of collectivization (R.W. Davies and Stephen Wheatcroft), and the most hard-hitting indictment of the Stalinist regime in Ukraine (Robert Conquest). Students should be exposed to different views and then sort out the issues for themselves. Our university motto is *Quaecumque vera* – whatsoever things may be true. I subscribe fully. The university classroom is for exploration and intellectual growth, not for indoctrination.

In the course of these interventions, a few questions emerged concerning what might be called my location. To begin with, for instance, I felt strongly that I should not try to intervene in Ukraine itself, that it was not my place; I thought I should restrict my commentary to the diaspora, since that is where I am located. This self-imposed limitation can be discerned in a number of pieces,[34] but I realized later that this stance was impossible to maintain. Much of what I wrote in the diaspora was read in Ukraine, and things I published in Ukraine and even in Ukrainian were being read in the diaspora. I had failed to understand that we live in a highly transnational era.

Another, related location question was: Am I a Ukrainian? Grzegorz Rossolinski-Liebe, himself a demythologizer, criticized me for making this self-identification. I believe his objections stem from his

---

[33] The controversy started when a leading Canadian nonfiction writer who sat in on a seminar I gave about the famine wrote up her experience: Kostash, "Genocide or 'a Vast Tragedy'" The discussion also took place in Balan, "Gullible Leftists Play into the Hands of Putin's Neo-Soviet Apologists" and John-Paul Himka, "Alternatives to Self-Deluding Campaign Exist in Calling Attention to the Famine," and Klid, "Haiti Is a Vast Tragedy, Ukraine Famine Was Genocide."

[34] Himka, "Apocalypse Tomorrow"; Himka, "War Criminality"; Himka, "Antysemityzm, diialoh, samopiznannia."

low opinion of ethnicity and national identity. But I disagree for two reasons. One is that identity location makes some difference in the kind of demythologizing in which I am engaging: challenging core myths from the inside. By example I demonstrate that one need not identify with OUN-UPA to identify, and be identified, as a Ukrainian. I have to admit that I sometimes wavered on this point, feeling so discouraged by the nationalist hegemony that I wondered what I had in common with such people. I wrote to my close friend Alan Rutkowski on April 29, 2010: "I think I may be done crusading. But my crusade was not anti-OUN-UPA as such, it was a crusade to keep OUN-UPA from becoming a central point of Ukrainian identity. I think I lost that battle. To be 'Ukrainian' today means to embrace their heritage."

The second reason why I identified as Ukrainian is that I am actually so benighted as to have a Ukrainian identity. I have worked on Ukrainian history for over forty years; before that I studied to become a Ukrainian priest; my wife and I raised our children to speak Ukrainian; I attend a Ukrainian Orthodox church; I visit Ukraine and have close friends and relatives there; I like to eat Ukrainian food and drink *horilka*; I like to listen to various kinds of Ukrainian music, along with other music; I pursue a deep interest in Ukrainian sacral art. How am I not Ukrainian? (I can hear the chorus of my critics: "Because you are a traitor!").[35]

The last point I would make about strategy is that I sometimes had offers from people to help me by joining in the debates, but I did not encourage them to do so. It was actually quite rare for someone to support me in a public venue rather than in a private email. Partly this was because I could argue from the advantageous position of being well versed in the documentation and historiography, a position few share. Still, perhaps I should have encouraged my supporters to take more of a public stand, even if only on the issue of the right to and value of free inquiry and free debate. Being a rather lone voice helped the opposition to deal with my arguments by simply isolating and vilifying me as an individual. A somewhat larger movement would have been more effective. Perhaps I should have organized a coordinated campaign, but we are all limited by our personalities and abilities.

---

[35] After I published an article critical of Shukhevych, Mykola Kulishov sent me an email (dated March 20, 2008). The subject heading was *zrada*, i.e., treason.

Costs and Coping

I do not like conflict. I am not combative. I have found the whole experience of being at the center of controversy to be emotionally difficult. It has caused tensions in the family and ruptured old friendships. When I began my more intense work on the Holocaust, I knew it would be upsetting for me. I had in mind, however, the disturbing material I would have to work through. I have had many nightmares after reading sources, particularly first-hand testimonies. I expected that there would be friction with some nationalists, but I was not at all prepared for the hegemony of the nationalist worldview in the Yushchenko government, North American diaspora, and the organized Ukrainian studies community. Nor was I prepared for the vehemence of the response to my interventions and scholarship. I had imagined that I belonged to a different kind of community. I am not going to recount everything here. Instead, I will use two examples to suggest the kind of opposition I, and others who have been active in demythologization, have been facing.

First I will discuss the activities of the Ukrainian Canadian Congress. The UCC from the start actively supported and opposed any revision to the OUN-UPA-Holodomor account of Ukrainian history. After Myrna Kostash published an article on my seminar on the famine in *The Literary Review of Canada*, the president of the UCC, Paul Grod, wrote a letter in which he defended the orthodox genocide version and objected to "the philistine musings" of "contemporary Holodomor-deniers and their enablers cited by Kostash and approvingly introduced by John-Paul Himka."[36] On February 1, 2010 the UCC called upon "the Government of Canada to make changes to Canada's War Veterans Allowance Act by expanding eligibility to include designated resistance groups such as OUN-UPA."[37] This appeal, which was a direct result of Yushchenko's Hero award to Bandera, was what led a group of us to protest in our local paper, *The*

---

[36] His letter is on the *LRC* online version, http://reviewcanada.ca/magazine/2009/12/#letters. Characteristically, he appropriates Holocaust language ("deniers," "enablers") for the famine.

[37] *UKL*, no. 441: 3.

Edmonton Journal. David Marples wrote an opinion piece on the posthumous award to Bandera, in which he wrote, among other things, that "members of the OUN-B [i.e., the faction of OUN led by Bandera] spearheaded pogroms in L'viv in the summer of 1941." The editor of the opinion page gave David's piece the heading "Hero of Ukraine Linked to Jewish Killings."[38] Among many responses to this from the Ukrainian community was a letter to the *Journal* from the president of the local branch of the UCC. She said that her office was "receiving calls from respected individuals in Alberta society who are being harassed at work as a result of an inaccurate, inappropriate and sensational headline and column." She denied the complicity of Bandera and the OUN in the Holocaust.[39] This kind of public interchange is fair enough, and I wish there could have been more of it.

Very soon thereafter, however, the UCC decided to respond in other ways. It organized a series of teleconferences that began on March 8, 2010;[40] the participants were constituted as a UCC Task Force for "Developing Community Strategy regarding Recent Attacks on Ukraine's Liberation Movement." Among the suggested actions from that meeting were to "organize a meeting with the Editorial Board of the Edmonton Journal" and "put pressure on North American academic institutions which are funded by community money (Harvard [Ukrainian Research Institute], CIUS [Canadian Institute of Ukrainian Studies], Chair of Ukr[ainian] Studies [at the University of Ottawa]" (Grod to Grod et al., March 14, 2010). Already before these teleconferences, community pressure had made the *Edmonton Journal* drop the issue. Per Rudling and I had written our own analysis of the UCC's recommendation to give Canadian veteran benefits to members of OUN-UPA, and it had been accepted by the *Journal*. It was supposed to have been published soon after David Marples's piece appeared. Instead, it was withdrawn. The editor of the opinion page, David Evans, wrote to Per Rudling on February 19: "I spoke to Jean-Paul Himka this morning and told him I am inclined to hold off now and let the white-hot fires

---

[38] Ibid., 3, 5.
[39] Luciw, "Full Text of the UCC-APC Letter."
[40] Email of Lesia Demkowicz to [name withheld], March 2, and of Jars Balan to Lesia Demkowicz et al., March 14, 2010. I know that at least two such teleconferences took place.

on this subject die down a bit. We did get your letters in this weekend,[41] and to judge from the reaction, running your op-ed might seem like firing one shot too many. I understand there is already a considerable debate going within the Ukrainian-Canadian community about Bandera and competing pictures of the period of history in which he was a part, and my instinct is to see where that goes for a bit. I hope you understand...[42] and I'll let you know the moment my reading on this changes." Needless to say, that moment never came.

I do not know if the UCC acted on the suggestions formulated during the teleconferences and I cannot ascribe all pressure on academic institutions to the UCC. I do not know if the UCC had anything to do with the letter of the Petro Jacyk Educational Foundation to the dean of the Faculty of Arts where I teach. I never saw the letter, only my dean's reply to it (Colleen Skidmore, interim dean of the Faculty of Arts at the University of Alberta, to Oksana Kovalenko, administrator of the Petro Jacyk Educational Foundation, April 20, 2010). The Jacyk Foundation, which has been a multimillion-dollar donor to CIUS, mainly to its Toronto branch, was expressing its displeasure with my debate with the CIUS director, Zenon Kohut. An associate dean called and asked me to "keep the temperature down." The nationalist community's mobilization of financial and human resources against me is something I cannot compete with. It has avoided open debate, where the playing field would be even; it does not want to confront the issues, relying instead on behind-the-scenes influence and the denigration of an individual.[43] Essentially, diaspora publication outlets, on paper and online, have now been closed to me.

Such methods are not surprising coming from persons and organizations who consider themselves heirs of OUN and UPA. What has surprised me more, and disappointed me more, has been the behavior of some of my colleagues in Ukrainian studies, with whom I had thought I shared a belief in free inquiry. Here I will limit my remarks

---

[41] See *UKL* no. 442: 2–4.
[42] Ellipse in the original.
[43] Andrew Sorokowski wrote to me: "I have heard and read various *ad hominem* responses to your recent writings on this subject [Ukrainian nationalist complicity in the Holocaust], but never a reasoned and fact-based refutation." Email of September 20, 2010.

to the case most painful for me, that of the Canadian Institute of Ukrainian Studies. Within CIUS I head up a research program (on Religion and Culture) and so does David Marples (Stasiuk Program for the Study of Contemporary Ukraine). David and I run small-budget programs, with no salary from the Institute; we do not have any decision-making power outside our own programs. The leadership of CIUS consists of three individuals: Zenon Kohut, the director; Frank Sysyn, the director of the Peter Jacyk Centre for Historical Research within CIUS; and Bohdan Klid, assistant director of CIUS. Jars Balan, who will also be mentioned in what follows, is the administrative coordinator for the Kule Ukrainian Canadian Studies Centre within CIUS.

After Myrna Kostash published her account of my famine seminar in *The Literary Review of Canada,* Jars Balan responded at some length in the Edmonton-based newspaper *Ukrainian News.* His attack was primarily directed against Kostash, and the rhetoric was heavy-handed. Stalin, he wrote, "knew exactly what he was doing when he used famine as another weapon in the arsenal that he unleashed in a multipronged and genocidal campaign. To argue otherwise is to ignore overwhelming facts about the known history of the USSR, and to play into the hands of the neo-Soviet apologists who are flourishing in Putin's Russia and have obviously found allies among gullible leftists in the West."[44] A few weeks later, after I responded to Balan, Bohdan Klid joined the debate in *Ukrainian News,* responding this time directly to me. He stated that I exhibited "what amounts to an indulgent approach toward the Soviet state and its leadership." He was later to apologize for writing here, incorrectly, that I had never referred to the acts of the Stalinist regime as "crimes."

My main disagreement with the piece, however, was that it presented such a distorted version of my argument. Klid accused me of "trivialization of the famine," charging that I regarded it as a tragedy on the order of the Haitian earthquake which had recently occurred. Readers were left to think that I maintain that the famine was an act of God, not a condemnable act of the Soviet leadership. Zenon Kohut also responded to the Kostash article, again defending the line that it

---

[44] Balan, "Gullible Leftists."

was genocide. It appeared in the *Literary Review of Canada* over his signature as "Director, Canadian Institute of Ukrainian Studies." Coming just after Paul Grod's letter, which was signed "President, Ukrainian Canadian Congress," it looked very much like an official response. Right after David Marples wrote his article on Bandera in *The Edmonton Journal*, Kohut wrote a letter to the editor over his directorial signature denying that Bandera had any connection with the Lviv pogrom ("Bandera was not in Ukraine at the time") and denying Marples's assertion that OUN was a typical Fascist organization.

Several things bothered me about all these responses coming out of CIUS. For one thing, I had the distinct impression that the Institute had now assumed the role of policing dissident views on twentieth-century Ukrainian history. None of those who responded to Kostash, Marples, and me were themselves specialists in that field. Kohut is an excellent historian of seventeenth and eighteenth century Ukraine; Klid wrote his dissertation on nineteenth century Ukrainian intellectual history and then went on to study Ukrainian hip hop; and Balan is an expert on Ukrainians in Canada. To my knowledge none of them has taught a university-level course on either the famine or the Holocaust or published a scholarly article on these themes. What motivated them to take such strong stands? Clearly, they believe in the mythologized history. CIUS has featured leading proponents of the OUN-UPA-Holodomor line in its annual Shevchenko Lectures and in its seminar series: Peter Potichnyj, Mykola Riabchuk, and Roman Serbyn. Critical opinions have been entirely absent, at least on our two crucial themes. It is also evident that CIUS does not feel that part of its mandate is to raise the level of Ukrainian discourse and thinking. Rather, it conforms to the community's orthodoxies—pure *khvostizm*, to use Lenin's term. I stand by my reply to Kohut in *The Literary Review of Canada*: "It is better if scholars and intellectuals complicate and challenge the nationalist mythologies of their communities, not enlist as their apologists."[45]

At the same time, I will point out, those who were so quick off the mark when they saw the myths under threat had nothing to say about the innumerable antisemitic interpretations of twentieth-century Ukrainian history that emerged in the course of the subsequent

---

[45] http://reviewcanada.ca/magazine/2009/12/#letters.

debates. Askold Lozynskyj, for example, in an article that appeared in *Kyiv Post* and was widely circulated on various diaspora electronic lists, an article directed against both Marples's and my views on OUN-UPA and the Holocaust, wrote: "And even those agents who themselves for many years were stateless and often oppressed, continue to seek out new demons to escape blame for a not so blameless past and to keep the fire of remembrance burning for their own tragedies, i.e. the Jews."[46] And further: "While there is divergence in various accounts of the Lviv incident as to the identity of the perpetrators, the indisputable facts are that the Soviets left a gory landscape, prisons replete with corpses of their Ukrainian prisoners accumulated over almost two years from the Molotov-Ribbentrop pact until the Nazi invasion of Western Ukraine. What is also indisputable is that many Jews served in the Soviet secret police during that period of Soviet rule in Western Ukraine. Naturally, Mr. Himka fails to mention the Jewish complicity which may have pointed to the motive of any number of oppressors."[47] Marco Levytsky, the editor of *Ukrainian News*, published a letter of rebuttal to Marples in *The Edmonton Journal*, which said: "Prior to the German invasion, the Soviet NKVD, in which Jews had disproportionate membership, was involved in the killing of 4,000 to 8,000 civilian prisoners—a fact the Nazis hoped would provoke Ukrainian retaliation."[48] Per Rudling called him on this, also in the *Journal*, saying that he was invoking "the spectre of Judeo-Communism." Levytsky "proved" his point by saying that while Jews constituted only 1.78 percent of the Soviet population, they accounted for 3.92 percent of the leading cadres of the NKVD.[49] The argument expressed by Lozynskyj and Levytsky, and indeed by other defenders of the nationalists, is the

---

[46] A subtheme in the nationalist polemics against me is that I am a paid agent of the Russians or the Jews or both. A little later in his article, Lozynskyj writes: "To his credit Prof. Himka did acknowledge that his paper [on UPA and the Holocaust] was paid for with a fellowship from the Holocaust Memorial Museum. This goes to motive. Simply put, Mr. Himka for his remuneration had to produce one or more demons." I mention this, because Lozynskyj was later to deny that he meant I was being paid by the Jews, but the reference to "demons" in both sentences leaves no doubt.

[47] Lozynskyj, "Rewriting History."

[48] *UKL* no. 441: 7.

[49] *UKL* no. 442: 6.

very same as the OUN and UPA put forward when they killed the Jews in the first place—that the Jews were Communist criminals. None of the debaters from CIUS felt the need to correct the Judeo-Bolshevik interpretation of modern Ukrainian history. To me, that indicates very skewed priorities.

But the activities of the CIUS leadership did not stop at written polemics. There was also a "whispering campaign" launched against me, but it was a very loud whispering campaign. A friend, a historian, whose name I will withhold, wrote to me on December 15, 2009: "I also want to let you know something in confidence,[50] I didn't want to say anything [the] first time but I have heard this a second time. I think you may have ruffled a few feathers in certain quarters (to be congratulated), as two leading figures from Canada in Ukrainian historical work have been saying rather nasty things about you and your motivations in your work regarding Jewish-Ukrainian relations and holodomor. This was said to [...] in [...] and also in [...] recently by another person. Essentially its being said your motivation is your 'Christian Marxism,' and, they are basically smearing your work as having ulterior motives." Later, on September 30, 2010, that same person, when reminded of this email, wrote to me: "I did not say at the time but one of those concerned is a leading light at CIUS." I know from a number of mutual friends that one person from CIUS who is saying things against me is Frank Sysyn, the director of the Jacyk Centre and head of the Toronto office. My close friend Alan Rutkowski wrote to me on April 29, 2010: "Frank sent me an email telling me that our friendship is over because of my friendship with you. It's a pretty passionate conflict when collateral damage occurs this far afield."

I attribute this personalization of the debate to the very nature of mythological thinking. The elements that make up the myth are not supposed to be subjected to rational scrutiny, hence the one who does so is demonized as a profaner of sacred mysteries. Whatever their source, however, I found the attacks very stressful. I had known Zenon Kohut since 1974 and felt close to him. Frank Sysyn and I had known each other even longer, and I used to stay at his apartment in Cambridge in the old days. Bohdan Klid wrote his doctorate under

---

[50] I subsequently obtained permission to quote the letter.

my supervision. Jars Balan and I had worked closely together in the Ukrainian-Canadian left for many years. I am sad to find these friendships destroyed.

I coped the way most people do—I had help from my friends, from other friends. I am most grateful to Marco Carynnyk, David Marples, and Per Rudling. Other colleagues in Holocaust studies and East European history from around the world sent me words of encouragement or took me aside and promised their support. I was blessed with encouragement from eminent Canadian writers of Ukrainian heritage, not only Myrna Kostash, but also Janice Kulyk-Keefer and Erin Mouré. I am doubly grateful to my wife, Chrystia Chomiak. Her own resistance to the history I was uncovering and perspectives I was developing helped me appreciate how hard it is for many diaspora Ukrainians to reconsider received views. But when she crossed over to my corner, she was steadfast in her support. I had many restless nights, but I also had people who helped me get by.

Misery loves company—I can vouch for it. I felt much better when I realized that there are other challengers of nationalist myths around and that they have been facing the same kind of vilification and marginalization. Judy and Larry Haiven, who used to be our neighbors some twenty years ago, returned to Edmonton recently for a lecture on the plight of the Palestinians in Israel. They have long been outspoken in condemning elements of Israeli policy.[51] No one in Larry's family will speak to him anymore. Only Judy's mother will talk to her, and only about subjects other than politics. I had known, but only in the course of my own experience did I fully understand, that Srdja Pavlovic, a Montenegrin who also did his doctorate under my supervision, was an outcast in the Serbian community—he was too vocal in his condemnation of the war crimes committed during the wars of the Yugoslav succession. He often consoled me when I was downhearted. I have a doctoral student now, Nina Pavlovic, who is writing a brilliant thesis on the Holocaust in Slovakia. She too has felt the coolness that comes from looking at the darker side of the national history. Sometimes it can be comforting to know that one is part of a larger trend.

---

[51] They are active in Independent Jewish Voices, http://ijvcanada.org/.

Results to Date

The debates are not yet over, and the major revisionist works are yet to appear. I am writing a book on "Ukrainian Nationalists and the Holocaust: Pogroms, Police, and National Insurgency, 1941–1945." Per Anders Rudling has basically the draft of a book on the *Schutzmannschaften* that shows the complicity of both factions of OUN in war crimes. Marco Carynnyk, a powerful writer, is well into a book on the NKVD murders and the pogroms. Grzegorz Rossolinski-Liebe is finishing a dissertation, which will also be a book, on the Bandera legend. Jeffrey Burds has been working on a book on Ukrainian nationalist violence and atrocities for some time. When all these tomes, based on archival research in many languages, are available, it will only be the True Believers who will defend the old myths.

At the moment, however, I feel that the biggest accomplishment of our activities is that we have forced the debate on these important issues. It is no longer so comfortable to hold on to the illusions. Marco Carynnyk was correct when he wrote to me (February 10, 2010) in reaction to my two responses to Kohut: "If this isn't a declaration of war, then it's at least a trumpet call for a battle royal. When the smoke blows away and the screaming of the wounded horses dies down, we'll know what positions a lot of people defended." The holder of the Chair of Ukrainian Studies at Ottawa, Dominique Arel, who was also very supportive and published my texts when no one else would, wrote me a week later: "However painful, it is healthy that Ukrainian studies is able to have this debate."[52]

Have I changed anyone's views? I think so. I have had some people write to me that my articles have had an effect on their evaluation of the nationalist heritage. I am pleased to note that the debate has spread from the diaspora to Ukraine itself. In June 2010 I was in Kyiv and lectured on the Holocaust and the famine. While I was there, I was approached by one of the editors of *Krytyka*, Andrii Mokrousov, to authorize Ukrainian translations of some of my essays and to write a new one for the paper. More important, he wanted to publish

---

[52] Email of Dominique Arel to John-Paul Himka, February 17, 2010, in the author's possession.

a collection of my articles on the famine and the Holocaust in Ukrainian translation. As we planned out what to include in the volume, I realized I had already written 450 printed pages on these topics, and this was aside from the monograph I was currently working on. The book was endorsed also by *Krytyka*'s founder and co-editor, Harvard professor George Grabowicz. Grabowicz also attended my lecture in Kyiv. During the discussion period he expressed bafflement about why the diaspora was so much up in arms against me and my views. He said he found very compelling a point I was making in the debates, that there was no reason that all Ukrainians and everything Ukrainian had to be burdened with crimes committed by a particular political tendency, namely OUN. I took heart, because I saw I was making progress.

The Ukrainian community in North America is fond of "action items." Their organizations and electronic lists regularly set in motion letter-writing and telephone campaigns—now to a periodical to use "Kyiv" instead of "Kiev," then to a congressman or member of parliament to recognize the Holodomor as a genocide. There is an unending mobilization for such "action items." I have proposed a "thinking item." I hope it meets with success.

Bibliography

Balan, J. "Gullible Leftists Play into the Hands of Putin's Neo-Soviet Apologists." *Ukrainian News*. December 28, 2009–January 19, 2010.

Bartov, O. *Erased: Vanishing Traces of Jewish Galicia in Present-Day Ukraine*. Princeton and Oxford: Princeton University Press, 2007.

Boshyk, Y. ed. *Ukraine During World War II: History and Its Aftermath: A Symposium*. Edmonton: Canadian Institute of Ukrainian Studies, University of Alberta, 1986.

Bruder, F. *"Den ukrainischen Staat erkämpfen oder sterben!" Die Organisation Ukrainischer Nationalisten (OUN) 1929–1948*. Berlin: Metropol, 2007.

Carynnyk, M. [Marko Tsarynnyk], "Zolochiv movchyt'," *Krytyka* no. 10 (2005): 9–10.

Dietsch, J. *Making Sense of Suffering: Holocaust and Holodomor in Ukrainian Historical Culture*. Lund: Media Tryck, Lund University, 2006.

Himka, J.P. "Alternatives to Self-Deluding Campaign Exist in Calling Attention to the Famine." *Ukrainian News*, January 20–February 3, 2010.

———. "Antysemityzm, diialoh, samopiznannia," *Krytyka* vol. 9, no. 5 (May 2005): 18.

———. "Apocalypse Tomorrow: Some Remarks on Two Texts on the Ukrainian Elections." *aaus-list* (American Association for Ukrainian Studies), 29 October 2004 at http://www.ukrainianstudies.org/aaus-list/0410/msg00027.html (accessed 7 October 2010).

———. "Be Wary of Faulty Nachtigall Lessons." *Kyiv Post*, March 27, 2008.

———. "Dostovirnist' svidchennia: reliatsiia Ruzi Vagner pro l'vivs'kyi pohrom vlitku 1941 r.," *Holokost i suchasnist'* no. 2, vol. 4 (2008): 43–79.

———. "The Holodomor in the Ukrainian-Jewish Encounter Initiative," paper presented at the meeting of the Ukrainian Jewish Encounter Initiative, Ditchley Park, England, December 14–16, 2009.

———. "How Many Perished in the Famine and Why Does It Matter?" *BRAMA: News and Community Press*, February 2, 2008. Available at http://www.brama.com/news/press/2008/02/080202himka_famine.html.

———. and Kurylo, T. "Iak OUN stavylasia do ievreiv? Rozdumy nad knyzhkoiu Volodymyra V"iatrovycha." *Ukraina Moderna* vol. 13 (2008): 252–65.

———. "In Memoriam: Janusz Radziejowski (1925–2002)." *Krytyka* vol. 6 no. 11 (November 2002): 31.

———. "The Lviv Pogrom of 1941," *Kyiv Post*, September 23, 2010. Available at http://www.kyivpost.com/news/opinion/op_ed/detail/83452/ (accessed 7 October 2010).

———. "True and False Lessons from the Nachtigall Episode." *BRAMA: News and Community Press*, March 19, 2008. Available at
http://www.brama.com/news/press/2008/03/080319himka_nachtigall.html

———. "Ukrainian Collaboration in the Extermination of the Jews during the Second World War: Sorting Out the Long-Term and Conjunctural Factors," in *The Fate of the European Jews, 1939–1945: Continuity or Contingency*, ed. Jonathan Frankel (New York, Oxford: Oxford University Press, 1997), *Studies in Contemporary Jewry* vol. 13 (1997): 170–189.

———. *Ukrainians, Jews and the Holocaust: Divergent Memories*. Saskatoon: Heritage Press, 2009.

———. "Ukrainian Past and Ukrainian Future," *Kyiv Post*, September 20, 2010, at http://www.kyivpost.com/news/opinion/op_ed/detail/83019/ (accessed 7 October 2010).

———. "War Criminality: A Blank Spot in the Collective Memory of the Ukrainian Diaspora." *Spaces of Identity* 5, no. 1 (April 2005) at http://spacesofidentity.net/ (accessed 6 October 2010).

Hoffman, E. *After Such Knowledge: Memory, History, and the Legacy of the Holocaust.* New York: Public Affairs, 2004.

Hrachova, S. "Vony zhyly sered nas?" *Krytyka* vol. 9, no. 4 (April 2005): 22–26.

Klid, B. "Haiti Is a Vast Tragedy, Ukraine Famine Was Genocide," *Ukrainian News*, February 4–17, 2010.

Kostash, M. "Genocide or 'a Vast Tragedy': University Students in an Alberta Classroom Try to Decide." *Literary Review of Canada*, December 2009. Available at http://reviewcanada.ca/essays/2009/12/01/genocide-or-a-vast-tragedy/; and see the letters about this, http://reviewcanada.ca/magazine/2009/12/#letters.

Lozynskyj, A. S. "History Should Be Written by Objective and Competent Scholars," *Kyiv Post*, September 22, 2010, at http://www.kyivpost.com/news/opinion/op_ed/detail/83306/ (accessed October 7, 2010).

———. "Rewriting History: An Evidentiary Perspective," *Kyiv Post*, February 16, 2010, at http://www.kyivpost.com/news/opinion/op_ed/detail/59650/ (accessed October 7, 2010).

———. "Where's the Evidence of Ukrainian Wartime Atrocities against the Jews?" *Kyiv Post*, September 27, 2010, at http://www.kyivpost.com/news/opinion/op_ed/detail/83945/ (accessed October 7, 2010).

Luciw, D. "Full Text of the UCC-APC Letter Submitted to the Editor of the Edmonton Journal," Ukrainian Canadian Congress, Alberta Provincial Council website. Available at http://www.uccab.ca/default-archive.asp (accessed 8 October 2010).

Mendelsohn, D. *The Lost: A Search for Six of Six Million*, photographs by Matt Mendelsohn New York: HarperCollins, 2006.

Pohl, D. *Nationalsozialistische Judenverfolgung in Ostgalizien 1941–1944: Organisation und Durchführung eines staatlichen Massenverbrechens.* Munich: R. Oldenbourg Verlag, 1997.

Rybakov, D. "Marko Tsarynnyk: Istorychna napivpravda hirsha za odvertu brekhniu," *Lb.ua*, November 5, 2009. Available at http://lb.ua/news/2009/11/05/13147_marko_tsarinnik_istorichna.html (accessed October 6, 2010).

Caught Between History and Politics: The Experience of a Moldovan Historian Studying the Holocaust

DIANA DUMITRU

In 2003, while a visiting fellow at the University of North Carolina at Chapel Hill, I managed to read Jan Gross' *Neighbors*.[1] Gross' study is focused on a single event, which occurred on July 10, 1941, when in a Polish town, Jedwabne, local Poles murdered the entire local Jewish population—men, women, and children—without mercy, using "primitive, ancient methods and murder weapons: stones, wooden clubs, iron bars, fire, and water."[2] After reading this book I wondered what happened in the summer of 1941 in Moldova—the country where I was born—and how my compatriots behaved towards Jews, after the Soviets left and Romanian and German troops entered.

My family is not Jewish, and I could be considered a typical "product" of both Soviet and post-Soviet education. During Soviet times I studied in a regular Moldovan village school and was well aware of the Fascist brutality towards "Soviet citizens." While in school, I went for excursions to the "hero-cities" of Brest, Kyiv, Sevastopol, as well as to a memorial in Katyń (Belarus), where, as I then managed to learn, the entire population of the village (149 residents) was burned alive during a Nazi reprisal action. I read the novel of Vasily Grossman, *Life and Fate*, the book of Anatoly Kuznetsov, *Babi Yar*, and my memory was marked by terrifying pictures of the Nazi concentration camps, as shown in the Soviet documentary *Ordinary Fascism*.[3] However, the issue of Jewish genocide during WWII did not have a central place in

---

[1] Gross, *Neighbors*.
[2] Ibid., 80–81.
[3] Grossman, *Zhizn' i sud'ba* and Kuznetsov, *Babi Yar. Roman-dokument*.

my awareness about history. Presumably, I was not too much different from a typical Soviet teenager of the era.

In this naive ignorance I remained during the first part of the 1990s, when I was an undergraduate student in Chișinău, majoring in history. During those times Moldovan professors were doing a great job in recovering the "white pages" and correcting the distortions of the Soviet history. We, the first graduates from History Departments in independent Moldova, were set to read and be lectured about the crimes of Stalinism, Katyń, the Molotov-Ribbentrop Pact, as well as about the suffering of the Moldovan people, such as deportations, the 1946–1947 famine, forced collectivization, destruction of the churches, Russification, etc. None of the classes and the recommended books touched upon the history of local Jewry during WWII. Moldovan universities and school history programs omitted mention of the Holocaust during the 1990s.[4] In part, this situation was a reverberation of the state of affairs in Romania, where initially the issue of Holocaust study raised serious debates and denial of it surfaced both in historiography and political declarations.[5] After intense professional and social debates, and pressured politically by the West, the attitudes towards the issue of the Holocaust in Romania suffered visible changes in the late 1990s. Curiously, this transformation did not have any impact on the Holocaust study in Moldova.

While in graduate school, I researched nineteenth century diplomatic history, again failing to learn about tens of thousands of Jews killed in Bessarabia, Bukovina, and south of Ukraine in the summer of 1941 by Romanian soldiers. I did not know about the deportations organized by the Romanian authorities and the imprisonment of the Jews, who survived the murder campaign, into ghettoes and camps in Transnistria.[6] Meanwhile significant publications about the Holocaust in

---

[4] Regarding the study of the subject of the Holocaust in schools of Moldova see Dumitru, "V labirinte politizatsii," 27–38.

[5] On this topic see the chapter "Holocaust Denial in the Post-communist Public Discourse" in the International Commission on the Holocaust in Romania, *Final Report*, 349–379.

[6] During WWII the territory between the rivers Dniester and Bug, which in August 1941 came under the civilian-military administration of Romania, was named Transnistria. The region was comprised of the contemporary territory of Transnistria—part of the Republic of Moldova, as well as

Romania started to appear in the West at the end of 1990s–early 2000s. At the first encounter with the literature on the Holocaust in Bessarabia, I was startled by the fact that while I was a trained historian, I had no previous knowledge about the tragedy that had occurred, for example, in villages were my parents were born. Still, there was no available research on the attitude of Moldovans towards Jews during World War II.

I learned that numerous archival materials copied from various European archives, including Moldovan, were located in Washington D.C., at the United States Holocaust Memorial Museum. During a short visit to the USHMM, I found difficult to orient myself in the immense ocean of available documents, and asked for advice from specialists regarding the relationship between Jews and gentiles in Bessarabia during the war. It seemed that nobody had approached this particular subject. This is how I became the first researcher of the attitude towards Jews in Bessarabia during World War II.

In the year 2005, while already an Assistant Professor at the Chişinău State Pedagogical University, I left for ten months to the USHMM for a study visit. I had to combine my archival research with the reading of the literature of the Holocaust, since my historical knowledge about the subject was clearly scanty. Subsequently, I worked at the archives in Yad Vashem, Jerusalem, where I collected memoirs and testimonies of Jewish survivors. The more I was learning about the Holocaust in Romania, the more complicated was becoming my professional life at home.

The Opposition

As I had to learn from my personal experience, the topic of the Holocaust was not simply understudied—my fellow historians were clearly trying to stay away from it. The politicization of history, caused by the issue of identity in Moldova, touched the majority of historians and

---

territories of Nikolaev, Vinnitsa, and Odessa regions, which are today part of Ukraine. Regarding the Holocaust on the territories administered by Romania in 1941–1944 (including Bessarabia and Transnistria) see: Friling et al. *Final Report*); Ancel, *Contribuţii la istoria României*; Ancel, *Transnistria, 1941–1942*; Ioanid, *The Holocaust in Romania*.

divided them into two opposing groups: of pro-Romanian orientation (they form a majority amongst professional historians) and pro-Soviet/pro-Russian orientation (later became known as "Moldovenists"). At stake in this fight between these two groups was the formation of the national identity in the Republic of Moldova. Pro-Romanian historians were defending a concept of national identity which was based on the common Romanian descent, while "the Moldovenists" argued for a separate Moldovan identity, different from the Romanian one. Immediately after the declaration of independence, the community of Moldovan historians—primarily driven by pro-Romanian feelings—managed to get the upper hand and introduced in schools and higher education programs which backed their ideology. History courses, as taught in the universities of Moldova, were divided into two parts: the History of Romanians, and World History.

In 2001, after of period of relative independence and the triumph of the "spirit of nationalism," the Communist Party came to power and professional historians from Moldova were confronted with a new agenda from the authorities. The government attempted to change the incumbent concept of historical education and to impose an alternative model of identity for the population of Moldova.[7] The majority of historians made it clear that they did not intend to interact or assist the authorities in this project, further disquieting Communist politicians. In the conditions when a part of population had a visible propensity towards Romania, or were identifying themselves with the Romanian state or Romanian nation, and the Bucharest authorities were making statements about the existence of "two Romanian states,"[8] the Communist administration firmly decided to prevent the consolidation of "Romanian" identification. For this purpose it intended to exclude from educational programs the course of "History of Romanians," to introduce the mandatory study of the Russian language, and to support the historians form the "Moldovenist" side. Among numerous "historical" and "democratic" arguments that Chișinău used in its confrontation with the opposition and the pro-Romanian historians, the

---

[7] For more details see Musteață, "Identitatea națională între istorie și politică," 175–190; also Musteață, "Predarea istoriei în Republica Moldova," 376–392.

[8] For more information about the relationship between Moldova and Romania see Weiner, "The Foreign Policy of the Voronin Administration," 541–556.

issue of the Holocaust became handy, especially in the framework of the cultivation of a good image in the West. It was in this specific context that the Moldovan leadership showed an interest in the research and recovery of the memory of the Holocaust.

In October 2003, Alexei Tulbure, the permanent representative of the Republic of Moldova in the Council of Europe, visibly irritated by the interest of Romania towards the issues of teaching of history and Romanian language in Moldova, declared that "the Romanians should mind their own business and take care of their own textbooks," because "our [Moldovan] xenophobes and antisemites were inspired from those [Romanian textbooks]."[9] Soon after that, Andrei Neguța, the president of the Moldova's Parliamentary commission on foreign policy, launched an accusation which claimed that Romanian textbooks were attempting to "rehabilitate the crimes" committed during the years of World War II and were denying the Holocaust, simultaneously contributing to the "preservation in the Romanian society of a nationalistic, anti-Semitic, and xenophobic spirit, which is directly contradictory to the values of contemporary Europe."[10] This accusation was rejected by the Committee of Ministers of the Council of Europe; in its official response to Moldovan authorities it was indicated that the Romanian government at that time already undertook a number of measures to modernize history textbooks, in accordance with the advice of this European forum. The Committee of Ministers also reminded that in schools in Romania "the problem of the Holocaust is studied since 1999, in the textbooks for grades 7, 8, and 12, under the topics dedicated to World War II."[11]

Moldovan historians who followed with enthusiasm their Romanian colleagues in study of other historical subjects, when it came to the study of the Holocaust chose a distinct way, which was leading them to denial or even justification of the Holocaust in Romania under the governance of Ion Antonescu.[12] In 2005, a book published

---

[9] Coman, "Chișinăul încearcă disperat să provoace România."
[10] Ibid.
[11] Written Question No. 435 to the Committee of Ministers by Mr. Neguță: "Modernisation of history teaching in Romanian schools."
[12] At the time Romanian researchers made serious progress in research and debate related to the Holocaust. In 2003 an International Commission of

by Sergiu Nazaria[13] on the topic of the Holocaust caused among Moldovan historians furious reactions, which practically meant the denial of the Holocaust in Romania.[14] Many regarded Nazaria as being politically engaged, since he served as vice-Minister of education (2001–2002) under the Communist government and was a supporter of the governmental policy of introduction in schools of mandatory study of Russian language, and the substitution of the course "History of Romanians" with the "Integrated History." In light of the allegations about Nazaria's bias, his research conclusions to the effect that Romanian administration is responsible for the destruction of local Jewry in 1941–1944, were perceived by pro-Romanian historians as "political," being designed to discredit the "pro-Romanian" forces in contemporary Moldova.

Certainly, the accusations against Nazaria were also of political, but not of academic character. They underlined his "Romanophobia" and accused him of playing up to the Communist leadership by his position on the Holocaust.[15] Moreover, since many historians defended the idea of belonging of Moldovans to Romanian ethnocultural group, any attempt to cast aspersions on the Romanian state caused a sharp reaction.

Even without the possession of the information on the Holocaust on Bessarabian territory, at least part of historians were able to guess that the research of this topic can reveal quite repugnant actions of the Romanian administration during World War II. Bogged down in political battles, historians of Moldova were viewing the Holocaust as an "undesirable" and "dangerous" topic, which has the potential for tarnishing Romania and pushing away Moldovans from their ethnic kin;

---

the Holocaust in Romania was established by the Romanian president Ion Iliescu and in late 2004 the Commission released a report on the actual history of the Holocaust in Romania. (International Commission on the Holocaust in Romania, *Final Report*).

[13] Nazaria et al. *Kholokost v Moldove*, 222.

[14] Read about the scandal caused by Nazaria's book in Prisăcaru, "Un istoric neagă că a scris 'Holocaustul in Basarabia'; Moraru, "Aparută recent cartea 'Holocaustul in Basarabia' este un eşec"; Marinescu, "Afacerea 'Holocaustul evreiesc în Moldova'. Toate episoadele."

[15] Political opponents could not fail to notice that the Communist government was supporting the interest towards the subject of the Holocaust; that President Voronin visited the memorial to the victims of Chişinău ghetto, or that state money was used to erect memorials to Jews killed in 1941.

as well as a political weapon which can be used by Communists for whipping up anti-Romanian sentiments.[16]

For years I managed to stay away from the political debates around history, but when I began researching the Holocaust this detachment became truly difficult. My colleagues wanted to know "on whose side I was standing," and the answer that I was exclusively pursuing my academic interests was not accepted as a satisfactory answer. My attempts to argue that the denial of the Holocaust was senseless, since everybody could learn about it just by talking to elderly people from Moldovan villages, were to no avail. Arguments usually fail to convince those for whom conviction remains more important than knowledge. It felt like being in a "historical solitude" when most of my historian colleagues did not approve on my academic interest.

The prospects for me at the time were as follows: if I defend this position alone (or even worse, with the help of historian Sergiu Nazaria), as an historian I will have to face isolation and maybe ostracism among historians from my country. A historian from Moldova, who had been living for some years in the United States, after learning that I have been researching the Holocaust, and was not planning to move across the ocean, told me that in his opinion what I was doing was "professional suicide." Nevertheless, I planned to survive, and started to look for allies and to consider a plan of action.

The Strategy

By 2005 the dominant professional and public opinion was that there was no Holocaust on the territory of Moldova, and even if there was "something," this was merely a "political punishment" of Jews for their hostile behavior towards the Romanian army, when it was withdrawing after the Soviet ultimatum of 1940.[17] The idea that the Romanian

---

[16] Regarding the issue of politicization of the Holocaust in Moldova and the corresponding debates see Dumitru, "The Use and Abuse of the Holocaust," 49–73.
[17] This idea is explicitly supported in the book of the renown Romanian dissident and writer Paul Goma. See Goma, *Săptămâna roşie 28 iunie – 3 iulie 1940 sau Basarabia şi evreii*.

state was responsible for the destruction of Jews of Bessarabia, Bukovina, and Transnistria was perceived as politically "dangerous," while its author would be classified as "Moldovenist," despite their actual political views. This was quite an unpleasant perspective, because the majority of historians of Moldova were of pro-Romanian orientation, while the "Moldovenists" were few; besides, the prestige of the latter was deplorable in professional circles.

There was a need for support from specialists with an international reputation and ones that would not have any connections with Moldovan politics. I shared my thoughts and concern with colleagues and friends from the USHMM, who agreed to take part in the organization in Moldova of the first international conference dedicated to the issue of Jewish destruction in Bessarabia, Bukovina, and Transnistria in 1941–1944.[18]

The conference was attended by experts from the U.S. and Romania. They all spoke Romanian and none of them could be suspected of Romanophobia or being sympathetic to the Communist government of Moldova. Moldova historians who gave presentations included Anatol Petrencu, the head of the National Association of Historians of Moldova, and Sergiu Nazaria, Igor Cașu, and myself. The conference was attended by local historians, political analysts, representatives of NGOs, state officials, and other professionals. Journalists actively questioned the speakers about the fate of Jews in Bessarabia in 1941–1944. Several presentations mainly consisted of historical photographs and Romanian archival documents. These materials documented in a truly visible manner the responsibility of Romanian administration for the

---

[18] The conference was organized in Chișinău by the Ion Creangă State Pedagogical University, the United States Holocaust Memorial Museum from Washington D.C., and Elie Weisel National Institute for Studying the Holocaust in Romania. The author of this article, a member of the World History Department from Ion Creangă State Pedagogical University, organized it. Five international experts presented at the conference: Paul Shapiro, the director of the Center for Advanced Holocaust Studies; Radu Ioanid, the director of the archive of the USHMM; Dennis Deletant, Professor at University College London; Mihail Ionescu, the director of Elie Weisel National Institute for Studying the Holocaust in Romania (Bucharest); and Alexandru Florian, vice-director of Elie Weisel National Institute for Studying the Holocaust in Romania.

extermination of the Jews and the deliberate nature of their actions. Massive killings of Jews started in the summer of 1941 immediately after the entrance of German and Romanian troops into Bessarabia and Bukovina. Those who survived the first wave of extermination were sent to local camps and ghettoes, and later were deported by foot to the East, to camps placed in Transnistria, where they were kept until the end of war. About 154,000–170,000 Jews of Bessarabia and Bukovina walked hundreds of kilometers, during the summer, autumn, or winter of 1941.[19] Upon their arrival these were locked in barns and stables, without food and medical care.[20] In November 1943 only 49,927 out of these deportees were still alive, primarily due to food provided by local peasants.[21] The others died because of hunger, typhus, extenuated by hard labor, or were killed by Romanian soldiers. Another 150,000–180,000 Jews natives of Transnistria were killed by German or Romanian soldiers during the first actions of mass murder, or died because of the same intolerable conditions in the same camps and ghettoes of Transnistria.[22]

At the conference various points of view were voiced, and some criticism was directed towards the speakers. However, none of the participants tried to deny openly the deliberate extermination of Jews in Bessarabia, Bukovina, and Transnistria during World War II.[23] The demonstration of photos of women and children chased by Romanian gendarmes to Transnistria seriously shook the position of those who affirmed earlier that nothing happened to the local Jews. A subtle change of views was possible to observe already during the conference

---

[19] *Final Report*, 176.
[20] The conditions of detention of Jews from Bessarabia and Bukovina at the places of deportation (in Transnistria), in 1941–1944, are described in detail in Ancel, *Transnistria*.
[21] *Final Report*, 177. About the relationship between Jews and gentiles, see Dumitru, "The Attitude of the Non-Jewish Population of Bessarabia and Transnistria towards the Jews during the Holocaust."
[22] Ibid., 178.
[23] One of the journalists, who took part at this forum, made the following remark: there is an impression that between the scandal caused by the book of Nazaria and this conference passed "not months, but years: such different are these in their approach of the subject and seriousness of the proposed investigations." See Luk'anchikova, "Sud'ba evreev Bessarabii, Bukoviny i Transnistrii v 1941–1944 godakh."

itself.²⁴ Late in the evening the local radio broadcast an interview with a participant of the conference, while on the next day one of the national newspapers published an article with the title "Holocaust in Bessarabia?"²⁵

Certainly, I did not expect this or any other similar event to change the opinion of an established generation of historians. Many more possibilities were offered by teaching at the university. Some of my students after graduation teach history in secondary schools, so my knowledge about the Holocaust could be widely spread through this particular channel.

For six years I have been teaching a course entitled "The Holocaust in Romania: Texts, Theories, and Memories." In my classes the students analyze Romanian documents of the era, get familiar with interview materials of the witnesses of the Holocaust and Jewish survivors, and have numerous discussions on this topic. Communication with my students gives me a sense of confidence in the future of the historian's profession in Moldova.

As frequently happens in many other countries, in Moldova the recognition of one's work in the West can facilitate one's endorsement at home, so one of my goals was to publish in reputable Western academic journals. Most of my publications appeared abroad: in the U.S., Israel, Romania, Germany, and Ukraine.²⁶ My colleagues gradually got

---

²⁴ For example, the head of the National Association of Historians of Moldova in his talk marked the necessity to clarify the definition of the Holocaust: "until not too long time ago the Holocaust meant physical destruction of Jews, nowadays it means repressive policies, including deportations, camps, etc." Ibid.,10–11.

²⁵ Moraru, "Holocaust in Bessarabia?"

²⁶ Dumitru, "Attitudes towards Jews in Odessa"; Dumitru and Johnson, "Constructing Inter-Ethnic Conflict and Cooperation"; Dumitru, "The Attitude of the Non-Jewish Population of Bessarabia and Transnistria towards the Jews during the Holocaust"; Dumitru, "Atitudinea populaţiei ne-evreieşti din Basarabia şi Transnistria către evrei în perioada Holocaustului"; Dumitru, "The Use and Abuse of the Holocaust"; Dumitru, "V labirinte politizatsii: prepodavanie Holokosta v shkolakh Respubliki Moldova"; Dumitru, "Moldawien seit 1990"; Dumitru, "Moldova: Holocaust als Spielball. Der schwierige Umgang mit dem jüdischen Erbe"; Dumitru, "In Memoriam: Jean Ancel, 1940–2008"; Dumitru, "Educarea toleranţei la lecţiile de istorie?"

used to my commitment to the study of the Holocaust and started to show a more balanced attitude towards my research interest. Today, my research findings even meet a certain interest in both formal and informal settings. In part this can be explained by the legitimacy of an expertise which results from more than six years of research, and by the recognition of these studies in the West.

These encouraging changes did not occur exclusively in the academic sphere. Moldovan TV and radio prepared several broadcastings on the issue of the Holocaust. In 2010, the Chișinău publishing house "Cartier" published the translation of the German book *The Holocaust at the Peripheries*, which focuses on the Holocaust in Bessarabia, Bukovina, and Transnistria.[27] A local TV station proposed a discussion of this book, for which I was invited. The TV presenter asked in great detail about those historical events that until recently were silenced by majority of historians. Meanwhile a Moldovan newspaper noted the publication of the book dedicated to "these very sensitive issues," and announced that its authors indicate that 45,000–60,000 Jews were killed by the Romanian and German troops in Bessarabia and Bukovina.[28] The very first comment to the online version of this material was signed by a known Moldovan historian and reads as follows: "In Bessarabia and Transnistria WAS NO so-called holocaust!"[29]

Perspectives

Today I have reason to believe that in Moldova there are occurring—even if slowly—certain shifts in the perception of the Holocaust as part of our history. These changes are still timid, and tremendous efforts are necessary for society to understand the inadmissibility of Holocaust denial. For me it is especially difficult to talk about the Holocaust with school teachers: at seminars with them I frequently encounter teachers'

---

[27] Benz, Mihok, eds., *Holocaustul la periferie. Persecutarea și nimicirea evreilor în România și Transnistria în 1940–1944*.
[28] "O carte despre Holocaust a fost lansată la Chișinău," *Timpul*, May 16, 2010.
[29] http://www.timpul.md/articol/o-carte-despre-holocaust-a-fost-lansata-la-Chișinău-10718.html (viewed on October 6, 2010). Capital letters as in the original version.

aversion to teaching about the Holocaust; this often comes with accusations against Jews, who are declared to be the cause for their own misfortune. Over and over I have been asked these types of questions: "Don't you think that behind the discussion about the Holocaust is the desire of Jews to get compensation from Romania?," "Weren't Jews the NKVD officers who took our grandfathers to Siberia?," "Why don't you study the deportation/famine/repressions against Moldovans? Why are you so interested in the fate of Jews?" etc. Several years ago, during one of the seminars with history teachers, I mentioned a testimony included in the book of Jean Ancel, where a Jewish survivor told how in some Moldovan villages local peasants were waiting for columns of deportees and were "buying" from Romanian gendarmes those prisoners who were nicely dressed. Afterwards they would kill them and rob them of clothes and shoes.[30] The audience refused to believe it. Instead, they insinuated that Jews might have invented this story in order to present themselves as the exclusive victims. In the last several years I interviewed over two hundred Moldovans who were eyewitnesses to the Holocaust in 1941. Without any knowledge about Ancel's book, or other testimonies of Jews who survived, these villagers recounted similar episodes, which they witnessed in person.[31]

Meetings with school teachers tend to be strenuous. Teachers from Moldovan schools support pro-Romanian historians and trust their version of national history.[32] In general, the representations of teachers about the Holocaust were formed by the older comments of professional historians on this subject, which were replicated by mass-media. As a result, the majority of Moldovan teachers continue to believe that teaching and researching the Holocaust goes against national interests and benefits only Romanophobes. Until university professors declare a change in their previously held views, one can hardly expect any change in the schools. This may be possible only with the changing of generations.

---

[30] Ancel, *Documents Concerning the Fate of Romanian Jewry during the Holocaust*, 579.

[31] These episodes were reported in Ochiul Alb, Lencăuți, Gârbova, Vălcineț, Scăieni.

[32] The situation is different in schools for national minorities, where a pro-Russian approach of history interpretation is dominant.

Yet in recent years I enjoy the companionship of a small circle of like-minded people. These are young historians, most educated in the West, who believe that the historian's work is not to get involved in political struggles, but to undertake the painstaking research of resources. Their support and encouragement make a serious difference in my academic life.

BIBLIOGRAPHY

Ancel, J. *Contribuții la istoria României: problema evreiască. 1933–1944.* Vol. 2. Bucharest: Hasefer, 2001.
———. *Documents Concerning the Fate of Romanian Jewry during the Holocaust.* Vol. VIII. New York: Beate Klarsfeld Foundation, 1986.
———. *Transnistria, 1941–1942. The Romanian Mass Murder Campaigns.* Vol 3. Tel Aviv: The Goldstein Goen Diaspora Research Center, 2003.
Benz, W. and Mihok, B. eds. *Holocaustul la periferie. Persecutarea și nimicirea evreilor în România și Transnistria în 1940–1944.* Chișinău: Cartier, 2010.
Coman, G. "Chișinăul încearcă disperat să provoace România." *Ziua,* Oct. 16, 2003.
Dumitru, D. and Johnson, C. "Constructing Interethnic Conflict and Cooperation: Why Some People Harmed Jews and Others Helped Them during the Holocaust in Romania." *World Politics* vol. 63, no. 1 (January, 2011): 1–42.
Dumitru, D. "Educarea toleranței la lecțiile de istorie? Predarea Holocaustului în școlile din Republica Moldova" in *Valorile multiculturalității. Lucrări prezentate la Simpozionul Internațional "Valorile Multiculturalității," 16–18 noiembrie 2007,* edited by B. Layslo, V. Sibianu. Miercurea Ciuc: Editura Status, 2007, 217–229.
———. "Attitude Towards Jews in Odessa: From Soviet Rule through Romanian Occupation, 1921–1944," *Cahier du monde russe,* vol. 52, no. 1 (2011): 133–162.
———. "In Memoriam: Jean Ancel, 1940–2008," *Holocaust and Genocide Studies* vol. 22, no. 3 (Winter 2008): 605–606.
———. "The Attitude of the Non-Jewish Population of Bessarabia and Transnistria towards the Jews during the Holocaust: A Survivors' Perspective." *Yad Vashem Studies* vol. 37, part 1, (Spring 2009): 53–83.
———. "Atitudinea populației ne-evreiești din Basarabia și Transnistria către evrei în perioada Holocaustului: o perspectivă a supraviețuitorilor." *Holocaust. Studii și cercetări* vol. 1, no. 2, (2009): 35–58.
———. "Moldawien seit 1990" in *Handbuch des Antisemitismus. Judenfeindschaft in Geschichte und Gegenwart* vol. I. "Laender und Regionen." Edited by W. Benz, W. Bergmann, J. Heil, J. Wetzel, U. Wyrwa. Munich: K.G. Saur Verlag, 2008, 235–236.

———. "Moldova: Holocaust als Spielball. Der schwierige Umgang mit dem jüdischen Erbe." *Osteuropa* vol. 58, no. 8–10 (August–October 2008): 481–492.

———. "The Use and Abuse of the Holocaust: Historiography and Politics in Moldova." *Holocaust and Genocide Studies* vol. 22, no. 1 (Spring 2008): 49–73.

———. "V labirinte politizatsii: prepodavanie Kholokosta v shkole." *Голокост і сучасність в Україні і світі* vol. 1, no. 3 (2008): 27–38.

Goma, P. *Săptămâna roşie 28 iunie – 3 iulie 1940 sau Basarabia si evreii.* Chişinău: Editura Museum, 2003.

Gross, J.T. *Neighbors. The Destruction of the Jewish Community in Jedwabne, Poland.* Princeton, NJ: Princeton University Press, 2001.

Grossman, V. *Zhizn' i sud'ba.* Moscow: Knizhnaia palata, 1990.

International Commission on the Holocaust in Romania, *Final Report.* eds. Friling, T., Ioanid, R., and Ionescu, M. Iaşi: Polirom, 2005.

Ioanid, R. *The Holocaust in Romania: The Destruction of Jews and Gypsies under the Antonescu Regime, 1940–1944.* Chicago: Ivan R. Dee, 2000.

Kuznetsov, A. *Babi Yar. Roman-dokument.* Moscow: Molodaia gvardia, 1967.

Luk'anchikova, M. "Sud'ba evreev Bessarabii, Bukoviny i Transnistrii v 1941–1944 godakh. Reportazh s mezhdunarodnoi konferentsii." *Istoki Zhizni* no. 2, (October 2006): 10.

Marinescu, G. "Afacerea 'Holocaustul evreiesc în Moldova. Toate episoadele." *Moldova Noastră* June 16, 2005. Available at www.mdn.md/historical.php?rubr=1242.

Moraru, A. "Aparută recent cartea 'Holocaustul în Basarabia' este un eşec," *Flux* no. 61 (April 27, 2005).

Moraru, L. "Holocaust in Bessarabia?" *Flux* (Oct. 10, 2006).

Musteaţă, S. "Predarea istoriei în Republica Moldova. Între reformă şi antireformă," in *Contribuţii în căutarea unui nou mesaj. Profesorului Ion Stanciu la împlinirea vârstei de 60 de ani*, edited by Iu. Oncescu, S. Miloiu. Târgovişte, 2005. 376–392.

———. "Identitatea natională între istorie şi politică: un studiu de caz Republica Moldova (2001–2005)," in *Stat slab, cetăţenie incertă. Studii despre Republica Moldova,* edited by M. Heintz (Bucharest: Editura Curtea Veche, 2007, 175–190.

Nazaria, S., Danu D., and Zagorcea, Y. *Kholokost v Moldove.* Kishisnev: CEP USM, 2005.

Prisăcaru, I. "Un istoric neagă că a scris 'Holocaustul în Basarabia,'" *Timpul* (April 29, 2005).

Written Question No. 435 to the Committee of Ministers by Mr. Neguţă: "Modernisation of history teaching in Romanian schools." Reply of the Committee of Ministers. Website of the Committee of Ministers of the Council of Europe, document CM/AS(2004)Quest435finalE/ 23 January 2004. Available at https://wcd.coe.int/ViewDoc.jsp?id=109319&Site=CM&BackColorInternet=9999CC&BackColorIntranet=FFBB55&BackColorLogged=FFAC75.

Weiner, R. "The Foreign Policy of the Voronin Administration." *Demokratizatsiya* vol. 12, no. 4, (2004): 541–556.

The Turns of Russian Historical Politics, from Perestroika to 2011

ALEXEI MILLER

The relationship between history and politics in Russia experienced many dramatic changes since the beginning of Perestroika over 25 years ago. One such dramatic U-turn began in 2009–2010. The purpose of this article is to analyze the causes of the surge of historical politics in Russia at the beginning of the 21st century, and its current revision.

From the Fervor of Perestroika to the Indifference of the 1990s

It is highly unlikely in the foreseeable future that public interest in history in Russia will be anywhere near the level that was typical of the perestroika era. At that time, new trends had a clear political relevance, such as the discovery of "blank spots" in history concerning the crimes of the Communist regime—above all, Stalinism—and the widespread usage of such terms as "empire" and "totalitarianism" in reference to the Soviet Union, which had been previously banned. Even perestroika's idiomatic language was largely borrowed from historians' vocabulary, such as the use of phrases like "opting for a historical path," "historic alternatives," etc. [1]

The public began to crave all things historical. The situation was generally very unhealthy and showed signs of fervor—it was a period when demand definitely outweighed quality supply. At the same time the impression that the whole country decided to adopt a critical attitude towards Stalin and Stalinism was false—those who kept their pro-Stalin views simply were not active in public sphere.

---

[1] See Atnashev. "Transformation of the Political Speech under Perestroika."

The first half of the 1990s was marked by shocks resulting from the collapse of the Soviet Union and dramatic deterioration of material conditions for the majority of Russians. This coincided with a noticeable drop in public interest in history. The so-called trial of the Communist Party in 1992 revealed a profound split in society over the perception of its own past.[2] The Soviet Union's victory in World War II was the sole element of collective memory that evoked an emotional response across various social groups. Russian politicians sensed this and did not make many references to history in their key speeches.[3]

Boris Yeltsin, who remained a staunch proponent of anti-Communist rhetoric until the end of his presidency, no longer sought to make this position the only legitimate one. In the second half of the 1990s, the authorities stopped exploiting the subject of history for political goals and left history for the historians.

In contrast, the 1990s and the beginning of 2000s were very productive years for historians. The "archive revolution" defined this period, when many documents were made accessible for the first time and a considerable number were published. Russian historians started to actively cooperate with their foreign counterparts—mostly Americans and Western Europeans—in studying the events of the 20th century. Dozens of scholarly books on the Soviet period were published, even though society paid far less attention to them than in the perestroika era. Overall, the Russian media did not cope with the job of focusing the public's attention on new historical research. More precisely, it did not set this objective for itself.

Hundreds of monuments to the victims of political repression were erected at the time, most often at sites of mass executions or at Gulag camps.[4] Yet these monuments did not occupy a central place in public space and public consciousness, as they were located on the outskirts of urban areas, or even in hard-to-reach places.[5] No national rituals

---

[2] Materialy dela o proverke konstitucionnosti ukazov Prezidenta RF, kasaiuschihsia deyatelnosti KPSS I KP RSFSR, a takze o proverke konstitucionnosti KPSS I KP RSFSR. Moscow, Spark, 1996–1998, vol. 1–6.

[3] Malinova. "Tema proshlogo v ritorike prezidentov Rossii,"106–122.

[4] The most important role in organization of research of the history of the crimes of the Soviet regime and commemoration of its victims belongs to "Memorial" society, founded in 1991.

[5] Roginskii. "Pamiat' o stalinizme."

for commemorating the victims of the Soviet regime ever materialized. The criminal nature of the Soviet state was fixed neither in juridical nor official political documents.

The assessment of 20th century history, coined in this period, was reflected—with some distinct, but not principal differences—in the wide range of school textbooks.[6] These textbooks assessed the Soviet regime as totalitarian and mentioned many of its crimes. However, this was not to diminish in any way the achievements of the Soviet era or the heroism of the Soviet people at work or on the frontlines.

The nationalization of history was also evident in the textbooks. In Russia's case, this meant that information about those regions of the Soviet Union that had gained independence in 1991, was omitted. However, unlike other former Soviet republics, such nationalization was not accompanied by a radical revision of the pantheon of outstanding personalities. Rather, the pantheon was replenished with figures from the "White camp" (the anti-Bolshevik forces that were forced to emigrate after 1920). Often it was supplemented by physical transfer of their remains to Russia.[7] Attempts to expand the national "list of glorious people" with the names of those who had collaborated with Nazi Germany proved unsuccessful, but their all-out demonization gave way to "discussions, with a shade of understanding." This distinguished Russia from its Western neighbors, above all, the Baltic countries and Ukraine, where wartime collaborators were portrayed as fighters against Soviet occupation and became important part of the national pantheon.

2003–2008: The Escalation of Historical Politics

Former (and future) Russian President Vladimir Putin employed a "reconciliatory comprehensive approach" to history at the beginning of his first presidential term when he resolved the legal problem of state symbols. In order to establish the tricolor Russian flag,

---

[6] Zagladin, et al. *Istoriia Rossii*; Chubarian, *Otechestvennaia istoria*; Levandovskii et al, *Istoria Rossii*.
[7] The remains of Ivan Shmelev were reburied in Donskoi monastery in 2000, the reburial of Ivan Il'in and Anton Denikin took place there in 2005.

he joined a coalition with the liberals and democrats in 2000, ignoring protests from the Communist party. A year later, however, he teamed up with the Communists to reinstate—despite liberal protests—a slightly revised version of the Soviet national anthem. It looked as if the main idea was to accept the past in its entirety as "a common heritage." The result was not a synthesis, but a construct full of controversies, based on the principle of ignoring problems and disregarding responsibility. Attempts to use past events as symbols of reunification proved extremely awkward. This was graphically manifested by the introduction of a new national holiday, the Day of National Unity, in 2005. The "negation" part of the plan worked well—to replace a date linked with the 1917 October Revolution, which was viewed by the authorities as irrelevant. But the "positive" message of national unity failed, the new holiday became, instead, the day of demonstrations by extreme nationalists.

There was growing concern in Moscow over the intensification of Eastern European historical policies targeted at Russia in the 2000s. There were many international incidents during celebrations of the anniversary of the victory in World War II (especially in 2005), when some former Communist countries refused to send delegations to the festivities in Moscow. As a result, Moscow decided to issue no invitations for the festivities in 2010, just welcoming those who expressed the wish to come.

The Reactive Nature of Russian Historical Politics

Subsequently, Russia started drafting a response. The government's first reaction was fairly traditional—tightening the screws inside the country, "rebuffing slanderers abroad," and setting up similar institutions to the ones that other countries used to badmouth Russia. In Russia there was talk of setting up an Institute of National Remembrance modeled after similar institutions in neighboring countries.[8] As early as 2003, Putin said at a meeting with historians at Moscow's Rumyantsev Library that "concentration on negative facts," which was

---

[8] http://www.hrono.ru/statii/2008/shwed_pam.html

justified while the old system was being dismantled, should be replaced by the pathos of creativity and instilling pride in one's own history. "We need to get rid of the gibberish and scum that have accumulated over these past years," he said.

All the countries of Eastern Europe undertook a simple and rather fraudulent operation of "exclusion" of Communism from national history as, allegedly, totally alien to national tradition. That meant total "export" of responsibility to Russia and rejection of any achievements of the Communist period.[9] In Russia such move was impossible, because the central place in national historical mythology belongs to "Victory" (in World War II), which doesn't have analogies in any neighboring countries, except Belarus and South-East Ukraine. The situation demanded a more complex solution. However, politicians first tried a simple one—the legacy of the Soviet period should be protected, particularly the traditional interpretation of Great Patriotic War, while the problem of historical responsibility of the Communist regime should have been neglected.

The period from 2003 to 2006 can be described as a covert phase in the elaboration of Russia's historical politics. That was a reaction to the escalation of historical policies in the neighboring countries, but also to the growth of tensions in relations with the West, particularly the USA and "the new Europe." "The Orange Revolution" of 2004 in Kyiv scared the Kremlin both as a possible scenario for Russia herself, and as a challenge to Russian influence in a key country of post-Soviet space. That caused serious changes in Kremlin policies in many spheres. The acme of tensions was in 2007–2008, which included Putin's famous Munich speech, the conflict around missile defense structures in the countries of Central Europe and the plans of NATO enlargement to Ukraine and Georgia, and, finally, the Russian-Georgian military conflict in August 2008.

Conflicts with Poland, where the very notion of historical politics came into being, became the catalyst for the process. Relations between Moscow and Warsaw, troubled by a tragic past, deteriorated in 2004 due to Poland's active involvement in Ukraine's Orange Revolution. Moreover, Russian-Polish relations grew into a full-blown crisis

---

[9] See Andrei Cusco's article in this volume for a description of the history museum in Kishinev.

in 2005 after the election of Lech Kaczyński, a proponent of a tough anti-Russian policy, as president. Moscow scaled back cooperation with Warsaw over the Katyń massacre, which had become a token element of historical politics in both countries. Moscow displayed a tough reaction to any gesture that had an anti-Russian tint in relations with Ukraine and the Baltic countries.

In 2006, a team of textbook authors, led by Alexander Filippov and Alexander Danilov, was assigned the task of writing a fundamentally new set of Russian history textbooks.[10] We can assume with high degree of probability that the project was commissioned by the presidential administration. The first products in the series, a teacher's manual titled *Russian History: 1945–2007* and a user's guide for the period from 1900–1945, were published in 2007.[11] In June 2007, an all-Russian conference "The Urgent Issues of Teaching History and Knowledge about Society (*Obschestvoznanie*) at School" took place. There new textbooks were presented by the Minister of Education, Andrei Fursenko and the first deputy of the Head of the Presidential Administration Vladislav Surkov. The participants of the conference met President Putin in his country residence in Novoogarevo.

Soon the textbook *History of Russia: 1945–2007*, and the teacher's manual for the period of 1900–1945 were published.[12] Alexander Danilov's own summary of the concept of the textbooks contained the following significant statements:

> – "The main cause of the 'Great Terror' was resistance to Stalin's policy of rapid modernization and Stalin's fear that he might lose control over the country."

---

[10] Danilov defended his first dissertation under the title "Komsomol—an active assistant of the Communist Party in the upbringing of the working youth. 1966–1980's" in 1986, and his doctorate "The Party leadership in the development of creative activity of young working people. 1960–1980's" in 1990. Filippov works as a deputy director of an NGO, the "National Laboratory of Foreign Policy," which defines its task as "assistance to the government structures in the realization of foreign policy" (http://www.nlvp.ru/laboratory/).

[11] Filippov, *Noveishaia istoria Rossii.*

[12] Danilov et al, *Istoria Rossii. 1945–2007*, (second edition: *Istoria Rossii. 1945–2008*); Danilov, *Istoria Rossii. 1900–1945.*

- "There was no organized famine in the rural areas of the Soviet Union."
- "In talking about victims of repression, it would be correct to devise a formula that would include only those who were sentenced to capital punishment or were executed."
- "It should be emphasized that the Red Army's campaign in September 1939 concerned the liberation of territories transferred to Poland under the 1920 Treaty of Riga; in other words, it meant the liberation of part of the homeland."
- "Although there is no justification for the massacre of Polish prisoners of war at Katyń, it should be noted that from Stalin's point of view the executions went far beyond the problem of political rationality, and were a response to the deaths of thousands of Red Army soldiers held in Polish captivity after the war of 1920."[13]

These quotes convey that many postulations (e.g. on 1939, the Katyń massacre or the famine) were motivated by the historical policies of the neighboring countries and worded in the same propaganda-tainted mode of politicized history.

The authors said their textbooks were based on renouncing totalitarianism as a non-scientific tool borrowed from the Cold War era and on an analysis of the Soviet period from the viewpoint of modernization theory. It must be mentioned that preference of modernization theory or the concept of *modernity* to the concept of totalitarianism in analysis of the Soviet period is nothing new. Quite respectable historians argued for such an approach in the early 2000s.[14] But even in the usage of the purposefully primitive version of such an approach in a textbook Danilov and Filippov were not pioneers. They had as a predecessor Yakov Tereschenka, a Belarussian historian close to Alexander Lukashenka, who edited a textbook, published in 2005.[15] This textbook speaks about modernization, implemented in "force

---

[13] См.: http://www.prosv.ru/umk/ist-obsh/info.aspx?ob_no=15378 (последнее посещение 3 февраля 2011 г.).
[14] Kotkin. "Modern Times: the Soviet Union and the Interwar Conjuncture," 111–164.
[15] Tereschenka, ed., *Istoria Balarusi v 2 chastiah*. I am grateful to Alexey Bratochkin for bringing my attention to this book.

major conditions,"[16] it argues that "Soviet totalitarianism—is generally a myth, coined in political, and, as it becomes more and more clear, also civilizational confrontation between the East and the West,"[17] and even claims that the "the deeds of NKVD and the activities of the McCarthy Commission in USA are quite comparable."[18] It is clear that both textbooks had common agenda—"normalization" of Stalinism and legitimization of the contemporary authoritarian leader.

Essentially, the Danilov-Filippov textbook is remarkably similar to the post-Stalin, Soviet narrative, with the exclusion of Communist rhetoric. It suggests that the crimes committed during the Soviet era were unavoidable because Russia was surrounded by enemies and was going through a wartime mobilization. Furthermore, these crimes were kind of justified by the success of modernization, without which Russia's victory in World War II would have been impossible. The public presentations of the textbook by the editors promoted the gloomy mentality of a besieged fortress and stylistically were total déjà vu of Soviet times.[19]

The interests of the commissioner of the textbook were most clearly reflected in the last chapter of the manual, which bears the title "Sovereign democracy."[20] The concept of "sovereign democracy" (in the textbook without quotation marks) was used in the textbook to describe the nature of political regime in Russia, which, according to the authors, ensured the successful development of the country since 2000. As a matter of fact, the textbook was promoting one of the key elements of the ideological platform of the "United Russia" party, coined by Vladislav Surkov.

The number of printed copies of Danilov-Filippov textbook reached 250,000 during the first year. Other textbooks are usually printed in 10,000–15,000 copies per year. 250,000 copies clearly signal political involvement, as none of the publishing houses would print that many, risking several million dollars, if guided exclusively

---

[16] Ibid., 7.
[17] Ibid., 9.
[18] Ibid., 7.
[19] See Danilov and Filippov speeches during the conference in Khabarovsk: http://history.standart.edu.ru/info.aspx?ob_no=12080; http://history.standart.edu.ru/info.aspx?ob_no=12081
[20] Filippov. *Noveishaia istoria Rossii,* 421–485; *Istoria Rossii: 1945–2007.* Chapter 6, esp. 328–329.

by commercial reasons. Formally, Russian schools are free to choose between several textbooks, and the publishing house "Prosveschenie" must have received clear and convincing assurance that it will not encounter problems with distribution. The use of administrative resources to promote this textbook as the "correct one" at the expense of the other textbooks is a classical attribute of historical politics. [21]

The organizers of preparation and publication of the new textbooks for history and "knowledge about society" (the last one got less public attention)[22] clearly aimed at making them dominant at schools. Pavel Danilin, the author of the chapter on "sovereign democracy," at the moment employed at the Fund for Effective Politics—directed by Gleb Pavlovsky who has close links to the Kremlin—and the member of Political Council of "The Young Guard of United Russia" since 2010 has been employed in the Presidential administration. During the public debate about the new textbook he wrote in his blog, addressing the critics: "You can write what you want about me, but you will teach children based on the textbooks we give you and the way Russia needs. All those silly things, which you have now in your goat-bearded heads, will dissapear, otherwise you will disappear from educational institutions."[23]

Attempts to regulate historical issues with legislation, so typical of historical politics, can also be traced in Russia. In the winter of 2009, Emergency Situations Minister Sergei Shoigu, one of the leaders of the ruling United Russia party, was the first to speak out about the need to pass a law threatening criminal prosecution for "incorrect" remarks about World War II and the Soviet Union's role in that war.[24] Two bills pursuant to this idea were soon submitted to the Russian parliament.[25]

---

[21] On administrative mechanisms of imposing the textbook on schools see Miller, "Rossia: vlast' i istoria," 6–23, and my public lecture "Historical policy: update" (http://www.polit.ru/lectures/2009/11/05/istpolit.html).

[22] Obschestvoznanie. Globalnyi mir v XXI veke. Moscow: Prosveschenie, 2008.

[23] As cited in Borisov, "My vas nauchim rodinu lubit'."

[24] Serguei Shoigu suggested to treat as criminal offence attempts to "deny the victory of the USSR in the Patriotic War." *Newsru.* February 20, 2009. (http://www.newsru.com/russia/24feb2009/srokzavov.html).

[25] See "Rossii garantirovano proshloe," *Kommersant* No. 88 (4143). May 20, 2009 (http://www.kommersant.ru/doc.aspx?DocsID=1172771).

In May 2009, Russian President Dmitry Medvedev signed a decree to set up a presidential commission on fighting historical falsification.[26] This was the culmination of the historical politics that had gained momentum since 2003. The document not only fueled a wave of criticism from professional historians and the public at large, but also signaled the start of an aggressive propaganda campaign by those who supported the decree and saw it as a tool to put a check on professional historians. The above mentioned Danilin argued that professional community of historians was irritated by the decree because it was unable to fight against falsifications of history and in many case was sharing the "revisionist" attitude with the enemies of Russia: "Revisionists have raised their heads and use the mainstream media as if under Goebbels."[27] This rhetoric was consciously transforming the debates about history as *res publica* into a clash between the patriots and the traitors, in which the "traitors" had to be silenced and punished.

Many rank and file activists of historical politics were attacking the academic establishment for passiveness, inability or unwillingness to "fight falsifications," claiming that state should support "independent historians," who could do the job much better. The real issue here was an attempt to give the leading role (and the lion's share of funding) in the implementation of the historical politics to newly created NGOs, which were focusing on agressive propagandist efforts as a response to historical policies of Russia's neighbors.[28] Instead of creating an Institute of National Remembrance according to the Ukrainian model, Russian authorities opted for a solution that was technologically more sophisticated.[29] They used the efforts of formally independent public

---

[26] http://президент.рф/%D0%B4%D0%BE%D0%BA%D1%83%D0%BC%D0%B5%D0%BD%D1%82%D1%8B/4121

[27] Danilin. "Kak reagirovat na komissiiu po bor'be s falsifikaciiami," (http://russ.ru/pole/Kak-reagirovat-na-komissiyu-po-bor-be-s-fal-sifikaciyami).

[28] One of such organizations is the foundation "Historical memory," directed by Aleksandr Dyukov. His support to the decree see at http://www.liberty.ru/Themes/Aleksandr-Dyukov-Boyat-sya-deyatel-nosti-Komissii-po-bor-be-s-fal-sifikaciej-istorii-mogut-tol-ko-te-kto-etu-istoriyu-fal-sificiruyut

[29] The creation of an institution similar to Polish Institute of National Remembrance in Russia is impossible, as FSB maintained continuity with KGB, including control of the archives.

organizations that could be assigned various tasks and given selected archival materials. In essence, this was a modification of the familiar technology for media leaks, in which case leaked information is not necessarily altogether false, but is often manipulated. This way historical research loses its scholarly nature and turns into a political-technological contract; decisions on funding and assessing works are not transparent and are made by the political authorities, not by the professional community.

Thus, all the key elements of historical politics, as defined in the introduction to this volume, can easily be found in Russian practices of the 2000s. First, there was an attempt to introduce a standardized history textbook edited by the political center. Second, there were specialized politically engaged institutions that combined the tasks of organizing historical research with control over archives and publications. Third, an attempt was made to regulate interpretations of history through legislation. Finally, all of these practices were supported by methods of legitimization and ideological support typical for historical politics. Historical politics was targeted at people inside Russia.

Although some organizational solutions were quite original, Russian historical politics, in spirit and style, was in line with that of its neighbors. This was fraught with serious consequences for Russian international relations, since the promoters of an anti-Russian historical politics in post-Communist countries expected exactly such reactions from Moscow. The political atmosphere inside Russia was becoming quite depressing.[30]

2009–2011: Contradictory Trends, International Aspect

By autumn 2009 some events signaled certain hesitations about historical politics on the very top of the Russian pyramid of power. Cautious contacts with Polish leadership began almost immediately after Donald

---

[30] At the same time, one shouldn't overestimate the dominance of this tendency to normalize Stalinism in public space and media. The main TV channels were offering almost simultaneously an apologetic serial "Stalin-life" and another based on Solzhenitsyn "In the First Circle," and documentaries with clear anti-Stalinist message.

Tusk, the political opponent of the Kaczyński brothers, became the prime minister of Poland in autumn 2007. The Russian-Polish group for "difficult questions" first met in summer 2008 under the chairmanship of the former Polish minister of foreign affairs Adam Rotfeld and the Rector of Moscow State Institute of International Relations Anatoly Torkunov.[31]

In June 2008, Torkunov published an article, "Paradoxes and Dangers of 'Historical Politics'" in *Nezavisimaia Gazeta*, in which he opposed the then dominant line in Russian historical politics. He spoke about Perestroika as the time when "correct things had been said about the crimes of the [Stalinist] regime." He stated that "in our discussions with revisionists we often use too simplistic, primitive arguments, which are wrongly interpreted within Russia. We shouldn't use the same weapon as our enemies! The answer should be assymetrical. The strive for total uniformity in interpretation of our history can become a corner stone for new totalitarian ideology, even if we are motivated by the wish to refute slanderers."[32] It is important to stress that the first steps towards revision of historical politics in Russia took place in 2008, before the general political context had changed due to the "reset" of relations between Washington and Moscow.

Still, the trend towards "normalization" of Stalinism had remained dominant for some time. The colossal international conference on the history of Stalinism, which took place in Moscow in December 2008 with financial support of Boris Yeltsyn's foundation, was practically ignored by the main TV channels and accompanied with hostile publications in press and websites, close to the Kremlin.[33] During the conference, Minister of Education and Science Andrei Fursenko continued to defend the Danilov-Filippov textbook in spite of devastating criticism from the other participants.[34]

The further dynamic of revision of the government line in historical issues was closely entangled with the development of Russian-Pol-

---

[31] See more about the Group in Torkunov and Rotfeld, *Belyie piatna*.
[32] http://www.ng.ru/ideas/2008-07-18/7_istpolitika.html Compare the article to my public lecture on April 24, 2008 in Moscow for some striking similarities. http://www.polit.ru/lectures/2008/05/07/miller.html
[33] Pavlovsky, "Ploho s pamiat'u = ploho s politikoi."
[34] http://www.memo.ru/2008/12/10/Stalinizm_Conference.htm

ish relations, where Moscow had found a constructive partner since 2007. Prime Minister Putin ex officio became the main partner for Donald Tusk in the developing political dialog. He visited Westerplatte, the symbol of the Polish Army's resistance to Nazi occupation, together with other European leaders on September 1, 2009, the 60th anniversary of the beginning of World War II. This was a significant event for bilateral relations, as September 1 is directly related to the Molotov-Ribbentrop Pact and the Soviet invasion of Poland on September 17, 1939.

On the eve of Putin's visit, the Russian media launched a full-scale "preliminary bombardment" in the spirit of historical politics and tried to depict Poland as a country that had to share responsibility for the outbreak of the war. Naturally, the Molotov-Ribbentrop theme was widely exploited on the eve of the anniversary in historical politics discussions in Russia's neighboring countries as well.

Amid these events, Putin offered an unexpectedly constructive approach in an article titled "Pages of History: A Pretext for Reciprocal Claims or a Basis for Reconciliation and Partnership?" that was published in *Gazeta Wyborcza*, Poland's leading newspaper, on the eve of his visit to Poland.[35] Putin made a reconciliatory speech at Westerplatte in which he unequivocally denounced the Soviet-German treaty of 1939. Also constructive was the speech of Tusk, who said that in 1945 the Soviet soldiers had saved Europe from Nazism, but couldn't bring freedom as they were not free themselves. Russian opponents of historical politics cautiously welcomed Putin's speech, while outspoken proponents of historical politics condemned it as a senseless concession to the Poles, who ostensibly do not have the ability to appreciate such gestures. The Kaczyński camp also rushed to take steps towards fueling the tensions and restoring the confrontational atmosphere that had begun to settle down. All of this clearly showed that the advocates of a confrontational historical politics in both Russia and Poland actually played into each other's hands, using the provocative statements of their opponents to legitimatize their own policies.

The events of the spring of 2010 had a strong impact on the general situation. On April 7, 2010 Tusk and Putin met in Katyń to

---

[35] See the original Russian text at: http://premier.gov.ru/events/news/4814/

commemorate the Polish officers who were shot there in 1940. Putin called this event the "crime of a totalitarian regime" and stood on his knees at the monument to the Polish officers.[36] At the same time Putin declared that the Katyń crime had already got its legal evaluation, which signaled that at that moment he was not prepared to revise the decision of 2004, when the authorities had closed the investigation without making public 116 volumes of materials of the case. Even the government newspaper *Rossiiskaia Gazeta* stated after the ceremony that the "final of the tragedy is still open. The word reconciliation was pronounced by both sides, but only as something to be achieved in future."[37]

President Lech Kaczyński was not invited to the ceremonies on April 7, and decided to go to Katyń on April 10, officially on the "pilgrimage." His plain crashed in Smolensk. The Russian authorities weathered the tragedy with dignity, among other things opting for more decisive revision of the previous historical policy. On the eve of the meeting of prime ministers, on April 2, the Russian television channel "Kultura" which is available to a rather small portion of the country, had shown without previous announcement the much acclaimed film of Andrzej Wajda *Katyń*, which had remained "on the shelf" for more then two years. Already on April 11 the main Russian television channel "Rossia" had shown the film in prime time, making it known to the whole country.

The Kremlin ignored incendiary statements by some Polish media claiming that Russia should bear complete responsibility for the crash. Instead, Russia said it was ready to take further steps towards normalizing relations regarding the most painful issues of their common history. The Russian Ambassador in Warsaw Alexander Alekseev announced in February 2011, that the Russian side was prepared to find the way to "rehabilitate" the victims of Katyń execution, which had been one of the demands of the families of the Polish officers, and continue the declassification of the rest of the volumes of the Katyń documents.[38]

---

[36] http://novayagazeta.ru/data/2010/037/06.html.
[37] "To overcome Katyń," *Rossiiskaia gazeta*. Central edition. No. 5152 (73). 2010. April 8. (http://www.rg.ru/2010/04/08/katyn.html).
[38] See: http://www.echo.msk.ru/news/748814-echo.html.

Significant changes characterized the behavior of those Russian media which are in some way controlled by the Kremlin. Previously any anti-Russian points of Polish politicians and journalists were met with immediate and angry "response." Now media tended to ignore such occasions, in spite of the fact that they were quite numerous at that time. As a result, without constant bombardment with news about Russophobia of the neighbors, public opinion in Russia became more receptive to the reasonable demands of the Polish side, including the issues of history. In general the Russian leadership proved to be willing to search for rapprochement with Warsaw as soon as it had got a partner for this process on the Polish side.

On their side, Donald Tusk and his supporters were persistent in their commitment to reconcile with Russia, even though they have had to pay a large political price. Jarosław Kaczyński and his Prawo i Sprawiedliwość (PiS) party made the "betrayal of Polish dignity and interests" their main point in criticizing the government. It is quite obvious that Lech Kaczyński's "murder" and Russia's responsibility for "genocide in Katyń" will remain on the agenda of PiS party for quite a while. The word "genocide," which in reference to Katyń is questionable even for many Polish historians, has once again proven its efficiency as an instrument of historical politics. The power of the emotions it arouses blocks any rational reasoning.

The Moscow-Warsaw dialogue embraced people on both sides of the debate who wanted to ease tensions, while historical politics advocates sought to push the discussions back into verbal bickering. Both Russia and Poland (and probably the majority of other countries too) have distinct groups consistently targeted towards reconciliation, as well as no less coherent communities that want an escalation in confrontation. Both camps are seeking to win over the majority of people who have no clear position. The success of those who want reconciliation largely depends on whether their partners across the border are ready to ignore provocations, pushing them to the periphery of the public sphere and collective consciousness. Although tensions have not disappeared, they are no longer a decisive factor on the political agenda.

Withdrawing from a confrontation caused by historical politics is a long and difficult process with inevitable setbacks, like any recovery from a severe illness. In the early stages the proponents of reconciliation often have to face a difficult challenge: how to minimize the damage inflicted by attacks from their competitors who are betting on a confrontational historical politics while keeping the trust of their foreign partners. The conduct of Civic Platform representatives in 2010 and 2011 can be seen as a good example of such maneuvering. Moreover, the simple logic of political struggle appears to be an important factor in reconciliation: once politicians start the reconciliation process, they find it difficult to stop since they would have to acknowledge then that their political opponents were right. That is why proponents of reconciliation will abide by it strategically, even if they conduct various political maneuvers.

Russian-Ukrainian relations also changed considerably in 2010. Ukrainian President Victor Yanukovich and his team sought to remove the elements of historical politics that Russia found especially irritating.[39] Moscow was also ready to ease tensions. On May 17–18, 2010, soon after the inauguration of Victor Yanukovich as President of Ukraine, Dmitry Medvedev paid an official visit to Kyiv. Both presidents had visited the memorial to the victims of the famine of 1932–1933. It was the same memorial the opening of which during the presidency of Victor Yushchenko, Medvedev refused to visit in spite of invitation, answering instead with angry comments.[40]

Only Patriarch Kirill had visited this memorial together with Yushchenko in 2009. He condemned the crimes of the Communist regime, stated that starvation "was caused by quite clear political decisions" and called for not using this tragedy for the "historiosophy of hatred."[41] It is clear that both in Russia and in Ukraine the Russian Orthodox Church had become an independent actor in the domain of politics of memory, taking, particularly under Kirill, a resolute anti-Stalinist and anti-Communist position.[42]

---

[39] See more in Georgiy Kasianov's article in this volume.
[40] See Medvedev's statement at http://www.regnum.ru/news/1083713.html
[41] http://www.vesti.ru/doc.html?id=305478
[42] Metropolitan Kirill played an important role in organization of the first visit of president Putin to the site of mass executions in Butovo on October 30, 2007. That was the first visit of the highest Russian official to the site of mass shootings and graves on the Day of commemoration of the victims of political persecutions.

Although there was no political rapprochement with the Baltic countries, the principle of "avoiding extra tensions" was extrapolated there as well. For the most part, the media simply ignored provocative acts on the part of Russia's neighbors. It was the same case in relations with Moldova, although historical politics intensified sharply in that country in 2010, along with a surge in internal political strife.[43] The "reset" in Russia-USA relations, proclaimed in 2009, did not start the politics of reconciliation between Russia and her western neighbors, but had created a favorable climate for consolidation of this trend.

2009–2011: Contradictory Trends, Domestic Aspect

Some politicians in Russia started making statements in 2010 that contrasted sharply with the government's historical politics of the previous years. After Polish President Lech Kaczyński's death, Dmitry Medvedev and an influential part of the establishment started using anti-Stalinist gestures and rhetoric. Commenting on the plan of Moscow Major Yury Luzhkov to decorate Moscow with posters with the portrait of the Commander-in-Chief Joseph Stalin as part of preparations for the anniversary of the Victory in in 2010, the Minister of Culture Alexander Avdeev angrily remarked: "Stalin is a butcher, he is responsible for our country loosing almost a century in its development. He is fully responsible for the first two years of defeats in the Great Patriotic War."[44]

On May 7, 2010, on the eve of Victory celebrations, President Medvedev in an interview with *Izvestia* stated: "It is impossible to say that Stalinism returns, that we return Stalinist symbols, that we plan to use certain posters, etc. This will not happen. This is absolutely unacceptable. This is our state ideology and my position as a President of the Russian Federation… Concerning evaluation of Stalin in the recent year, our position is very clear—Stalin committed massive crimes against his own people." Medvedev also spoke about the USSR as a "totalitarian society" and mentioned the Soviet policy in Katyń investigation as an example of falsification of history. Thus he signaled

---

[43] For more see the article of Andrei Cusco in this volume.
[44] http://echo.msk.ru/news/666986-echo.html

his wish to change the previous historical policy, which, as he admitted, made people talk about renaissance of Stalinism.[45]

In autumn 2009, speaking on his official video-blog, Medvedev condemed the logic, according to which "numerous victims could be justified with some superior state goals." He said that "repressions can't be justified." "We pay much attention to the fight against falsification of our history. But for some strange reason we think that it concerns only the attempts to revise the results of the Great Patriotic War. But no less important is to prevent acquittal of those who killed his own people,"—these words clearly signaled the wish of Medvedev to change the line of historical politics, which was aimed at normalization of Stalinism.[46] In spring 2010, after the tragic events in Smolensk, the political leadership desided to intensify anti-Stalinist rethoric, and Medvedev nailed this change with the words about "state ideology."

Some events in public life of 2010 also signaled the change of general atmosphere. Two of them made particular resonance. In December 2010, the Academy of Sciences had to elect a new director of the Institute of Russian History, formally—the main academic institution for research of Russian history. The frontrunner was Alexander Danilov, the author of the infamous textbook. He had the support of the leadership of the Academy and of the Presidential Administration. Unexpectedly, the members of the historical-philological section of the Academy voted against Danilov.[47] That was a clear signal that servility of the Academy has its limits and that diligent implementation of political commissions doesn't necessarily bring expected benefits.

Another important episode was the discussion of the textbook for university students, written by Alexander Vdovin and Alexander Barsenkov.[48] The book had been approved by the Scientific Council of the Department of History of Moscow State University. It was sharply

---

[45] http://www.izvestia.ru/pobeda/article3141617/
[46] http://blog.kremlin.ru/post/35/transcript
[47] Avtor skandalnogo uchebnika ne vozglavil Institut rossiiskoi istorii, http://polit.ru/country/2010/12/15/daniloff.popup.html; "Akademiki nadenut belye halaty," *Rossiiskaia gazeta*. December 15, 2010. (http://www.rg.ru/2010/12/15/ran.html)
[48] Barsenkov and Vdovin, *Istoriia Rossii. 1917—2009.*

criticized in several journals for xenophobic statements and normalization of Stalinism.[49] Unlike in previous years the case provoked fast reaction by the Public Chamber, which made the book a subject of investigation of a special commission and sharply criticized it for "radical nationalism."[50] The Chair of the Department Sergei Karpov had to apologize. The proponents of the pro-Stalinist trend tried to present the events an assault of "non-Russian liberal mafia" on "Russian historians."[51] The whole story served as yet one more signal of change in the position of authorities, who keep the Public Chamber under strict control.

It is difficult to assess the role of different factors in the reorientation of rhetoric and—potentially—of the government's policies that occurred in 2010. One can only list them without trying to define their significance. In the foreign policy sphere, the "reset" in Russian-U.S. relations luckily coincided with the arrival of political leaders in Poland and Ukraine who want to normalize relations with Russia. The easing of tensions offered a chance to abandon verbal wars over historical issues and Moscow clutched at this opportunity, together with Warsaw and Kyiv. Concerns about improving Russia's image abroad have forced the authorities to admit that attempts "to normalize Stalinism" are seen by Russia's foreign policy partners as scandalous and are used by politicians and the media, who are driven by anti-Russian sentiments.

A few events that took place in early 2011 can be seen as attempts to establish cooperation between a public that finds it necessary to give a clear derogatory political and legal assessment to the wrongdoings committed by the Communist regime, and that part of the establishment ready to make that theme an element of its policy. Some of the members of the Presidential Council for the Development of Civic Society and Human Rights, led by Mikhail Fedotov and Sergei

---

[49] Sokolov and Golubovsky, "Chemu uchat uchitelei istorii"; Svetova, "Specificheskaia istoriia."

[50] http://www.oprf.ru/files/280910453342.doc, see also http://www.echo.msk.ru/news/708657-echo.phtml. History of the polemic about this textbook is described in a special article in Wikipedia: http://ru.wikipedia.org/wiki/История_России._1917—2009

[51] See http://poiskpravdy.com/istoriya-rossii-vdovin-barsenkov/

Karaganov, and the Memorial human rights group, have drafted proposals to implement a national state-public program for commemoration of victims of the totalitarian regime and work towards national reconciliation. In February 2011, this document was presented to President Medvedev during a meeting of the Council in Yekaterinburg.[52] Along with erecting monuments, opening museums and research centers, and establishing national commemorative dates, the authors have suggested holding a competition for a new history textbook and called on the government to support academic research in this field. The project also specifies important political and legal steps, such as juridical assessment and political condemnation of crimes committed by the Communist regime. Furthermore, the project presupposes a ban on the denial and/or justification of these crimes. The authors of the project wanted to write their own anti-Communist views into the president's political agenda. The preamble of their brainchild mentions, among other things, the task of modernization and fantastical ideas about the consolidation of CIS countries. The somewhat awkward preamble and a number of inaccurately formulated practical proposals have made the draft an easy target for criticism from its opponents.

The Crystallization of Positions

The future of the document remains unclear. Through the irony of politics, Medvedev handed the program to Chief of the Presidential Administration Staff, Sergei Naryshkin, who is also head of Medvedev's commission on historical falsification, and instructed him to analyze "the important proposals." Yet some things can already be stated. The draft has marked a transition in the public debate on history to a new quality level, where there are two opposing positions that are stringently formulated and politically anchored.

One position suggests that the condemnation of crimes committed by the Communist regime should be reduced. First of all, it should not overshadow the achievements of the regime, which include, in addition to the victory in World War II, industrialization, space research,

---

[52] http://news.kremlin.ru/transcripts/10194

successes in atomic energy, the eradication of illiteracy, etc.[53] Second, the recognition of the crimes of Communism will weaken Russia's foreign policy positions and may result in unpredictably large compensation payments to the victims of repression and their descendents. Finally, the implementation of the program is allegedly untimely, as it will split society and lead to a "civil war." The latter argument is based on the conviction that today, almost a hundred years after the Bolshevik revolution and more than fifty years after Stalin's death, which marked an end to mass repression, it is still useful to abide by the tactics of "superseding oblivion."[54]

This camp is quite heterogeneous—it includes Communists, who are still prepared to wave Stalin's portraits at public rallies, but also the "gosudarstvenniki" (proponents of a strong state), who may dislike Stalin, but detest his critics and the West even more. It was in precisely this vein that historical politics developed in 2003–2009. It progressed under the motto of a struggle against libels of the past and sought to understate the scale of repressions (Danilov's proposal to rank only those who were executed as victims) or to present them in a relativist way (on the principle "others had sins too"). In many ways this was an attempt to rehabilitate the Communist-era discourse on the balance of Soviet achievements and faults, and criticism of the personality cult, more in tradition of Brezhnev's era rather than Khrushchev's, but without defending Communism as an ideology. This discourse resonates with the frustrated part of the population, which loads into "Stalin" as into an empty container the nostalgia for "superpower," "friendship of peoples," "social security" and their protest against quite real and often glaring social inequality, corrupt government and other vices of today's Russia.

The other side posits that society and politics should make the condemnation of Communist crimes an integral part of the political

---

[53] This position is clearly formulated in the blog of one of the activists of historical politics: "1937–1938. If not for these events, the Stalin period would stay in history as absolutely normal." (http://a-dyukov.livejournal.com/933487.html?view=23216239).

[54] The main medium of the opponents of the project is the web-portal "Regnum," which offers plenty of critical texts about the text and its authors. See http://www.regnum.ru/dossier/1747.html

discourse about the past and a key element in the government's political legitimization. Unless the remembrance of crimes and commemoration of their victims is limited to self-identification with the victims—the simplest and most dangerous path[55]—and if memory raises the issue of national responsibility for past sins, it may serve as an important lever in revamping social relations. Russian liberals have traditionally been most active in criticizing historical politics of normalization of Stalinism. Their opponents usually present it as a conspiracy of anti-national liberals, which might be an effective propagandistic move, but deliberately distorts reality. The liberals are not the only group who want to strongly condemn the crimes of Communism. *Russian History: the Twentieth Century* (edited by Andrei Zubov), a strongly anti-Communist book, was published recently.[56] It became a bestseller and has produced a widespread public response. The book was written on the basis of religious—and partly conservative—positions. Another major project, *History of Stalinism*, launched in 2008 by the ROSSPEN publishing house and the Boris Yeltsin Foundation, currently includes 50 volumes reflecting a wide range of opinions.[57] More than 800 commemorative sites (museums, monuments, memorial plaques, etc.) dedicated to those who were killed in political repressions and erected across Russia mostly through local initiatives, show that the problem concerns not only "liberals who live in downtown Moscow."

Public opinion surveys show that only 30 percent of the population supports the politics of de-Stalinization, but this figure needs proper interpretation.[58] The 45 percent of respondents who say that de-Stalinization is a myth and empty words are not necessarily opponents of de-Stalinization as such, because only 26 percent of respondents believe that Stalin made more good then bad for Russia. In order to consolidate public support for de-Stalinization, people must be convinced that proposed measures are not yet another momentary political

---

[55] Focusing of historical discourse of victimhood allows totally externalize the responsibility for past crimes and can even become a basis for aggressive behavior, as the case of Yugoslavia perfectly illustrates.
[56] Zubov, *Istoriia Rossii. XX vek.*
[57] The author of this article counts himself among the non-liberal (in terms of political views) adherents of this program. See Miller, "Istricheskaia pamiat'."
[58] See VCIOM poll on April 27, 2011.

manipulation, but a serious attempt to address crucial moral and political issues.

Anti-Stalinist trends in politics of memory can lean on a broad coalition of forces that are far apart on many other issues. The Russian Orthodox Church, particularly under the leadership of Patriarch Kirill, has been persistently anti-Stalinist and anti-Communist. When discussions of the draft program for commemorating the victims of political repressions were underway, the Russian Orthodox Church strongly supported its main idea—the political and legal assessment of the crimes committed by the Bolshevist regime. "It's clear for me, that such suggestions should have been done long ago. It is necessary to establish political and legal evaluation of the crimes of the Bolshevist regime. We should remember that these were the crimes not only of Stalin, but also Lenin, Dzierzynski, Trotsky. We should commemorate the victims of the bloody Bolshevist coup. We can't continue naming streets after butchers"—said the head of the department of public relations of the Russian Orthodox Church Vsevolod Chaplin.[59]

It turned out that many people in the establishment have strong anti-Communist sentiment, although they are not necessarily consonant with liberal viewpoints. There are also people who are ready to support this policy out of momentary tactical considerations. For instance, in January 2011 a group of United Russia party officials said they were in favor of burying Lenin's body.[60] The party is ready to support the anti-Communist memorial policy by and large if it brings political rewards. Given this situation, the memorial policy may become an important element in the overall political agenda and an important distinctive element of Medvedev's positioning in the upcoming years.

Most importantly, it may help tap new ideas for legitimizing and transforming the incumbent regime, whose ideology has obviously become tattered. The condemnation of illegitimate repression and the Bolshevist class-based terror falls perfectly in line with the idea of a state ruled by law, democratization and political nation-building—a slogan that Medvedev has put at the center of his platform. It is difficult to predict where this discussion will lead. The opponents of con-

---

[59] http://www.regnum.ru/news/1393655.html#ixzz1KHx9xUCP
[60] Fishman. "Obschestvennyi interes: zhivoi ili mertvyi."

demnation of the Communist regime's crimes have mobilized to put the polemics back on the track of habitual historical politics—personalized attacks against opponents, purported distortions of their position and complaining about high treason. There is a chance, however, that efforts to defile the discussion will fail. It seems that both supporters of an anti-Communist memorial policy and its opponents have enough people ready for an essential dialogue.

Naturally, one cannot help but notice the absence of a traditional infrastructure for public discussion in Russia, which David Art has analyzed using Germany and Austria. He highlighted the significance of printed media as the arena where different viewpoints confront each other and where shifts in public consciousness regarding collective memory and norms of politically correct speech are fixed.[61] Russia does not have a single printed medium that might play the role of this kind of moderator. Attempts continue to give this role to the internet, and that is where the main action is taking place.[62] In this sense further progress on memorial policy is of special interest to researchers, as this is one of the first instances of an internet-based process.[63]

Russia has escaped the outburst of historical policy that seemed inevitable in 2009. Today one can hardly expect that the tendency—whose culmination came with the creation of Medvedev's commission on historical falsification and the Filippov-Danilov textbook—would successfully regain its previous power, audacity and confidence. It is equally obvious, however, that the heated public debate over the memorial policy will continue to gain momentum. This will likely become an important, if not decisive, ideological element in reformatting the entire social and political sphere—something that is practically inevitable twenty years after the collapse of the Soviet Union and because the related emotions and images are gradually disappearing from most peoples' short-term memories. It is impossible to figure out,

---

[61] Art. "The Politics of the Nazi Past in Germany and Austria."

[62] That is clearly visible in the footnotes to this article, where internet sources dominate.

[63] In Poland, for instance, two newspapers (*Gazeta Wyborcza* and *Rzeczpospolita*), hostile to each other but still maintaining a dialog, provide traditional infrastructure for discussions about memory politics.

however, the historical myth that might appear in place of what has been the focal point of polemics over the past two decades.

BIBLIOGRAPHY

Art D. *The Politics of the Nazi Past in Germany and Austria*. Cambridge; N. Y.: Cambridge Univ. Press, 2006.
Atnashev. T. *Transformation of the Political Speech under Perestroika. Free Agency, Responsibility and Historical Necessity in the Emerging Intellectual Debates (1985-1991)*. PhD Dissertation. Florence: EUI, 2010.
Barsenkov A.S., A.I. Vdovin. *Istoriia Rossii. 1917-2009. 3rd edition*. Moscow: Aspekt Press, 2010.
Borisov M. "My vas nauchim Rodinu lubit,'" *Otechestvennye zapiski* no. 4, vol. 36 (2007). Available at http://www.strana-oz.ru/print.php?type=article&id =1530&numid=38.
Chubarian A.O. ed. *Otechestvennaia istoria XX—the beginning of the XXI century. 3rd edition*. Moscow.: Prosveschenie, 2006.
Danilin, P. "Kak reagirovat na komissiiu po bor'be s falsifikaciiami." Available at http://russ.ru/pole/Kak-reagirovat-na-komissiyu-po-bor-be-s-falsifikaciyami.
Danilov A.A. *Istoria Rossii. 1900-1945*. Moscow: Prosveschenie, 2008.
Danilov A.A., A.I. Utkin, and A.V. Filippov, eds. *Istoria Rossii. 1945-2007*. Moscow: Prosveschenie, 2007. (Second edition: *Istoria Rossii. 1945-2008*. Moscow: Prosveschenie, 2008).
Filippov A.V. *Noveishaia istoria Rossii: 1945-2006: A manual for teacher*. Moscow: Prosveschenie, 2007.
Fishman, M. "Obschestvennyi interes: zhivoi ili mertvyi." *Vedomosti* no. 14, January 28, 2011. Available at www.vedomosti.ru/newspaper/article/253920/ zhivoj_i_mertvyj.
Kotkin S. "Modern Times: the Soviet Union and the Interwar Conjuncture." *Kritika: Explorations in Russian and Eurasian History* vol. 2, no 1. (New Series) (Winter 2001): 111-164.
Levandovsky A.A. Schetinov Ju.A., Mironenko S.V. *Istoria Rossii: XX–the beginning of the XXI century*. Moscow: Prosveschenie, 2009.
Malinova, O. "Tema proshlogo v ritorike prezidentov Rossii." *Pro et Contra*, no. 3-4, (2011): 106-122.
Miller, A. "Istricheskaia pamiat': neobhodimaiia programma." *Vedomosti* no. 62, April 8, 2011. Available at http://www.vedomosti.ru/newspaper/article/258134/neobhodimaya_programma
———. "Rossia: vlast' I istoria." *Pro et Contra* no. 3-4. (2009): 6-23.
Pavlovsky, G. "Ploho s pamiat'u = ploho s politikoi. Politika pamiati." *Russkii zhurnal*, December 9, 2008. Available at www.russ.ru/pole/Ploho-s-pamyat-yu-ploho-s-politikoj

Roginsky, A. "Pamiat' o stalinizme." Paper at the conference "History of Stalinism," Moscow, December 5, 2008. Available at http://www.hro.org/node/3916).

Sokolov, N., A. Golubovsky. "Chemu uchat uchitelei istorii." *Iskusstvo kino* no. 4. (2010).

Svetova, Z. "Specificheskaia istoriia. Uchebnik kak posobie po ksenofobii." *The New Times*, no. 21. June 21, 2010.

Tereschenka, Y. ed. *Istoria Balarusi v 2 chastiah. Uchebnoe posobie dlia studentov uchrezdenii, obespechivaiuschih polucheniie vysshego obrazovaniia.* Vol. 2 *(From February Revolution to Our Days)*. Mogilev: Mogilev State University, 2005.

Torkunov, A., V. Rotfeld, eds. *A. Belyie piatna – chernyie piatna. Slozhnyie voprosy v rossiisko-polskih otnosheniiah.* Moscow: Aspekt Press, 2010.

Zagladin N.V, et al. *Istoriia Rossii: XX–the beginning of the XXI century* (8th edition). Moscow: Russkoe slovo, 2008.

Zubov, A., ed. *Istoriia Rossii. XX vek.* Vol. 1–2. Moscow: AST, 2009.

Politics of History in Turkey: Revisionist Historiography's Challenge to the Official Version of the Turkish War of Liberation (1919–1922)

Şener Aktürk

Introduction

History writing has been highly politicized and closely monitored in Turkey, not only during the authoritarian founding period of the Republic (1923–1950) under the one-party dictatorship of the Republican People's Party (CHP), but also in the sixty years since Turkey's transition to multiparty democracy (1950–2010). On the other hand, Turkey has not been a totalitarian state, even during the period of one-party rule, and definitely not since the 1950s, and this allowed for continuous traditions of revisionist historiographies, which flourished in particular since the end of the last period of military government in 1983.

Despite Turkey's pluralistic civil society and quasi-democratic political regime, the hegemony of the official version of Turkey's history has been maintained and reinforced by a mix of legislative measures, criminal codes, funding and subvention decisions, and repression against unrepentant critics of the official historiography along with the inclusion of formerly revisionist scholars and figures into the official structures as a reward for good behavior.[1] Nonetheless, especially

---

[1] Therefore we see that the state has sometimes been receptive towards and rewarding of formerly revisionist scholars, if they changed their views at least in part and started defending aspects of the official historiography against its detractors. In such behavior we see the authoritarian intention of wanting to control not only the government but also the opposition. The hegemony of the official view is therefore maintained not only by repression but also through rewards to former revisionists who accept and defend aspects of the official view. Similarly, in the Soviet Union, Yitzhak Brudny argued that the

with the legalization of multiple political parties in 1945, and the coming to power of the Democratic Party in the first free and fair elections in 1950, different political parties and factions were able to produce their own versions of and challenges to the official Turkish history, with different degrees of success and differentiation. But what have been the historical episodes of contention?

The narration and interpretation of many historical episodes have been of immediate concern and direct attention by the state authorities, including but not limited to the history of Atatürk's secularizing reforms starting with the Lausanne Treaty (1923), the legislative act that abolished the Caliphate and the Ministry of Sharia and Foundations and unified the education system (1924),[2] the conduct of the Independence Tribunals (*istiklal mahkemeleri*) in the 1920s and the 1930s, Kurdish rebellions including that of Sheik Said (1925), Ağrı (1930), and Dersim (1938) in particular, episodes of minority discrimination such as the Wealth Tax (1942) against non-Muslims, the three military coups (1960, 1971, 1980), Turkish-Soviet relations under Atatürk, and even pre-Republican episodes such as the constitutional "revolution" of 1908 and the reaction to it epitomized in the uprising of "March 31" (1909), mass deportation and massacres of the Ottoman Armenians (1915), and the nature of the Arab revolt (1916–1918).

Naturally, the representation of the historical figures involved in these episodes has also been extremely politicized, especially since the value judgments about contested historical episodes are usually transmitted through the overly negative or positive depictions of key figures. However, no single episode is more central to the politics of history and identity in modern Turkey than the War of Liberation (*Kurtuluş Savaşı*, 1919–1922), which was a struggle between the resistance fighters spread across Anatolia and Thrace, who eventually came under the

---

Soviet leadership employed strategies of inclusion vis-à-vis the Russian nationalist movement that emerged during and after Khrushchev's thaw. See Brudny, *Reinventing Russia*.

[2] In Turkish, *Şeriye ve Evkaf Vekaleti*, and *Tevhid-i Tedrisat Kanunu*. Along with the abolition of the Caliphate, all three of these historic reforms occurred in March 3, 1924, making this date perhaps the most important milestone of Turkey's secularization.

leadership of the Ankara government led by Mustafa Kemal (Atatürk), against the Greek, British, French, and Italian occupation forces, and their local collaborators, including the last Ottoman sultan and his government in Istanbul. The War of Liberation is, as such, the "master narrative" of modern, post-imperial, republican Turkish national identity.

In this master narrative, according to the official historiography, the key actor is Mustafa Kemal (Atatürk), who enjoys probably the most resilient "cult of personality" in a post-authoritarian, democratic country in the modern world. The official narrative of the war depicts it as the independence struggle of an ethno-linguistically defined Turkish nation, whose aspirations for modern secular statehood are represented by Atatürk, who is depicted as the most important military and political genius of the 20th century credited with almost single-handedly planning, launching and winning the war as well as conceiving and implementing a multitude of reforms in the aftermath of the war. Therefore, any challenge to the official version of the history of the War of Liberation, and Mustafa Kemal's role in it, is a challenge to the very heart of the official identity narrative, and treated as such.

There are two different types of revisionism: one about reinterpreting Mustafa Kemal so that his myth would support a particular political agenda; and a second one aiming at undermining Kemal's myth as such. My primary focus in this chapter is the latter, what I think of as the "fundamental revisionism." Among the revisionist scholars covered in this chapter, all the Islamist and Kurdish nationalist revisionists, most of the liberal critics, and a small minority of socialist critics are fundamental revisionists. The former type, on the other hand, is what we may call "pragmatic revisionism," where a political party or a group argues that Mustafa Kemal was in reality a supporter of *their* political ideology and program. Pragmatic revisionism as such supports the personality cult of Kemal Atatürk even as it challenges the official interpretation of Mustafa Kemal's life and ideas. In this chapter, most socialist revisionist figures fall into the "pragmatic revisionist" category.

The Official History of the War of Liberation and Its Discontents: Personal, Islamist, Socialist, Kurdish Nationalist, and Liberal Challengers

It is therefore most apt to focus on the partisan, political and politicized controversies around the history of the War of Liberation, and Mustafa Kemal's role in it, in discussing the politics of history in Turkey. Since the very founding of the Republic there emerged at least four major ideological-interpretive groups of challengers to the official historiography of the War of Liberation: Islamist, socialist, liberal, and Kurdish nationalist critics. These four strands have not been of equal strength; the Islamist one has been more resilient and popular among the masses throughout than the other three; but the socialist and liberal ones were more popular among the intellectuals, and the Kurdish nationalist interpretation has been, unsurprisingly, popular among Kurdish intellectuals.

All four challenged the official historiography to differing degrees on two key issues: first, the nature of the War of Liberation, and second, the role of Mustafa Kemal in it. In this chapter, I will first discuss the institutional, legal, and informal regulations and parameters, which for a long time helped to maintain the hegemony of the official interpretation, and structured the politics of history in modern Turkey. I will then focus on the primary sources, the earliest, original challenges to the official historiography that emerged in the writings of key leaders of the War of Liberation who were marginalized and pushed out of the political arena (and in some cases out of Turkey). These include most importantly two leading military and political leaders in the War of Liberation, as well as one of the two negotiators of Turkey's independence in the Lausanne Conference who was also a long time minister of health in the first parliament.[3] Their criticisms of the official historiography had a "personal" dimension in addition to ideological differences, and have been extensively used by both liberal and Islamist critics in their revisionist accounts of modern Turkish history. In the third and final part, I will briefly present the Islamist, Kurdish nationalist, socialist,

---

[3] Respectively, Kazım Karabekir, Rauf Orbay, and Rıza Nur.

and liberal interpretations of the War of Liberation and its aftermath that emerged in the more pluralistic and permissive environment of multiparty politics since the 1950s, and especially since the 1980s.

The Institutional, Legal, and Informal Parameters of Turkey's Politics of History

There are institutional, legal, and informal parameters that structure and regulate politics of history in Turkey. To begin with, the Turkish History Institute (*Türk Tarih Kurumu*, TTK) in Ankara has been the standard bearer of the official doctrine on Turkish history. Along with the Turkish Language Institute (*Türk Dil Kurumu*, TDK), TTK was founded by Mustafa Kemal himself. The two are cherished as some of Mustafa Kemal's most important institutional legacies, also because he left a certain share of his personal inheritance for the funding of TTK and TDK. The very first goal of TTK under the one party regime was the propagation of the Turkish History Thesis, a controversial assertion by the Kemalist regime that the ancestors of Turks migrated from Central Asia across the Eurasian landmass and accounted for the spread of civilization in these places. It counted various peoples and civilizations such as Hittites in pre-Islamic Anatolia and Etruscans in pre-Roman Italy as having proto-Turkic origins. A somewhat less extensive but still ambitious list of historic empires and peoples were studied as being "Turkish," going as far back as to the Scyhtians, Huns, Khazars, and Avars, among others. Thus, political control of the TTK should be considered as part of the politics of history.

TTK maintained some kind of an institutional "autonomy," which somewhat sheltered it from elected officials' influence after the transition to multiparty democracy in 1950, when CHP, the founding party of the Republic, lost power to the Democratic Party (DP). DP became the touchstone of social, economic, cultural, and political grievances against the 27-year long one-party regime of CHP. Never again after losing power in 1950 could the CHP garner enough votes to come back to power without a coalition. However, a cursory look at TTK's institutional history and leadership strongly suggests that TTK remained the preserve of CHP and its version of Kemalist truisms well into the multiparty period. This is evident in the directors of TTK.

For example, a figure who even served as a prime minister during the one-party regime of CHP was the director of TTK for 20 years (1941–1961), continuing in this position for more than a decade after the transition to multiparty politics.[4] A doctor of medicine who was also a racial anthropologist interested in cranial measurements, succeeded him for the next decade (1962–1973).[5] The next director (1973–1982) was previously appointed as a member of the parliament and the constitutional commission by the military dictatorship of 1960–1961, and was also strongly associated with the CHP.[6]

In summary, although the country transitioned to democracy in 1950, and conservative parties of the right that were implicitly or explicitly critical of the official Kemalist interpretation of history came to power over the next decades, the institutional pinnacle and standard bearer of Turkish history, TTK, remained in the hands of scholars who subscribed to the official interpretation that prevailed since the 1930s, due to its institutional autonomy. However, while TTK might give a direction or a signal to other historians who are willing to follow its lead in terms of the acceptable and desirable historiography, it neither dominates nor controls the writing of history by Turkish scholars and non-scholars at large. Therefore, its existence alone would not be sufficient to sustain the hegemony of the official historiography for so long.

Most importantly, there are laws that criminalize certain historical interpretations, which, by definition, constrain the freedom of expression and the politics of history, forcing many political actors and intellectuals to censor themselves. For example, there is the law number 5816, which is the "Law on the Crimes Committed against Atatürk."[7] The law was curiously legislated by the Democratic Party (DP) in 1951, a year after its historic electoral victory against the CHP, in order to prove the Kemalist credentials of DP against mounting attacks and pressure from the CHP. These laws were responding to a concrete

---

[4] This figure was Şemsettin Günaltay. Official website of the TTK. http://www.ttk.org.tr/index.php?Page=Sayfa&No=182. Accessed in October 8, 2010.

[5] Ibid. This was Şevket Aziz Kansu, who served between April 28, 1962 and April 21, 1973.

[6] This was Enver Ziya Karal. See Demirer, "Iki Referandum: 9 Temmuz 1961-12 Eylul 2010."

[7] The law was ratified in July 25, 1951, and published in the Official Gazette in July 31, 1951. Also available at http://www.mevzuat.adalet.gov.tr/html/956.html.

development, the rising attacks by a new religious order called the *Ticanis* on the busts of Atatürk around the country. Also curiously, CHP was in a covert alliance with this new religious order in the run up to the 1950 elections; therefore, CHP even resisted the passage of the law. Interestingly, Ticanis heightened their attacks and activities after DP's election victory and CHP blamed DP for the attacks, accusing the new DP government of allowing the rise of religious reactionary groups. The law was passed in 1951. Ticanis were given prison sentences and their leader was exiled to an island, which he appears to have turned into his economic fiefdom over the years, until he was finally arrested again, this time for sexually molesting young boys.[8] The Ticani religious order virtually disappeared and left these curious and horrendous crimes behind it; but the law that was passed in reaction to one of their activities is still in place.

The law stipulates from one to three years prison term to anybody who "insults or curses at Atatürk's legacy." For a person damaging, destroying, blemishing, or polluting representations of Atatürk such as his statues, busts, or memorials, a prison sentence from one to five years is prescribed. Those who encourage or incite others to commit the acts listed above are subject to the same punishment as the one who does it.[9] If the crime is committed by two or more persons together or in a public manner, the prison sentence is increased by half (e.g., six years in prison instead of four).[10] Many intellectuals and politicians of conservative-Islamist inclination have been given prison sentences for defaming and insulting Atatürk.[11]

Another example is the infamous Article 301 of the Turkish Penal Code, which criminalizes "insulting Turkishness," and prescribes a prison sentence from six months to three years for this offense.[12] The prison term is increased by a third if the crime is committed by

---

[8] Hür, "CHP, Ticaniler ve Atatürk'ü Koruma Kanunu."
[9] Ibid, Article 1.
[10] Ibid, Article 2.
[11] These include Necip Fazıl Kısakürek (in 1960–61), Mustafa İslamoğlu (1995–96), Hakan Albayrak (in 2003), Cuma Bozgeyik (in 2008), and Atilla Yayla (in 2008).
[12] Turkish Penal Code, Article 301/1. Turkish Penal Code is available at the official website of the Grand National Assembly (parliament) of Turkey at http://www.tbmm.gov.tr/kanunlar/k5237.html.

a Turkish citizen outside of Turkey.[13] Article 301 was used most often in recent years to indict Turkish citizens who would describe the deportation of Ottoman Armenians in 1915 as a "genocide."[14] Turkish-Armenian journalist Hrant Dink was among those found guilty on the basis of Article 301, but he was murdered before serving a prison sentence. It was suspected that the "deep state" seeking to create the conditions for a military coup was involved in the murder of Hrant Dink. The application of Article 301, however, is certainly not limited to expressions regarding the fate of Ottoman Armenians, and both Islamist and Kurdish nationalist intellectuals were put on trial for insulting Turkishness.[15]

The way the fate of Ottoman Armenians in 1915 is addressed in Turkish public and academic community brings together many elements of Turkey's politics of history in a somewhat ironic way. Perhaps the first thing one notices about the "discussion" is that it stimulated a tremendous publication boom in Turkey in the first decade of the 21st century. Not a month passes without multiple books published on the "Armenians." A casual search in a Turkish online bookseller returned 297 books with "Armenian" in their title as of November 2010.[16] Almost all of these books deal with the deportation of Armenians in 1915 with some also on the previous rebellions and massacres, and a large majority, but definitely not all, are aimed at refuting the allegations of "genocide." It is noteworthy that an overwhelming majority of them were published in the 2000s, that publications of TTK and other state organs are prominently represented among these although the majority are definitely private publishers, organizations, and persons.

Equally noteworthy however is the fact that several dozen books making the argument of genocide, implicitly or explicitly, have appeared in Turkish, also in recent years. What is most noteworthy, however, is that many if not most historians in the leading public and private universities in Turkey are highly critical of the official view and they implicitly

---

[13] Ibid, Article 301/3.
[14] These include very prominent artists and intellectuals such as Orhan Pamuk, Hasan Cemal, and Murat Belge. But none of these were found guilty.
[15] These include Abdurrahman Dilipak, a very prominent Islamist, Ismail Beşikçi and Ferhat Tunç, among others.
[16] www.kitapyurdu.com. Search term "Ermeni." Last accessed November 27, 2010.

or explicitly accept the thesis that the Committee of Union and Progress dictatorship decided to rid Anatolia of its Armenian population. This also created, or rather augmented, a widespread anti-intellectualism among those subscribing to the official view. When three leading Turkish universities, one of them being the leading public university in Turkey, organized an international conference in September 2005 on the fate of the Ottoman Armenians, participants of the conference, which included some of the highest profile historians and intellectuals in Turkey, were heavily criticized and stigmatized in major newspapers such that some of them started traveling with bodyguards for their personal safety. There are many opportunities to talk about the deportations and how tens if not hundreds of thousands died or were killed during this process, but the word "genocide" is a taboo. Therefore one often sees that even the official authorities, including textbooks, admit that tremendous human suffering and mass deaths occurred as a result of this decision, but they argue that this was not the goal of the Ottoman government, which was simply trying to relocate them from Eastern Anatolian provinces to Syria, another Ottoman province.

Beyond the institutional and legal constraints against revisionist historians of modern Turkey, there are also informal parameters and constraints that are at least as important. For example, often it seems as though the content of what is being said is less important than the political position and value judgment of the one who said it. A typical example is the leader of the Marxist-Maoist Workers' Party, who wrote a book, where it was implied that Atatürk was an agnostic or even an atheist, based on Atatürk's own personal and public writings on religion.[17] If a conservative or an Islamic intellectual claimed Atatürk to be an atheist or an agnostic, he would likely be imprisoned for insulting Atatürk's memory under Article 5816. But when a Marxist-Maoist atheist makes the same claim as a way to praise Atatürk and to endear him to the Marxist-Maoist intelligentsia, he goes unpunished, since he serves the purpose of strengthening the admiration of Atatürk within his political constituency.

Following on the same theme of Atatürk's views on religion, at the other end of the spectrum one finds books about Atatürk's deep reli-

---

[17] Perinçek, *Atatürk: Din ve Laiklik Üzerine*.

giosity, exemplified in a recent book on "Atatürk's Quranic Culture."[18] The goal of the book is to repudiate Islamists' allegations that Atatürk was a bad Muslim or worse, an atheist and an enemy of Islam. This, too, is a purpose in conformity with the official historiography, even if the underlying factual claim is the polar opposite of Perinçek's book mentioned above. On the other hand, when an Islamist columnist claimed that Atatürk might not have had an Islamic funeral (more specifically, an Islamic "funeral prayer" before burial),[19] he was sentenced to 15 months in prison for insulting the memory of Atatürk, and served six months in the Kalecik prison in 2004. These examples illustrate that factually similar assertions can be subjected to completely different treatments, while assertions in opposite directions can be treated similarly. What matters most is whether their value judgment is in conformity with the official historiography.

Despite legal, institutional, and informal constraints on criticizing the official historiography, many dissidents developed their own critiques and alternative views of history, often under the protection of different political parties and intellectual groups that emerged, especially after the transition to multiparty politics in 1950. However, even during the one party regime (1923–1950), there were few political figures who had a personal stature powerful enough to challenge the emergent official historiography. Within the constraints of this chapter, one can briefly review some of most notable dissident, revisionist personalities of this era.

"Personal" Challenges to the Official History of the War of Liberation: Memoirs of Kazım Karabekir, Rauf Orbay, and Rıza Nur as Dissident Narratives

Some of the first challenges to what later became the official history of the War of Liberation came from the major figures who organized and led the war together with Mustafa Kemal. The closest one gets to the "beginning" of the War of Liberation is a revolutionary declaration issued and signed by five military officers including Mustafa Kemal in the town of Amasya in June 1919, which is a key turning

---

[18] Kasapoğlu, *Atatürk'ün Kur'an Kültürü*.
[19] Hakan Albayrak, "Bir Cenaze Namazı," *Milli Gazete*, June 20, 2000.

point in the centralization and nationalization of isolated and regional instances of resistance to the occupation forces of Britain, France, Italy, and Greece. This declaration called for a congress of people's deputies in the town of Erzurum in July 1919, which took place as scheduled. What is noteworthy for our purposes is that four signatories of the Declaration of Amasya (*Amasya Tamimi*, or in modern Turkish, *Amasya Genelgesi*), namely every signatory other than Mustafa Kemal himself, was politically marginalized after the victory in the war as opponents of Mustafa Kemal and the new Kemalist regime.[20]

As in other self-identified revolutionary situations in modern history, the national revolutionaries' victory against foreign occupation and the Ottoman dynasty rapidly gave way to a struggle between different leaders and factions among the victors themselves. Of the five signatories of the Declaration of Amasya, four joined in founding the first opposition party of the new republic, the Progressive Republican Party (*Terakkiperver Cumhuriyet Fırkası*, TCF), which was closed down for its alleged involvement in the Kurdish-Islamic Sheikh Said rebellion in Eastern Anatolia in 1925.[21] Moreover, they were later accused of plotting the assassination of Mustafa Kemal. Although they were acquitted, the clearly contrived accusation was the pretext for their political marginalization. One of them, Rauf Orbay lived in exile, mostly in London, for over a decade until 1935, when he returned but never again met Mustafa Kemal (by then renamed "Atatürk"), who died on November 10, 1938. Another, Kazım Karabekir, lived under police surveillance around the clock, until the death of Atatürk. The memoirs of Karabekir, Orbay, and others, who lost the leadership struggle against Mustafa Kemal, therefore provide a crucial resource for alternatives to the official historiography in Turkey's politics of history.

Memoirs of Kazım Karabekir (1882–1948)

Kazım Karabekir is perhaps the most prominent military-political leader who later came out strongly and openly against Mustafa Kemal.

---

[20] The other four signatories were Kazım Karabekir, Rauf Orbay, Refet Bele, and Ali Fuat Cebesoy.
[21] These four were again Karabekir, Orbay, Cebesoy, and Bele.

Karabekir left Istanbul for Anatolia earlier than Mustafa Kemal, and he established a de facto autonomous state in Erzurum with an army under his command. He continued to be the uncontested organizer of the Eastern front (against Armenians, Georgians, and potentially Russians) throughout the war, and it is under his auspices (and definitely his military protection) that the first national congress of people's deputies was convened in Erzurum, and formed the Committee of Representatives (*Heyeti Temsiliye*), which functioned as the chief executive body of the national struggle until the founding of a permanent parliament, the Grand National Assembly, in Ankara in April 23, 1920. This much is conceded in the official historiography. The story of how he was discredited was also summarized above. Karabekir, however, has a radically different view of Mustafa Kemal's role in the war, which put him in irreconcilable opposition with official historiography during his lifetime. Already in the second paragraph of a book of his memoirs, he states that:

> "But Mustafa Kemal Pasha did not choose this path and instead chose the opposite path: He hid the truths [of the war] and by doing so he did not concede the historical rights of persons. Just as the significance/worth [of these persons] was suppressed, the [honor/prestige of] services rendered during the War of Liberation were distributed to various persons, as if to distribute important positions and wealth to this or that person, and as such, he [Mustafa Kemal] tried to give the impression that he thought and did everything [in the war]. In order to impress this in public memory as such, the publication of memoirs was also not permitted. Government wasted its strength and secret powers for this purpose."[22]

Tellingly, the subtitle of the opening section of Karabekir's book quoted above is, "It is a Great Danger to Falsify Our History."

Karabekir's account of the War of Liberation is full of assertions that are heretical at best and traitorous at worst by the standards of official historiography. He argues, most importantly, that the idea to

---

[22] Kazım Karabekir, *Paşaların Hesaplaşması: İstiklal Harbine Neden Girdik, Nasıl Girdik, Nasıl İdare Ettik?*, edited by İsmet Bozdağ, (Istanbul: Emre, 1993), 7.

launch the War of Liberation from Anatolia was originally his idea, and not Mustafa Kemal's; that Karabekir tried, at first unsuccessfully, to convince Mustafa Kemal to join such a war of liberation, but Kemal only later joined Karabekir in Anatolia after much hesitation; and that the idea to abolish the Sultanate and the Caliphate in order to establish a Republic was originally Karabekir's idea, which Kemal rejected and resisted for a long time because Kemal wanted to become the Sultan-Caliph after the war.[23] In sum, Karabekir claims two of the key achievements of Mustafa Kemal for himself: the idea for the war of liberation in Anatolia, and the declaration of a secular republic accompanied by the abolition of the Sultanate and the Caliphate.

Karabekir argues that in November 29, 1918, he told Ismet İnönü, the second president after and a close ally of Atatürk, about his plans to launch a war of liberation, as well as the military and political master plan of such a war.[24] Karabekir also claims that prior to departing Istanbul for Anatolia, he visited Mustafa Kemal in Şişli, Istanbul, in April 11, 1919, and told him about his plans for launching a war of liberation, and urged Kemal to leave Istanbul and join him in Anatolia. The detailed diaries of Karabekir published by a well-known publisher very recently concur that he indeed met İnönü in November 29, 1918, and Kemal in April 11, 1919, in Istanbul.[25] Karabekir's diaries and memoirs also indicate remarkable hesitation on the side of Mustafa Kemal and Ismet İnönü about launching a new war. According to Karabekir, in their meeting of November 29, 1918, İnönü suggested starting a new life by "becoming peasants" to Karabekir, to which Karabekir replied that he "would continue [the struggle] even if I have to do it all by myself."[26]

Apart from claiming the original idea of launching the war of liberation, abolishing sultanate and the caliphate, and declaring a republic, Karabekir also alleges certain attitudes and decisions to Mustafa Kemal that would certainly hurt Mustafa Kemal's charisma in the eyes of the Turkish public in particular. Karabekir claims, for example,

---

[23] Ibid., 29.
[24] Ibid.
[25] Kazım Karabekir, *Günlükler (1906–1948)*, Volume I (Istanbul: Yapı Kredi Yayınları, 2009), 565 and 587.
[26] Ibid, 565.

that the Ottoman Empire surrendered in late October 1918 because of a telegraph Mustafa Kemal sent from Syria to Istanbul, where he stated that the Ottoman "armies are lacking the power to fight."[27] Karabekir claims that the signature slogan of the war, "either independence or death," was first coined by him, and not by Mustafa Kemal.[28] Even more, he claims that Mustafa Kemal was in favor of seeking the support, if not the mandate, of the United States, because Kemal believed that "starting a war of liberation with our own forces alone would bring bigger troubles."[29]

The fate of Karabekir's efforts to publish his memoirs is a good indicator of the nature and evolution of the politics of history in Turkey in the 1930s and the 1940s. Karabekir was politically marginalized with the show trials of 1925 conducted by the Independence Tribunals with the allegation that the Progressive Republican Party (TCF) led by Karabekir was somehow involved in the Sheik Sait Rebellion in Eastern Anatolia, although TCF did not even have chapters in the Eastern provinces where the rebellion occurred, and was later also accused (but acquitted) of being involved in an assassination plot against Mustafa Kemal in 1926. Thereafter, he lived in de facto house arrest until Atatürk's death in 1938. Provoked by the publication of a series of articles narrating the War of Liberation that, in Karabekir's opinion, severely falsified real history at the expense of diminishing his role in the war and exaggerating Mustafa Kemal's, he first tried to publish articles in the same newspaper countering some of the claims made. Once the newspaper stopped publishing the articles Karabekir was sending, he decided to write a book of memoirs, which were published in Istanbul in 3,000 copies. The night these books were published, Kılıç Ali, a close friend of Mustafa Kemal, entered the publishing house and burned all 3,000 copies except one that he missed.[30]

Atatürk's death in November 1938, however, changed the political calculus, and unexpected opportunities arose for dissidents and revisionists. İsmet İnönü, who succeeded Atatürk as the second president, in his scramble to prop up his new found power, brought Karabekir

---

[27] Ibid., 31.
[28] Ibid., 31.
[29] Ibid., 49, and 52.
[30] Karabekir, *Paşaların Hesaplaşması*, 12.

into the parliament as a representative of Istanbul in January 1939, and later made him the chair of the parliament in 1946, the second ranking political post in the protocol after the president. It is in the 1940s that Karabekir, completely freed from his remaining inhibitions seen in his previous memoirs, wrote the frank account of the War of Liberation cited earlier. He died in 1948. It impossible to discuss the full extent of Karabekir's memoirs within the constraints of this chapter; but suffice it to say that the changing political balance after Atatürk's death allowed for the first fissures in the politics of history of the new republic.

Memoirs of Rauf Orbay (1881–1964)

Rauf Orbay's memoirs are also a critical resource vis-à-vis the official historiography. One of the five original signatories of the Declaration of Amasya, Orbay was also well-known beforehand for his legendary success as a naval commander at the time of the Balkan Wars (1912–1913).[31] Following the occupation of Istanbul, he was imprisoned in Malta by the British as the leading member of the last Ottoman parliament who sided with the resistance in Anatolia. Following his release, he briefly served as a Prime Minister of the Ankara government during the war. Along with Karabekir, Orbay was the leader of the "Second Group" in the parliament in Ankara, who were critical of what they saw as the building of an authoritarian one party (CHP) dictatorship under the leadership of Mustafa Kemal. According to the editor of Karabekir's and Orbay's memoirs, Mustafa Kemal, Rauf Orbay, and Kazım Karabekir were the three indispensable leaders without whom the War of Liberation could not have succeeded; the role of all the other field commanders and political figures were secondary and could be fulfilled by others in their absence.[32]

In Orbay's memoirs, there is a latent ideological counter-current going beyond his personal disputes with the Kemalist leadership. Apart from the unofficial "Second Group" in the first parliament during the war, Orbay was also a prominent leader of the TCF, the first official opposition party of the new republic. The party was accused of being

---

[31] He was known as the "Hero of Hamidiye [the name of his battleship]."
[32] Ismet Bozdağ in his introduction to, Orbay, *Cehennem Değirmeni*, 9.

linked to the Sheik Said rebellion. Orbay argued that the CHP government used the rebellion as a pretext to close down the TCF and suppress every kind of opposition to the emerging one party dictatorship. He even suggested that there were various provocations to implicate TCF members, including himself, in violent plots against the CHP government, so as to justify suppressing them later on. For example, he mentions a mysterious letter he received from a certain other "Rauf," who pledged allegiance to Orbay and offered to join and help him along with his "guards."[33] The obvious goal of this thinly veiled trap was to secure a positive response from Rauf Orbay, which could then easily be used against him in public and at court in substantiating the claim that Orbay was organizing an armed rebellion against the government.

The two other ideological dimensions of the allegations against Orbay were related to Islamism and Kurdish nationalism, the two most resilient fears of the Turkish republic. On the one hand, among the military-political elite of the time, Orbay was well known as a relatively devout, pious Muslim. This led the judges of the Independence Tribunals to allege pro-Caliphate political activities to Orbay.[34] Moreover, Orbay was doubly suspect on the ethnic question, since he was perhaps the most politically prominent Circassian at the time, and was married to the daughter of a very prominent and assertive Kurdish leader. Both Circasssians and Kurds had nationalist movements seeking separate independent states with the aid of the British and other European powers during the War of Liberation.[35]

Rauf Orbay argues that ultimately the CHP leadership was blindly focused on suppressing any form of political or intellectual opposition under the pretext of suppressing the Sheik Said Rebellion. Using the martial law and the extraordinary powers they acquired with the infamous "Restoring Order" laws in 1925, the government indeed closed down TCF, silenced the Istanbul-based media that was critical of CHP and the new regime being built in Ankara, and politically marginalized Karabekir, Orbay, Refet Bele, Ali Fuat Cebesoy, and any other

---

[33] Orbay, *Cehennem Değirmeni*, 183. *Fedailer* is the word used for "guards."
[34] Ibid., 188.
[35] Kurdish nationalism and a series of Kurdish rebellions are well known. On the less known case of Circassian nationalism and separatism, see Gingeras, *Sorrowful Shores*.

prominent figures who resisted the rapid slide towards one party dictatorship.[36] Orbay's memoirs as such include a condemnation of and a critical perspective on the origins of the Turkish Republic, and were used by both Islamist and liberal dissidents of the official Kemalist historiography.

Memoirs of Rıza Nur (1879–1942):
An ethnic Turkish nationalist and a secularist

Rıza Nur served as Minister of Education in the first parliament, and also as Minister of Health later on, while he was also one of Turkey's two chief negotiators of the Treaty of Lausanne (the other one was Ismet Inonu), which established modern Turkey as an independent state with its internationally recognized borders in 1923. Nur was one of the most enigmatic, controversial, erratic, and colorful characters of that time: he was a vehement ethnic Turkish nationalist and a secularist (and privately an atheist), and though some of his claims in his lengthy memoirs are incredible or at least exaggerated, they provided a resource for revisionist historiography and drew the ire and wrath of official authorities at various times.

Among many other claims, most of which we cannot review here, Rıza Nur claims that he came up with the name of the new country: "Turkey" (*Türkiye*), which replaced the "Ottoman State" (*Devleti Aliyeyi Osmaniye*) and the "Ottoman Empire."[37] Rıza Nur also claims that he was the first one to publicly demand the secularization of the state in the very first parliament, when the various ministries and the composition of the government was being decided upon: "I made the following suggestion: 'All is well but let us take this opportunity to separate religion and the state. Let's have a secular (*laik*) government. This is a great opportunity, let's not miss it.'"[38] As such, he mentions in his memoirs that, "[i]n fact I do not have a religion; but I am not opposed to religion."[39]

Rıza Nur alleges that Mustafa Kemal enthusiastically suggested Turkey to be officially Bolshevik, and it was only his intervention that

---

[36] Ibid., 193. These laws were known as *Takrir-i Sukun* laws in Turkish.
[37] Nur and Ellison, *İlk Meclisin Perde Arkası 1920–1923*, 49.
[38] Ibid., 50.
[39] Ibid., 51.

prevented Turkey from becoming a Bolshevik country. "He [Mustafa Kemal] almost made the country Bolshevik. Can this be the deed of a sane person?!."[40] Rıza Nur relates the following anecdote: "One day the cabinet was deliberating. Mustafa Kemal began talking in the following manner: 'Friends! As you know I have been busy with building a Communist organization for a while, we did everything on this account. As a perfect force, we formed the Green Army. This country can only be liberated with Bolshevism (*Bolseviklik*). The time has come. Make your decision. I will declare to the world that Turkey is Bolshevik and Communist.'"[41] While everybody in the meeting was pressured to consent and agree with this plan, Rıza Nur fervently intervened and objected. He made the argument that there is no bourgeoisie ("factories") in Turkey to target and that it would be counterproductive to close down the few shops there existed in dire times of war. Moreover, he argued, since the common people associate Bolshevism with atheism, they would completely turn against the Ankara government, which was challenging the Sultan-Caliph's government in Istanbul at the time, and they would lose the war before even starting it. Refet (Bele), the minister of the interior, seconded Rıza Nur's opinion, and Turkey was saved from becoming Bolshevik, according to Rıza Nur.[42]

Rıza Nur also makes some controversial claims about the foreign relations of the new republic, in particular its relations with Russia and the Caucasus. As an ethnic Turkish nationalist, he has a tendency to overemphasize the ethnic origins of the political elite around Mustafa Kemal. Ankara government's first foreign minister, Bekir Sami (Kunduk) was an Ossetian, and when he was sent to Moscow to negotiate the relations of the Bolshevik regime with the Ankara government, he conceded to give Van to the Armenians in return for the promise of Ossetian independence, Rıza Nur alleges.[43] Just like Rauf Orbay, Rıza Nur also left Turkey in 1926 during the wave of show trials against the opposition under the pretext of the failed plot to assassinate Atatürk in Izmir, and he only returned to Turkey following Atatürk's death in 1938. Rıza Nur died in Istanbul in 1942. His memoirs, which he

---

[40] Ibid., 55.
[41] Ibid, 81.
[42] Ibid., 81–82.
[43] Ibid, 111–114.

entrusted to the British Museum in 1935 only to be published twenty-five years after his death, were published posthumously in Turkey in 1968. They were banned and collected by the official authorities, but currently are in circulation both in university libraries and in some bookstores. In Turkey's politics of history, his memoirs remained a notable reference point not only for secular ethnic Turkish nationalists, but also for Islamist and liberal critics of Kemalist one party state.

Islamic Interpretation of the War: Jihad of the Anatolian Muslims

In Turkey's politics of history, the most popular and resilient of the revisionist historiographies has been that of the Islamist critics. They also constitute the most notable exception to the broad consensus around glorifying Atatürk, because in their criticisms, they don't portray him as an Islamist hero, but rather, as an impostor who exploited Islamic religiosity throughout the war and then turned against it once the victory was won. In other words, Islamists constitute the largest group of fundamental revisionists.

Among other sources, they rely on all three of the historical figures we reviewed above, as well as official publications including Mustafa Kemal's speeches and the parliamentary proceedings. The Islamist version of history, suppressed during the one party regime (1923–1950), resurfaced with particular vigor in the 1950s under the DP government, which itself heavily relied on a criticism of Kemalism that was at times implicit and at other times explicit, and continued to grow to the present day, especially since the 1980s.

The Islamist perception of the War of Liberation, and its aftermath, can be briefly summarized as follows: the war was a jihad of the Anatolian Muslims, regardless of their various ethnic backgrounds, against European Christian occupation forces (British, French, and Italians), and their local Christian collaborators (Greeks, Armenians, and others).[44] Not only the composition, but also the ideological justifications and the discourse of the war effort were also decidedly Islamic, and as such, the war can easily be described as an Islamic *jihad* (defensive

---

[44] Also see, Aktürk, "Persistence of the Islamic *Millet* as an Ottoman Legacy," 893–909.

war), rather than a "national" liberation struggle in the ethnic or secular understandings of the nation. However, once the war was won, Mustafa Kemal chose a path of radical secularization in seeming contradiction to the deeply Islamic nature and rhetoric of the war, Islamists allege.

The interpretations of two Islamist dissident intellectuals are exemplary here for their radically revisionist views. First one is Kadir Mısıroğlu (1933–), and the second one is Abdurrahman Dilipak (1949–). In terms of the periodization of Turkey's politics of history, they represent two different generations of dissidents: Mısıroğlu took advantage of the democratic opening created by the first free and fair elections that brought DP to power in 1950, whereas Dilipak took advantage of the political opening created by Turgut Özal's economic liberalization in the 1980s and the rise of Islamism in the late 1980s and the early 1990s. Therefore, one of them rose to prominence already in the 1950s and the 1960s, while the second one became popular in the 1980s and the 1990s. As of late 2010, both are active and popular Islamist public figures, Dilipak as the chief columnist of the newspaper *Yeni Akit*, and Mısıroğlu as a regular commentator in TVNET, among his other public appearances.

Mısıroğlu argues in his book, *Mujahedeen with Turbans in the War of Liberation*, published in 1967, that the war was mostly the work of Islamist warrior preachers, who sustained the popular support that the Ankara government enjoyed throughout the war. Among such "heroes with turbans" (sarıklı kahramanlar), he describes in detail the activities of eight leading religious figures who were important active participants in the war.[45] Emblematic in this regard is the opening of the parliament in Ankara in 1920, which had the appearance of a very religious ceremony, including recitations of the Quran, and other religious literature such as the *Mevlid*, along with chants of "God is great" (*Allahu Ekber*).[46] Mısıroğlu argues that such Islamic discourse

---

[45] Kadir Mısıroğlu, *Kurtuluş Savaşında Sarıklı Mücahitler* (Istanbul: Sebil, 1967). These figures were Ahmed Hulusi Efendi, Hafız İbrahim Demiralay, Şükrü Çelikalay, Bediüzzaman Said Nursi, Mehmed Akif Ersoy, Sheik Ahmed Sunusi, Esat Hoca, and Ali Rıza Acara.

[46] Ibid., 191–194. This depiction, which is confirmed and emphasized in the works of Dilipak and Akyol (to be discussed later), is historically accurate by all accounts.

was quickly abandoned following victory in the war, and in particular, with the Lausanne Treaty, where he alleges that Britain, France, and the international community at large accepted Turkey's independence only with the provision that it would become a secular state, abolish the Caliphate, and never pursue a Pan-Islamist foreign policy.[47] Mısıroğlu was sentenced to seven years in prison by a military tribunal in 1970 for insulting Atatürk's legacy under Article 5816, and he served four years of his prison sentence before being freed with the general amnesty of 1974. While the court cases against him were piling up, the 1980 military coup occurred and Mısıroğlu fled to Germany, and later to Britain, where he was given asylum as a politically persecuted person. After the removal of Article 163 criminalizing activities against secularism, which was often broadly interpreted to imprison many Islamic intellectuals, Mısıroğlu returned to Turkey in 1991.

Abdurrahman Dilipak likewise emphasizes the composition and the discourse of the first parliament, quoting at length the very "first day" the parliament opened in Ankara, with incessant prayers and religious chants. Dilipak also quotes passages from Atatürk's speech where he praised Islamic veiling of the women.[48] This first parliament officially banned the production, sale, and consumption of alcohol, also on a religious basis. Atatürk even gave a famous Friday sermon in a mosque, where he used a phrase that can, and has been understood by some people as meaning, "our constitution is the Quran alone."[49] In short, Islamist critics made their case that the War of Liberation was first and foremost an Islamic struggle.

Socialist Interpretation of the War: Bolsheviks and the First Anti-Imperialist War

According to a book by a Turkish Maoist socialist, in January 1921, Mustafa Kemal said that, "personally I and many of my comrades are advocates of Communism, but the situation and the conditions require

---

[47] Mısıroğlu, *Lozan: Zafer mi Hezimet mi?*.
[48] Dilipak, *Bir Başka Açıdan Kemalizm*, 77–90.
[49] This was a Friday sermon he gave in the Zağanos Pasha mosque in Balıkesir in February 7, 1923.

that we remain silent on this matter. If I declare myself to be a Communist tomorrow, there will not be anything left of my influence."[50] Since the beginning of the war, both some supporters of Mustafa Kemal and many of his opponents claimed that the Ankara government had strong socialist tendencies as evidenced by its close relations with the Soviet Union. Indeed, although non-state actors such as the Indian Muslims also provided substantial financial and political support to the war of liberation, the Soviet Union was the only independent state—and the only great power—that openly supported the Ankara government financially, militarily, and politically throughout the war.

Soviet leadership and Turkish socialists alike depicted the war first and foremost as an anti-imperialist one, but the Turkish socialists went a step further by anointing the War of Liberation as the first and decisive anti-imperialist war that turned the tide against imperialism by providing the first example of an Eastern power defeating Western colonial powers in the 20th century. The many works of the famous Turkish intellectual and poet Attila Ilhan harp on this theme in particular.[51] From Mustafa Kemal writing his first ever diplomatic letter to Lenin in April 26, 1920, to Voroshilov's visit to Turkey in October 1933, a particularly significant date in the Kemalist hagiography since it was the 10th anniversary of the founding of the Republic; from Turkey's adoption of the first Five Year Plan in 1932 after the Soviet model, to the building of its major textile plants with Soviet credits, there are many spectacular and meaningful examples of Turkish-Soviet friendship in the 1920s and the early 1930s.[52]

However, somewhat like Islamists' argument about the regime turning its back to Islam after victory in the war, socialist critics also argue that Turkey started to turn its back to the Soviet Union starting in 1936 with the Turkish-British rapprochement evident in the Montreux Treaty, and continuing with Turkey's cozy relations with Nazi Germany in the earlier part of World War II, and the Turkish-American alliance in the postwar (Cold War) period, which made Turkey a bastion of pro-American, anti-Soviet military-political grand strategy.

---

[50] Akyol, *Ama Hangi Atatürk?*, 214; quoting from Perinçek, *Atatürk'ün Sovyetlerle Görüşmeleri*, 272–273.
[51] İlhan, *Hangi Atatürk?*
[52] Akyol, 216.

There are two versions of this socialist revisionism; the first and more dominant one is a pragmatic revisionism that amounts to a reinterpretation of Kemalist myths so that they would support a socialist agenda ("Mustafa Kemal as a socialist at heart"), which does not undermine but in fact even reinforces Kemalism as such. This view sees all successors of Atatürk, starting with İnönü, as having betrayed the original, proto-socialist, anti-imperialist ethos of the War of Liberation. In reaction to but also aided by the economic and political liberalization of the 1990s and the 2000s, this socialist revisionist view of the War of Liberation also found ample room and a receptive audience for its expression.

The second type is a fundamental revisionism that depicts Kemalism as a Fascist regime that turned its back against socialists in solidifying its dictatorship, by drowning Mustafa Suphi, the chairman of the Central Committee of the Communist Party of Turkey and his friends, in the Black Sea—allegedly with the support of the Ankara government led by Mustafa Kemal. In discussing the international political context of this murder, E.H. Carr argues that, "[f]or the first, though not for the last, time it was demonstrated that governments could deal drastically with their national Communist parties without forfeiting the goodwill of the Soviet Government, if that were earned on other grounds."[53] This view, which seeks to undermine Kemalism by depicting it as a murderous regime, is much less pronounced and limited to some left-liberal socialists in Turkey.

Kurdish Nationalist Interpretation of the War: A Story of Broken Promises

Kurdish nationalists have been vociferous critics of official historiography in Turkey since the founding of the Republic. Many among them argue that going into the War of Liberation as supporters of the Ankara government, Kurdish leaders were promised a kind of ethno-federal arrangement, but that the Kemalist government rescinded this promise once the war was won.[54] The Kurdish-Islamic Sheik Said rebellion is

---

[53] Carr, *The Bolshevik Revolution, 1917–1923*, vol. 3, 301.
[54] Kutlay, *21, Yuzyila Girerken Kurtler*, 81–87.

interpreted as an expression of the righteous anger of Kurds who were incensed by the Ankara government's volta face after the war, according to Kurdish nationalist historians. Some socialists, liberals, and Islamists also partially endorse this view by pointing out that ethnic identities were very prominent, public, and recognized in the deliberations of the first parliament, whereas they were gradually but eventually categorically suppressed after the establishment and consolidation of the new republic in the 1920s and the 1930s, such that by the time of the military dictatorship in the 1980s it became a crime to claim that a people called Kurds exist.[55] Like its Islamist and socialist counterparts, Kurdish nationalist revisionist historiography also flourished in the 1990s and the 2000s.

Liberal Interpretations of the War: From Popular Resistance to One Party Dictatorship

Liberalism has a derogatory connotation in the official Kemalist historiography and therefore it is sometimes used as a generic label for any dissident who does not readily fit into the groups reviewed above. Here I describe as liberals those who think what was fundamentally wrong with the Kemalist regime was not its disregard or "betrayal" of its Islamic or socialist origins and Kurdish allies, but its departure from and suppression of a relatively pluralistic, quasi-democratic, competitive political scene in order to build a one party dictatorship. In this, the liberal critics resemble Karabekir and Orbay, who criticized the emergence of the one party dictatorship after 1925, not based on a heavily ideological critique of that regime, but rather from the vantage point of leading personalities of a collective political effort, the War of Liberation, whose contributions were disregarded and who themselves were politically sidelined and personally treated with contempt.

Hence, when Ayşe Hür, the historian columnist of the unabashedly pro-Western left-liberal *Taraf*, critically depicts the trials of Karabekir, Orbay, and other leading personalities in connection with the plot to assassinate Atatürk in Izmir in 1926 as show trials aimed at

---

[55] Aktürk, "Regimes of Ethnicity," 115–164.

purging the opposition against the emerging Kemalist one party regime, she does not state that either Karabekir or Orbay, or the more Islamic, socialist, or Kurdish political leadership would have governed Turkey better at the time.[56] Liberal critics do not like the official historians' retrospective depiction of all the rivals of Atatürk as being reactionaries and counter-revolutionaries who wanted to keep Turkey in—what is often described as—"the darkness of the Middle Ages," with an unaccountable, despotic monarchy allied with a repressive, obscurantist religious clergy. Far from it, Karabekir, Orbay, and most other prominent leaders of the war also genuinely supported the decision to establish a republic and most secularization efforts. However, since they saw and accepted Mustafa Kemal only as the *primus inter pares*, they virulently opposed later developments that turned him into the uncontested and unquestionable leader with a personality cult around himself as the officially anointed "Atatürk" (Father of the Turks). In order to have a sense of whether and where, beyond academic and intellectual circles, these revisionist views find a voice in the popular media, one has to look at the structure of the Turkish media, which is a topic the next section briefly takes up.

Structure of the Media in Present-Day Turkey: Economy, Politics, and Ideology

Turkey has a very vibrant media as of late 2010, with at least thirty-five national newspapers reaching a daily circulation of four and a half million, and hundreds of local newspapers, with dozens of privately owned national TV channels along with hundreds of local TV and radio stations.[57] Going beyond this façade of wild diversity, however, one notices that about a dozen financial industrial media groups own the most popular newspapers and TV stations, as well as other enterprises.[58] This does not, of course, indicate a lack of diversity;

---

[56] Hür, "İzmir Suikastı ve muhalefetin tasfiyesi."
[57] Current newspaper circulation reports can be found in http://www.medyatava.com/tiraj.asp. Last accessed in December 3, 2010.
[58] Notable among them are *Doğan, Çalık/Turkuvaz, Ciner, Çukurova, Koza, Doğuş,* and *Feza* media groups.

after all, a dozen nodes of private financial-industrial-media power is better, for example, than five, three, one, or none. However, until 1990, only state-owned TV channels existed; but after the opening of Star TV later in that year, private TV and radio stations mushroomed around the country both at the national and the local level at a dizzying pace. This was one of the many consequences of the neoliberal reforms undertaken by Turgut Ozal in the 1980s, and continued in the 1990s.

However, until recently, the state and the military in particular were able to exert considerable influence over the media, and hence successfully maintained the hegemony of the official views on history even in the private media. Both legal and informal methods were used to discipline and punish media outlets that went beyond what was considered permissible criticism by the military and the state. For example, several Islamist and Kurdish nationalist newspapers, like their political parties, were repeatedly closed down. A very high profile Islamist columnist was subjected to heavy fines that resulted in the confiscation and auctioning of his house by the courts. The 1990s also witnessed an inordinate number of assassinations of journalists, mostly of secular Kemalist orientation, but also some Kurdish journalists. In an infamous episode simply known as the "Warning" (Andic), the military allegedly warned newspaper owners to fire several high profile columnists for their criticisms of the military, which the newspaper editors did. The episode is now almost universally condemned but politically motivated firing of journalists may still occur. Even as of late 2010, dozens of journalists are on trial for their reporting, some of them facing a hundred or more years of jail if found guilty.

Given the unusually long term in office of the current AKP government (2002–present), the current media groups are most often classified according to their attitudes vis-à-vis government; whether they are generally supportive of the AKP or the main opposition party, CHP. AKP's rise to power has given revisionist historians tremendous opportunities to voice their views in major national media outlets, which they made ample use of, because AKP itself originated from an Islamist political movement highly critical of Kemalism and its depiction of Turkish history. The Turkish nationalist MHP and the Kurdish nationalist BDP do not have any major media outlets affiliated with them, though the latter have larger media outlets among the Kurdish diaspora in Europe. Therefore, in present-day Turkey, one finds critical views of the official historiography most prominently in conservative, Islamic-inspired, and liberal newspapers sympathetic if not supportive of the AKP government.[59]

History Education and Textbooks: Democracy and the Bureaucracy at the TTKB

Although AKP's rise to power led to the mass dissemination of revisionist and critical views on Turkey's official history through newspapers and TV channels sympathetic to or allied with AKP, paradoxically, this does not necessarily indicate a change in the official history found in school textbooks and curricula. Education and textbook selection is strictly controlled and monitored by the Presidency of Training and Discipline Council (*Talim ve Terbiye Kurulu Başkanlığı*-TTKB) under the Ministry of Education.[60] No textbook can be used in Turkey's schools, unless it is previously approved by the TTKB, which makes the TTKB bureaucracy the ultimate authority governing the billion dollar textbook market. There has been incessant and highly publicized turmoil in the TTKB under the JDP government, since one TTKB president resigned after another, citing widespread irregularities, corruption, and insufficient attention paid to Atatürk's principles.[61] Since the bureaucracy, like the judiciary and the military, has been the preserve of more secular, Kemalist cadres historically, the turmoil might indeed have an ideological dimension to it, or it might result from disputes over the sharing of the textbook market, or both. There was, for example, the accusation that the government is pushing the TTKB to approve textbooks of a publisher that is allegedly connected to a religious order, which then combines ideological and economic aspects of a perceived competition in the textbook market.

All social science books in primary and secondary schools, such as history, geography, and national security, have pictures and sayings of Atatürk at the beginning, and often also thematic sections on Atatürk's

---

[59] These include *Sabah, Star, Taraf, Vakit, Yeni Şafak,* and *Zaman.*
[60] Its official website is at http://ttkb.meb.gov.tr.
[61] Öztürk, "Talim Terbiye'de Gidenler Gelenler."

views on various topics. Therefore, although many hundreds of thousands and even millions of newspaper reading adults and TV viewers have been exposed to highly critical views of Kemalism, history curriculum is unlikely to become significantly critical of the past policies of the state in Turkey.

For example, in 2011 the AKP government criticized in the harshest terms the bloodshed that accompanied the suppression of a rebellion in Central Eastern Anatolia in 1937–38. Some even describe this internal operation of the military, undertaken during the one party dictatorship, as being genocidal. These high-level condemnations by the government were condemned in return by the main opposition party CHP, which defended this military operation. What is noteworthy is that even though the AKP government condemned the actions of the Turkish state in 1937–38 as being cruel and unjustified, and even though a large swath of the intellectual establishment and the media joined in this opinion, it is very unlikely that any Turkish history textbook that is critical of the Turkish state's actions as such would be approved and used in mass education. This example also highlights both the extent and limits of revisionist historiography within Turkey's politics of history today.

Politics of History in a Post-Kemalist Turkey? Growing Revisionist Historiographies amidst the Hegemony of the Official View

Strictly contained or outright suppressed for most of the 20th century, revisionist views on Turkish history enjoyed a tremendous efflorescence and popularity since the coming to power of the Justice and Development Party (AKP) in November 2002. This is in great part due to the Islamist origins of AKP, which makes it sympathetic not only to Islamist and Islamic-motivated, but also liberal, Kurdish, and even socialist criticisms of Kemalism. AKP, in this respect, provided a large umbrella or a tent for all those critical of the official historiography, and one might even speak of a "post-Kemalist era" in Turkey's history since 2002.

However, the legal-criminal and institutional framework described in detail earlier in this chapter is still formally in place, and sometimes activist judges might and do intervene by prosecuting critics of the official historiography, and in particular, the person of Atatürk. One should not forget that even the globally popular internet media, *YouTube*, was banned in Turkey for two and a half years due to the existence of some videos defaming Atatürk. The ban was finally lifted in October 31, 2010, after the removal of all such videos.

On the one hand, revisionist historiographies, although repeatedly punished and suppressed, did not disappear, and thanks to the transition to multiparty democracy in 1950, found political benefactors and protectors who sometimes sheltered them against official persecution. On the other hand, although revisionist historiography is definitely enjoying an unprecedented upsurge, especially among the intellectual elite and the newly rising, Islamic oriented Anatolian bourgeoisie that is associated with the current AKP government, the official historiography is still well entrenched in the legal, institutional, and educational structures of present-day Turkey.

BIBLIOGRAPHY

Aktürk, S. "Persistence of the Islamic *Millet* as an Ottoman Legacy: Mono-Religious and Anti-Ethnic Definition of Turkish Nationhood," *Middle Eastern Studies* vol.45, no.6 (November 2009): 893–909.

———. "Regimes of Ethnicity: A Comparative Analysis of Germany, Soviet Union, Russian Federation, and Turkey." *World Politics* vol.63, no.1 (January 2011): 115–164.

Akyol, T. *Ama Hangi Atatürk?* Istanbul: Dogan, 2008.

Brudny, Y. *Reinventing Russia: Russian Nationalism and the Soviet State, 1953–1991* Cambridge, MA: Harvard University Press, 2000.

Carr, E.H. *The Bolshevik Revolution, 1917–1923,* vol. 3. New York: W. W. Norton, 1985.

Demirer, M.A. "Iki Referandum: 9 Temmuz 1961-12 Eylul 2010." *Anayurt,* 12 Temmuz 2010. Available at http://www.anayurtgazetesi.com/default.asp?page=yazar&id=9490.

Dilipak, A. *Bir Başka Açıdan Kemalizm.* Istanbul: Beyan, 1988.

Gingeras, R. *Sorrowful Shores: Violence, Ethnicity, and the End of the Ottoman Empire.* New York: Oxford University Press, 2009.

Hür, A. "İzmir Suikastı ve muhalefetin tasfiyesi," *Taraf,* June 22, 2008.

———. "CHP, Ticaniler ve Atatürk'ü Koruma Kanunu," *Taraf,* February 10, 2008.

Karabekir, K. *Günlükler (1906–1948),* vol. 1. Istanbul: Yapi Kredi Yayinlari, 2009.

Karabekir, K. and P. Hesaplaşmasi. *İstiklal Harbine Neden Girdik, Nasıl Girdik, Nasıl İdare Ettik?* edited by İ. Bozdağ. Istanbul: Emre, 1993.
İlhan, A. *Hangi Atatürk?* Istanbul: Bilgi, 2003.
Kasapoğlu, A. *Atatürk'ün Kur'an Kültürü.* Istanbul: İlgi, 2009.
Kutlay, N. *21. Yüzyıla Girerken Kürtler.* Istanbul: Peri, 2002.
Mısıroğlu, K. *Kurtuluş Savaşında Sarıklı Mücahitler.* Istambul: Sebil, 1967.
———. *Lozan: Zafer mi Hezimet mi?* Istanbul: Sebil, 1964.
Nur, R. and Ellison, G. *İlk Meclisin Perde Arkası 1920–1923,* İstanbul: Örgün Yayınevi, 2007.
Orbay, R. *Cehennem Değirmeni—Siyasi Hatıralarım.* Istanbul: Emre, 1993.
Öztürk, S. "Talim Terbiye'de Gidenler Gelenler," *Hürriyet,* March 6, 2008.
Perinçek, D. *Atatürk: Din ve Laiklik Üzerine.* İstanbul: Kaynak, 1997.
Perinçek, M. *Atatürk'ün Sovyetlerle Görüşmeleri.* Istanbul: Kaynak, 2005.

The Politics of History in Contemporary Japan

Jeff Kingston

Japan's shared history with Asia is a continuing source of tensions, recrimination and denial featuring inadequate efforts in Japan to acknowledge and atone for its imperial aggression in the region. As in many other countries, the shameful past is often minimized, mitigated, glorified and otherwise distorted in service of contemporary political agendas. It is worth bearing in mind, however, that opinion polls over the past twenty years show that most Japanese accept Japan's war responsibility, acknowledge past misdeeds and favor further and fuller atonement. Thus there is a lack of consensus within Japan about its shared history with Asia, a fault-line that separates conservative nationalists from majority opinion, a divide that conveys mixed messages to countries victimized by Japanese imperialism and undoes any goodwill generated by the numerous apologies issued by Japanese leaders regarding previous transgressions.[1]

Essentially, this fault line pits those favoring a vindicating and exonerating narrative against those who see no dignity in denial or shirking the burdens of history. The "Dr. Feelgoods" of Japanese history represent few Japanese, but they are disproportionately represented in the corridors of power, ensuring that their views gain prominence in the international media, reinforcing misleading images regarding Japan's collective amnesia.[2] In this chapter I examine the controversies over war memory, apology, Yasukuni Shrine, Emperor Showa's war responsibility and the 2010 centennial of Japanese

---

[1] See Yamazaki, *Japanese Apologies for WWII*.
[2] On this misleading image and disproportionate representation see Seaton, *Japan's Contested War Memories* and Sven Saaler, op.cit.

colonialism in Korea in order to elucidate how political agendas are shaping history and how history is influencing politics.

I. War Memory and Apology Discourse

In 2010, Naoto Kan became the first prime minister in twenty-five years to instruct his cabinet to refrain from visiting Yasukuni Shrine on August 15, the anniversary of Japan's surrender in 1945 when the shrine holds a public commemoration ceremony honoring Japan's war dead. Kan's Democratic Party of Japan (DPJ) promised a moratorium on shrine visits by high ranking politicians soon after gaining power in the 2009 lower house elections. The Liberal Democratic Party (LDP) that dominated Japanese politics since it was established in 1955 has long favored shrine visits and its party leaders did visit on August 15, 2010. The LDP's Prime Minister Junichiro Koizumi (2001–2006) visited the shrine six times while premier, provoking an angry reaction from China and the Korean peninsula because his visits were seen to show support for the Yasukuni narrative emphasizing Japan's sacrifices and the nobility of its imperial quests. Many Japanese were also angered and disappointed by the shrine visits because they contravened the separation of religion and State mandated in Article 20 of the Constitution, and they also do not agree with Koizumi's political agenda, one aimed at turning the page on history and rendering such pilgrimages normal gestures freed from the shackles of the past. They expressed their opposition in opinion polls where Yasukuni visits are opposed by a majority of Japanese and by filing lawsuits.[3]

For critics, Yasukuni and the adjacent Yushukan Museum represent unrepentant militarism and a vindicating and exonerating historical narrative about Japan's rampage through Asia 1931–1945. For proponents, the shrine and museum validate their view that Japan's Holy War in Asia fought in the name of Emperor Showa (Hirohito) was just, motivated by the benevolent desire to liberate Asians from the yoke of western imperialism.[4] The conflicting meanings of Yasukuni are rooted

---

[3] Kingston, *Contemporary Japan*.
[4] For a comprehensive rebuttal of such Pan-Asian fantasies see Goto, *Tensions of Empire*. Also Kratoksa (ed.), *Asian Labor in the Wartime Japanese Empire*.

in the broader historical debate about war memory, responsibility and reconciliation.[5]

The past still casts long shadows over contemporary Japan, and time has not yet buried memories of the bloody history that continues to divide Japan from its Asian neighbors, because there is a widespread perception, partially accurate, that Japan has shirked its war responsibility. While there is truth in the allegation that the Ministry of Education has encouraged a collective amnesia about Japan's record as imperial overlord and invader in Asia, it is also true that Japanese scholars, educators, politicians, and journalists have robustly challenged such efforts to whitewash the past.[6] And while many Japanese may nurture a keen sense of victimization regarding the Pacific War that baffles its Asian victims, the very public debates about the past have forced the nation to confront inconvenient evidence and memories that undermine the more exonerating versions of this traumatic era. The domestic rift over Yasukuni is part of this larger discourse.

The 1990s was a time of reckoning when the past suddenly caught up with the Japanese, largely unprepared by their schooling to confront the unsavory truths of what the imperial forces were engaged in when they were not "liberating" Asians from the yoke of western imperialism. Although there had been important revelations about this dark past prior to Emperor Showa's death in 1989, this grew from a trickle to a cascade. While he was alive (and widely venerated by a war generation raised to believe he was a god), mainstream discourse elided his war responsibility and many of the horrors carried out in his name; following his death these constraints quickly faded. Equally important has been the sustained pressure applied from the late 1980s by Asian activist groups seeking redress and a more forthright depiction of Japan's sordid past involving abuses and atrocities such as the comfort women system, the slaughter in Nanking, slave laborers, and the chemical and biological warfare experiments at the notorious Unit 731.[7] As a result of these mutually reinforcing domestic and regional developments,

---

[5] Seaton, *Japan's Contested War Memories*.
[6] Nozaki, *War Memory, Nationalism and History in Japan*; Yoshida, *The Making of the "Rape of Nanking"*; Seraphim, *War Memory and Social Politics in Japan, 1945–2005*.
[7] Tanaka, *Japan's Hidden Horrors*.

during the 1990s the Japanese learned more than they were prepared for about their history. This sudden flood released from the cesspool of Japan's past proved shocking and unsettling to a people accustomed to a less troubling narrative. In terms of the politics of history, the conservative consensus denying, minimizing, and shifting responsibility that had prevailed since the U.S. Occupation ended in 1952 was overwhelmed by a torrent of disturbing and credible revelations in the 1990s that supported progressive critiques of the war. The pendulum swung rapidly in favor of Saburo Ienaga and other progressive intellectuals who had been fighting to force the government and nation to embrace a more forthright reckoning. This is where I think Jennifer Lind misunderstands the politics of history in Japan.

Lind asserts that Japan's apologies and contrition trigger a nationalistic backlash in Japan, provoking comments by Japanese conservatives aimed at undoing the apologies. She asserts that these remarks fuel and fan resentment in Korea and China, and thus apologies have been counterproductive.[8] This is confusing the symptoms for the cause. The absence of a national consensus in Japan about what happened, and whether Japan's actions were wrong, continues to this day and these battles precede apology diplomacy.

In Germany, there has been no question about whether the Nazi's wartime misdeeds were wrong, so even if Germany showed limited contrition initially, and focused on its own suffering like Japan, it was not denying or justifying what Germany did during the war. In Japan, conservatives and progressives have fought bitterly for the past six decades over what happened and conservatives continue to assert that Japan was engaged in a noble Pan Asian mission to liberate Asians from the yoke of western colonialism. They have contested the substance of wartime history, fighting a forthright reckoning. Their reactions to gestures of contrition and apologies are symptoms of the more fundamental issue of war memory. The politics of war memory in Japan, a longstanding battle, drive and define the subsequent battles over apologies and acts of contrition, and thus it is misleading to suggest that apologies are the source of rancor and suspicion. Japanese conservatives are upset that their narrative is losing credibility and that

---

[8] Lind, *Sorry States*, and "Apologies."

the progressives' candid narrative they managed to sideline for much of the post-WWII era is gaining momentum at home. The apologies bother them because they represent a shift in what is being acknowledged, a revision with implications for the rectitude of Japan's wartime actions. Apology denial is merely continuing the pattern of denial that has animated conservatives' longstanding approach to war memory. It is also important to note that Chinese and Koreans have long resented Japanese equivocations about war memory and responsibility and thus are predisposed to discount the apologies and view the apology denials as part of a larger longstanding pattern of Japan's failures on history. In this sense, apology denials only reconfirm what neighbors already believe (and dislike) about Japan's selective amnesia.

Understandably there has been resistance to these revelations and efforts to deny, justify, and shift responsibility for the more gruesome tragedies.[9] However, during the cathartic 1990s the self-vindicating narrative that focused on noble sacrifice and victimization of the Japanese people has been vigorously challenged and in some important respects irreversibly discredited. While many will continue to prefer a more comforting version of their history, the exhumed past is here to stay.

Recrudescent nationalism in contemporary Japan runs the risk of trapping politicians into an escalating war of words and gestures that undermine reconciliation. Former PM Nakasone warns, "the problem is that a resurgence of nationalism in Japan is bound to clash with the nationalisms of its Asian neighbors. As politicians trumpet nationalism,

---

[9] In post-Tiananmen Square China, the Communist Party sought to shore up its legitimacy by nurturing patriotic education that emphasized its role in defeating the Japanese and teaching Chinese students in gruesome detail about Japanese wartime atrocities. This nationalistic historical discourse in China had reverberations in Japan where conservatives were angered by this fanning of anti-Japanese sentiments. Moreover, Japanese conservatives resented what they viewed as distorted depictions that tarnished and discredited the vindicating and exculpatory narrative they had propagated in post-WWII Japan. The emergence of a revisionist historical movement in Japan known as the Society for the Creation of New History Textbooks (Atarashi Rekishi Kyokasho oTsukuru-kai) represents, inter alia, a Japanese backlash against this patriotic education in China. Certainly the Tsukurukai was also reacting to the more forthright reckoning at home about Japan's rampage in Asia that emerged after Emperor Showa's death in 1989.

people tend to follow unhealthy nationalism. As a result, politicians become more responsive to such popular sentiments. This will create a mood of confrontation between the government leaders of the countries involved, as illustrated by Japan's present relations with China and South Korea."[10] True, but nationalism remains muted in Japan and Nakasone, known as a very conservative, ardent nationalist, reveals the sensible, internationalist inclinations of many right-wing politicians who counsel more responsible diplomacy. Thus many conservatives agree with left wing concerns about treading carefully on history issues with neighboring countries and aggressive nationalism gets little traction in mainstream politics.

Yasukuni represents Japan's failure to come to terms with its war history and the futility of attempting to assert a one-sided, exculpatory narrative while commemorating the war dead there resonates with political purpose.[11] It embodies a war memory that emphasizes that Japan's long war in Asia was justified and fought to liberate Asians from colonial rule. In this vindicating and valorizing narrative on display at the Yushukan Museum adjacent to Yasukuni Shrine, there is no mention of Japanese atrocities or its victims. Neither facility enjoys government designation as the national war memorial or museum, but they remain at the heart of Japan's war remembrance and rituals of commemoration. The 1978 enshrinement of 14 Class A-war criminals at Yasukuni, the architects of the war under whose authority the excesses were committed, next to the sanitized remembrance displayed at the Yushukan is an eloquent political statement bristling with historical mischief. The war is depicted as a legitimate act of self-defense and the judgment at the International Military Tribunal for the Far East (IMTFE), accepted in Article 11 of the San Francisco Peace Treaty signed by Japan in 1951, is repudiated. The renovation of the museum in 2002 embellished and updated Yasukuni's image

---

[10] Nakasone, *Japan Times*, September 21, 2006

[11] See Takahashi, "The National Politics of the Yasukuni Shrine," Also, Columbia University's Gerald Curtis in testimony to the U.S. Senate in September 2005 said, "Yasukuni is not simply a shrine to honor the young men who fought and died for their country. Yasukuni honors the ideology and the policies of the government that sent these young men to war." As quoted in *Japan Times*, August 12, 2006.

as a symbol of Japan's failure to promote reconciliation by asserting a narrowly nationalistic narrative concerning divisive issues of war memory.

PM Koizumi Junichiro justified his six visits while in office on the grounds that it is unseemly to discriminate among the dead and thus he honored all equally, including the war criminals. This perhaps reflects a widespread perception among Japanese that the IMFTE (1946–48) also known as the Tokyo Tribunal, was a kangaroo court that served up a biased "victor's justice" even as a majority recognize that Japan's military forces committed extensive atrocities. Conservatives have long chafed under the victor's war narrative that denigrates Japan's Pan-Asian aspirations as empty rhetoric justifying its own imperial ambitions in the region. For many Japanese, the Class-A war criminals put on trial were remote from the things of which they stood accused: they were not convicted of actually committing the atrocities, but rather were held responsible for crimes against peace and leading Japan into war. Thus some Japanese consider that their convictions were unjust and that the tribunal failed to recognize Japan's legitimate reasons for going to war, including a variety of western provocations and colonial domination of Asia.

Yasukuni is also a touchstone for domestic controversy because it is a Shinto religious facility and official visits ignore the division between the state and religion enshrined in Article 20 of the Constitution. This is a sensitive issue because during the war, state-sponsored Shinto was linked with Emperor worship and was used as a vehicle to inculcate loyalty to the government and mobilize popular support for the war. Shinto is thus tainted, in the eyes of some Japanese, by its dubious links with imperialism; and Yasukuni, as the focal point of wartime Shinto, is considered the temple of ultra-conservative nationalism where the most regrettable aspects of Japan's military past continue to be venerated.

Yasukuni is thus laden with symbolism that reverberates loudly and divisively both within and outside Japan. Powerful right-wing lobby groups such as the War Bereaved Veteran's Family Association (Nihon Izokukai) and the Association of Shinto Shrines (Jinja Honcho) pressure politicians to pay respect to the nation's war dead at Yasukuni in exchange for well-organized electoral support and generous funding. Both have longstanding ties with the LDP, and party leaders regularly serve as the president of Nihon Izokukai.[12] Paying obeisance at Yasakuni is for such associations a political litmus test, but their influence is fading as membership ages and dwindles.

It is important to bear in mind that there is considerable domestic opposition to Yasukuni visits. New Komeito, a coalition partner in several LDP cabinets, publicly opposes the visits, as does the Japan Communist Party and the Social Democratic Party. New Komeito's support base is the Soka Gakkai, a Buddhist lay organization that has also called for an end to Shrine visits. State-sponsored Shinto has been associated with systematic discrimination against Buddhism since the Meiji era, and there is a lingering wariness about government ties to Shinto among the vast Soka Gakkai membership. The mainstream press also carries critical commentary about Yasukuni, especially the conservative *Yomiuri*, the liberal *Asahi* and *Mainichi*, but also NHK, the quasi-government broadcasting corporation and various weekly magazines. Thus, there is a rich array of countervailing views that belie simplistic notions of the Japanese nation monolithically defending Yasukuni visits and embracing a dangerous nationalism. Unlike in Europe where fringe parties tend to be the standard-bearers for controversial nationalistic sentiments, visits to Yasukuni Shrine are favored by the LDP, Japan's dominant party from 1955–2009.

Emperor Showa, the chief priest of Shinto and the man for whom so many soldiers gave their lives, made no more visits to Yasukuni once the Class-A war criminals' enshrinement in 1978 became known. His son, Emperor Akihito, maintains the boycott and the unspoken repudiation. For conservatives, this inconvenient symbolism undermines their efforts to promote an unrepentant, glorifying history and highlights that they are acting in defiance of His Majesty's wishes. On the eve of his sixth visit, Prime Minister Koizumi shrugged off revelations in July 2006 that the Emperor Showa in 1988 confided his misgivings about the enshrinement of Class-A war criminals at Yasukuni to Tomita Tomohiko, the grand steward of the Imperial Household Agency, stating that this is why he discontinued his annual pilgrimages

---

[12] For analysis of right-wing politics in Japan see Wakamiya, *The Postwar Conservative View of Asia* and Ruoff, *The People's Emperor*.

to the shrine.¹³ In the wake of this bombshell, vacillating public support for Shrine visits by prime ministers plummeted to 20 percent.¹⁴

In the wake of Koizumi's 2001 visit, more than 900 Japanese citizens joined suits against the prime minister across the archipelago, charging him with violation of the constitutional separation of state and religion. The government was placed in the awkward position of arguing that the visits were not official and thus the line of separation between religion and state had not been breached. In response to charges that the prime minister had signed the visitors' book with his official title, traveled to the shrine in an official car and laid a wreath bearing his official title, the government disingenuously responded that these gestures were personal and private. In this case, "personal" was certainly a flexible term as Koizumi was accompanied to the site by dozens of other lawmakers and the whole event had been given substantial prior publicity, ensuring a crowd of onlookers and blanket media coverage.

The court cases brought against Koizumi drew on similar litigation against PM Nakasone, the last Japanese leader to visit the shrine in his official capacity. In 1992, the nation's three high courts in Tokyo, Sendai and Osaka all found that Nakasone's official visit in 1985 had been unconstitutional, thereby making it problematic for subsequent prime ministers to follow in his footsteps. Rulings concerning Koizumi's visits were mixed. On September 29, 2005 the Tokyo High Court ruled that Koizumi's visits were private affairs while the next day the Osaka High Court ruled that he made his visits in his

---

[13] On July 20, 2006 an article in *Nihon Keizai Shimbun* reported that the Emperor "believed Yasukuni Shrine erred when it decided to include Class-A war criminals from WWII on its list of people honored there." Emperor Showa is quoted from the 'Tomita memo' saying, "That's why I have not visited the shrine... [again]. This is from my heart. July 24, 2006. *Nikkei Weekly*. Emperor Showa visited Yasukuni Shrine eight times after WWII but never after the Class-A war criminals were enshrined there in 1978. His son, Emperor Akihito has never visited the shrine since ascending to the Chrysanthemum Throne. *Asahi Shimbun*, July 21, 2006.

[14] In the Emergency poll conducted by *Asahi Shimbun*, July 22 and 23, 2006 right after the Emperor's reservations were reported, only 20 percent favored a visit to Yasukuni Shrine by the next prime minister while 60 percent opposed a visit. See Asian opinion polls at: http://www.mansfieldfdn.org/

official capacity and thus violated the constitution. Rulings in 2007 skirted the constitutionality issue and instead summarily rejected damage claims by the plaintiffs. However, even with these judicial setbacks, Article 20 continues to cast a long shadow over prime ministerial visits, explaining why alternative proposals for paying tribute emphasize a secular option. The politics of Yasukuni ensure that it will remain an important symbol of Japan's militaristic past. Nationalists bridle at suggestions of alternative sites to pay respect to the war dead precisely because the issue is not the souls of fallen soldiers. The issue of the shrine is about national pride and sustaining a more glorious, unapologetic narrative of Japan's past.

In contrast, Ienaga Saburo, a noted historian who led the fight against reactionary distortions of the nation's history for more than four decades until his death in 2002, argued that while the souls of the fallen soldiers must be honored, it should not be by deifying them. In his view, Japan must ensure that the mistakes of the past are not repeated by exposing the crimes of leaders who sacrificed these soldiers as cheap cannon fodder for unworthy reasons; only then will the war dead be truly honored.[15] Ienaga insists that by conflating the issues of nationalism, patriotism and filial piety, those who support retaining Yasukuni as the de facto national war cemetery seek to defend an outmoded and reactionary national ideology.

By invoking atavistic symbols of nationalism aimed at reawakening pride in nation, politicians are responding to a sense of fading glory, growing insecurity and a loss of faith in the government. They are also seeking to rally the public and cultivate a sense of shared purpose. In such an atmosphere it is not surprising that some people and politicians seek refuge in reassuring symbols and gestures of nationalism. However, these siren songs from the past sound more like a last gasp than a call to arms.

Predictably, pundits suggest that Koizumi's visits reflect a resurgent nationalism, but what is interesting is that Koizumi was rather isolated on Yasukuni. In 2005, five former prime ministers publicly advised him to refrain from visiting. The head of Keidanren, Japan's leading business federation, urged him not to go and even

---

[15] Ienaga, *Japan's Past, Japan's Future*.

the conservative newspaper *Yomiuri Shimbun* weighed in against further visits. Perhaps even more surprising was the statement in 2005 by Koga Makoto, a conservative LDP lawmaker who at the time headed the War Bereaved Families Association, suggesting the prime minister reconsider his visit in light of Asian sensitivities. The Japan Association of Corporate Executives (Keizai Doyukai) also urged Koizumi to stop his visits to Yasukuni, terming them the main obstacle to improving bilateral relations with China. Thus, a broad spectrum of conservatives opposed Koizumi's visits to Yasukuni Shrine.

Koizumi went anyway, saying that he wanted to honor all the war dead, believing that it was the right and natural thing for a national leader to do. His agenda was to render such observances normal, and thus turn the page on history and show that Japan would no longer be held hostage by its past in the present. In this respect he certainly failed because such visits are still seen as unacceptable in Korea and China, and by a majority at home.

Interpreting the causes of the war, what actually happened during the war and the aftermath remain divisive questions in contemporary Japan. Just because some groups in society favor air-brushing the inconvenient and unappealing aspects of Japan's wartime record does not mean that this is a widely embraced point of view. The exculpatory junior high school textbook written by the Society for the Creation of New History Textbooks (Atarashi Rekishi Kyokasho oTsukuru-kai) and approved by the Ministry of Education, was adopted by fewer than one percent of junior high schools both in 2001 and again in 2005, reflecting the good sense that prevails.[16]

Japan is seen to be shrinking from the onus of its history to the extent that it continues to embrace a self-vindicating narrative that casts the nation as victim and relegates competing narratives to the margins. Why have many Japanese clung so tenaciously to a sanitized version of its past and only belatedly recognized—and that tentatively and intermittently—their nation's role as victimizer? Surely Japan would gain stature in the eyes of the world, and facilitate its own regional integration, if it came clean about its devastating wartime record and stopped caviling about details that make it look eager

---

[16] For analysis of the Tsukurukai see McCormack, "The Japanese Movement to 'Correct' History," 53–73.

to evade responsibility. The reasons for continuing denial are various. For many Japanese, the vilification of Japan and ceaseless demands for apologies reflect a double standard; many countries have committed horrible crimes on an enormous scale that they minimize or ignore. For younger Japanese, the burdens of history seem unfair and irrelevant; grandfather did those things and that is his problem. For pragmatic government officials, there are worries that the tab for compensation could prove very expensive. There is also concern, based on several incidents, that confronting ultra-nationalists over the past could provoke violent retribution. For many older Japanese, moreover, the exoneration of Emperor Showa has clouded the issue of war responsibility; if the man in whose name a sacred war was waged was never held accountable, why should anyone else be?

II. Guilty?

The Women's International War Crimes Tribunal (WIWCT or Tokyo Women's Tribunal) convened in Tokyo in 2000 represented a belated attempt by Japanese civil society activists and international jurists to hold Emperor Showa accountable for his role in Japan's escalating and widening war in Asia 1931–45. The tribunal was aimed at rectifying the silence of the Tokyo Tribunal (1946–1948) regarding the Emperor's war responsibility and to delve into the experiences of women caught up in that maelstrom. The tribunal attracted protests by rightwing groups eager to keep a lid on this past and considerable media attention, including a subsidiary of Japan National Broadcasting (NHK) that negotiated the rights to film the proceedings.

On January 30, 2001, NHK screened a 40-minute film, part two of a series entitled, "How to Judge Wars." The documentary film featured the proceedings of the Tokyo Women's Tribunal that was convened in December 2000 to examine issues involving violence against women in war, most notably the system of sexual slavery known as the comfort women system. Presiding over the court was an international team of prosecutors and judges, some of whom had participated in the Bosnian and Rwandan war crimes trials.

The Tokyo Women's Tribunal was convened because acts of violence committed against women during WWII were neglected crimes at the Tokyo Tribunal convened soon after the war ended. Advocates of re-examining this dark era were returning to the territory of the Tokyo Trials precisely because they reject the dominant rightwing narrative that absolves Japan of war responsibility by dismissing the verdicts as "victor's justice." Instead, those who convened the Tokyo Women's Tribunal believe that the original Tokyo Tribunal did not go nearly far enough in assessing Japan's war responsibility, letting too many Japanese off the hook for heinous crimes they committed, especially those involving women. The controversy over the tribunal and the NHK documentary provides insights on the fundamental fault-line of post-WWII Japanese history that divides Japanese; unfairly condemned for challenging an international order that subjugated Japan and other Asian nations, or, guilty of perpetuating myths that seek to justify extensive war crimes committed by Japan's Imperial Armed Forces acting at the behest of the Emperor that have not been sufficiently acknowledged or atoned for.

In the Treaty of Rome (1998) an International Criminal Court was established and empowered to try genocide, rape, and sexual slavery as major war crimes. Animated by similar concerns, the Tokyo Women's Tribunal represents an attempt by civic groups to judge past crimes and determine state responsibility for them. Since the early 1990s, when victims finally came forward and researchers found archival evidence proving state and military involvement in recruiting the comfort women and running the comfort stations, debate in Japan about the entire issue has been highly charged and controversial. The battles have been fought over whether to include reference to the comfort women in school texts and to what extent the state should bear responsibility and atone. In 1993, Kono Yohei, the chief cabinet secretary at the time, acknowledged state responsibility, proffered an apology and promised to make amends, riling right-wing groups opposed to acknowledging Japan's wartime crimes and excesses much less atoning for them.[17]

In 2005, the *Asahi* newspaper, based on reports by a whistleblower, alleged that NHK censored its 2001 documentary covering the Tokyo Women's Tribunal because of political pressure from senior

---

[17] http://www.mofa.go.jp/policy/women/fund/state9308.html. Last accessed August 31, 2010.

politicians in the LDP. Four presiding judges declared that Japan's system of military sexual slavery, known as the "comfort women" system, constituted a crime against humanity; they further found the Showa Emperor guilty of this crime, and the Japanese government to have incurred state responsibility.[18]

The TV program's producer stated, "We were ordered to alter the program before it was aired. I would have to say that the alteration was made against the backdrop of political pressure."[19] The censored version of the documentary that was aired eliminated testimony by soldiers and references to the verdict finding Emperor Showa guilty of allowing the comfort women system to operate.

NHK aired the documentary film on the tribunal on its educational channel, one that typically attracts less than one percent of all TV viewers, so it is only because of the censorship scandal that many Japanese actually became aware of the tribunal's finding and the degree to which NHK is politicized. The documentary, originally prepared by an independent production company under a sub-contracting agreement with NHK, was subject to a last minute "in-house" editing process at a time when NHK was besieged by right-wing protestors and sound trucks demanding the entire program to be cancelled. During this phase of editing, NHK incorporated the critical comments of a prominent conservative historian, Hata Ikuhiko, well known for his minimization of Japanese responsibility for the comfort women system. Then, shortly before the film was shown, a meeting was allegedly held between senior executives of NHK and two prominent LDP politicians, Abe Shinzo, then deputy chief cabinet secretary and later prime minister, and Shoichi Nakagawa. Following this meeting, major changes were then made, adding new material while cutting the 44 minute film to 40 minutes only hours before the broadcast. This final cut deleted all references to the emperor's guilt even though this was the main finding of the tribunal.

Abe and Nakagawa (since deceased) were members of the "Association to Consider the Future Path for Japan and History Education."

---

[18] Statement of Protest to NHK: VAWW-NET Japan, http://www1.jca.apc.org/vaww-net-japan/english/backlash/statement_by_vaww.html

[19] Gavan McCormack, "How the History Wars in Japan Left a Black Mark" on NHK TV, February 2005 http://hnn.us/articles/printfriendly/9954.html

This organization, founded in 1997 with 107 Diet members, embraces an exonerating narrative about Japan's wartime past totally at odds with the tribunal and its conclusions not to mention Japanese public opinion. Political intervention in the media is forbidden by both Article 21 of the constitution and Article 3 of the Broadcasting Law, but it is standard procedure for NHK executives to meet with Diet members because politicians must approve NHK's annual budget.

Abe defended his meeting with NHK executives, saying he had heard that the tribunal was biased and was naturally concerned about possible misrepresentations. He explained, "Because I was told that the mock trial was going to be reported in the way that the organizers wanted it to be, I looked into the matter. I found out that the contents were clearly biased and told [NHK] that it should be broadcast from a fair and neutral viewpoint, as it is expected to."[20]

The NHK censorship controversy ended up in the courts. The Supreme Court in June 2008 reversed a lower court ruling and dismissed a suit filed in 2001 by one of the seven NGO's that organized the tribunal, Violence Against Women in War-Network Japan (VAWW-NET Japan). The NGO demanded that NHK and two affiliated production companies pay compensation for altering the documentary and deleting discussion of the emperor's responsibility for the comfort women system. The NGO claimed cutting this crucial conclusion constituted breach of trust.[21]

The top court ruled the three media firms involved were not obliged to produce a documentary in accordance with the plaintiffs' expectations because broadcasters are free to edit their productions. It also rejected the plaintiff's complaint that NHK had betrayed their trust and expectations since the public is aware that TV programs are normally edited.

At issue, as the court defined it, was whether NHK and the two production companies were obliged to explain to VAWW-NET Japan about the changes they made before the program was broadcast. In the court ruling, Justice Yokoo Kazuko, the presiding judge, said legally

---

[20] "NHK censored TV show due to political pressure," *Japan Times*, January 14, 2005.
[21] *Japan Times*, June 13, 2008.

protecting the trust and expectations of people who become the subjects of broadcast productions would impinge on press freedoms.

Regarding political pressures by LDP politicians and rightist demonstrators, the Supreme Court acknowledged NHK executives met with Abe one day before the program was broadcast and that rightists demanded that NHK not air the show, but did not rule on whether this was inappropriate. The high court concluded that there was no evidence Nakagawa met NHK officials before the airing.

NHK was thus vindicated, although in 2007 the Tokyo High Court acknowledged that NHK changed the content of the program after taking politicians' remarks into account. In that decision, since overturned, the court awarded VAWW-NET damages of two million yen, fining NHK for failing to properly explain the changes made to the documentary before airing it.

This censorship case highlights political intervention in shaping perceptions of history and how this has been contested by civil society. NHK was absolved in the courts, but the censorship scandal and the appearance of kowtowing to conservative politicians about the emperor's war responsibility has further tarnished a reputation already suffering from a series of embezzlement scandals. More importantly, in 2009 the Broadcasting Ethics and Program Improvement Organization criticized NHK's handling of the documentary, stating that for the sake of independence and autonomy NHK should cease the practice of consulting with politicians about program content. This ethics committee specifically criticized NHK for the meeting with Shinzo Abe prior to airing the program, but refrained from concluding that political meddling influenced the editing process. The panel's surprising recommendation that NHK stop consulting politicians over specific programs is not legally binding, but does carry moral authority within the industry and the public at large. So just as it thought that the issue had been resolved to its satisfaction, NHK yet again found itself in the dock of public opinion, its journalistic standards, ethics and editorial independence still questioned. Certainly the millions of Japanese who refuse to pay their mandated dues to NHK are not doing so because it covered up the emperor's war guilt, but it does provide them with a convenient reason to claim conscientious objector status.

III. Legacies of Colonial Rule in Korea

The 100th anniversary of the signing of the Treaty of Annexation in 1910 between Japan and Korea provides insights on the state of bilateral relations and the politics of history.[22] Although sixty-five years have passed since colonial rule ended, the scars have not healed and Japan's relations with Seoul and Pyongyang remain vexed by history. Numerous apologies by Japanese politicians and Emperor Akihito have been undone by discordant voices of denial and unrepentant justification. These mixed messages reflect a lack of consensus within Japan about its colonial era and help explain why Koreans remain seething and indignant, unconvinced by Japan's sincerity, unwilling to extend a hand to the perpetrator.

On August 10, 2010 Prime Minister Kan Naoto issued an apology to South Korea regarding colonial rule, expressing deep regret over the suffering inflicted, stating, "the people of South Korea at the time were deprived of their nation and culture, and their ethnic pride was deeply harmed by colonial rule that was against their will." He added, "those who render pain tend to forget it while those who suffered cannot forget it easily." Although more specific about Japanese transgressions in Korea, and helpfully forthright on the issue of wounded ethnic pride, the apology was to South Korea alone, neglecting North Korea. Kan's statement draws heavily on the 1995 Murayama Statement, one that has become a mantra for subsequent Japanese expressions of remorse about its rampage through Asia.[23] In his statement, Murayama apologized for Japan's "colonial rule and aggression, [that] caused tremendous damage and suffering to the people of many countries, particularly to those of Asian nations." This is also similar to the 2005 Koizumi Statement issued on the sixtieth anniversary of the end of WWII.

Given that Murayama was the head of a coalition government including the LDP and Koizumi was party president when he issued

---

[22] http://search.japantimes.co.jp/cgi-bin/ed20100829a1.html. Last accessed August 31, 2010.
[23] For the text of the Murayama Statement see: http://www.mofa.go.jp/announce/press/pm/murayama/9508.html. Last accessed August 31, 2010.

his apology, the LDP's peevish criticism of Kan smacks of hypocrisy and politics. Acknowledging Japan's transgressions while ignoring its contributions proved an unacceptable version of war memory for conservatives. Former Prime Minister Abe Shinzo (2006–07) took off the gloves, ridiculing Kan's statement as foolish and ignorant, strong criticism from someone who speaks with authority on both charges.

Abe, during his brief tenure as premier, became an object of derision when he quibbled about the level of coercion involved when recruiting teenage Korean girls as comfort women and a national punching bag when he tried to rewrite and sanitize the history of the Battle of Okinawa and the role of Japanese troops in instigating group "suicide" by Okinawans.[24] Perhaps Kan feels vindicated that the nationalist goon squad was offended.

These conservative ideologues are called the "revisionists," those who are eager to revise what they see as a masochistic history imposed on Japan following WWII. They favor instilling pride in nation through a more favorable assessment of Japan's colonial and wartime actions and bridle at the repeated apologies that they feel tarnish the nation's honor. In response to Kan's apology, the conservative press called for a more balanced and less self-flagellating history, pointing out that Japan's colonial rule was not only negative and contributed to the modernization of the peninsula.[25]

Tobias Harris observes, "As Kan himself noted, there is nothing cowardly about frankly acknowledging one's transgressions without hedging or equivocating. And while the list of apologies to Japan's neighbours is lengthy, it is precisely because conservatives question the legitimacy of those apologies—most notably the Murayama statement—that prime ministers are compelled to keep issuing new ones. The revisionist right believes that a 'proper' and 'truthful' historical perspective are critical for national pride, which it

---

[24] The Battle of Okinawa was one of the bloodiest in the Pacific War. The U.S. suffered 50,000 casualties while Japan lost some 100,000 soldiers. It is estimated that some 125,000 Okinawan civilians, about one quarter of the population, were also killed in the conflict. This battle is a bitter memory for many Okinawans who resent that Japan used them as a sacrificial pawn to buy time to defend the inner islands. Oral testimony of eyewitnesses implicates the Japanese soldiers in some of the group suicides.

[25] *Sankei Shimbun,* August 11, 2010.

believes to have been corroded by the left-wing academics and media personalities and pusillanimous politicians. While they claim to be interested only in historical fact, their selective reading of history belies a blatantly opportunistic approach to Japan's imperial past that belittles the claims of Japan's victims and presents a blatantly self-serving narrative in which Japan was not a colonizer, and even if it was, it was a benevolent one that hastened the demise of those wicked European empires."[26]

Harris adds, "Since Abe's downfall in 2007 the revisionists have been increasingly marginalized in Japanese politics, their influence virtually non-existent under the DPJ despite having sympathizers within the party. Indeed, their influence may be inversely proportional to the amount of noise they are capable of generating through various media outlets."

The Kan Statement thus aims to put historical issues behind the two countries and focus on the future, but there is little chance that Koreans will let Japan off the hook of history even if they do appreciate the sentiments. No apology could ever be enough, as Koreans cling to past injustices as part of their national identity and value actions above words. Christian Caryl, contributing editor to *Foreign Policy* argues that, "part of the problem is a Korean nationalism that is built around a deep-seated notion of Korean victimhood. Koreans need to get over this if they're ever going to have a healthy relationship with their neighbors."[27]

Conservative Japanese call for an end to masochistic history and endless apologies, preferring a vindicating, airbrushed history. But few Japanese seek refuge in such a glorifying narrative, understanding there is little dignity in denial. Former ambassador to the Netherlands (and grandson of wartime Foreign Minister Togo Shigenori) Togo Kazuhiko states, "I don't think that Japan suffers from apology fatigue nor is the Japanese people's willingness to do more exhausted. There is a big hole in the Murayama statement. He acknowledged that Japan did bad things including aggression and colonial rule, but did not determine

---

[26] http://www.eastasiaforum.org/2010/08/18/the-politics-of-japans-prime-ministers-apology. Last accessed August 31, 2010.
[27] Interview August 2010. Subsequent attributions to Caryl draw from this interview.

who was responsible and as long as this issue remains unanswered, reconciliation will not proceed."[28]

A Japanese expert on Korea, requesting anonymity, observes that, "Japan must be made to perpetually apologize and there can be no resolution and no gesture can ever be enough." As the victim, the Koreas are in a position to decide about how to deal with the colonial past and sees few incentives in reconciliation. Given that apologies are offered, but shunned, and gestures of contrition never quite measure up, the odds against reconciliation are high. Rather than seeking a dramatic breakthrough, several experts recommend that Japan should pursue concrete measures dealing with outstanding issues such as forced labor, the comfort women, textbooks, Yasukuni Shrine and the disputed islands of Dokdo/Takeshima. Pursuing this agenda is the best chance for giving some momentum to a healing process that eventually may create an opening. Not to do so will only prolong the stalemate.

Normalization?

There is no shortage of issues dividing the Koreas and Japan, and habits of recrimination remain resilient on the Korean peninsula because there is a sense that Japan has not fully taken the measure of the torments it inflicted during the colonial era (1910–45) nor atoned sufficiently for them. The Treaty of 1965 normalizing relations between South Korea and Japan is often invoked by the Japanese government as evidence that it has not neglected this shared past and point to the $800 million in loans and aid it provided at that time as a concrete gesture of contrition. They also cite the 1965 agreement to fend off individual claims for reparations, arguing that the South Korean government was obliged to distribute a portion of the settlement to individuals and that any further claims were waived. Koreans counter that at that time the Japanese government withheld information regarding forced labor, and the comfort women issue was buried until the 1990s, so the waiver does not pertain to these claims.

---

[28] Interview August, 2010. Subsequent attributions to Togo draw on this interview.

Given that South Korea was a military dictatorship until the late 1980s, and civil rights were routinely suppressed under a succession of generals, the Japanese legal position may be solid, but it is also politically awkward. In 2005, the South Korean government released the normalization negotiation documents, sparking public fury and highlighting the difficulties of relying solely on a legalistic approach to the extremely emotional issues of colonial subjugation. The reality of a lingering, widespread sense of injustice among South Koreans makes Japanese assertions that the 1965 treaty can be a lockbox for history little more than wishful thinking.

Compensating Forced Labor

Togo contends that the Japanese government and companies now have a chance to live up to their moral responsibility regarding claims for forced labor compensation. He states, "In May 2007 the Supreme Court ruled that neither the Japanese government or companies bear any legal liability and are not criminally responsible for forced labor, but I think that this opens up an opportunity to consider the moral point of view. It behooves Japan to establish a joint fund by government and the private sector to provide individual compensation to victims... but the problem is determining the criteria and which victims are eligible."

Seizing this chance may not be easy, because it has implications for Chinese forced laborers, POWs and others who seek individual compensation, but in 2010 Mitsubishi has agreed to compensate some 300 conscripted Korean women workers at its wartime Nagoya aircraft factory. According to William Underwood, a historian who has conducted groundbreaking research into the forced labor issue, this decision "is potentially Copernican... the big factors were the committed demonstrations against Mitsubishi in Seoul and Tokyo and well-coordinated transnational activism at the community level. Then there was a petition signed by more than 130,000 South Korean citizens and 100 members of the National Assembly, and talk of a boycott, that put this effort over the top. It is hard to see how Mitsubishi will now draw a line between the *teishintai* (Conscripted Women's Brigade) and other Korea citizens conscripted into working for its various companies.

A Mitsubishi program for compensating its former labor conscripts would up the ante for other companies to follow suit."²⁹

Underwood also finds it encouraging that in March 2010 the Japanese government finally provided "the long sought civilian name rosters and payroll records that the South Korean government needs to carry out it its own program for compensating former conscripts and their descendants." The list has 175,000 names of Korean forced laborers and details about some $3 million of their money held by the Japanese government. Why it took sixty-five years to turn over this list reveals much about Japan's mishandling of reconciliation and why Koreans remain so resentful.

Standing in the way of compensation is the unawareness and denial in Japan concerning forced labor and abuses. It is astonishing, Underwood says, that "Prime Minister Aso could contend with media support that the 10,000 Koreans at Aso mining were well-treated and not unduly coerced. The Japanese media, which rarely covers the vigorous activism within Japanese society that seeks to resolve historical issues... barely covered the Mitsubishi announcement. It is also amazing that Keidanren has been able to completely ignore the myriad claims upon Japanese industries by taking a *mokusatsu* (ignore with contempt) stance, especially in this age of corporate social responsibility and despite Keidanren's charter on ethics valuing human rights." Underwood also points out that a comprehensive settlement of forced labor compensation is complicated by claims of conscripts from North Korea with which Japan does not have diplomatic relations. Unlike with South Korea, there are no treaty waivers.

Enshrinement

Koreans are also incensed that some of their countrymen have been enshrined at Yasukuni without permission. Given that Koreans were forced to serve in the Imperial Armed Forces, and were subsequently stripped of any veterans' benefits, the enshrinement at Japan's ground zero for bellicose nationalism only adds insult to injury. Before the

---

²⁹ This and subsequent statements attributed to Underwood draw from an interview in August, 2010.

end of WWII, 415 Korean conscripts were enshrined at Yasukuni, but beginning in 1958, an additional 21,000 Korean souls were enshrined without permission and without notification of bereaved families. Curiously, the Ministry of Health and Welfare provided the list of war dead to this private religious facility that was used for their enshrinement. The government's evasive justifications notwithstanding, its role in facilitating deification breached Article 20 of the Constitution regarding separation of religion and the State while also, in many cases, offending bereaved families.

The Yasukuni Shrine has explained that the Koreans were actually Japanese at the time they died and thus remain so after they died. Alas, enshrinement is something of a consolation prize as this logic has not helped any Korean veterans or their survivors obtain pensions after the government rescinded their Japanese nationality following WWII. The shrine maintains that the Koreans were enshrined also "because they fought and died believing that they would be enshrined as deities of the Yasukuni Shrine when they die as Japanese soldiers." Perhaps, but this argument has not convinced many Koreans about the virtues of soul-snatching. Kim Hee Jong, an octogenarian veteran, was surprised in 2007 to find that he was enshrined at Yasukuni and complained to authorities that he is still alive and wanted his soul back, but apparently this is an exorcism too far. In 2001, relatives of enshrined Koreans sued the government to expunge the names and liberate the souls of their deceased relatives from Yasukuni, arguing that, "the souls of the victims, who were forcibly mobilized and killed during Japanese colonial rule, were enshrined as deities for the war of aggression against the religion of the victims themselves and the will of the bereaved families and have been violated for over a half century."[30] This case was dismissed in 2006 with the judge falling back on the 1965 treaty and justifying the handing over of names to the shrine as ordinary administrative procedure. In 2007, relatives sued the shrine directly for inappropriate consecration and are seeking one yen as symbolic compensation and an apology.[31]

---

[30] http://english.historyfoundation.or.kr/?sub_num=49. Last accessed Sept. 4, 2010.

[31] *Japan Times*, February 27, 2007.

Taiwanese have also had no success in gaining dis-enshrinement for the very good reason that shrine officials do not want to set a precedent. In resisting pressure from some quarters to remove the Class-A war criminals, one of the main "attractions," shrine priests maintain that deification is a one-way ticket. Purging the shrine of colonial souls might open the floodgates for other restless souls and shift attention to establishing a national war cemetery without Yasukuni's historical baggage.

Islands of Eternal Dispute

A French whaling ship, Le Liancourt, was nearly shipwrecked in 1849 on a cluster of ninety islets and reefs that are located in between the Korean peninsula and Japan, explaining why they are known to some as the Liancourt Rocks. The Rocks, comprise twin, jagged islets surrounded by rocky outcrops and reefs that both Japan and the Korean governments claim, referring to them as Takeshima and Dokdo respectively. The South Koreans maintain a Coast Guard presence and an octopus fisherman and his wife permanently reside there. Both nations maintain that their claims are stronger and better documented, but discussion of Takeshima is relatively muted in Japan, with the exception of Shimane Prefecture which in 2005 declared February 22 Takeshima Day to commemorate the seizure of the islands back in 1905. And so on February 22 in Matsue there are annual festivities attracting nationalists from around Japan who try, with little success, to stir up some primordial emotions among an indifferent public that goes about its business while the deafening "hate buses," blare out patriotic songs and exhortations.[32]

In South Korea, Dokdo is a very big deal and much more than a territorial dispute. While taking the ferry to Dokdo passengers can get in the mood by watching an anime featuring a massive robot repelling Japanese invaders. South Korea's (and North Korea's) assertion of sovereignty over Dokdo enters the realm of the sacred and is indisputable while Japan's claim is profane, a groundless legacy of colonial

---

[32] Julian Dudden has coined this vivid expression to denote the uyoku (ultranationalist) buses festooned with loudspeakers that loudly circulate through city centers in Japan.

rule and imperial arrogance. Any suggestion of submitting the rival claims to international arbitration is rejected because to do so would be tantamount, from the Korean view, to rewarding colonial aggression. While international lawyers certainly could find some merit in the competing claims, this is to ignore the vehemence that animates public discourse in South Korea about the dispute that renders legal hairsplitting irrelevant. The seizure of Dokdo in 1905 was the opening act of Japanese colonial aggression and as such an unforgivable perfidy and non-negotiable.

The Japanese government is keenly aware of Korean sensitivities and, in order to avoid provoking uproar during the fraught centennial, delayed release of the 2010 Defense White Paper because it refers to the taboo Takeshima. If this all seems a bit over the top, remember that in July 2010 a Korean threw a rock at the Japanese ambassador in Seoul and some Koreans have cut off fingers to register their anger about Japan's conceit over Dokdo. The fact that the Japanese government maintains its claims and middle school textbook guidelines now require teaching about Japan's "spurious" sovereignty outrages Koreans.

Togo, who once served as Director General of the Treaties Bureau in the Foreign Ministry, explains, "Korea's position is there is nothing to talk about. But in order to resolve the dispute, it is necessary to talk. Track 2 (non-official) efforts by academics, scholars can open discussions and it is possible to have good exchanges. There is room to learn from the confidence building measures (CBMs) such as fishery agreements, no visa visits and humanitarian assistance that helped change the context of negotiations between Japan and Russia regarding the Northern Territories. CBMs can help shift perspectives and allow actors to see the situation from a different angle and break the impasse. They do not have to be islands of eternal dispute." Perhaps, but as Christian Caryl, editor of *Foreign Policy*, points out, "North Koreans publish their own set of Dokdo postage stamps; any smidgen of compromise by Seoul on territorial issues will immediately be seized upon by the North for its own propaganda purposes."[33]

Russia and China also have island disputes with Japan that appear just as intractable. In Japan, the "northern territories" or southern

---

[33] Personal communication. August, 2010.

Kurile islands (Kunashiri, Etorofu, Shikotan and Habomai) just north of Hokkaido, remain a symbol of Soviet perfidy. Japan focuses on how the Soviets continued fighting the war beyond the surrender on August 15, 1945, invading and seizing the northern territories while Japan lay prostrate, and while the 1941 bilateral non-aggression pact still remained in force. From a Japanese perspective, this "lost" territory was illegally seized from it under dubious circumstances and there is almost no public recognition that Russia has any legitimate claim to sovereignty.

By the mid-1950s there were signs of a deal with the Soviet Union on the disputed northern territories, but Tokyo killed the deal by suddenly increasing its demands from two to all four islands. Rightwing groups also organized protests against the deal, wanting to avoid a breakthrough with Moscow that might bolster left-wing groups in Japan. In a sense, right-wing zealots hijacked Japanese foreign policy, forcing the government to abandon compromise and demand all of the islands. To this day, right-wing hate buses armed with loud speakers frequently circulate in Tokyo berating the Russian government and asserting that the northern territories must be returned. Prospects for a resolution of the dispute seem remote given how rightwing pressure groups eliminate any scope for compromise that might facilitate a deal. But there are precious few signs of such an inclination in contemporary Japan anyway. In a press conference on September 30, 2010 Foreign Minister Seiji Maehara, known as a pro-Washington hawk in the relatively liberal DPJ government, stated, "It is important to have a strong political will to conclude a peace treaty while firmly discussing the territorial issue." Moscow responded by stating that Japan's raising of the territorial issue is a dead-end and asserted that Japan was undermining bilateral ties by issuing warnings against President Medvedev visiting the islands during his regional tour. Ironically, the Russian view that there is no territorial issue echoes that of Japan regarding the Senkaku islands, a polarizing position that poisons prospects for compromise.

China and Japan have been locking horns over the Senkaku/Diaoyutai Islands. The arrest of a captain of a fishing trawler that rammed two Japanese Coast Guard ships in September 2010 sparked a major crisis in bilateral relations. The Japanese public was led to believe that Japan's claims are legitimate and that "greedy" China was only belatedly asserting sovereignty to lay claim to natural resources in the surrounding seabed. Legitimate questions about Japan's claims were ignored in the mainstream media while China's inept diplomacy and overreaction conceded Japan the moral high ground while undermining a decade of diplomacy trying to convince neighbors that a rising China was not threatening. The Japanese government released the captain in the face of escalating Chinese threats and sanctions, helping to defuse the row, but PM Kan drew sharp criticism from many conservatives for kowtowing to China.

The stakes of managing the northern territories dispute with Russia are decidedly smaller than managing relations with China, Japan's largest trading partner and most dynamic export market. Japan can live without Russia, but even though anger and distrust towards China is high, there is a pragmatic recognition that sustaining a working relationship is essential to Japan. In that sense, because the stakes in the northern territories are less and Russia is not as important to Japan, nationalist groups in Japan have more leeway to influence this agenda while politicians can posture assertively about these islands of eternal dispute without much risk. Putin's resumption of the presidency in 2012 has raised hopes in Japan of a breakthrough, but there is a history of missed opportunities.

Nullification?

At the crux of colonial controversy lies the 1910 Treaty of Annexation. Koreans maintain that the treaty was never valid principally because it was negotiated under coercion and there are procedural flaws and discrepancies involving the signatures and state seal on the Treaty and royal edict that promulgated the treaty. The 1965 Treaty of Normalization states that all treaties signed before August 22, 1910 are already null and void, but the Japanese government maintains that the treaty was valid at the time it was signed until Korea's liberation in 1945.

Haruki Wada, professor emeritus of the University of Tokyo known inter alia for his prominent role in the Asia Women's Fund, has played a key role in pressuring the Japanese government to nullify the 1910 treaty of annexation, but to no avail. He along with colleagues in Japan and South Korea gathered over 1,000 signatures of intellectuals from each nation on a joint statement calling for official recognition that Japanese colonialism in Korea was illegal. In doing so, the hope is to open the door for individual compensation, heightened awareness about the specific crimes of colonial rule in Korea in Japan while igniting a wider debate about colonialism. The petition also calls on the government to normalize ties with North Korea.

Alexis Dudden, states that "the point isn't whether or not the annexation was legal or illegal, but rather to understand what constituted 'legality' in 1910, thus, even though it is possible to demonstrate that the annexation was legal at the time, that doesn't mean it was 'good.' Japan's annexation of Korea was legal because forced and forged treaties, assassinations, bribes, and deceit were the colonial game. In the summer of 1907, the world sided with Japan to agree collectively that the Koreans were 'unfit to rule themselves.'"[34] And thus Korea was abandoned to Japanese violence and ambitions.

Peter Duus does not see much hope in the nullification movement, arguing, "the recent movement to have the Japanese government declare the annexation treaty 'null and void' from the start seems quixotic at best, and questionable as a matter of international law unless there is evidence that Yi Wan-yong, the Korean prime minister at the time, was bribed or signed the treaty at gun point. All the major world powers, U.S. included, accepted the treaty as legitimate, and most thought that Korea would be better off under Japanese guidance."[35] Andrew Horvat, Director of the Stanford program in Kyoto, is equally skeptical, describing the nullification movement as the polarizing equivalent of Jane Fonda going to Hanoi during the Vietnam War.[36] Horvat argues that reconciliation depends on forging a consensus within Japan about the colonial era, one that will lead to concrete acts of contrition. In his view, the nullification movement will

---

[34] Interview, August 2010. Subsequent statements attributed to Dudden draw from this interview. She is author of *Japan's Colonization of Korea* (University of Hawaii, 2005) and *Troubled Apologies* (Columbia University, 2008).

[35] Interview, August 2010. Subsequent statements attributed to Duus draw from this interview. He is author of *Abacus and the Sword* (University of California,1998).

[36] Interview, July 2010. Subsequent statements attributed to Horvat draw from this interview. Horvat previously served as Director of the Asia Foundation's Tokyo office and sponsored and participated in numerous conferences on reconciliation between Japan and Korea.

divide domestic actors and prevent any consensus, thereby derailing reconciliation initiatives.

Another expert requesting anonymity comments, "for a movement with overt political aims, its organizers dizzying lack of political acumen on multiple fronts will likely yield unnecessary backlash to a worthy and necessary aim: historical understanding between Japan and Korea."

Imperial Visit?

In September 2009 President Lee Myung-bak of South Korea invited Emperor Akihito to visit on the occasion of the centennial, in the hope this would facilitate a future-oriented relationship. Imperial visits have played an important role in promoting reconciliation, but the government is mindful that the 1992 visit to China was premature and did little to appease public opinion or ease tensions over history. Any incidents during a visit also carry the risk of causing a significant setback for bilateral relations.

Dudden suggests another option. "If Japan is serious about moving on from the so-called 'history problems' in productive and substantive ways befitting East Asia's most successful democracy, the answer lies *not* in sending Emperor Akihito to Seoul, but first in having him address the Japanese nation on TV and apologizing (with a bow) to those in Asia and in Japan (in that order) whose lives were devastated by the course of the Japanese empire and war."

Kenneth Ruoff acknowledges that Japan was slow to own up to its wartime behavior and make amends, but thinks this has changed, "beginning with Emperor Akihito's apology to President Roh Tae-woo during his 1990 visit." Subsequently, Akihito made reference to his Korean ancestry, "a statement with tremendous symbolic importance because it mocked the notion that the Japanese are a 'pure' race. A visit, if carefully choreographed by both governments might improve relations. The emperor is Japan's national symbol after all, and it was also in the name of the emperor that Japan's colonial policies were executed."[37]

---

[37] Interview, August 2010. Subsequent statements attributed to Ruoff draw from this interview. He is, author of *The People's Emperor* (Harvard, 2001) and *Imperial Japan at its Zenith* (Cornell, 2010). In 2001 in his annual

Prospects for Reconciliation

It won't happen soon and may take until the centennial of liberation in 2045 before the Koreas and Japan manage to alleviate the miseries of the shared past. Mark Caprio notes that colonial officials believed it would take a century to assimilate a people they regarded as inherently inferior.[38] The wounds of belittling and eradicating Korean cultural identity and trampling ethnic pride remain painful and healing them could take just as long.

The flawed attempt to compensate the comfort women through the Asia Women's Fund (1995–2007) helped relatively few victims (364) while stoking anger and disappointment in both nations. It was an equivocal effort over an issue demanding a grand gesture, thus provoking recrimination and underscoring how important a problem it remains for Japan.

Redress is hostage to domestic politics and general heedlessness. Ruoff observes, "Although more and more Japanese have a general sense that their country's colonial rule over Korea was exploitative, they still lack a sense of just how dreadful it was for Koreans." The same could be said for attitudes towards China and other victims of Japanese aggression as well. Duus notes the lack of "a willingness on both sides to take the other's point of view into account, but unfortunately those with extremist views often seem to speak with the loudest voices—or maybe just attract the most media attention." And as Horvat points out, giving the Japanese their due might help, saying, "much also depends to what degree Koreans are willing to gaze steadfast into a past in which economic progress took place in a period of national humiliation."

Speech from the Throne, the Emperor acknowledged his ancestors' Korean ancestry, a surprising admission to most Japanese if they read about it. Only the liberal *Asahi* newspaper reported this part of his lengthy speech. His frank admission was aimed at improving relations in the run up to the joint hosting by Japan and Korea of the FIFA World Cup Soccer Championships in 2002. Given that popular Japanese attitudes towards Koreans are fairly negative, and ethnic Korean residents in Japan (zainichi) suffer from discrimination, his suggestion that "they" are "we" was not entirely welcome, especially among conservatives.

[38] Caprio, *Japanese Assimilation Policies*.

Howard French, former *New York Times* bureau chief in Tokyo and Shanghai, asserts that "Japan's acts of reconciliation have been inadequate in scope, in terms of the weight of the language or the drama of the acts themselves... never rising to the level of a consensus wholly embraced among the mainstream political class. Japanese governments have come and gone, and their ardor for reconciliation has varied considerably ... the impression this leaves others is of insincerity."[39] But, he adds, "there is a responsibility incumbent on Japan's neighbors to extend their hand of friendship, to make it easier, in effect, to make the definitive magnanimous gestures that are needed. This means giving up the cynical use of war issues and flag waving to energize the base. It means accepting the idea that real reconciliation requires generosity from all parties. It requires a willingness to expend some political capital to end an unsightly and ultimately harmful state of affairs."

Conclusion

The politics of history in Japan prevents Japanese reaching a consensus about their shared past with Asia and sends a mixed message to victims of Japanese imperial aggression that raises legitimate questions about the sincerity of Japanese apologies and depth of contrition. Unable to agree what happened and why, the Japanese state and public remain uncertain about what to acknowledge and take responsibility for, thus conveying a disturbing degree of fecklessness about this past that precludes reconciliation with neighbors. As a result, rapprochement in Asia between Japan the perpetrator and its victims has been in prolonged abeyance, marred by dilatory and inadequate deeds of atonement, a process suffering from an absence of any grand gestures. Dithering over acknowledging war responsibility, followed by half-hearted gestures of contrition, has complicated reconciliation because it has generated bad will and suspicion among Japan's victims. Many Chinese and Koreans believe Japan is now trying to hastily bury the past before taking its full measure, and are thus disinclined to let Japan off the hook of history and accept proffered olive branches. The

---

[39] Interview, August 2010.

demonstrated inability to forge a consensus within Japan and forthrightly assume responsibility without quibbling, legalistic caveats and equivocation ensures that history will remain divisive in Asia. Japan's failure to promote reconciliation is not entirely its fault alone, but it is largely responsible for this state of affairs. As a result, contemporary disputes within the region over a range of issues remain hostage to history and the rancor it inspires, rendering resolution elusive.

The politics of history within Japan sustains a vigorous debate that precludes a consensus about the wartime past as conservatives and progressives contest the substance and implications of this history, arguing about whether Japanese troops committed atrocities, whether Japan was an aggressor and if its actions were wrong. The credible cascade of revelations about Japan's record in Asia that have emerged after Emperor Showa's death in 1989 support the more critical views of progressives towards Japan's actions, while undermining the conservative assertion that Japan was engaged in a noble mission to liberate Asia from the yoke of western imperialism. Pan Asian liberation has long served as an ideological refuge for Japan's conservative deniers and minimizers, ennobling ignoble deeds and justifying Japan's imperial expansion. The discrediting of this valorous and glorifying narrative in the 1990s, and frank acknowledgement of what has long been denied, triggered a backlash. So it is not, as Lind argues, the apologies for these past misdeeds that have provoked a nationalistic backlash in Japan that has irked Korea and Japan, but rather it is the more forthright reckoning about this past that has long been resisted by Japanese conservatives.

Apologies are not sufficient to heal the wounds of history, but they are a necessary part of that process. To deny the importance of apology in reconciliation in northeast Asia, and to suggest it is an obstacle to that process, is to ignore expectations and realities. Official apologies stem from a less blinkered reckoning, and the acknowledgement of misdeeds that undermine the exonerating nationalistic narrative. Thus it is the belated but candid evaluation of the past, not the apologies per se, that is the taproot of discord within Japan and between Tokyo and its victims.

In terms of party politics, history is not a central campaign issue, but for certain core constituencies, nationalistic gestures such as whether or not a candidate plans to visit Yasukuni Shrine remain a litmus test. But these aging lobby groups have declining clout in electoral politics and the political revolution in 2009 sweeping the long dominant

LDP from power may have implications for the evolving politics of history. The DPJ cabinet refrained from visiting Yasukuni Shrine on August 15, 2010 and endorsed an apology to South Korea marking the centennial of Japanese colonialism in Korea. Prominent LDP members such as former premier Abe immediately repudiated the apology, but the mass media mostly endorsed this gesture of contrition. The escalating tension with China over the Senkaku Islands dispute has poisoned Japanese perceptions of China, but the overt nationalistic backlash has been muted in terms of demonstrations or actions targeting Chinese or Chinese institutions in Japan. The LDP has tried to politicize this dispute to attack PM Kan's leadership, but the odd development in this dispute is how history has taken a backseat despite competing claims based on history. The discourse in Japan is mostly about the Chinese overreaction and bullying and the implications of China's growing power, while the divisive past remains simmering on the backburner.

The politicization of Japan's modern history is nothing new, and indeed was a core concern of the Meiji oligarchs from the time they restored the Emperor and assumed power in 1868; invoking history has long served political purposes because of the power to influence how people think and act. Throughout the era of Japan's imperial expansion, history was heavily politicized and in some respects intensified when the embers of WWII were still warm and Japanese bureaucrats carried out orders by burning incriminating documents ranging from the coercive recruiting of comfort women and management of comfort stations providing sex to Imperial soldiers to maltreatment of POWs, forced labor, and battlefield excesses. The Tokyo Tribunal (1946–1948) further politicized Japan's war memory through flawed proceedings that did not meet international judicial standards, casting a cloud over the entire endeavor. Perversely, the botched tribunal has enabled revisionist apologists to portray Japan's militarists as victims of "victor's justice" and to argue that these war criminals were in fact noble martyrs. Moreover, in excluding Emperor Hirohito from prosecution, the U.S. complicated the whole issue of war responsibility for a Holy War waged in his name.[40] If he could be exonerated, or at least

---

[40] During the Occupation, the U.S. believed that it was far more useful to mobilize the Emperor in support of democratizing reforms such as the new Constitution than making him into a martyr for nationalists to rally around.

overlooked, why would anyone else in Japan feel compelled to assume responsibility? The U.S. further politicized Japan's colonial and wartime history during the Cold War (1947–1989), effectively encouraging Japan to imagine that the Tokyo Tribunal was a sufficient reckoning and could look forward while insulating it from demands for a more thorough judgment, especially from China, the country that had suffered most from Japanese depredations.

From 1949 when Mao's forces prevailed in the civil war and took power until Nixon's famous diplomatic gambit in 1972, the U.S. and its subordinate protégé Japan were cut off from China, a Cold War inspired hiatus that allowed resentments over history to fester on the mainland while memories faded in the archipelago. In normalizing relations with Japan in the 1970s, Beijing also downplayed its grievances and restricted blame to wartime militarists while renouncing reparations, making it easier for Japan to remain complacent about the past. Japanese insensitivities about wartime transgressions was reflected in the enshrinement of Japan's 14 Class A war criminals at Yasukuni Shrine in 1978. This and subsequent tensions over textbook content regarding the shared past in the early 1980s, and Prime Minister Nakasone's 1985 official visit to Yasukuni, divided Japanese while also arousing nationalistic fury in Korea and China.[41]

1989, however, proved a pivotal year in politicizing modern Japanese history that resulted from a confluence of developments in Japan, China and South Korea. Emperor Hirohito died, removing a significant obstacle to a forthright reckoning. Following his passing, the archives began to yield their secrets, historians "found" documents, soldiers retrieved "lost" diaries, and the context for a reappraisal of the wartime and colonial past became more favorable. The sanitized version of this past that had prevailed in Japan came under scrutiny within and was found wanting as evidence emerged and contesting narratives gained attention. This revision of history and the cascade of revelations about various atrocities, especially the comfort women, took the nation by surprise. There was a collective shock as people awoke to the magnitude of what had been inflicted. While many welcomed the embrace of

---

[41] In the aftermath of the textbook imbroglio, the Ministry of Education adopted guidelines indicating that textbooks must take neighboring countries sensitivities into consideration.

a more forthright reckoning and assumed responsibility for Japan's traumatizing rampage in Asia, others sought to reassert a more benign narrative emphasizing noble motives and Japan's own suffering. Ironically, those favoring this exonerating and glorifying narrative are referred to as the "revisionists." They oppose "apology diplomacy" and what they see as "masochistic" history, arguing that Japan has been unfairly vilified in a narrative shaped by the "victor's justice" meted out at the Tokyo Tribunal. They also have been incensed by what they see as the "instrumentalization" of history in China and Korea since the early 1990s. From a revisionist view, the incessant criticism of Japan is a cynical ploy to win concessions, keep Japan kowtowing, extort apologies, and undermine Japan's global standing by tarnishing its image.

Also in 1989, after the debacle in Tiananmen Square, the Chinese Communist Party revised school textbooks in order to shore up its legitimacy. It sought to remind the public about the decisive role that the party had played in "saving" the nation from the invading Japanese. In this new patriotic narrative, Japanese barbarism and outrages figured more prominently, meaning that younger Chinese know and care more about this tragic history, thus inflaming anti-Japanese sentiments. This has heightened sensitivities about Japan's apparent insouciance about the past and left Chinese with a misleading image of public discourse within Japan. The controversial remarks of denial, minimization and justification uttered periodically by prominent conservatives are seen to represent a Japanese consensus, one at odds with public opinion polls showing that the Japanese are not in denial, not eager to shirk their responsibility, and favor gestures of atonement.

The battle of words between nationalists in China and Japan stirs resentment and recrimination in both nations. Japan's revisionists wrap themselves in the flag, claiming they are protecting Japan's honor and dignity from exaggeration and distortion, provoking the expected (and desired) backlash. Revisionists depicted Chinese criticism of PM Koizumi's repeated visits to Yasukuni as intrusive meddling in Japan's domestic affairs even as many Japanese agreed with such criticism. Bilateral relations soured while mutual hostility and suspicions increased due to disputes over history. Since Koizumi left office in 2006, however, there has been a conscious decision by leaders in Beijing and Tokyo to dial down the rhetoric about history. There is a broad recognition that mutual economic interests are far too important to hold hostage to history and pragmatic accommodation has trumped patriotic history. Agreeing not to disagree, however, remains a very long step away from reconciliation and means that managing discourse over history remains vulnerable to politics and fraught with peril.

The emergence of democracy in the late 1980s in South Korea also heated up battles over history as a more robust civil society put a spotlight on the comfort women and forced laborers and lobbied for redress. The 1965 Treaty of Normalization, and the waiving of further reparations, has not convinced Koreans to forgive and forget. The lifting of military repression lead to a flowering of a vibrant democracy in South Korea and greater attention to historical wrongs and the absence of individual redress let alone apology or acknowledgement of responsibility. Emperor Akihito did apologize to visiting President Roh Tae-woo in 1990 for the colonial era, but this did little to quench the Korean thirst for a fuller accounting. So just as South Korea was awakening from the darkness of authoritarian rule, Japan too was shedding the denial and half-truths that shaped memories of colonial rule among Japanese.

The obscured past suddenly jumped to the fore and became the focus of intense battles both bilaterally and within Japan, especially over the comfort women. The coercive recruitment of tens of thousands of teenage Korean women at the behest of Japanese military authorities to serve as sex slaves for Imperial soldiers was a long suppressed story, one that has ignited a strong backlash among Japanese conservatives because it is one of the most damning episodes subverting their preferred narrative. Civil society groups in both nations disinterred this story and lobbied for redress. Revisionist denial has targeted the 1993 Kono Statement for acknowledging Japanese state responsibility for the horrors endured by comfort women and the Asian Women's Fund (1995–2007) precisely because these gestures contradict their political agenda of "rescuing" Japanese history from the damning revelations that have accumulated since the early 1990s. Efforts within Japan and South Korea to expose more about the tribulations of the colonial past are met by revisionists emphasizing and seeking refuge in focusing on Japan's contributions to Korea's modernization.

There are few signs that the long shadow that politics casts over Japan's shared history with Asia is dissipating, and in many ways the politics of history has intensified. This carries some benefits as over the past twenty years there has been an incredible outpouring of revelations and history has become the subject of vibrant public discourse. History has been unshackled from past constraints, contesting narratives have drawn attention to historical controversies, taboos have been trampled, previous inadequate narratives have been subverted and efforts to take the measure of Japan's shared history with Asia have gained considerable momentum. Although there is no doubt that the revisionists have been media savvy and attracted attention disproportionate to their influence, enabling them to propagate their version of events, the greater scrutiny this has attracted has also exposed significant shortcomings in their narrative that undermines their agenda and educates the public to be more keenly observant regarding the interplay of politics and history.

In short, it has become more difficult to bamboozle the public with selective truths under the glare of the political limelight even as this also complicates a coming to terms and reaching an accommodation over the past. Perhaps the greatest benefit of a politicized history is a vigorous, contested remembering within Japan that guards against the dangers of forgetting, "unhappening" and complacency.[42]

Bibliography

Caprio, M. *Japanese Assimilation Policies in Colonial Korea.* Seattle: University of Washington, 2009.

Goto, K. *Tensions of Empire.* Athens, OH: Ohio University Press, 2003.

Ienaga, S. *Japan's Past, Japan's Future.* Lanham, M.D.: Rowman & Littlefield, 2000.

Kingston, J. *Contemporary Japan: History, Politics and Social Change.* London: Wiley, 2011.

Kratoksa, P., ed. *Asian Labor in the Wartime Japanese Empire.* Singapore: Singapore University Press, 2006

---

[42] Koji Wakamatsu's award-winning *Caterpillar* (2010) is a mordant satire of Japan's wartime patriotism, exploring the devastating impact of war and loss on individuals. His film is an unforgettable remembering, one that implicates Emperor Showa and a society that inculcated unquestioning loyalty and deference to the state. As such it constitutes a valuable memorial, one that ends with a grim tally of destruction and death in Japan and Asia that resulted from Japanese aggression.

Lind, J. "Apologies in International Politics." *Security Studies* vol. 8, no.: 517–556.

———. *Sorry States*, Ithaca, N.Y.: Cornell, 2008.

McCormack, G. "The Japanese Movement to 'Correct' History." In *Censoring History: Citizenship and Memory in Japan, Germany, and the United States* edited by Hein, L. and M. Selden. Armonk, NY: East Gate, 2000.

Nakasone, Y. *Japan Times*, September 21, 2006

Nozaki, Y. *War Memory, Nationalism and History in Japan: Ienaga Saburo and the History Textbook Controversy, 1945–2005*. London: Routledge, 2006.

Ruoff, K. *The People's Emperor: Democracy and the Japanese Monarchy 1945–1995*. Cambridge, M.A.: Harvard University Press, 2001.

Seaton, P. *Japan's Contested War Memories*. London: Routledge, 2007.

Seraphim, F. *War Memory and Social Politics in Japan, 1945–2005*. Cambridge, M.A.: Harvard, 2006.

Takahashi, T. "The National Politics of the Yasukuni Shrine," translated by P. Seaton. No. 2272, available at www.japanfocus.org.

Tanaka, Y. *Japan's Hidden Horrors*. Boulder, CO: Westview Press, 1997.

Yamazaki, J. *Japanese Apologies for WWII*. London: Routledge, 2005.

Yoshibumi, W. *The Postwar Conservative View of Asia*. Tokyo: LTCB International Library Foundation, 1999.

Yoshida, T. *The Making of the "Rape of Nanking": History and Memory in Japan, China and the United States*. New York: Oxford University Press, 2006.

List of Contributors

ŞENER AKTÜRK, assistant professor, Department of International Relations, College of Administrative Sciences and Economics, Koç University

ALEXANDER ASTROV, associate professor, Central European University, Budapest

STEFAN BERGER, director, Institute of Social History, Ruhr University, Bochum

ANDREI CUSCO, senior lecturer, Chişinău State Pedagogical University; research fellow, Moldova State University

DIANA DUMITRU, associate professor, Chişinău State Pedagogical University

GÁBOR GYÁNI, visiting professor, Central European University, Budapest

JOHN-PAUL HIMKA, professor, University of Alberta, Edmonton

MACIEJ JANOWSKI, recurrent visiting professor, Central European University, Budapest; professor, Institute of History, Polish Academy of Sciences, Warsaw

GEORGIY KASIANOV, chair, Department of Contemporary History, Institute of Ukrainian History, National Academy of Sciences, Kyiv

JEFF KINGSTON, professor, Temple University, Tokyo

ALEXEI MILLER, recurrent visiting professor, Central European University, Budapest; senior research fellow, Institute for Scientific Information in Social Sciences, Russian Academy of Sciences, Moscow

DARIUSZ STOLA, professor, Institute of Political Studies, Polish Academy of Sciences; professor *Collegium Civitas,* Warsaw

Index

A

Abe, Shinzo, 322, 324, 326
Adenauer, Konrad, 23
Alekseev, Alexander, 266
Ancel, Jean, 250
Ansip, Andrus, 128
Antall, József, 92, 93, 106
Antonescu, Ion, 195, 196, 202, 243
Arel, Dominique, 235
Arnold, Agnieszka, 61
Art, David, 276
Atatürk, Mustafa Kemal, 19, 280, 281, 282, 283, 284, 285, 287, 288, 289, 290, 291, 292, 293, 295, 296, 297, 298, 299, 300, 301, 302, 303, 305, 307, 308
Avdeev, Alexander, 269
Ayers, Bill, 132
Azarov, Nikolai, 166

B

Bachman, Klaus, 65
Balan, Jars, 230, 231, 234
Bandera, Stepan, 158, 159, 163, 164, 169, 219, 220, 222, 223, 228, 231, 235
Barsenkov, Alexander, 270
Bartov, Omer, 218
Belarus, 7, 64, 65, 214, 239, 257, 259
Bele, Refet, 294, 296
Berman, Paul, 133, 134

Bessarabia, 176, 182, 183, 188, 193, 195, 196, 206, 207, 240, 241, 246, 247, 248, 249
Biden, Joe, 123
Bikont, Anna, 62, 70, 72, 81, 82, 83, 87
Bildt, Carl, 123
Birthler, Marianne, 48
Bismark, Otto von, 27, 34
Błoński, Jan, 61
Bobrzyński, Michal, 83
Boniecki, Adam, 80, 81
Brandt, Willy, 28, 29
Brezhnev, Leonid, 273
Browning, Christopher, 60, 69, 70
Brudny, Yitzhak, 279
BStU, 47, 49, 51
Bukovina, 240, 246, 247, 249
Bulba-Borovets, Taras, 222
Burds, Jeffrey, 235
Bush, George, 123

C

Canada, 19, 219, 220, 227, 230, 231, 233, 234, 237
Caprio, Mark, 338
Carr, E. H., 301
Caryl, Christian, 327, 333
Carynnyk, Marco, 218, 234, 235
Caşu, Igor, 246
Catherine II, 159
Cebesoy, Ali Fuat, 294

Cenckiewitz, Slawomir, 7
China, 310, 312, 313, 314, 319, 333, 334, 335, 337, 338, 341, 342, 343
Chirtoacă, Dorin, 198
Chodakiewicz, Marek Jan, 72, 73, 77
Chomiak, Chrystia, 234
Churchill, Winston, 137
Cichy, Michal, 61
Cohn-Bendit, Daniel, 132
Cojocaru, Gheroghe, 201, 202, 204
Connerton, Paul, 97
Conquest, Robert, 225
Courtois, Stéphane, 130, 133
Czarnowski, Stefan, 69

D

Danilin, Pavel, 7, 261, 262, 277
Danilov, Alexander, 12, 258, 259, 260, 264, 270, 273, 276
Davies, R. W., 225
Deák, István, 101
Demnjanjuk, John, 217
Derrida, Jacques, 123
Dilipak, Abdurrahman, 298, 299
Dink, Hrant, 286
Dmitrów, Edward, 68
Dudden, Alexis, 336, 337
Duus, Peter, 336, 338
Dyukov, Aleksandr, 7, 119, 124, 262, 273
Dzierzynski, Felix, 275

E

Eichmann, Adolf, 27
Emperor Akihito, 316, 317, 325, 337, 344
Emperor Showa (Hirohito), 309, 310, 311, 313, 316, 317, 320, 322, 340, 341, 342, 345
Engelking, Barbara, 84
Estonia, 6, 10, 16, 17, 19, 117, 118, 119, 120, 121, 123, 124, 125, 126, 127, 128, 131, 132, 133, 135, 136, 137, 158

European Union, (EU) 18, 38, 105, 120, 126, 128, 131, 136, 137, 139, 158
Evans, David, 228

F

Fedotov, Mikhail, 271
Fest, Joachim, 33
Filat, Vlad, 197, 199
Filippov, Alexander, 12, 258, 259, 260, 264, 276
Finkelstein, Normal, 75
Finkielkraut, Alain, 134, 135
Fischer, Joschka, 132, 133, 139
Fonda, Jane, 336
Foster, Norman, 14, 38
Frederick the Great, 27
French, Howard, 339,
Fülberth, Georg, 34
Furet, Francois, 125, 138
Fursenko, Andrei, 258, 264

G

Gauck, Joachim, 9, 47, 48, 49, 55
genocide, 10, 16, 22, 29, 33, 37, 40, 70, 92, 93, 96, 119, 133, 134, 151, 153, 155, 156, 157, 162, 163, 164, 165, 177, 190, 209, 212, 213, 214, 215, 219, 220, 224, 225, 236, 237, 239, 267, 286, 321
Georgia, 10, 17, 134, 137, 257, 290
Germany, 2, 5, 9, 18, 19, 21, 22, 23, 24, 25, 26, 27, 28, 29, 30, 31, 32, 34, 35, 36, 37, 38, 39, 40, 41, 42, 43, 47, 92, 123, 124, 125, 126, 248, 255, 276, 277, 299, 300, 307, 312, 346
Ghimpu, Mihai, 7, 10, 197, 198, 199, 206
Glemp, Józef, 80
Glucksmann, André, 124, 134, 135
Goebbels, Joseph, 262
Goldhagen, Daniel, 70
Goma, Paul, 245

Index

Gontarczyk, Piotr, 7, 73, 76
Grabowitz, George, 236
Grabowski, Jan, 84
Grachova, Sofia, 218
Grass, Günter, 28, 39
Graziosi, Andrea, 225
Grod, Paul, 227, 228, 231
Gross, Jan Tomasz, 59, 60, 61, 62, 63, 64, 65, 66, 67, 68, 69, 70, 71, 72, 73, 74, 75, 76, 77, 78, 79, 80, 81, 82, 83, 84, 85, 86, 239
Grossman, Vasily, 239
Grudzińska-Gross, Irena, 83
Gustloff, Wilhelm, 39

H

Habermas, Jürgen, 32, 33, 35, 123, 125, 132, 136
Haiven, Judy and Larry, 234
Hammarberg, Thomas, 159
Harris, Tobias, 326, 327
Hata, Ikuhiko, 322
Havel, Vaclav, 123
Hegel, Georg Wilhelm Friedrich, 119, 135
Herkel, Andres, 135
Hildebrandt, Kurt, 33
Hillgruber, Andreas, 32, 33, 35
Himka, John-Paul, 15, 19, 215, 216, 217, 218, 227, 228, 232
Hindenburg, Paul von, 27
Historians' Controversy (Historikerstreit), 22, 32, 33, 34, 35, 36, 38, 40, 41, 124
Historical Memory Fundation, 7
Hitler, Adolf, 24, 25, 27, 31, 66, 69
Hochhuth, Rolf, 28
Hoffman, Eva, 219
Holocaust, 2, 11, 22, 24, 25, 26, 27, 29, 31, 32, 33, 35, 36, 37, 38, 40, 41, 42, 68, 69, 75, 76, 84, 85, 92, 93, 95, 109, 124, 130, 132, 153, 155, 157, 158, 176, 178, 193, 195, 196, 209, 211, 213, 214, 215, 216, 218, 219, 221, 225, 227, 228, 229, 232, 234, 235, 236, 237, 239, 240, 243, 244, 245, 246, 247, 249, 250, 251
Holodomor, 10, 14, 150, 151, 153, 155, 157, 158, 162, 163, 164, 165, 166, 169, 170, 212, 215, 220, 222, 227, 231, 233, 236, 237
Horvat, Andrew, 336, 338
House of Terror, 10, 93, 107
Hungary, 6, 16, 19, 91, 92, 93, 94, 95, 96, 101, 102, 103, 105, 106, 107, 108, 109, 111, 112
Hür, Ayşe, 302

I

Ienaga, Saburo, 312, 318
Ignatiew, Radosław, 70
Ilves, Toomas Hendrik, 123, 135, 136, 138
Inönü, Ismet, 291, 292, 295, 301
Institues of National Remembrance, 7, 12, 53, 55
Institute of National Remembrance, IPN, 46, 47, 48, 50, 51, 52, 53, 54, 55, 56, 57, 70, 78, 81

J

Japan, 2, 11, 18, 309, 310, 311, 312, 313, 314, 315, 316, 317, 319, 320, 321, 322, 323, 324, 325, 326, 327, 328, 329, 330, 331, 332, 333, 334, 335, 336, 337, 338, 339, 340, 341, 344, 345, 346
Jászi, Oszkár, 106
Jedwabne, 8, 51, 59–89, 96, 239, 252
Jenninger, Philipp, 21
Judt, Tony, 178, 216

K

Kaczynski, Andrzej, 61
Kaczynski, brothers, 1, 10, 13, 15, 53, 62, 88, 158, 258, 264, 265, 266, 267, 269

Kaczyński, Jaroslaw, 267
Kaczyński, Lech, 13, 15, 158, 258, 266, 267, 269
Kádár, János, 95, 96, 98, 99, 100, 102
Kagan, Robert, 138
Kan, Naoto, 310, 325, 334
Kant, Immanuel, 30, 136
Karabekir, Kazim, 282, 288, 289, 290, 291, 292, 293, 294, 302, 303
Karaganov, Sergei, 272
Károlyi, Mihály, 106
Karpov, Sergei, 271
Katyń, 15, 57, 239, 240, 258, 265, 266, 267, 269
Kelam, Tunne, 136, 137
Khrushchev, Nikita, 273, 280
Kieres, Leon, 47
Kim Hee Jong, 331
Kissinger, Henry, 134
Klid, Bohdan, 230, 231, 233
Kohl, Helmut, 1, 30, 31, 32, 35
Kohut, Zenon, 219, 222, 224, 229, 230, 231, 233, 235
Koizumi, Junichiro, 310, 315, 316, 317, 318, 319, 325, 343
Kolesnichenko, Vadim, 163
Kolodzinksy, Mykhailo, 222
Kono, Yohei, 321
Konsalik, Heinz G., 24
Kostash, Myrna, 211, 225, 230, 231, 234
Kotovskii, Grigorii, 179
Kouchner, Bernard, 132, 133
Kovács, Éva, 111
Kozłowski, Krzysztof, 46
Kravchuk, Leonid, 142, 146, 220
Kreisky, Bruno, 29
Kremlin, 7, 167, 257, 261, 264, 266, 267, 270, 272
Kuchma, Leonid, 153, 162, 163, 166, 220
Kühnl, Reinhard, 34
Kula, Marcin, 65

Kulesza, Witold, 48
Kulyk-Keefer, Janice, 234
Kuroń, Jacek, 86
Kurtyka, Janusz, 57
Kuznetsov, Anatoly, 239
Kwaśniewski, Aleksander, 47, 81

L

L. Nagy, Zsuzsa, 110
Laar, Mart, 118, 128, 135
Latvia, 6, 17, 158
Lazo, Sergei, 179
Lee Myung-bak, 337
Lenin, Vladimir Ilyich, 179, 194, 231, 275, 300
Leociak, Jacek, 85
Lévy, Bernard-Henri, 134, 135
Levytsky, Marco, 232
Lezsák, Sándor, 106
Libionka, Dariusz, 79, 85
Lind, Jennifer, 312, 340
Lipski, Jan Józef, 61
Lithuania, 10, 17, 64, 145
Lozynskyj, Askold, 222, 224, 232
Lucinschi, Petru, 183
Lüdtke, Alf, 35
Luik, Jüri, 129, 130, 131, 132, 133, 135, 138
Lukashenka, Alexander, 259
Lupu, Marian, 197, 198
Lustration laws, 15, 45, 56, 52, 53, 54, 203, 204, 205
Luther, Martin, 34
Luzhkov, Yury, 269

M

Machcewicz, Paweł, 62, 78, 84
Macierewicz, Antoni, 46
Maehara, Seiji, 334
Maier, Charles S., 22, 178
Mao Zedong, 242
Marples, David, 220, 228, 230, 231, 232, 234
McCain, John, 123, 133
Medgyessy, Péter, 100

Medvedev, Dmitry, 157, 164, 166, 262, 269, 270, 275, 276, 334
Meinecke, Friedrich, 24, 43
Memorial Human Rights Center, 7, 272
Milewski, Jan M., 65
Mısıroğlu, Kadir, 298, 299
Mokrousov, Andrii, 235
Moldova, 6, 10, 16, 19, 175–200, 202–209
Möller, Horst, 33
Molotov, Viacheslav, 59, 165, 180, 232, 240, 265
Murayama, Tomiichi, 325, 326, 327
museums, 7, 8, 10, 30, 31, 32, 38, 43, 93, 106, 107, 153, 155, 167, 168, 192, 193, 195, 205, 211, 214, 232, 241, 246, 252, 257, 272, 274, 297, 310, 314
Musiał, Bogdan, 69, 72, 73, 76, 77, 78
Musiał, Stanisław, 61

N

Nagy, Imre, 96, 98
Nakagawa, Shoichi, 322
Nakasone, Yasuhiro, 313, 314, 317, 342
Naruszewicz, Adam, 83
Naryshkin, Sergei, 272
NATO, 4, 17, 118, 120–126, 129, 131, 133, 257
Nazaria, Sergiu, 196, 202, 244, 246, 247
Neguta, Andrei, 243
Nihon Izokukai, 315, 316
Nolte, Ernst, 31, 32, 33, 35, 125, 138
Nora, Pierre, 216
Nowak, Andrzej, 78
Nowak, Jerzy Robert, 75
Nur, Riza, 288, 295, 296, 298

O

Obama, Barack, 17, 18, 132, 133
Orange Revolution, 17, 161, 221, 257

Orbán, Viktor, 105
Orbay, Rauf, 282, 288, 289, 293, 294, 295, 296, 302, 303
Organization of Ukrainian Nationalists, 158, 170, 213, 214, 215, 216, 218, 219, 220, 222, 223, 224, 226, 227, 228, 229, 231, 232, 233, 235, 236
Ormos, Mária, 110
Ozal, Turgut, 304

P

Palubicki, Janusz, 48
Patriarch Kirill, 268, 275
Pavlicenco, Vitalia, 203
Pavlovic, Nina, 234
Pavlovsky, Gleb, 261
Persak, Krzysztof, 62
Plawiuk, Mykola, 142
Pohl, Dieter, 218
Poland, 1, 6, 7, 8, 9, 13, 15, 16, 17, 18, 19, 20, 47, 48, 49, 50, 51, 57, 58, 59, 62, 63, 64, 65, 72, 74, 75, 77, 79, 80, 82, 83, 84, 85, 86, 87, 88, 89, 115, 158, 257, 259, 264, 265, 267, 271, 276
Pope John Paul II, 94
Posokhov, Serhii, 153
Potichnyj, Peter, 231
Putin, Vladimir, 15, 230, 255, 256, 257, 258, 265, 266, 268, 335

R

Radziejowski, Janusz, 237
Raffay, Ernő, 106
Reagan, Ronald, 31
Riabchuk, Mykola, 231
Ritter, Gerhard, 24, 25
Roh Tae-woo, 337, 344
Romania, 6, 175, 176, 179–199, 206, 207, 208, 209, 213, 239, 240–250
Romsics, Ignác, 103, 110
Rossolinski-Liebe, Grzegorz, 223, 225, 235

Rothfels, Hans, 25
Rudling, Per Anders, 220, 228, 232, 234, 235
Rumsfeld, Donald, 17, 122, 123
Ruoff, Kenneth, 337, 338
Russia, 6–10, 12, 14, 15, 16, 17, 19, 27, 30, 39, 117, 118, 119, 120, 124, 125, 126, 128, 134, 136, 137, 139, 141, 150, 151, 157, 158, 161, 162, 164, 165–169, 171, 172, 193, 194, 199, 202, 206, 212, 222, 230, 232, 242, 244, 250, 254–280, 296, 333, 334, 335, 347
Rutkowski, Alan, 226, 233
Rüütel, Arnold, 127
Rzepliński, Andrzej, 48

S

Saakashvili, Mikheil, 134
Sapozhnikova, Galina, 120
Schmidt, Mária, 107
Schöttler, Peter, 35
Sebald, W. G., 38
Serbyn, Roman, 231
Sheik Said, 280, 289, 294, 298, 301
Shevchenko, Taras, 163
Shoigu, Sergei, 261
Shukhevych, Roman, 158, 163, 164, 169, 219, 223, 226
Shultz, George, 134
Siklová, Jirina, 102
Slovakia, 105, 234
Snegur, Mircea, 181, 182, 187
Solonari, Vladimir, 196
Solzhenitsyn, Aleksandr, 133, 263
Soosaar, Enn, 128
Stalin, Joseph, 159, 165, 169, 178, 211, 225, 230, 258, 259, 269, 270, 273, 274, 275
Stalinism, 141, 142, 240, 253, 260, 263, 264, 269, 270, 271, 274, 278
Stepaniuk, Victor, 184, 191
Sternberger, Dolf, 33

Stetsko, Yaroslav, 219, 223
Stola, Dariusz, 64, 67, 68, 69, 86
Strzembosz, Tomasz, 61, 64, 65, 66, 74
Stürmer, Michael, 30, 32, 33, 35
Sułek, Antoni, 63, 65, 69
Suphi, Mustafa, 301
Surkov, Vladislav, 258, 260
Symonenko, Rem, 146
Sysyn, Frank, 230, 233
Szabó, István, 100, 101
Szarota, Tomasz, 66, 68, 76, 79
Szőcs, Géza, 107
Szujski, Józef, 83

T

Tabachnyk, Dmytrov, 163, 168
Tarand, Kaarel, 120
Tereschenka, Yakov, 259
textbooks, 3, 12, 96, 145, 150, 152, 161, 168, 169, 173, 190, 191, 196, 243, 255, 259, 260, 261, 287, 305, 313, 328, 342, 343
Thalmann, Ernst, 26
Tkachuk, Mark, 202
Togo, Kazuhiko, 327
Togo, Shigenori, 327, 329, 333
Tomohiko, Tomita, 316
Torkunov, Anatoly, 264
Transnistria, 6, 180, 188, 195, 240, 241, 246, 247, 248, 249, 251
Trianon, 91, 93, 95, 97, 99, 101–115
Trotsky, Leon, 275
Tulbure, Alexei, 243
Turkey, 2, 11, 16, 18, 279–283, 285–289, 291, 293, 295–301, 303, 305, 306, 307
Tusk, Donald, 15, 17, 264, 265, 267
Tymoshenko, Yulia, 162

U

Ukraine, 6, 7, 9, 10, 15–19, 66, 141–174, 178, 211–232, 235, 237, 240, 241, 248, 255, 258, 268, 271

Underwood, William, 329, 330
Ungvári, Tamás, 94
Ungváry, Krisztián, 111
UPA, 15, 150, 151, 152, 158, 167, 169, 170, 176, 213–220, 222, 224, 226, 227, 229, 231, 232, 233

V

Várszegi, Asztrik, 94
Vdovin, Alexander, 270
Velliste, Trivimi, 126
Verhoeven, Michael, 35
Volosiuk, Volodymyr, 154
Von Hagen, Mark, 148
Voronin, Vladimir, 181, 189, 191, 195, 197, 202, 242, 244
Vyatrovych, Volodymir, 7

W

Wada, Haruki, 335
Wajda, Andrzej, 266
Wakamatsu, Koji, 345
Wasersztejn, Szmul, 60
Wheatcroft, Stephen, 225
Wierzbicki, Marek, 66, 71

Wildt, Michael, 35
Winkler, Heinrich August, 36, 38

Y

Yakovenko, Natalia, 172
Yanukovych, Viktor, 161, 162, 163, 164, 165, 166, 167, 168, 170, 220, 268
Yasukuni shrine, 309, 310, 314–319, 328, 330, 331, 332, 340, 341, 342, 346
Yeltsin, Boris, 254, 274
Yi Wan-yong, 336
Yokoo, Kazuko, 323
Yushchenko, Viktor, 15, 149, 150, 151, 153, 154, 155, 156, 157, 158, 161, 162, 163, 164, 165, 166, 167, 168, 170, 173, 199, 212, 213, 219, 220, 221, 222, 223, 227

Z

Zabily, Ruslan, 7, 167, 168
Zakowski, Andrzej, 68, 76
Zbikowski, Andrzej, 65, 66
Zitelmann, Rainer, 36
Zubov, Andrei, 274
Zyzak, Pawel, 7